Killers, Clients and Kindred Spirits

EDINBURGH STUDIES IN EAST ASIAN FILM
Series Editor: Margaret Hillenbrand

Available and forthcoming titles

Killers, Clients and Kindred Spirits: The Taboo Cinema of Shohei Imamura
Edited by Lindsay Coleman and David Desser

Independent Chinese Documentary: Alternative Visions, Alternative Publics
Dan Edwards

Tanaka Kinuyo: Nation, Stardom and Female Subjectivity
Edited by Irene González-López and Michael Smith

Worldly Desires: Cosmopolitanism and Cinema in Hong Kong and Taiwan
Brian Hu

The Cinema of Ozu Yasujiro: Histories of the Everyday
Woojeong Joo

Eclipsed Cinema: The Film Culture of Colonial Korea
Dong Hoon Kim

Moving Figures: Class and Feeling in the Films of Jia Zhangke
Corey Kai Nelson Schultz

Memory, Subjectivity and Independent Chinese Cinema
Qi Wang

Hong Kong Neo-Noir
Edited by Esther C. M. Yau and Tony Williams

'My' Self on Camera: First Person Documentary Practice in an Individualising China
Kiki Tianqi Yu

edinburghuniversitypress.com/series/eseaf

Killers, Clients and Kindred Spirits

The Taboo Cinema of Shohei Imamura

Edited by Lindsay Coleman and David Desser

Edinburgh University Press is one of the leading university presses in the UK. We publish academic books and journals in our selected subject areas across the humanities and social sciences, combining cutting-edge scholarship with high editorial and production values to produce academic works of lasting importance. For more information visit our website: edinburghuniversitypress.com

© editorial matter and organization Lindsay Coleman and David Desser, 2019, 2021
© the chapters their several authors, 2019, 2021

First published in hardback by Edinburgh University Press 2019

Edinburgh University Press Ltd
The Tun—Holyrood Road
12 (2f) Jackson's Entry
Edinburgh EH8 8PJ

Typeset in 10/13 Chaparral Pro by
IDSUK (DataConnection) Ltd

A CIP record for this book is available from the British Library

ISBN 978 1 4744 1181 3 (hardback)
ISBN 978 1 4744 8136 6 (paperback)
ISBN 978 1 4744 1182 0 (webready PDF)
ISBN 978 1 4744 1183 7 (epub)

The right of the contributors to be identified as authors of this work has been asserted in accordance with the Copyright, Designs and Patents Act 1988 and the Copyright and Related Rights Regulations 2003 (SI No. 2498).

Contents

List of Figures vii
Notes on the Contributors ix

1 Introduction 1
   Lindsay Coleman and David Desser

2 The Making of an Auteur: The Early Films (1958–1959) 21
   Jennifer Coates

PART I   KILLERS

3 Confronting America: *Pigs and Battleships* and the Politics of
   US Bases in Postwar Japan 41
   Hiroshi Kitamura

4 Insect Men and Women: Gender, Conflict and Problematic
   Modernity in *Intentions of Murder* 56
   Adam Bingham

5 Hidden in Plain Sight: The False Leads and True Mysteries of
   Vengeance Is Mine 75
   John Berra

6 *The Eel*: Trauma Cinema 92
   David Desser

PART II   CLIENTS

7 *The Insect Woman*, or: The Female Art of Failure 115
   Michael Raine

8 The Obscene in the Everyday: *The Pornographers* 139
   Lindsay Coleman

9 Shohei Imamura's Profound Desire for Japan's Cultural Roots: Critical Approaches to *Profound Desires of the Gods* 159
   Mats Karlsson

10 "Products of Japan": *Karayuki-san, The Making of a Prostitute* 177
   Joan Mellen

11 The Female Body as Transgressor of National Boundaries: The History of Postwar Japan as Told by a Bar Hostess 192
   Bianca Briciu

PART III KINDRED SPIRITS

12 Better Off Being Bacteria: Adaptation and Allegory in *Dr. Akagi* 213
   Lauri Kitsnik

13 Time Out of Joint: Shohei Imamura and the Search for an "Other" Japan 228
   Bill Mihalopoulos

14 Promotional Discourses and the Meanings of *The Ballad of Narayama* 246
   Rayna Denison

15 Boundary Play: Truth, Fiction, and Performance in *A Man Vanishes* 267
   Diane Wei Lewis

16 *Why Not?* Imamura, Nietzsche, and the Untimely 287
   David Deamer

17 *Kuroi Ame:* An Anthropology of Suffering 308
   Dolores P. Martinez

18 The Symbolic Function of Water 326
   Timothy Iles

Index 343

Figures

5.1	The power of reconstruction and the potential for interpretation	80
5.2	Achieving upward mobility by adopting an academic persona	83
5.3	Breaking the rules to visualize the presence of the restless spirit	88
6.1	A long-take, deep-focus shot of the layout of the house	99
6.2	The priest's traditional house, shot from the low level characteristic of Yasujiro Ozu	102
6.3	Of eels and women; the longest take in the film	105
6.4	It's all done with mirrors	108
7.1	Newsreel footage of the demonstrations against the America–Japan Security Treaty in June 1960, with superimposed text	118
7.2	Freeze frame of Tome counting her money after she has been tricked into becoming a prostitute	119
7.3	Chūji's sudden looming behind Matsunami creates a kind of ironic visual punchline	120
7.4	*The Insect Woman* press sheet	121
7.5	Tome, followed by Nobuko, in the middle ground	128
7.6	Tome urinates in a mulberry field	134
8.1	Ogata spies on Keiko through multiple frames-within-frames	150
8.2	An establishing shot of star Anthony Perkins, as the character Norman Bates	151
8.3	Hitchcock then allows the camera to adopt the perspective of Norman as we spy on an undressing Marion Crane (Janet Leigh)	151
8.4	Ogata is briefly tempted by young Keiko	153
8.5	Kevin Spacey's Lester Burnham invests in a complex erotic fantasy life	154
8.6	Angela is eroticized not only for Burnham, but also for the audience	155
8.7	The final seeming consummation of Burnham's desire is framed classically and romantically	155
8.8	A father's incestuous relationship with his own daughter is discovered in a blackly comic moment in *The Pornographers*	156

8.9	The titular characters engage in a semi-absurd, and again blackly comic, exchange on the relative virtues of incest	157
9.1	Rentaro Mikuni as an islander with his own ideas in *The Profound Desires of the Gods*	159
9.2	Nekichi's Sisyphean labor	160
9.3	Kariya goes native	165
9.4	The Rock appears to budge	166
9.5	The masked villagers closing in for the kill	167
11.1	Akaza and her daughter walking arm in arm with GIs	195
11.2	Newsreel footage shows General MacArthur descending from a plane and Occupation troops marching on Japanese soil	196
11.3	Newsreels of violent protests show the divided nation and the public opposition to Occupation in contrast to the discourse of peaceful democratization	197
11.4	Akaza watching documentary footage showing people's reaction to the emperor's announcement of defeat	198
11.5	Akaza tells how she explained to her American lovers that the imperial family are not gods	199
11.6	Imamura shows pictures of atrocities committed by the Americans in the Vietnam War but she denies their reality	200
12.1	Dr. Akagi running through streets to meet another patient	216
12.2	Dr. Akagi presenting the results of his research on liver disease	219
12.3	A dream sequence about Dr. Akagi's son in Unit 731	221
12.4	Dr. Akagi and war prisoner Piet setting up research equipment	223
12.5	Witnessing the end of the war	225
13.1	Akeem, a former Japanese soldier who converted to Islam and lives in a close-knit Muslim community in Malaysia	237
13.2	The "wild boy" from Nagasaki, Fujita Matsukichi	239
13.3	"Outlaw Matsu" returns to Japan	240
14.1	Location shooting	252
14.2	Imamura as the exaggerated center of *The Ballad of Narayama*	256
14.3	Tatsuhei and Orin in helicopter downdraft	259
15.1	An ad for *A Man Vanishes* in the August 1967 issue of *Eiga hyōron*	268
17.1	Yasuko with her aunt and uncle, making their way through Hiroshima	317
17.2	Yasuko and her uncle Shigematsu see the king carp	318

Notes on the Contributors

John Berra is a lecturer in Film and Language Studies at Renmin University of China. He is the co-editor of the *Directory of World Cinema: Japan* (2010/12/15). He has also contributed to *World Film Locations: Tokyo* (2012) and *Ozu International: Essays on the Global Influences of a Japanese Auteur* (2015). His articles have been published in *Asian Cinema, Film International, Geography Compass,* and *Journal of Science Fiction Film and Television.*

Adam Bingham is a Senior Teaching Fellow in Japanese Film Studies at SOAS in London. He has taught film at various institutions around the UK and has published widely on Japanese and Hong Kong cinema. His book *Japanese Cinema since Hana-Bi* was published by Edinburgh University Press in 2015, and he has been a regular contributor to *Film Comment, CineAction,* and *Asian Cinema*. He recently completed studies of Ozu Yasujiro and representations of prostitution and of female filmmakers in Japan.

Bianca Briciu is an instructor in film studies and communication at Carleton University and St. Paul University, Ottawa. She has a PhD in Cultural Mediations and an interdisciplinary formation in film studies, gender studies, and social psychology. She has done extensive research on the representation of gender and sexuality in Japanese cinema and has published six articles in peer reviewed journals. She is pursuing research on the representation of affect and the body in cinema and other media.

Jennifer Coates is Senior Lecturer in Japanese Arts, Culture, and Heritage at the Sainsbury Institute for the Study of Japanese Arts and Cultures, University of East Anglia. She is the author of *Making Icons: Repetition and the Female Image in Japanese Cinema, 1945–1964* (2017). Her current ethnographic research focuses on early postwar film audiences in Japan.

x Notes on Contributors

Lindsay Coleman is a writer, academic, and educator based in Melbourne, Australia. His books include *Transnational Cinematography Studies* (2016), co-edited with Daisuke Miyao and Roberto Schaefer; *Contemporary Film Music* (2017), co-edited with Joakim Tillman; and *Sex and Storytelling in Modern Cinema* (2015). He is presently developing a television series on the history of visual effects with Richard Edlund and Leslie Iwerks. His three major areas of research are film technique, gender and sexuality, and Japanese Cinema

David Deamer is a writer and freelance scholar associated with Manchester Metropolitan University, UK. He is the author of *Deleuze's Cinema Books: Three Introductions to the Taxonomy of Images* (Edinburgh University Press, 2016) and *Deleuze, Japanese Cinema and the Atom Bomb: The Spectre of Impossibility* (2014), and is currently writing a book on Nietzsche and film. He has published in various edited collections and journals and occasionally blogs online at davideamer.com.

Rayna Denison is a Senior Lecturer in the School of Art, Media, and American Studies at the University of East Anglia. She is the author of *Anime: A Critical Introduction* (2015) and the editor of *Princess Mononoke: Understanding Studio Ghibli's Monster Princess* (2018). She is the co-editor of the Eisner Award–nominated *Superheroes on World Screens* (with Rachel Mizsei-Ward, 2016). Her scholarly articles can be found in many leading journals, including *Cinema Journal*, *Velvet Light Trap*, *Japan Forum*, and the *International Journal of Cultural Studies*.

David Desser is Emeritus Professor of Cinema Studies, Comparative and World Literatures, and East Asian Languages and Cultures at the University of Illinois. He has published twelve books, many of them on Japanese cinema. He is the founding co-editor of the *Journal of Japanese and Korean Cinema* and a former editor of *Cinema Journal*. He has done DVD commentary on Japanese films for Criterion and Arrow Academy.

Timothy Iles is an Associate Professor of Japanese Studies at the University of Victoria, Canada. He teaches on a range of issues related to Japan in particular and Asia in general, including history, ideology, literature, film, language, and popular culture. His primary area of research is Japanese cinema, both live action and animated, and the constellation of social critiques with which it engages. He is the author of *The Crisis of Identity in Contemporary Japanese Film: Personal, Cultural, National* (2008).

Mats Karlsson researches and teaches on Japanese literature and film at the University of Sydney. He is currently working on a project dealing with popular film during Japan's Period of High Economic Growth in the fifties and sixties. For a representative article related to this project, see his "Kinoshita Keisuke's Film at the End of the Rainbow: Love, Labour, and Alienation at the Yahata Steel Works" in the *Journal of Japanese and Korean Cinema*.

Hiroshi Kitamura is Associate Professor of History at the College of William and Mary. He is the author of *Screening Enlightenment: Hollywood and the Cultural Reconstruction of Defeated Japan* (2010). He is currently working on a biography of film critic Yodogawa Nagaharu and a study of post–World War II Japanese cinema in relation to economic and industrial growth.

Lauri Kitsnik is Japan Society for the Promotion of Science Postdoctoral Research Fellow at Kyoto University. His research interests include Japanese film history and theory, stardom, adaptation, and screenwriting. His work has appeared in *Asian Cinema, Japanese Studies, Journal of Japanese and Korean Cinema, Journal of Screenwriting*, and several edited volumes, including *Tanaka Kinuyo: Nation Stardom and Female Subjectivity* (Edinburgh University Press, 2018).

Diane Wei Lewis is an Assistant Professor in Film and Media Studies at Washington University in St. Louis. Her research on Japanese film and media cultures focuses on cinema's connections to mass media, capitalism, and modernity. Her articles have appeared in *Cinema Journal, positions*, and *Feminist Media Histories*, and she is completing a book on cinema, identification, and emotion in interwar Japan.

Dolores P. Martinez is Emeritus Reader in Anthropology at SOAS, University of London and a Research Associate at ISCA, University of Oxford. She has written on maritime anthropology, tourism, religion, gender, and popular culture in Japan. Her latest publications include *Remaking Kurosawa*; *Gender and Japanese Society* and, with Griseldis Krisch and Merry White as co-editors, *Assembling Japan*. An edited collection, *Persistently Postwar* (co-edited with Blai Guarne and Artur Lozano), will be published in 2019.

Joan Mellen retired as Professor Emerita from Temple University after fifty-nine years of teaching literature and creative writing. In 2004, she was a recipient of Temple's "Great Teacher" lifetime achievement award. She is the author of twenty-four books, ranging from film criticism, Japan studies, biography, sports, fiction, history, and investigative reporting. She has been a whistle blower in search of unresolved historical issues, from the JFK assassination (*A Farewell to Justice*, 2007) to the 1967 attack on the USS *Liberty* (*Blood in the Water*, 2018).

Bill Mihalopoulos is a Lecturer in Asian Pacific Studies at the University of Central Lancaster. He is the author of *Sex in Japan's Globalization, 1870–1930: Prostitutes, Emigration, and Nation-Building*. He fell under the cinematic spell of Shohei Imamura when he was an undergraduate at the University of Adelaide. He remains enchanted.

Michael Raine is assistant professor of film studies at Western University, Canada. He is editor, with Johan Nordström, of *The Culture of the Sound Image in Prewar Japan* and is writing *The Cinema of High Economic Growth: New Japanese Cinemas, 1955–1964*. He has worked extensively on Japanese cinema, including essays in the *Oxford Handbook of Japanese Cinema* (2014) and *Reorienting Ozu: A Master and His Influence* (2018).

Chapter 1
Introduction

Lindsay Coleman and David Desser

It is August 1945. A snake crawls across a dirt floor followed by a man similarly crawling snake-like. We learn that he is Yukichi Furuhashi, recently discharged from the Imperial Army due to his mental condition. Yukichi's father jokes that at least his son crawls very well. His wife, Sae, is horrified at her husband's condition but is having an affair with the local Buddhist priest. When Yukichi bites his mother's hand as she tries to feed him, the family determines to let him crawl away. But the townspeople, afraid of being embarrassed by him, seek him out. At the end, Sae sees him slither his way into a river where he will drown.

This is the basic situation of Shohei Imamura's contribution to the UNESCO Award- winning film at the 2002 Venice Film Festival, *11´09˝01/September 11*. Imamura was invited to contribute a nine-minute, eleven-second short along with films of the same length by the likes of international powerhouse directors like Youssef Chahine, Amos Gitai, Alejandro González Iñárritu, Claude Lelouch, Ken Loach, Samira Makhmalbaf, Mira Nair, and Idrissa Ouedraogo. This would be, sadly, Imamura's final film. That Imamura returned to the scene of World War II and the atomic bomb (alluded to in the film) is his attempt to understand the cultural trauma experienced by the United States—even the world—on 9/11. Certainly, Imamura makes direct reference to his earlier film on the subject: The name Yukichi should recall the name Yuichi, the World War II soldier stricken with PTSD in the film version of *Kuroi ame/Black Rain* (1989). The stars of the earlier film, Kazuo Kitamura and Etsuko Ichihara, appear here as villagers. And just for the sake of continuity, of insisting upon an authorial stamp, Imamura casts Tomorowo Taguchi as Yukichi, Mitsuko Baisho as his mother, along with Ken Ogata and Koji Yakusho as other villagers. The script was written by his eldest son, Daisuke Tengan. The village setting, the trauma of the war, the sense of shame for the wounded and the illicit sex that cannot be repressed—could Imamura have ended his career on a more appropriate note, continuing his ruthless yet humanistic examination of Japan's lower castes?

In 1978 Japanologist and film scholar Audie Bock published *Japanese Film Directors*. This survey of ten directors, drawn from three significant eras of Japanese film history, was intended to introduce and encapsulate the works of what Bock claimed were the filmmakers who represent the most consistently high achievements of Japanese cinematic art. Among these directors, categorized as part of "the New Wave and After," was Shohei Imamura. This section found Imamura linked with Nagisa Oshima and Masahiro Shinoda. Bock's choices of directors, both for the New Wave and throughout the book, have proven to be virtually canon-forming. Of course, by 1978 consensus had been formed around directors like Yasujiro Ozu, Kenji Mizoguchi, Akira Kurosawa, and Masaki Kobayashi along with the New Wave directors. To this group Bock added Mikio Naruse, Kon Ichikawa, and Keisuke Kinoshita—all of whom had some reputation in the West, if not as great as the likes of Mizoguchi, Ozu, or Kurosawa. What is astonishing about Bock's choices is the fact that only two directors from this cohort outside of her selections have been the subject of a full-length study since publication of her work. Of course, directors who began their careers much later have been the subjects of some study; but for those directors who worked in the 1920s–1970s, only two—Heinosuke Gosho and Seijun Suzuki—have been the subject of thorough review.[1] Some of her directors have been the object of study subsequently, with a handful of works devoted to the likes of Ozu, Kurosawa, Mizoguchi, and Oshima. One fine monograph has been devoted to Naruse; one excellent study of Kobayashi; one anthology on Ichikawa and one on Imamura.[2] Kinoshita and Shinoda remain merely in Bock's book.

Bock's work was preceded by two years by another pioneering work, Joan Mellen's *The Waves at Genji's Door*. With a subtitle of *Japan through Its Cinema*, it might have appeared to be merely a sociological survey of what could be learned of Japanese society via its movies. In fact, the book is far more than that. It is a reading of Japan through an ideological lens of criticism and critique, often from a feminist viewpoint. And in this book, still required reading for those new to the field, Shohei Imamura may be said to occupy a particular pride of place: a still from *The Profound Desire of the Gods* is reproduced on the book's cover. In fact, Imamura was nowhere near as well known in the West as classical directors like Ozu and Mizoguchi, modernist directors like Kurosawa and Kobayashi, or his New Wave colleague, Oshima. He was represented by only a handful of his films; almost two-thirds of his output at the time was unknown outside of Japan. What is more astonishing is that it may be argued that Imamura's best years were still ahead of him, certainly in terms of prizes within Japan, recognition outside of Japan, and wide festival and art house distribution. It is testimony to both Mellen and Bock that they had Imamura pegged so early in his career as a leading Japanese director.

The one full-length, English-language book dedicated to Imamura merely begins to appreciate the magnitude of his oeuvre and its significance. In fairness to the book and its estimable editor, James Quandt, it was designed to accompany a traveling retrospective of the director's work. Thus, about half of the book consists of interviews and essays by Imamura himself. No attempt was made to be thorough as regards each of his films, for instance. However one feels about this effort, there is surely room for many more. Sadly, however, such is not the case. This 1999 book remains alone on the shelf of Imamura studies, at least until the present volume.

There are so many surprising things about Imamura's career besides the fact of the early recognition given to him by pioneering scholars and the paucity of writings subsequently. For instance, Imamura won the prestigious Kinema Jumpo Best One award five times, second only to Ozu, who was a six-time winner.[3] Twice his films took the most coveted award of any film festival, the Palme d'Or from Cannes—the only Japanese director to have won the award more than once.[4] The traveling retrospective of 1997–1998 encompassed eleven venues in North America, including the Cinematheque Ontario, the Pacific Film Archive, the Museum of Fine Art, Boston, the National Gallery of Art, the UCLA Film Archive, the Pacific Cinematheque, Vancouver, the Film Center of the Art Institute of Chicago, and the Film Society of Lincoln Center. The Criterion Collection, the most important distributor of high-quality DVDs in the United States, most with a host of extras, has released a box set of three of Imamura's films along with interviews and essays. The Masters of Cinema series, the UK's equivalent of Criterion, has made no fewer than eight Imamura films available on DVD. A number of his films are or were available through mainstream outlets, like Amazon and Barnes & Noble.

Awards and retrospectives do not begin to scratch the surface of Imamura's importance as perhaps the preeminent examiner of the hidden, barely repressed underpinnings of Japanese society. As our title indicates, he has spent his career focusing on outsiders, those alienated by Japan's rush to its economic miracle. There are those men who turn to violence as an inchoate form of rebellion, who oppress women who are themselves in even more alienated circumstances but who ultimately must succumb to the greater society that surrounds them. And the oppression of women, which Imamura understands in ever more graphic terms than the great Mizoguchi, leads many of them into prostitution, the ultimate symbol of both the transactional nature of gender relationships and the monetary value placed on women and their bodies. But Imamura also knows that Japan and the Japanese people form something more than a nation; they are, in fact, a community of kindred spirits, bonded by their history and culture into a cohesive group, and his films work to examine these bonds yet at the same time look at the ways individual members of the group seek to break the chains of culture and escape.

It is no surprise that Imamura's films that most clearly depict and dissect Japanese society were those that received the greatest acclaim within Japan and distribution and discussion in the West. His clear-eyed examinations seem almost documentary-like and, indeed, many are documentaries. Within Japan his career was unprecedented for his having worked in both fiction film and documentary, including fiction films based on true stories. And perhaps that is one secret to his success: that unflinching search for the truth that makes for powerful but sometimes difficult cinema. But difficult in the sense of uncomfortable, not in the sort of postmodern way of many of the films of his contemporaries, especially Oshima and Kiju Yoshida. In his combination of documentary and fiction, then, he compares to directors like Wim Wenders and Werner Herzog, especially the latter.

With terms like anthropological, documentary, and documentary-like frequently applied to Imamura's cinema, it becomes important to examine the visualization of his insights, which is to say his style, the manner in which he expresses himself as a cinematic auteur. Because of the sometimes shocking nature of what he portrays and because clearly he is interested in society and culture, this aspect of Imamura's cinema has been overlooked. The style of directors like Mizoguchi, Ozu, and Kurosawa have often taken precedence over their content; Oshima and Yoshida, too, are sometimes prized for their manner and less so their meaning. But Imamura's documentary aesthetic is no less crucial than Mizoguchi's complex camera movements, Ozu's even-pacing and contemplative tone, Kurosawa's dynamic montage, and Yoshida's extreme distanciation. There is a kind of ruthlessness to Imamura's observing eye, a refusal to look away despite what is shown in front of the camera. No less than his anthropological interest, Imamura is a director defined by his deceptively stimulating style.

Imamura began his career, as virtually all Japanese directors did at the time, as an assistant director, in his case at Shochiku Studios in 1951. He worked as an assistant to Ozu on masterpieces like *Bakushu/Early Summer* (1951) and *Tokyo monogatari/Tokyo Story* (1953). Unhappy with Ozu's approach to the portrayal of Japanese life, he left Shochiku to work at Nikkatsu, where he had the good fortune to be paired up with Yuzo Kawashima, a contract director gently but insistently pushing the boundaries of genre. With Kawashima, Imamura co-wrote the screenplay for *Bakumatsu taiyo-den* (*Sun in the Last Days of the Shogunate*) in 1957. An often-raucous comedy with many implications regarding 1957 Japan as much as the last days of the Tokugawa era, the film's success earned Imamura his opportunity to direct. These early efforts—three films in 1958—already betray many of his directorial interests: sex, outsiders, rural Japan, and the strength of women. His first film, *Nusumareta yokujo/Stolen Desire*, was not quite what the commercially minded Nikkatsu desired. They kept their directors mostly in check during this period, and so Imamura was forced into a less critical stance in his other two films of the year.[5] With great subtlety and care he made his fourth film, *Nianchan*, into a study of poverty, the treatment of ethnic Koreans (zainichi) living in Japan, the strength of young women, and the lure of the outside world as seen from a slowly dying mining town. This year 1960 marks the beginning of the Japanese New Wave, termed at the time the Shochiku New Wave for the many films released that year by young directors, such as Oshima, Shinoda, and Yoshida, clearly pushing the boundaries of film style and social commentary. Imamura's *Nianchan* was not quite in that mode, though neither was it in the classical style of other social commentators like Ichikawa and Kinoshita.[6] But with his 1961 *Buta to gunkan/Pigs and Battleships*, there was no question that the New Wave label deserved to be expanded beyond the Shochiku imprint. His first masterpiece, *Pigs and Battleships* (Kinema Jumpo's #7, although for the year 1960, for some reason), is a darkly comic look at the effects of the American presence on the Japanese lower classes, the first of his films to truly focus on an underclass of weak-minded, foolish men and the strong women who love them nevertheless.

Imamura was clearly one of the most consistently interesting and skilled directors of the 1960s, with a powerful sense of cultural criticism, tying into what Bock calls "the irrational mythic consciousness of the Japanese" (1978: 287). In film after film in this decade he burnished his reputation as one of Japan's most important and insightful directors. In 1963, *Nippon konchuki/The Insect Woman* became the first of his five Kinema Jumpo-award winning films, also taking Best Director and Best Screenplay; his *Kamigami no fukaki yokubo/Profound Desire of the Gods* in 1968 took the Kinema Jumpo Best Film and Best Director awards once again. Meanwhile, controversial films like *Akai satsui/Intentions of Murder* (1964) netted a Kinema Jumpo #4, while in 1966 *Erogotoshi-tachi yori: Jinruigaku nyumon/The Pornographers* took #2 in the famed magazine poll (losing out to the now-forgotten *Shiroi kyoto/The Great White Tower* by Satsuo Yamamoto). It was in 1967 that he made his first foray into documentary production—Oshima of the Shochiku New Wave had also turned to documentary, though he would have far less impact with these films than would Imamura with his. Yet while Oshima would return to feature filmmaking toward the end of the 1960s and for the rest of his career, Imamura spent almost the entire decade of the 1970s making documentaries, including the famous *Nippon sengo-shi: Madamu Onboro no seikatsu/History of Postwar Japan as Told by a Bar Hostess* (1970); the World War II–themed *Muhomatsu kokyo ni kaeru/Muhomatsu Returns Home* (1973); and the deeply moving *Karayuki-san, the Making of a Prostitute* (1975).

To leave feature filmmaking at the height of his career was unprecedented. Also unprecedented was his formation of a professional academy, the Yokohama School of Broadcasting and Film (today the Japan Academy of Moving Images). He brought in industry professionals as well as film scholars (including Audie Bock) to teach the next generations of film and television professionals at a time when the assistant director system was becoming a thing of the past in light of the decline of the major studios. Perhaps their most successful graduate is the absurdly productive Takashi Miike. And then, again unprecedented, he returned to feature filmmaking at the end of the decade; we might say he returned with a vengeance, but that would be too obvious in light of the fact that the film was entitled *Vengeance Is Mine* (*Fukushu suru wa ware ni ari,* 1979). But return with a vengeance he did, with the film taking yet another Best One award from Kinema Jumpo. This film would mark an important collaboration not only with star Ken Ogata, but with co-star Mitsuko Baisho, who would be a presence in seven of his films, the most of any single performer.

Imamura would scale back his feature-film production in the 1980s, releasing only four films, but two of them would bring him the kind of international acclaim that had previously eluded him. Though *Eijanaika/Why Not?* of 1981, a return to the Bakumatsu era, made little impact, the same could not be said of *Narayama bushi-ko/The Ballad of Narayama* (1983), which received the first of his two Palme d'Or awards, #5 from Kinema Jumpo, and numerous awards from the Japanese Academy, including Best Film, Best Director, Best Actor for Ken Ogata, Best Supporting Actress for Mitsuko Baisho, and Best Screenplay. Though often cited as a remake of Keisuke Kinoshita's groundbreaking version of 1958, the two films could not be more different. The film would be the widest release that Imamura ever had around the globe—after Cannes it would get its North American debut at the Toronto International Film Festival and then be released around the world. *Zegen* (1987) was in official competition at Cannes, followed by minor festival playoff thereafter, but it never caught on. However, the same surely cannot be said for *Kuroi ame/Black Rain* (1989). Once again Imamura found himself in official competition at Cannes; received a Best One from Kinema Jumpo, and Best Film from the Japanese Academy. More significantly, the film became, along with Akira Kurosawa's *Hachi-gatsu no rhapusodi*/*Rhapsody in August* (1991), part of public discourse in the United States regarding the efficacy and ethics of the atomic bombings of Japan. Kurosawa's film was admittedly more controversial, mostly for the moment when Hollywood star Richard Gere, playing a Japanese American man from Hawaii, apologizes for the US bombing of Nagasaki. What most Americans missed about Imamura's film was the way in which it was a more devastating critique of the bomb not by its overt criticism (there is none), but by the way it invokes the style and theme of Ozu. Once rejected by Imamura, now Ozu became extremely useful as a way to talk about Japanese tradition and the family and the way in which the atomic bomb represented a rupture in Ozu's seemingly placid view of the continuity of Japanese life despite changes in culture and society.

As the years went by without another film from Imamura following *Black Rain*, it seemed as if illness and age had taken their toll on his career. Even so, Imamura's post–New Wave career had proven far more significant than his New Wave cohort. Oshima never made a truly important film after *In the Realm of the Senses* in 1976 (his career had taken a severe downturn even before his debilitating stroke in 1996); Shinoda never made a successful film after the well-received 1977 *Ballad of Orin*, though he kept working regularly through the 1980s, sporadically in the 1990s, and then retired in 2003; following his brilliant *Coup d'etat* in 1973, his last New Wave–style film, Kiju Yoshida worked only intermittently, and only his *Wuthering Heights* in 1988 met with any attention outside of Japan as it played in competition at Cannes—though it never received any distribution in Europe or the United States. So it came as something of a surprise when Imamura released *The Eel* in 1997. Winner of the Palme d'Or at Cannes and his fifth Kinema Jumpo Best One, Imamura suddenly found himself linked with the renaissance of Japanese cinema that began in the mid-1990s. With its long takes, minimalist dialogue, episodic structure, and low-key presentation of a highly dramatic story that begins with the murder of an adulterous wife by her husband, Imamura was now a filmmaker with much in common with a new generation of Japanese directors who fell under the sway of Ozu and Hou Hsiao-hsien. *Akai hashi no shita no nurui mizu*/*Warm Water Under a Red Bridge* (2001) was yet another of Imamura's films invited into competition at Cannes along with many other festival showings. In some ways this, his last feature film, was a return to his roots in the rural, the mythic, and the magical power of women. After more than forty years as Japan's "anthropologist," he would make only one more, short, film, as part of the international omnibus film exploring 9/11 with which this introduction began. He died in 2006 of the cancer he had long been battling, though by that time it was already clear that he was, as so many commentators noted upon his death, one of the most significant of Japan's postwar filmmakers.

As noted above, though long recognized as one of Japan's most significant filmmakers, there has been only one book in English devoted to Imamura. Many articles have appeared on individual films, while both Alexander Jacoby and Jasper Sharp devote entries to Imamura in their fine reference guides.[7] The awards he has earned, the wide distribution his films have received, and the scholarly attention devoted to him indicate that he is one of the most significant directors in Japanese film history. This book is an attempt not only to give sufficient space to the bulk of his career, but also to give the career a certain shape in order to understand Imamura's project as an investigator into Japanese tradition and culture and to understand the significance of his achievement. To this end, we have gathered together a number of very well known film scholars from Australia, the UK, and the US along with scholars associated with other humanistic and philosophical pursuits. We might say that the quality of the contributors is indicative of the stature of Imamura himself.

As related above, it took some time for the full effect of Imamura's legacy to be felt. The small number of films in distribution through the 1970s stunted the growth of his reputation. But from the time of the success of *Black Rain* in theaters, subsequent successful festival appearances of his films, and the current availability of many of his films on DVD, it is possible to see clearly the consistency of his vision and the powerful way it is conveyed. Though he remains associated with the Japanese New Wave, and his films made during the height of that exciting movement are reckoned among its best, his post–New Wave career far exceeds that of his contemporaries. A career span of over forty years, numerous awards domestically and in the international arena, box office success, and critical acclaim demand a fuller account of his singular achievement. This book is that attempt.

Killers, Clients and Kindred Spirits: The Taboo Cinema of Shohei Imamura is divided into three sections, each with a specific theme, with the films arranged chronologically within each section. It is always possible to discuss a group of films from many different perspectives, including the most obvious one: in strict chronological order. Though many monographs devoted to the work of an individual auteur utilize such a structure, that often implies a kind of Platonic ideal toward which a director's work aspires. There is no reason to imagine that a director cannot move around in his or her interests, working on some issue, abandoning it, circling back to it later, etc. Similarly, the vicissitudes of financing and film funding often necessitate making compromises in one's overall plan. Working for the most part independently and on an ad hoc basis, this was less an issue for Imamura as his career progressed, but it is certainly apparent in his early filmmaking efforts. And while we have grouped the films according to overarching themes in each section, it is not impossible to imagine that other scholars could arrive at other groupings—this is all to the good. We hope merely that our grouping has validity and the ability to shed light on each film and Imamura's overall accomplishment.

Previous to our groupings we have an initial chapter that focuses on the very early output of the director. Jennifer Coates's chapter, "The Making of An Auteur: The Early Films (1958–1959)," examines his first four works. These have received significantly less academic and critical attention than his work from 1960 onward. *Stolen Desire*, *Ginza Station* (aka Lights of Night, *Nishi Ginza eki mae*, 1958), and *Endless Desire* (*Hateshinaki yokubō*, 1958), made at Nikkatsu Studios, have been largely dismissed, with *My Second Brother* (Nianchan, 1959) credited with bringing Imamura to critical and academic attention. This chapter takes a closer look at these early films, investigating their relation to critical and popular understanding of Imamura's present reputation and providing some context for the later critical groupings arranged in this book.

The first grouping is that of "Killers." This is probably one of the more obvious categories to create for Imamura's overall oeuvre as his protagonists are frequently murderers, or at the very least those who toy with the possibility of murder. The mindset and emotional landscape of the killer was both thematic and narrative terrain Imamura knew extremely well. The title "Killers" refers to these characters, as well as their preoccupations, and by default Imamura's own. For a closer understanding of what this might mean let us place Imamura's particular focus in a broader context of cinematic history. *The Silence of the Lambs* (1991), as an easy example, fetishizes, sensationalizes, glamourizes the act of killing and the killers who perpetrate these acts. Even a superlatively gifted filmmaker such as Jonathan Demme cannot help but create these killers, in the form of Buffalo Bill and Hannibal Lecter, as somewhat glorious monsters. Imamura places us squarely in the mind and heart of a killer as an individual whose pathologies, while extreme, are still symptomatic of forms of social and sexual alienation at least some of us can identify with. To describe his killers as "banal" would be unfair. They kill, but they also boast, bullshit, pine, lust, lecture, and bore their fellow men. Ken Ogata is the prototypical Imamura killer in his performance in *Vengeance Is Mine*. Here is a character who kills with ease and skill but saves his real disgust and hatred for his ineffectual father, and his ultimate coldness for his spurned wife. The closest mainstream Hollywood cinema has come to such a depiction would be Tom Noonan's superb evocation of the Tooth Fairy Killer in Michael Mann's *Manhunter* (1986), a character of mania, vulnerability, poetry, and odd hubris all at once. (There have been two other iterations of the character, but Noonan's is the only performance which captures a balance of traits comparable to Imamura.)

Imamura's skill in depicting killers as ordinary humans is not unique, of course. Fritz Lang's famed *M* (1931) achieved this in Peter Lorre's entirely sympathetic performance, but even Lang could not help but lean heavily on the notion of killers as pathological beings. Imamura's eye is colder, more anthropological than the theatrical Lang, the eclectic Demme, the lyrical Mann. Mann allows the Tooth Fairy moments of romance and emotional epiphany, even if that epiphany—in the form of a moment of bonding with his lover and a sedated tiger—is equally tied to his particular pathology for megalomania and grandiosity. What matters is that Mann lets his killer have an emotional life which makes, at the very least, powerful sense to him. Imamura arguably is one of the only filmmakers to craft portraits of killers who are not beings possessed by pathology, neurosis, or megalomania for its own sake, but rather sexual (or asexual), romantic, emotional and above all physical beings, subject to sequences of emotion and appetite readily identifiable by any member of the audience. Their resentments are terrifyingly familiar, their fragile egos and casual deceptions an ugly reminder of our own. Takuro Yamashita, the lead character of Imamura's *The Eel* (1997), is a sad man, a tragic figure, a thwarted romantic who struggles in his attempts at igniting an affair. These are the many colors Imamura reveals of the character, yet from our first instants of meeting him Imamura contextualizes him as the most brutal and misogynist of killers. Imamura spares us none of the gore, the audience witnessing him brutally dispatch his wife and wound her lover in a crime of passion. His actual act of killing, as David Desser notes in his chapter on the film, is a prime catalyst for ongoing characterization in the film. How he kills, why he kills, tells us much about the character as any other act he commits in the film. For Roger Ebert, Ogata's Iwao Enokizu in *Vengeance Is Mine*, is a portrait of a cold-blooded serial killer that "suggests a cruel force without motivation, inspiration, grievance" (2008). Ebert is partly correct. To say the character is without "grievance" is perhaps inaccurate; more that his "grievances" are not the specific pathology of Fritz Lang's killer, that of a murderer possessed by the need to dispatch children, but rather the kind of pique and resentment and contempt that can creep into any soul. They are not the kind of grievances one might connect to murder, more to the burning resentment we may find in Twitter trolls, men going through a divorce, the romantically and sexually spurned. These are the kinds of antisocial impulses hiding in plain sight. And so, too, are Imamura's characters. Even while he hates both his father and wife, and uses women as objects, Enokizu proffers bogus camaraderie to the men who surround him. These emotional attributes, the source of his misanthropy, may manifest in killings, but that is perhaps the only unique thing about them. Killers are, in Imamura, heroes, inasmuch as heroes are the proxies for the audience whom we cannot help but project our fears, ambivalences, even perhaps our dark fantasies onto.

The section on "Killers" begins with Hiroshi Kitamura's chapter "Pigs and Battleships, or the Paradox of Japan's Post-World War II Anti-Americanism." This chapter interrogates the cultural politics of Japan's postwar anti-Americanism by primarily exploring *Pigs and Battleships*, but also draws upon *Insect Woman* (1963), *History of Postwar Japan as Told by a Bar Hostess* (1970), *Black Rain* (1989), and *11'09"01/ September 11* (2002), Kitamura explores how Imamura presents postwar Japan as America's "client state" by framing Japanese life in relation to US military and sexual interventions. Yet in depicting the raw and energetic lives of the "low-end" Japanese (with such themes as sex, violence, rape, and crime), Imamura paradoxically offers prescriptions for survival under the American security and nuclear umbrella in an era of high-speed economic and industrial growth. This too elucidates the "killer" mindset so prevalent in Imamura's depictions of postwar Japanese masculinity.

In Adam Bingham's "Traveling by Rail with *Intentions of Murder*," the title film is examined on the basis of it being one of the director's most sociologically incisive pictures, touching as it does on seemingly extreme inequality—domestic servitude in an enforced relationship. The film is built around a female protagonist who (unlike those in numerous other Imamura films) seems to be a more overt victim of a patriarchal sociopolitical landscape. This leads interestingly, to the female lead's desire to poison her assailant and rapist, her pathology both justified and a central focus of the narrative. Here the "killer" is again a natural manifestation of the layers of social oppression they must endure, and again a powerfully relatable manifestation of everyday rage and resentment.

Where the "killer" of *Intentions of Murder* is an innocent, in John Berra's "Hidden in Plain Sight: The False Leads and True Mysteries of *Vengeance Is Mine*," the killer is similarly oppressed but anything but an innocent. Marking a return by Imamura to narrative filmmaking following a fruitful detour into documentary that lasted much of the 1970s, the serial killer saga *Fukushū suru wa ware ni ari/Vengeance Is Mine* (1979) represented a convergence between his nonfiction practices and the socially revealing, genre-riffing storytelling that firmly established him as a key figure in the Japanese New Wave in the 1960s. Imamura initially appears to undertake this task through a nonlinear puzzle structure that ostensibly dissects the relevant details of Enokizu's life. However, it soon becomes apparent that his procedural, no matter how methodically detailed, will shed little light on the motivations for its protagonist's depravity. This chapter examines Imamura's approach to his interrelated subjects of the sociopath and the society that Enokizu gleefully rebels against.

In David Desser's chapter "*The Eel*: Trauma Cinema," there is an exploration of the theme of redemption, the kind of redemption typically denied alienated outsider characters. A horrifyingly brutal murder climaxes the film's first scene and we think we are in the realm of Imamura's angry societal outcastes. An elided eight-year prison stint for the crime presages a change in tone as Imamura returns to the small-town life he so memorably depicted in earlier films. And Imamura joins the ranks of many art-cinema auteurs in depicting dailiness through the use of studied long takes. Yet there is a quirkiness of character and content that distinguishes the film from the more austere examples of mid-to-late 1990s art films. This chapter looks closely at the formal aspects of the film and demonstrates its relationship to Imamura's optimistic view of the possibility of redeeming a life through daily activities and comic incidents that overcome past trauma and tragedy. It presents the possibility that a man may be a killer and also still possess all the constituent parts of a human being still capable of love.

Hoping not to be overly reductive, and with the exception of *Intentions of Murder*, the characters cited in the "Killers" section are male and represent a definitively male perspective on society and relationships. Yet Imamura is equally acclaimed for the strong, sensual, and emotionally articulate women who populate his films, women who see themselves in broader terms than their connection to men. His perspective on women is considerably less in its scope, but more in the relative depth he demonstrates in seeing his women in great emotional, physical, and psychological detail. Paradoxically, much is revealed of the feminine perspective even as the point of view from which these women are seen by the director is obviously limited, specifically, to a male, Japanese, twentieth-century view on women, and in turn relations between the sexes. This in turn means that Imamura possesses a striking, equally anthropological perspective on women, seen within the expressly heteronormative male Japanese gaze that configures most relations between the sexes to those covering sex and love.

If Imamura's vision of his characters is blunt enough to allow their workaday misanthropy to curdle into homicidal rage, then equally his view on love and sex, and any other more sensual or whimsical moments between the senses, is equally overlaid with a bastardized extremity of the same sentiments. Love and lust devolve into the love of a prostitute for her pimp, or a john for his prostitute. Men, in Imamura's world, are "Clients," catered to both emotionally and sexually by the complex women in their lives. To Imamura, his men and women have one foot in, one foot out, of any of their significant relationships, afraid as they are to replace the brutish and transactional nature of their dealings with anything approaching an admission of tenderness. Love can mutate into rape, and rape can be eventually interpreted as love in such a fraught emotional environment. In *The Pornographers* (1966), Subuyan Ogata seduces/is seduced by his landlady, yet rather than admit to feelings of tenderness he must transform this scene into a hyperbolic, farcical declaration of potency, lust, and orgiastic invitation. Remarkably, however, it is not Ogata's own declaration that is most significant in this narrative, but the gradual characterization of his mistress that proves most intriguing in this comic tale.

Imamura himself is not exempt from this this perspective. While the gentleman filmmaker was certainly no killer, he, like his heroes, admitted to his attraction toward an objectified, biologically favored rendition of Japanese womanhood, an example of a typical Madonna-whore dichotomy that erred more toward the whore. Women in this paradigm could be brave, earthy, honest, emotional, but their biological assets ultimately would win out as their prime attraction, ironically on both an emotional and physical level. Imamura's women are defined by sex, but sex of the warmest, most human kind, and that which reveals a broad swathe of their unique psychology. The limit placed upon such characterizations is that they are seen through the lens of sex and sexual desire. This is sex from the male perspective, and inherent in it all of the anger, aggression, anxiety, and animal irrationality that might be expected. Imamura strands his women and men in a world where, biology and its transactional manifestations aside, little is articulated with any ease, even as much of the characters' burgeoning emotional complexity simmers beneath the surface. As such, they must struggle with their urges in a world of pitiless determinism and ceaseless transaction. This is what typifies the films of Imamura focused on "Clients," the second category we have chosen to focus on.

Lindsay Coleman's "The Obscene in the Everyday: *The Pornographers*" asserts that Imamura offers up a compelling portrait of Japanese society as permissive, profligate, and absurdly commercialized. The low-rent, industrialized processes of the film's title characters, all in an effort to feed the never-ending appetite for pornographic content, speak to such qualities within a society. Paradoxically, however, sexuality and sexual desire are presented not as commodified in the film, but rather as a shocking and ungovernable quantity. Their presence within the narrative triggers, conversely, the bemusement of the film's protagonists and an increasing incisiveness on the part of Imamura himself in his role as director. This chapter analyzes the means, via lighting, editing, composition, and the sequence of scenes, by which Imamura established a unique directorial approach to allow for the interrogation of taboos such as incest, sexual attraction toward minors, and indeed the manner in which sexuality may pervade a wide range of social and economic activities. It presents, to a degree, a notion of relations between the sexes ossified into a hyper-commodified state.

In Michael Raine's chapter on *The Insect Woman*, he observes that the film came at a turning point in the modernization of the Japanese economy and of the film industry.

The Insect Woman pits the *shomin* (the common people) against the bourgeois *shimin* (the citizen; the urban, westernized subject of political rights and duties), but in Imamura's hands the *shomin* become the *senmin* (outcasts; the exploited exploiters that make up the lower levels of both rural and urban Japan under high economic growth). Imamura heads a long line of filmmakers who sympathize with female protagonists whose suffering is caused by Japanese modernization, but unlike, say, Kenji Mizoguchi or Mikio Naruse, *The Insect Woman* foregrounds that protagonist's selfishness and materialism while refusing easy depictions of an untouched, authentic Japan.

In Mats Karlson's "Imamura Shohei's Profound Desire for Japan's Cultural Roots," the director's film, *The Profound Desires of the Gods* (1968), explores the origins of primordial Japanese culture. The dean of Japanese film criticism, Satō Tadao, while suggesting possible readings, claims that the film in the final analysis resists specific interpretation. Karlson suggests that the film is an "open" film, somewhat reminiscent of Hiroshi Teshigahara's *The Woman in* the *Dunes* (*Suna no onna*, 1964) in that it invites multiple interpretations from a reader-response perspective. Critic Saki Ryūzō identifies the film's message as a critique of all the Japanese, islanders per definition, who have willfully destroyed their "inner islands" and lost touch with their roots, enslaved to the transactional rudiments of postwar Japanese society, then still in its relative infancy. In identifying convergences and divergences in critical approaches to the film, Karlson seeks to address the contentious issues, such as the implied discourse on incest, it raises. The perspective advocated on Imamura's oeuvre here is not specific to male-female dynamics but does engage strongly with the notion of postwar Japan as a society in which all the more intimate elements of humanity had become commodified and subject to transaction.

In a similar vein, Joan Mellen's "'Products of Japan': *Karayuki-san, The Making of a Prostitute*" examines in depth the themes Imamura develops regarding the unknown and abandoned people of Japan's disastrous Pacific War. The karayuki-san of the title had been exploited and abandoned right from the start: as a woman and as a burakumin. She was even exploited by her own family before the war. Such a situation is ripe with so many of Imamura's favored themes, which this essay elaborates upon in detail.

Bianca Briciu's chapter, "The Female Body as Transgressor of National Boundaries in *The History of Postwar Japan as Told by a Bar Hostess*," suggests that while his fiction films have received a lot of critical attention, Imamura's documentaries made in mid-career in the 1970s are less well known but nevertheless epitomize his concern with marginal experiences. Two of his documentaries, *The History of Postwar Japan as Told by a Bar Hostess* (1970) and *Karayuki san, The Making of a Prostitute* (1975), describe the embodied experiences of low-status women, unpacking gender and class power relations.

Now for the twist, and the source of Imamura's greatness. The third major category explored is that of "Kindred Spirits" and suggests an oppositional strain in Imamura's films to the more cynical thematic focus of the previous two categories. Here is a filmmaker whose starting point for characterization can be, for a man, his basic bloodlust, and this bloodlust as a basic fact of his masculinity. Equally, Imamura may, literally, allow his vision of a woman's genitals to determine the kind of person she will be, how this may characterize her interplay with the man or men in her life. Yet from these bluntly contrived ingredients of character, Imamura conjures up dynamic, subtle, generically unclassifiable works whose emotional scope stretch from the limits of human response through all the most commonplace and natural responses and behaviors. How characters may spring to life from the most extreme of circumstances and journey toward normalcy is a cornerstone of Imamura's humanism. What is, arguably, a secret to Imamura's long-term appeal is how he foregrounds human and relatable stories against the most extreme of backgrounds. Think of Shigematsu Shizuma's efforts to secure a suitor for his niece in *Black Rain*. In itself this quest is relatable, emotionally charged, while also quotidian. The fact that such a request is set against the reality that his niece was exposed to the atomic fallout following the bombing of Hiroshima in 1945 fundamentally alters the setup. Where the original details of the scenario, that of a relative seeking a suitor for his niece, might perhaps be conducive to light sociological analysis such as that of Ozu, or even a comedy of manners in the hands of another filmmaker, Imamura's contrived "background" in *Black Rain* is that of a society shattered, of a social order haunted by death and destruction, of a population facing a lifetime of radioactive poisoning. Against this is set a quest, in the "foreground" for emotional and social survival in the form a successful matchmaking. In the midst of this juxtaposition we find the unlikely relationship of the niece Yasuko and the poor and traumatized Yuichi. In this most unlikely a combination of circumstances these two characters somehow find each other and fulfill E. M. Forster's famous dictum:

> Only connect! That was the whole of her sermon. Only connect the prose and the passion, and both will be exalted, and human love will be seen at its height. Live in fragments no longer.

There are plentiful further illustrations of this odd dynamic, two individuals finding one another, and bonding, in what would otherwise seem to be a hostile world. Only a filmmaker as richly ironic as Imamura would allow such an idealistic notion as espoused by Forster to play out in the following scene in *Vengeance Is Mine*, where Hisano Asano, the mother of Enokizu's love Haru, and a killer herself, confronts the killer in an oddly warm scene.

> Asano: Don't try to kill me, Enokizu. That's what you want to do, isn't it?
> Enokizu: Ever since you walked out last night.
> Asano: And this is the second time. The third time's the charm?
> (He smiles.)
> Asano: Wipe that smirk off your face! I suppose you think we're alike as fellow killers?
> Enokizu: Not really. But I sort of feel like you're a prison buddy.

Following this oddly comic exchange, the two crouch down and share in the drinking of water from an overflowing hose on the path they are walking. Later Enokizu does kill Asano, yet even the most cynical viewer cannot deny the genuine camaraderie of this scene in the face of the many other scenes in which Enokizu manufactures a semblance of warmth for his fellow man. This scene, and those shared by Yasuko and Yuichi, speak to the ability of Imamura characters to form the most unlikely connections, to articulate their humanity in moments unexpected to the characters themselves. Despite all in their characterization that would suggest otherwise, Imamura's characters have an ease in establishing basic kinship.

The final section of this book is dedicated to the varieties of kinship Imamura finds within Japanese society, in both his documentary and feature films. He evokes the collective spirit of Japan's rural people, family ties, the connections of Imamura himself to his cinematic subjects, and the shared bonds of those in the lower strata of society with his typical anthropological and incisive eye.

The first chapter of this section is Lauri Kitsnik's "Better off Being Bacteria: Adaptation and Allegory in *Dr. Akagi*." It looks at how certain alterations and shifts in emphases to the short story on which *Dr. Akagi* is based, coupled with the production process, enabled this adaptation to become a film unique to Imamura's style. It came to feature allusions to both the public and private, with the depiction of a war-torn rural community extending to Imamura's own family and professional background. By presenting allegories of state-induced violence and the perseverance of common people, *Dr. Akagi* is a humanist tale strongly consistent with the later output of Imamura.

Bill Mihalopoulos's "The Never-Ending Pacific War and the Ruse of Memory" offers a unique focus on a series of documentaries, "In Search of the Unreturned Soldiers in Malaysia," "In Search of the Unreturned Soldiers in Thailand," and "Outlaw-Matsu Returns Home," directed and produced by Imamura for NHK over a three-year period (1970–1971; 1973). All three documentaries are an investigation into the givens of a question which is hidden and wrapped up in the situation, and which the camera must extract, for the whole story to be told. For Imamura, the people at the margins of society offer hope and freedom. In his documentaries, Imamura attempts to identify the process of co-evolution between modern Japanese statehood and modern subjectivity, and, at the same time, to explore the possibility of finding a cultural framework in which the Japanese as a collective can define their embodied experience without recourse to the Japanese state. It is an effort to evoke their collective spirit.

Community is a central theme in Imamura's *The Ballad of Narayama* and is in turn explored in Rayna Denison's essay on the 1983 film. Imamura's adaptation presents a stark contrast to earlier versions of Shichirō Fukazawa's 1956 story of abandonment of the aged in a primitive, allegorical vision of Japanese society. Imamura interprets the tale through an anthropologically inflected and documentarian lens, thereby partially obscuring his excoriating appraisal of gender and aging within culture. This chapter investigates Imamura's adaptation process, using production-side discourse to assess the extent to which Imamura's version of *The Ballad of Narayama* was intentionally produced to contrast to earlier adaptations, and seeking to understand how and to what ends he remade this already well-known tale. The claims made in promotion and in reflective accounts of the production assess them in relation to the film text. By comparing production discourses to the film's content this chapter shows how Imamura's stylistic flourishes and moments of excess were used to offset a deeper, unflinching discourse about gender, societal functions, and aging, a powerful investigation of the unbreakable ties that tortuously hold a society together.

In *Ningen johatsu/A Man Vanishes* (1967), a documentary film crew led by Imamura follows a woman, Yoshie Hayakawa, nicknamed *Nezumi*, the Rat, who has been deserted by her fiancé, Takashi Oshima. Imamura helps Nezumi and family members investigate the man's disappearance. However, as the film develops, new information and unearthed secrets create an ever-denser web of intrigue, while Imamura progressively reveals that his "documentary" filmmaking has irreparably altered the "reality" it claims to report on. Imamura has a tryst with Nezumi, which weakens her motivation to find Oshima while strengthening her commitment to the film and filmmaker. In the middle of shooting, Imamura reveals that a scene is being staged within a studio set. Diane Lewis's

"Boundary Play: Truth, Fiction, and Performance in *A Man Vanishes*" examines the use of layered diegeses and sociological experimentation—particularly in their deployment of reenactment and role play in this film.

In David Deamer's "Cine-anthropology and Celebration: *Why Not?* and Nietzschean genealogy," Imamura is put forward as a genealogist, and his films as celebrations of moments in which values are questioned in order that the underlying disparate forces be exposed and explored. These essential tensions within Japanese society are further contextualized with a unique Nietzschean perspective.

Imamura's 1989 film *Kuroi Ame/Black Rain* is based on Masuji Ibuse's 1969 homonymous novel for which he had read numerous Hiroshima survivors' diaries. It forms the basis of Dolores Martinez's "*Kuroi ame*: An Anthropology of Suffering." Shot in radiant black and white, the film not only evokes the Japanese cinema of the 1940s, but also graphically depicts the horrors of the atomic bomb attack on Hiroshima in 1945. Cutting back and forth between the character Shigematsu Shizuma's memories of August 6 and the family's postwar life as *hibakusha* (lit. explosion-affected people) amongst villagers who are tired of hearing about the bomb, the film dissects Japanese society's attitudes toward difference. Through an analysis of the Shizumas' forbearance in the face of their neighbors' gossip and antipathy, this chapter considers the film as an anthropological depiction and exploration of suffering and of unlikely kinship.

In Tim Iles's chapter, "The Symbolic Function of Water," with its primary focus on *Warm Water under a Red Bridge*, there is an exploration of how Imamura creates a world in which both wonder and hope are possible. The fundamental humanism of Imamura's work sustains a community in which communication, redemption, and forgiveness merge with the absurd, the perverse, the supernatural, and the fantastic to demonstrate the dignity and value of each individual. The struggles of society's lowest strata provide the foundation for a reconceptualization of the contours of the human community, in which realization of aspirations becomes the shared project of all.

Any sharp-eyed observer will note the absence of *Zegen*. This is not any criticism of the film, of course. It simply reflects the problems in compiling collections. We could entice no commentator to work on the film. Good scholars are typically busy. We are ourselves amazed at the quality of our contributors and cannot complain about some few others who could not participate at this time. Of course, it is a shame that we could not include it. The film was invited to compete for the Palme d'Or at Cannes in 1987 and was Japan's official submission for the "Best Foreign Language Film" category at the American Academy Awards. Perhaps more to the point, this darkly comic look at a man who runs a string of brothels from Manchuria to Malaya at the turn of the twentieth century fits perfectly into our category of "Clients." The film, as Jasper Sharp notes in his useful review for *Midnight Eye*, takes place entirely outside of Japan and it seems if not indebted to, then at least a thematic extension of, *Karayuki-san* (Sharp 2001). If not a major Imamura film, we can say that it is nevertheless a typical Imamura film and thus worthy of our attention. Sadly, it could not be so.

Otherwise, we are very pleased to offer up this first-ever study of every Imamura film, from his little-seen early films through his exciting New Wave works, through his emergence as a filmmaker of international stature and status. We are equally pleased to have gathered together as knowledgeable a group of scholars of the Japanese cinema as one is likely to find in any one place devoted to the work of one filmmaker.

Lindsay Coleman, Melbourne, Australia
David Desser, Los Angeles, California

Notes

A Note on Names:

Japanese directors and stars are given in Western-style name order: given name first, family name second. Japanese works that have been translated into English are also listed in Western-style name order. Japanese names are rendered in Japanese fashion for those works that have not been translated.

1. See Arthur Nolletti Jr. *The Cinema of Gosho Heinosuke: Laughter through Tears* (Bloomngton: Indiana University Press, 2005); Tom Vick, *Time and Place Are Nonsense: The Films of Seijun Suzuki* (Washington, DC: Smithsonian Institution, 2015)
2. See Catherine Russell, *The Cinema of Mikio Naruse: Women and Japanese Modernity* (Durham, NC: Duke University Press, 2008); Stephen Prince, *A Dream of Resistance: The Cinema of Kobayashi Masaki* (New Brunswick, NJ: Rutgers University Press, 2017); James Quandt, ed., *Kon Ichikawa* (Cinematheque Ontario Monographs) (Bloomington: Indiana University Press, 2001); James Quandt, ed., *Shohei Imamura* (Cinematheque Ontario Monographs) (Toronto: Toronto International Film Festival, 1999).
3. Imamura's Best One award has gone to *The Insect Woman*, 1963; *The Profound Desire of the Gods*, 1968; *Vengeance Is Mine*, 1979; *Black Rain*, 1989; and *The Eel*, 1997.
4. These are *Ballad of Narayama*, 1983, and *The Eel*.
5. Even the great Seijun Suzuki, also often linked with the New Wave, would have to wait until the 1960s to unleash the full force of his fertile fancy.
6. Imamura's film is rather close in tone to a film he wrote for director Kirio Urayama, *Kyūpora no aru machi/Foundry Town* (1962), though the latter film also functions as a star vehicle for Sayuri Yoshinaga and Mitsuo Hamada.

7. See Alexander Jacoby, *A Critical Handbook of Japanese Film Directors* (Albany, CA: Stone Bridge Press, 2008), and Jasper Sharp, *Historical Dictionary of Japanese Cinema* (Lanham, MD: Scarecrow, 2011).

Works Cited

Ebert, Roger (2008). Rev. *Vengeance Is Mine* Jan. 17. https://www.rogerebert.com/reviews/vengeance-is-mine-2008 Accessed Sept. 5, 2018.

Jacoby, Alexander (2008). *A Critical Handbook of Japanese Film Directors*. Albany, CA: Stone Bridge Press.

Sharp, Jasper (2001). Rev. *Zegen* http://www.midnighteye.com/reviews/zegen/. Accessed September 5, 2018.

Sharp, Jasper (2011). *Historical Dictionary of Japanese Cinema*. Lanham, MD: Scarecrow.

Chapter 2

The Making of an Auteur: The Early Films (1958–1959)

Jennifer Coates

Shohei Imamura's first four films have received significantly less academic and critical attention than his work from 1960 onward. *Stolen Desire* (*Nusumareta yokujō*, 1958), *Ginza Station* (aka *Lights of Night*, *Nishi Ginza eki mae*, 1958), and *Endless Desire* (*Hateshinaki yokubō*, 1958), made at Nikkatsu Studios, have been largely dismissed, with *My Second Brother* (*Nianchan*, 1959) credited with bringing Imamura to critical and academic attention. This chapter takes a closer look at the contents and reception of these early films, investigating their relation to critical and popular understanding of Imamura's auteur persona and oeuvre.

For critics such as Jasper Sharp, these early films are "uncharacteristic" (2011: 93). Yet if we look closely at their themes, casting, language, and settings, we can see many central components of Imamura's later work evident in these early studio films. This chapter argues that this early career stage already exhibits Imamura's key thematic, stylistic, and political concerns. The final section takes a closer look at *My Second Brother* to understand how this fourth film enabled Imamura to win over professional film critics. While the dominant story of Imamura's career situates *My Second Brother* as the work in which he found his authorial voice, I want to suggest that this voice is discernible much earlier. Imamura's first three films are in fact strongly characteristic, not only of his later work, but also of his public-facing auteur persona.

The Auteur's Origin Story

In analyzing these early films in reference to Imamura's auteur persona, I am not necessarily subscribing to auteur theory itself, but rather practicing a kind of critical auteur studies. Mitsuhiro Yoshimoto has identified two strands of auteurist criticism in relation to writing on Japanese cinema: classical and revisionist (2000: 12). Classical auteurist criticism assesses the director's work as transcending the time and place of its making and understands the film text as an expression of its maker's consistent and coherent "personal expression" (Yoshimoto 2000: 55). Following Roland Barthes and Michel Foucault, who argued for the author as "a function of discourse" (Yoshimoto 2000: 57), poststructuralist critics challenged classical auteurism. Later revisionist auteurism such as that developed by Peter Wollen attempted to disengage auteur criticism from the person of the auteur, understanding the auteur instead as a kind of deep structure permeating films made by a particular director. Yoshimoto argues that the issue with Wollen's separation of the director as person from the director's name as an indication of a cluster of descriptive features is that the choice of the director's name to refer to a set of structural and stylistic features is still not explained or interrogated (2000: 58). Going back to the conception of the auteur as a function of discourse, I explore how Imamura's name became an indication of a set of stylistic and narrative components through the intervention of the popular press in the crafting of his auteur persona. In this case, the director's name and his public persona become inseparable from his film's style and content, as critics and journalists insist on the connection between these elements.

Following Yoshimoto's identification of "specific kinds of institutional constraint and disciplinary configuration" that have shaped Japanese cinema scholarship (2000: 54), I focus here on the role of Japanese print media in creating an auteur, and how the early work of a particular director may be used to create a distinct auteur persona. While I am arguing here that the qualities we associate with Imamura's later work and auteur persona are present in his first four films, I am not attempting to incorporate these works into the canon of Imamura's critically acclaimed oeuvre, in an attempt at rehabilitating these texts to fit a classical auteurist model. Instead, I focus on how critics and journalists used these texts to build an auteur persona around Imamura. A seemingly coherent public persona is built through film exhibition, criticism, and the appearance of the auteur or their film texts in popular media. I aim to demonstrate that the critical acclaim Imamura's fourth and subsequent films received was not necessarily contingent on Imamura becoming a better filmmaker, whatever that might mean. Rather, critical acclaim followed the building and marketing of a coherent auteur persona through the first three films and their media coverage.

I am approaching the persona of the auteur in a critical light here, inspired by Richard Dyer's work on star persona. Dyer argues for the star persona as constituted not only by the actor's actual work playing roles on film or television, but also by critical and journalistic coverage of the star and their imagined real life (Dyer 2004: 2–3). Japanese postwar film journals, newspapers, and gossip magazines published material on prominent directors as well as stars. In fact, journals such as *Kinema Junpō* participated in the creation and promotion of an auteur system similar to that recognized by *Cahiers du Cinéma*, which exerted some influence on global film criticism from its first issue in 1951. Of course, *Kinema Junpō* and *Eiga Geijutsu* (*Film Art*), the two high-brow film journals that ushered Imamura into the canon of Japanese auteurs, significantly predate the founding of *Cahiers du Cinéma*. Yet Jim Hillier argues that it is "a pretty widespread" contention that the development of this particular style of film criticism was greatly indebted to French film criticism, and particularly *Cahiers du Cinéma* (1985: 1). *Cahiers du Cinéma* and *Kinema Junpō* had a degree of cross-fertilization in the 1950s, as *Cahiers*, newly "discovering" Japanese cinema, reprinted translated material from *Kinema Junpō*, such as the filmography of Kenji Mizoguchi (Kriegel-Nicholas 2016: 228). Both magazines styled reviews in a similar manner, structuring an account of the critic's encounter with the film in question in terms of the critic's own expectations and preferences.

Cahiers du Cinéma, *Kinema Junpō*, and *Eiga Geijutsu* also printed yearly "Best Ten" rankings organized by studio and director. *Kinema Junpō* produced a number of special issues each year designed to rank directors by critical acclaim, from the "Who's Who" editions that listed the directors, actors, and writers considered most notable in the studio system, to the intermittent issues devoted to "Film Directors of the World" (*Sekai no eiga sakka zenshu*) that ranked acclaimed directors by fame and nationality. Whole issues were given over to selected auteurs with regularity; for example, Akira Kurosawa received a full issue of *Kinema Junpō* devoted to his work in January 1963, and another for his collaboration with Toshirō Mifune in September 1964, while Yasujirō Ozu's life and work were the subject of a special issue in February 1964.

Critical and journalistic coverage of the cinema was strongly auteurist in Japan in the years in which Imamura made his directorial debut and subsequent studio films. Like *Cahiers du Cinéma*, which printed critiques of auteur theory such as André Bazin's *De la politique des auteurs* (1957), individual writers were often reflexive about the auteurist claim that the director should be considered the sole author of a film text. Camera operators and producers were also invited to write articles or participate in round table discussions for publication in critical cinema journals. Yet the largest amount of coverage was devoted to film texts, stars, and directors, and directors in particular were most regularly invited to write or comment on their own work and that of other filmmakers. Maureen Turim has argued for the importance of understanding the work of Nagisa Ōshima as "the product of a certain period of auteurism's flowering," and at the same time "contemporaneous with, and arguably a part of, a deconstructive investigation of auteurism" (1998: 15). The same could be said of Imamura, who shared Ōshima's elite university background and working experiences, starting out as an assistant director at Shōchiku before leaving that studio, and later the studio system, to produce independent films.

Imamura was featured in the *Kinema Junpō* "Best Ten" yearly edition of 1959, and by 1963 was included multiple times in a *Kinema Junpō* anthology on the top films of the past eighteen years, which described *My Second Brother* as "full of energy" (1963: 58). His photograph even made the cover of the 1967 *Kinema Junpō* anthology of world film directors, and was included in the "Dictionary of World Film Directors" produced a month earlier by the same journal. Imamura's entry emphasizes his interest in humanity (*ningen ni kyōmi o motsu*), and his "strong tendency to depend on the idiosyncrasies of a subject" (*daizai no tokuisei ni tayoru*) (1967: 90). The dominant story of Imamura's career focuses on his speedy ascent into the circle of revered film directors in Japan, and his own idiosyncratic outlook. What this chapter aims to problematize is the idea that this ascent was precipitated by a distinct change in the content of his work. Instead, I want to suggest that Imamura's studio output laid the groundwork for an auteur persona and oeuvre of exactly the specifications desirable for critics and journalists in 1960s Japan.

After leaving Shōchiku to join Nikkatsu's training program in 1954, Imamura's first three films as director were released in quick succession throughout 1958. *Stolen Desire* was shown in roadshow Nikkatsu theaters from May 20, 1958, and introduced in *Kinema Junpō* as the first effort of the "newly promoted" director (1958: 93). Yet neither *Kinema Junpō* nor *Eiga Geijutsu* reviewed the film. In a later review for *Ginza Station*, *Eiga Geijutsu* critic Yūkichi Shinada described *Stolen Desire* as "having the attraction of showing a life full of vim and vigour" (*ōseina seiketsuryō no miryoku*) (1958: 59). Yet Imamura debuted relatively quietly.

Ginza Station, released just a month later, was introduced in *Kinema Junpō* (1958: 101) but once again not reviewed. Shinada reviewed the film for *Eiga Geijutsu* (*Film Art*), but dismissed it as a mere "supplement" (*soemono*) or knocked-together addendum (1958: 59). This kind of film was becoming more common in the late 1950s according to Shinada, as studios focused on producing material for double bills and providing opportunities for fresh talent to make their debuts (1958: 59). As the number of films produced increases, Shinada argued, the quality will decrease in inverse proportion (*Genzai no seisaku kikō no naka de seisan honsū ga sōkasureba, seisaku jōken wa hanbireiteki ni waruku naru ni kimatte iru*) (1958: 59). Shinada's association of increased production with decreased quality follows the auterist understanding, which seeks to restore the rarefied aura of the artwork to the medium of cinema. However, his concerns have a particularly postwar flavor, as he worries that "impoverished Japan" (*binbō kuni Nippon*) will not be able to make a good showing in the global cinema sphere with the kinds of films studios were churning out to fill double-feature programs (1958: 59). The first half of his one-page review of *Ginza Station* is therefore devoted to a public plea to the reader for support for his efforts to improve the quality of Japanese filmmaking.

The film itself is dismissed as a "vehicle for the popular title song" (*ryūkōka no daimei*). Shinada even likens the final product to an unexpected "illegitimate child" (*shoshi*), "though the film company may have expected a legitimate offspring before the birth, now they are burdened with this unexpected disaster" (1958: 59). He reports that no one is describing Imamura's direction or script as a great success, but nonetheless praises the second-time director for having endeavored to make an interesting (*omoshiroi*) film (1958: 59). Yet Shinada believes that the results are "meager" (*sasayakana sakuhin*) when compared to *Stolen Desire*, and that *Ginza Station* only partially (*bubunteki*) reflects the energy of the earlier film (1958: 59).

Shinada's mixed review nevertheless contributes something to Imamura's budding auteur persona, as he describes the filmmaker as "impudently taking an aggressive stance toward the bad conditions" of the film industry (*warui jōken no naka de zubutoku inaotte iru*) and showing "a promising attitude toward filmmaking" (*seisaku taidō wa tanomoshii*) (1958: 59). Overall, however, he found the film's "biggest flaw" (*saidai no kekkan*) to be that it "had no meaning" (*imi ga nai*) (1959: 58). Shinada's review reveals key criteria by which high-art film critics judged both film texts and film directors. Films without meaning are dismissed as light entertainment. However, the persona of the director is treated as a relatively separate matter, and it is possible for a filmmaker to win praise in spite of a disappointing film if he is perceived to have stamped something of his own character on the text.

Endless Desire fared better with critics when it was released in November 1958, though once again Imamura's effort was introduced but not reviewed in *Kinema Junpō* (1958: 88). In *Eiga Geijutsu*, Heiichi Sugiyama compared the film to renowned auteur John Huston's *Treasure of the Sierra Madre* (1948), which had been released in Japan as *Gold* (*Ōgon*) in May 1949. Comparing directors to one another as a means to analyze their auteur position is a classic *Cahiers du Cinéma* trope, as seen in the magazine's famous opposition of Mizoguchi to Kurosawa (Rivette 1958). Sugiyama argues that Imamura's film does not quite reach the level of Huston's and contains several unoriginal motifs. Neither the theme of a group slowly killing one another off nor the trope of murderous criminals chasing buried treasure is unusual (*mezurashikunai*), the former featuring in Huston's film and the latter in Minoru Shibuya's *Season of the Witch* (*Akujo no kisetsu*, 1958), released just a few months before. "Nonetheless, Imamura's *Endless Desire* is fresh and interesting" (*shinsen de omoshiroi*) (Sugiyama 1959: 67), and Sugiyama argues that making audiences laugh at violent and criminal scenes is "Director Imamura's precious talent" (*Imamura kantoku no kichōna sainō*) (Sugiyama 1959: 67). Imamura is credited with the power to draw the critic's interest (*Watashi wa taihen kanshinshita*) (1959: 67), and Sugiyama relates his sense that "this new director's originality really has a good feeling" (*atarashii kantoku no orijinaritei wa, makoto ni kimochi ga yoi*) (1959: 67). He regrets that the film gradually collapses into a criminal action picture (*jidai ni hanzai katsugeki ni kanyū*), echoing Shinada's desire for Imamura to focus on human (*ningenrashisa*) issues in the future (Sugiyama 1959: 67; Shinada 1958: 59). In the end, he argues, "the ending came to have an out of control feeling" (*te ni amatta to iu kanji ni natte shimatta*) (1959: 67).

Once again the critic's perception of Imamura's character colors his review of the film. Both Shinada and Sugiyama attribute key failings and successes of these first two films to an understanding of Imamura's character as mischievous and headstrong. His innovative technique produces a strong sense of originality; however, storylines can become tiresome or disappointing. It's clear that critical assessment of Imamura is further shaped by his relatively junior status. Criticisms such as "out of control" suggest a perception of the director as somehow immature, and critics focus on his future potential, emphasizing his recent promotion from assistant director.

Finally, in 1959 Imamura was credibly reviewed by *Kinema Junpō* for *My Second Brother*, released on October 28, 1959. The film was introduced in *Kinema Junpō* (1959: 78) and given a short review (1959: 88–89) before winning third place in the yearly *Kinema Junpō* Best Ten competition. Fuyuhiko Kitagawa introduces Imamura as an "up and coming director" (*shinei kantoku*), and praises the film's "simple and accurate realism" (*jimi de kokumeina riarizumu*) (1959: 88). The review is less than careful: Kitagawa freely admits he has neither read the original text on which the film was based nor seen Imamura's earlier work. Yet he credits Imamura with guiding (*shidō*) the young actors to excellent performances, and praises his direct approach to difficult issues (1959: 88). He critiques the pacing of the ending, however, stating a personal opinion that the penultimate scene should have been the last. Nonetheless, the review signaled that Imamura had made it into the elite circle of critically acclaimed Japanese directors.

Eiga Geijutsu had in many ways both intuited and contributed to Imamura's recognition. As early as 1958, he had been invited to join a roundtable discussion with up-and-coming directors Kō Nakahira and Yasuzō Masumura, hosted by Masahiro Ogi, for a feature titled "Film Is Advancing!" (*Eiga wa zenshinsuru!*) (1958: 33). Imamura is credited as "the director of *Stolen Desire*," though the magazine had yet to introduce or review the feature. The directors are invited to talk about "shouldering the burden of their generation's culture" (*sedai bunka no ninaite toshite kataru*), their pride in their work (*jibu*), their self-reflection (*hansei*), and their ambitions (*yashin*). However, for the first five pages Imamura is quiet, occasionally teased or chastised by Nakahira or Masumura, until he breaks forcefully into the discussion by calling the turn of the conversation "pretentious" (*kiza*), claiming to be "irate" (*iraira*) about the views the other directors express about writers (1958: 38), and reminding them that he also writes screenplays. Both Imamura and *Stolen Desire* are featured in photo insets (1958: 39), but overall he says little until the final page of the round table discussion, where he launches into a critique of "mass communication phobia" (*masu komi kyōfu*) (1958: 39). As an early introduction into the auteur's spotlight, this could have gone better, compared to the impressive oratorical performances of directors like Nagisa Ōshima. Yet it lays the groundwork for the popular understanding of Imamura's public persona as committed, bullish, and passionate in direct contrast to the quiet workmanlike persona of Ozu or the scholarly leftism of Kurosawa.

Every auteur persona is built on an origin story, and Imamura's training and debut provided rich details for his. From his criticisms of Ozu's working methods during his time at Shōchiku to his idolization of Yūzō Kawashima, and particularly his rebellious attitude toward the studio bosses (Desser 1988: 123), Imamura's outspokenness formed the base of his forthright and passionate auteur persona. In accounts of his troubles with studio personnel (Tessier 1997: 59), Imamura is framed as an iconoclast and deep believer in the artistic value of cinema. This profile fit perfectly into the New Wave auteur mode. Yet Imamura's auteur persona also had roots in his early work as well as his studio training.

Though *Stolen Desire* was based on a novel by Kon Tōkō, Imamura has claimed that protagonist Kunida, a young theater director played by Hiroyuki Nagato, was modeled on himself (Desser 1988: 58; Kehr 1997: 71). In many ways this first film is a kind of self-introduction, confronting viewers and critics not only with Imamura's particular visual and narrative style, but also with a number of themes and tropes relevant to the director's own personal and political concerns, publicized later in many interviews and personal writings. Drawing from elements of his personal life and upbringing, Imamura firmly situates his own persona as an indelible element of the film as a whole. The story focuses on a traveling theater troupe and the difficult lives of the actors. Imamura's eldest brother was a stage actor in Tsukiji sho Gekijō (Tsukiji Little Theatre) in Tokyo and the family frequently visited the stage. Furthermore, the narrative's love triangle between Kunida and the troupe leader's two daughters mirrors Imamura's own widely publicized romantic problems. Kunida and the younger daughter are eventually forced to leave the theater troupe, and Imamura has similarly attributed his departure from Shōchiku to his romantic relationship with a company administrator, whom he later married (Kim 2003). The conflicting pull of work and duty versus romance and sex was to become a key theme in Imamura's work as well as in accounts of his personal life.

Establishing Key Thematic Concerns

If *Stolen Desire* is Imamura's self-introduction, it is also the first example of a set of thematic concerns that form the backbone of every Imamura narrative thereafter. As many critics and writers have noted, Imamura's works are suffused with desire, and this first film is no exception. Nikkatsu studios insisted on the title, possibly due to several recent films with "desire" in the title having done well at the domestic box office in 1957 (*Kinema Junpō* 1963: 138–58). Imamura preferred *Tent Theatre*, and in fact left this working title at the top left side of the title screen, in a small sign of the defiance that would become a central trope of his auteur persona. In the roundtable discussed above, he claims he had no interest in a title that would attract viewers, but only hoped for one that would have them "watch with no expectations" (*kitai sarenai de mite morau*) (Imamura 1958: 39). Nonetheless, desire is the central theme of this first film. Kunida desires Chidori (Yōko Minamida), the eldest daughter of the troupe leader, and is desired in turn by Chigusa (Michie Kita), her younger sister. This leads to the break-up of the troupe, when Kunida tries to persuade Chidori to leave her husband, and instead is cast out with Chigusa while the troupe moves on without them. Chidori's husband, Eizaburō (Shin'ichi Yanagisawa), is himself an object of desire, becoming a local idol for screaming female fans. These screams are balanced in turn with the yells of the male fans of the troupe's strip-tease dancers, who open every show.

Desire abounds, and Imamura focuses on its destructive and disruptive aspects rather than its generative potential, romantic or otherwise. As Dave Kehr observes, the groups at the heart of Imamura's films "cannot contain the erotic energy of the individuals they hold together" (1997: 72). It is not only desire for romance or sex that endangers the structure of the groups that feature in Imamura's films, however, but desire more generally. The problems in *Stolen Desire* really begin when an old friend attempts to lure Kunida away from his tent theater troupe to work in television. Attracted by the money and opportunity, Kunida is swayed for a while, before deciding to remain with the troupe in a speech valorising the grass-roots efforts of the traveling actors in much the way Imamura himself, after tussling with the big business machine of Nikkatsu, began to vocally affirm his belief in the crafts of everyday people. David Desser has suggested that Kunida's "increasing disillusionment with the theatre and its rules" is a metaphor for the alienation felt by young filmmakers of Imamura's generation (1988: 59). This alienation is one side of the desire for novelty and adventure that characterizes Imamura's later career choices as well as the content of his future films.

The male fans of the strip-tease dancers are most clearly in pursuit of sexual satisfaction, tearing down the tent in which the dancers are changing. As the tent falls apart, the camera rests for a moment on a photograph of the popular actor Yūjirō Ishihara. As Ishihara was the biggest star in the Nikkatsu stable, this could be a kind of product-placement, or Imamura's ironic send-up of Nikkatsu's sexualized commercialism.[1] The inclusion of the photograph may even be a little of both, fusing commercial concerns with a touch of defiant humor in a similar manner to Imamura's insistence on including his original title above the Nikkatsu-approved title he was forced to accept in the opening sequence. The photograph also appears to reference female desire, as the dancers have pinned up the picture of Ishihara to enjoy his celebrated sexualized appearance (Raine 2000). At the same time, it hints at the fame and fortune at the pinnacle of the actor's pursuit of success. Desires for fame, recognition, money, and celebrity are as much to blame for the troupe's rocky future as Kunida's messy romantic life.

In *Ginza Station*, desire for a woman working in the store across the street from his wife's pharmacy gets the protagonist into trouble. This light-hearted musical film is perhaps the first nod toward a theme Isolde Standish has identified across Imamura's later work, which examines the conflicting demands of the family structure "on individuals living in the contemporary age of advanced capitalism" (2011: 81). Protagonist Jūtarō Ōyama (Shin'ichi Yanagisawa) is a "henpecked" husband with a wife who controls every aspect of his physical being. His friend Asada (Kō Nishimura) advises him "as a medical professional" (*isha toshite*) to take a lover to cure his fantastical daydreaming. Asada's seduction advice amounts to taking a woman for meals and shopping trips, and at the end of their expensive capitalist montage, Jūtarō finds that his would-be lover has been hired by his wife to keep an eye on him while she is away. The nuclear family has never been in any real danger from the desires coursing through *Ginza Station*, and yet, at the same time, Asada's duplicitous view of the world and Jūtarō's island fantasies suggest that the middle-class urban family life depicted in the film is not quite stable either. The wife strives to present a Japanese version of a modern Americanized democratic capitalist-compliant family unit, complete with a thriving middle-class family business, two perfectly dressed children, and a husband forced to consume all the latest health potions and supplements with the goal of continual self-improvement. While this public presentation appears successful, Jūtarō and Asada's respective dreaming and scheming undermine the performance, continually presenting the possibility of disruption, whether planned or inadvertent. Critics picked up on the darker themes underlying the comic story, noting that while the coupling of a henpecked husband (*kyōsaika*) and a terrifying wife is "common" (*afurete iru*), Jūtarō's daydreaming suggests something like shellshock from his participation in the recent war (*sensō boke*) (Shinada 1958: 59).

Imamura's concern with the darker aspects of desire, and the threat these pose to group structure, finds most explicit voice in *Endless Desire*. Crooked pharmacist Nakada (Kō Nishimura) worries aloud that the sexual desire all four male criminals express toward the female member of their gang will spell trouble. The gang have only five days to dig out a stash of morphine before the house above it is pulled down. Shima, the only woman, declares, "I'll give myself to the one digging the hardest." As the others fight, Nakada, who has been Shima's secret lover for eight years, worries, "This woman could destroy the harmony of our team." In the end, however, the desire of each gang member to keep the whole stash for themselves leads to them dying off one by one, until Shima dies alone on a bridge attempting to make off with the whole lot. Imamura's early films certainly show a fixation on desire, but a closer reading suggests that this desire can be other than sexual. In later films, such as the docu-fiction *A Man Vanishes* (*Ningen jōhatsu*, 1967), groups and alliances including the marital pair, a family of two sisters, and a film crew are threatened not only by sexual desire but also by the desire for fame exhibited by protagonist Yoshie Hayakawa. Before moving into documentary filming, however, Imamura established his own group in these first three films, building a team of actors and filmmakers with whom he would continue to work into his later career.

Building a Troupe

Hiroyuki Nagato, Yōko Minamida, Shin'ichi Yanagisawa, Kō Nishimura, and Shōichi Ōzawa, among many others, would continue to work with Imamura from these first three films throughout the rest of his oeuvre. Nagato and Minamida even married, forming a small family group within Imamura's wider group of filmmakers. *Endless Desire* was also Imamura's first film with Ensaku Himeda, the cinematographer he would work with for the next ten years. Imamura has connected his treatment of actors to his early experiences assisting Ozu, claiming the director's method of instructing actors was "repugnant" to him. "I don't have such blind faith in actors, I need to talk with them about family, education, etc. We talk about everyday life" (Imamura 1997: 148). From his first three Nikkatsu films, Imamura built a "stable" of actors with whom he would work again and again (much like Ozu). The stars who appear regularly in Imamura's films also inform his popular auteur persona, creating an image of a director who remains committed to his troupe and runs his filmmaking practice in a manner similar to earlier traditions of stagecraft. That many of these actors were unknown, conventionally unattractive, or otherwise unusual in the postwar studio system further supports a reading of Imamura's popular persona as iconoclastic and concerned with issues of an imagined authenticity rather than with superficial or business-friendly star qualities.

Even when working with actors outside his chosen group, particularly those visited on him by the studio, critics noted Imamura's skilful management of actors. Shinada praises his management of Hawaiian Japanese star Frank Nagai in *Ginza Station*, arguing that he "skilfully" (*kōmyō*) hides the weak points (*jakuten*) Nagai had previously displayed in leading roles in films such as *The 7:50 from Haneda* (*Haneda hatsu 7ji 50ppun*, Toshio Matsuda, 1958) (1958: 59). By drawing attention to the stronger attributes of a star popularly considered deficient in some respect, Imamura built a reputation as a director with a strong understanding of actors and the ability to get the best out of them. This trope is repeated in appreciations of his later work, such as *Intentions of Murder* (*Akai satsui*, 1964), in which he is said to have "rehabilitated" the star persona of Sachiko Hidari, known as an outspoken and not particularly attractive actress who refused to submit to the studio system. Hidari later became the third female director in Japanese cinema history, appearing to channel some of Imamura's nonconformism into an unusual career move.

Finding a Voice

As Max Tessier notes (1997: 46), many of Imamura's films feature nonstandard Japanese dialect, particularly from the Kansai region. In these first three films, Imamura's characters repeatedly quiz one another on their backgrounds and draw attention to differences between the speaking and behavioral habits of different regions. As the criminals of *Endless Desire* arrive in a run-down town across the bank from Shiohama, an elderly man asks Shima where she is from, noting her accent. "Tokyo," she replies. He counters, "That's no place to live!" (*amari ii tokoro ja nai*). Nonstandard Japanese appears to be a means to express not only outsiderness, but also the earthy qualities of the countryside and smaller towns of which Imamura often spoke. In fact, the "earthiest" characters, generally portrayed by older actors with strong nonstandard speaking habits and dialect, are the last ones standing at the end of a typically destructive Imamura narrative. The old man who makes circuits of the neighborhood in *Endless Desire* and the angry old woman who lends money to the characters of *My Second Brother* speak in strong dialects, and yet they are also given the roles of Greek chorus, providing commentary on the actions and beliefs of other characters.

Stolen Desire opens with a voiceover introduction set over an aerial view of Osaka, connecting the earthiness of the people with the area's Edo-period history. The "dry humor" of the area is specifically connected to the "ancient districts" of Settsu and Kawachi, and the "indefatigable" (*takumashii*) nature of the inhabitants who are "unchanged to this day" (*ai mo kawarazu*). These same themes are repeated from *The Insect Woman* (*Nippon konchūki*, 1963) through to *Ballad of Narayama* (*Narayama bushikō*, 1983), and feature in many interviews and writings by Imamura himself. *Ginza Station* takes the motifs of earthiness and nonstandard language to extremes in dream sequences where Jūtarō inhabits a remote island with a woman named Sally who speaks in grunts and whoops. This island paradise is an explicit contrast to his clean modern workplace, and Sally to his hyper-articulate and very vocal wife. Critics noted that the "contrasting" (*taihiteki*) "uninhibited" (*honbō*) nature of the island scenes should be "enjoyable" (*tanoshii*), but instead misfire (*fuhatsu*) and fail to produce laughter, going "too far beyond life's subtleties" (*jinsei no kibi*) (Shinada 1958: 59). Frank Nagai sutures over the join with a repeated jazz interlude channeling both the perceived earthy qualities of the genre and its fashionable reception in the Ginza area, in a narrative device Shinada described as "the only original point in the film" (1958: 59). Though Imamura insists that featuring Nagai was the idea of Nikkatsu studio personnel, Shinada describes the directorial decision to make use of Nagai's "comedic touch" (*kigeki tacchi*) as "a wise strategy" (*kenmeina sakusen*) (1958: 59). Here the critic's insistence on the auteur's originality and wisdom leads to attributing casting choices to Imamura in spite of the conflicting account provided by the director himself.

Imamura's troubles with management and preference for earthy characters blended seamlessly into his account of his own class identification. Though Imamura was born in Tokyo to a middle-class physician's family and attended elite schools before entering Waseda University, he was vocal about his dislike of the upper classes. From an early age, he remembered wanting to identify himself with "working-class people who were true to their own human natures" (Imamura, qtd. in Nakata 1997: 117). As a strong dialect or accent is often associated with working-class areas and peoples in Japan, Imamura's insistence on foregrounding different ways of speaking Japanese contributes to the crafting of his auteur persona as a director in touch with the working classes. Fellow directors recognized Imamura's specialized interest in dialect. From his first roundtable discussion for *Eiga Geijutsu*, he was invited to speak as a dialect specialist. Kō Nakahira asked him, "You know a lot about Osaka and Kansai people, right? Who has the most accurate Kawachi-ben?" (1958: 40). Imamura demurred with an uncharacteristic, "Well, that's a bit difficult . . ." (*Ee, aa iu koto wa chotto* . . .) (1958: 40). That this first introduction to Imamura's voice and personality focuses specifically on his interest in dialect suggests his affinity with outsiderness, an impression strengthened by his shyness in the face of the more established Nakahira's questioning.

Choosing a Setting

As the repeated theme of nonstandard dialect indicates, most of Imamura's films are set outside Tokyo and the major metropolitan hubs, focusing instead on marginal areas and themes of displacement and outsiderness. Many of Imamura's settings are temporary, as in the ever-moving tent theater of *Stolen Desire* or the village on the verge of relocation in *Endless Desire*. Protagonists are often further removed even from these marginal settings; the criminals of *Endless Desire* tunnel under the town to find a hidden stash of drugs, while Kunida spends much of his time on the roof or in the surrounding woods. Jūtarō of *Ginza Station* is physically located in the fashionable district around the train line, but spends much of his time imaginatively inhabiting a tropical island. While he returns to his "real" life at the end of the film, reconciliation with his wife is brokered at a tropical theme park, where his boat washes up after a night of drifting in the bay. From the positive critical reception of *Endless Desire* onward, film critics at the highbrow journals began to take Imamura's use of space seriously. Sugiyama suggested that the visual device of showing the criminals tunneling under the inhabitants of the neighborhood aptly depicted the divisions within human relations (*ningen kankei*) (1959: 67).

Though he was included alongside acclaimed directors in roundtables such as the one described above, Imamura has depicted himself as something of an outsider in his later writing and interviews. He has emphasized his disagreements with studio personnel and difference from critically acclaimed and studio-approved directors such as Ozu. This outsider persona demonstrates difference from both the studio system and mainstream Japanese society more generally, a position coherent with the recurring questioning and challenging of a perceived hegemonic version of Japanese self-representation in many of Imamura's films. Of course, his move from Shōchiku to Nikkatsu in 1954 and his battles with Nikkatsu after 1961, as well as his decision to set up Imamura Productions in 1965, form a picture of Imamura as working outside or against the studio system. His move from feature film to documentary from 1967 is similarly iconoclastic, casting him outside the commercial sphere to an extent. Yet this was a period when several directors were following similar paths in many parts of the world, most significantly Ōshima, who left Shōchiku in 1960 to set up his own company. As the Japanese New Wave generated ever more varied filmmaking modes, Imamura's heavily manipulated docu-fiction *A Man Vanishes* also seemed less the work of a complete outsider than the extension of an existing movement toward new film forms. By setting his films on the outskirts of an imagined mainstream society in Japan, however, Imamura's auteur persona could be associated with outsiderness even while he occupied a central place within critically acclaimed film history.

Recognition at Last! *My Second Brother*

Like his 1958 films, *My Second Brother* features Imamura's common narrative theme of desire distorting the structure of a group. While the previous films' protagonists desired fame, romance, or sex, however, the impoverished family at the heart of this fourth film desire only the financial security to live freely. Pursuit of these funds inevitably leads to the dissolution of the family, as the elder sister marries for a small dowry and moves away, and the elder brother goes to work in the major cities around the Kyushu area. Even the second brother of the title attempts to leave the coal-mining town in which the family has lived until their father's death. All of Imamura's key tropes are present in this fourth film: desire, a threatened group, nonstandard Japanese speech, and a poor outsider location. Unlike the first three films, which were either adapted from novels or written by Imamura himself, this fourth film was adapted from the best-selling diaries of a young *zainichi* Korean girl named Sueko Yasumoto. Yasumoto's diaries were published (seemingly without her consent) in 1958 and became a media phenomenon as readers rushed to express their sympathy and horror at the impoverished lives of Korean Japanese families during this era of rapidly increasing prosperity in the cities.

Kinema Junpō introduced the film specifically as an adaptation of Yasumoto's diary (1959: 78), and reviewer Fuyuhiko Kitagawa praised the director for not deviating from the original story (1959: 88). Imamura's film clearly benefitted from the popularity of Yasumoto's story and the sympathetic feelings directed toward her family.

Like the previous three films, *My Second Brother* was commissioned by Nikkatsu studios. In this sense the film is similar to *Ginza Station*, which was conceived as a vehicle for popular singer-comedian Frank Nagai. Nikkatsu instructed Imamura to structure the film around Nagai singing the title song three times, and the pacing of the film narrative is consequently secondary to these scenes. *My Second Brother* also circumscribes Imamura's storytelling within an already-known element; however, in this case that element is the tragic story of the suffering Yasumoto family. The Yasumotos are the classic suffering subjects beloved of critics and audiences alike, and Imamura's depiction of their suffering is "the kind of liberal indictment that Japanese critics laud" (Desser 1988: 59). Kitagawa argues for the universal importance of the film's themes, stressing the value of using cinema to depict "how people get by every day in hard times" (1959: 89). In this sense, the affect Imamura is forced to borrow from the structuring device of Yasumoto's diary is closer to the humanistic concerns prized by many postwar Japanese film critics than the stylish cool of Nagai's star persona.

Furthermore, as James Quandt has observed, while *Stolen Desire* and *Endless Desire* "are about classless people," *My Second Brother* is about "the proletariat" (1997: 18). Both the acting troupe of *Stolen Desire* and the criminals of *Endless Desire* have voluntarily opted out of mainstream society to pursue their own dreams. On the other hand, the Yasumotos and their neighbors have been rejected by society on the basis of their ethnic background and poverty in an ever-more vicious circle wherein one mode of suffering increases the other. When the second brother of the title goes to Tokyo to look for work, the people he encounters treat him like a strange animal. The mechanics in the bicycle shop where he applies for a job do not even attempt to explain to him that he is too young, instead going straight to the police. The Tokyo characters' bafflement at this young boy traveling alone to the capital to find work belies their conviction that Tokyo is civilization, and anything different therefore is uncivilized. Their ridicule at the boy's expectations is undercut by the viewer's understanding that in the coal districts of Kyushu, an elementary school student working a physically taxing job to support his family is not unusual in this era. Imamura's fourth film not only depicts the Yasumotos' situation in a sympathetic manner, but also works to shame viewers about their own ignorance of the situation of working-class and *zainichi* people, as the Tokyoites stand in for the audience. This kind of teaching function of popular cinema appealed to critics, who gave such educational humanist films as *Twenty Four Eyes* (*Nijūshi no hitomi*, Keisuke Kinoshita, 1954) unrestrained praise, and top prizes like the *Kinema Junpō* Best One award.

The Making of an Auteur

After establishing his critical reputation with *My Second Brother*, Imamura quickly returned to examining the strains that desire for sex, fame, and money place on group structures, in films such as *Pigs and Battleships*, *Intentions of Murder*, and *A Man Vanishes*. Following the critical and box office success of his fourth film, Imamura was frequently invited to write and interview for *Kinema Junpō* and *Eiga Geijutsu*, becoming part of a coterie of established auteurs who passed criticism and commentary on one another's work and place in the film industry, both in Japan and globally. I have argued here that Imamura's inclusion in this select group was not in spite of his first three studio films, but rather that those texts created and cemented an auteur persona that was absolutely of its time.

The kind of auteur persona the Japanese critical scene was ready to embrace was outlined in *Eiga Geijutsu* in critic Yūkichi Shinada's review of *Ginza Station*. The closing sentences read almost like advice to an aspiring auteur. Imamura's worries about pretentiousness are dismissed; Shinada has no problem with the use of "pretentious" (*keren*) techniques such as time-lapse photography (1958: 59). Banality is a greater crime—Shinada complains about the romantic reconciliation of the couple in the conclusion, which he calls "common as dog shit" (*gokuarifureta*) (1958: 59). Instead, Shinada recommends that Imamura's projects focus on the "attractive" (*miryoku*) "monster" (*kaibutsu*) characters like Kō Nakahira's, and avoid "ordinary" (*heibon*) characters like Jūtarō. Shinada argues that Imamura's "vivid" (*yakujo*) individual personality (*kosei*) should be boldly (*zubari*) displayed by making greater use of the widescreen format of Nikkatsuscope (1958: 59). In *Endless Desire*, Heiichi Sugiyama noted that Imamura used the full breadth of the wide screen admirably, sending characters onscreen from the right and left, and using the top and bottom of the screen space to increase visual interest (1959: 67). Imamura also appears to have followed Shinada's recommendations in his post-1960 work, which focused on monstrous personalities unleashing their desires on Japanese society. By presenting critics with exactly what they had asked for, Imamura became one of Japanese cinema's most lauded auteurs.

Note

1. With thanks to David Desser for this suggestion.

Works Cited

Bazin, Andre (1957). "*De la politique des auteurs*" [On the politics of the author]. *Cahiers du Cinéma* 70 (April): 2–11.
Desser, David (1988). *Eros Plus Massacre: An Introduction to the Japanese New Wave Cinema*. Bloomington: Indiana University Press.
Dyer, Richard (2004). *Heavenly Bodies: Film Stars and Society*. New York: Routledge.
Hillier, Jim (1985). *Cahiers du Cinéma: The 1950s: Neo-Realism, Hollywood, the New Wave*. Cambridge, MA: Harvard University Press.
Imamura, Shōhei (1997). "My Teacher." In *Shohei Imamura*, ed. James Quandt, 145–48. Toronto: Toronto International Film Festival Group,.
Kehr, Dave (1997). "The Last Rising Sun." In *Shohei Imamura*, ed. James Quandt, 69–88. Toronto: Toronto International Film Festival Group.
Kim, Nelson (2003). "Great Director Profiles: Shohei Imamura." *Senses of Cinema* 27. http://sensesofcinema.com/2003/great-directors/imamura/. Accessed April 10, 2017.
Kinema junpō henshu (1958). "*Nihon eiga shōkai*." *Kinema Junpō* 202 (April 15): 92–93.
Kinema junpō henshu (1958). "*Nihon eiga shōkai*." *Kinema Junpō* 210 (July 15): 98–101.
Kinema junpō henshu (1958). "*Nihon eiga shōkai*." *Kinema Junpō* 217 (November 1): 88–90.
Kinema junpō henshu (1959). "*Nihon eiga shōkai*." *Kinema Junpō* 244 (October 15): 78.
Kinema junpō henshu (1959). "*Nihon eiga hihyō: Nianchan*." *Kinema Junpō* 248 (December 15): 88–89.
Kinema junpō henshu (1963). *Nihon eiga sengo 18 nen sōmokuroku* [Index of 18 years of postwar Japanese cinema]. Kinema junpō sha: Tokyo.
Kinema junpō henshu (1967). *Sekai no eiga seisaku zenshu '67* [Film directors of the world]. Kinema junpō sha: Tokyo.
Kriegel-Nicholas, Isadora (2016). "The Historical Reception of Japanese Cinema at Cahiers du Cinéma: 1951–1961." PhD diss., Boston University.
Nakahira, K., Masumura, Y., Imamura, S., and Ogi, M. (1958). "*Eiga wa zenshinsuru!*" [Film is advancing!]. *Eiga Geijutsu* 8 (August 1): 33–43.
Nakata, Toichi (1997). "Shohei Imamura Interview." In *Shohei Imamura*, ed. James Quandt, 107–24. Toronto: Toronto International Film Festival Group.
Raine, Michael (2000). "Ishihara Yujiro: Youth, Celebrity, and the Male Body in 1950s Japan." In *Word and Image in Japanese Cinema*, ed. Dennis Washburne and Carole Cavanaugh, 202–25. Cambridge: Cambridge University Press.
Rivette, Jacques (1958). "Mizoguchi vu d'ici." *Cahiers du Cinéma* 81 (March):28–32.
Sharp, Jasper (2011). *A Historical Dictionary of Japanese Cinema*. Lanham, MD: Scarecrow.
Shinada, Y. (1958). "*Hihyō: Nishi Ginza Eki Mae*" [Criticism: Ginza Station]. *Eiga Geijutsu* 10 (October 1): 59.

Standish, Isolde (2011). *Politics, Porn, and Protest: Japanese Avant-Garde Cinema in the 1960s and 1970s*. London: Continuum.

Sugiyama, H. (1959). *"Hihyō: Hateshinaki yokubō*.: [Criticism: Endless Desire]. *Eiga Geijutsu* 2 (February 1): 67.

Tessier, Max (1997). "Shohei Imamura Interview." In *Shohei Imamura*, ed. James Quandt, 57–68. Toronto: Toronto International Film Festival Group.

Turim, Maureen (1998). *The Films of Oshima Nagisa: Images of a Japanese Iconoclast*, Berkeley: University of California Press.

Yoshimoto, Mitsuhiro (2000). *Kurosawa: Film Studies and Japanese Cinema*. Durham, NC: Duke University Press.

PART I
KILLERS

Chapter 3

Confronting America: *Pigs and Battleships* and the Politics of US Bases in Postwar Japan

Hiroshi Kitamura

The year 1960 was a time when Japan's anti-American sentiments had soared to their peak. On the surface, the United States and Japan had seemingly become inseparable allies by way of a bilateral security treaty, but the suppression of political freedom during the seven-year occupation (1945–1952), the extended presence of the US military, the testing of nuclear weapons in the Pacific, and the move to renew the US-Japan Security Treaty provoked considerable anger and rage among everyday citizens. Students, activists, and others took to the streets to mount fierce protests. This led to the resignation of Prime Minister Nobusuke Kishi, the so-called Hagerty Incident (wherein President Dwight Eisenhower's press secretary had to be rescued by helicopter to avoid being mobbed by angry protesters), and the cancellation of President Eisenhower's planned visit to Japan. The "roaring '60s" had barely begun, but the "season of politics" (*seiji no kisetsu*) was well underway. Much of the rage was directed at the United States.

This chapter is an attempt to understand how Shohei Imamura confronted the United States in this growing "season of politics." I do so by focusing on *Buta to gunkan/Pigs and Battleships* (1961). Made during the months when anti-security treaty protests were on-going, this satirical comedy boldly challenged the tense politics of the US-led international order by dramatizing crime, prostitution, and fraternization that pervaded in Yokosuka—the site of a major American naval base. Released in the aftermath of fierce political protests, this provocative film stirred controversy but earned wide acclaim. Over the years, critics have regarded it as the director's "first masterpiece" (Sato Tadao 1980: 39).

Scholars have treated Imamura as a rebellious director who, together with his "new wave" contemporaries, challenged and expanded the horizons of political and cultural expression in the 1960s and beyond.[1] Few, however, have explored how these filmmakers directly stood up against US power particularly at the height of Japan's anti-US opposition. While keeping a distance from protests unfolding on the streets, Imamura, in *Pigs and Battleships,* fought against charges that the film was "anti-American" (Imamura 2010a: 79) to depict the poverty and hardships that many Japanese faced in the shadow of US military expansion. He also used the motif and backdrop of the black market—usually a symbol of confusion and defeat—as a vehicle of empowerment in order to accentuate the resilience of the down-and-out Japanese. To accentuate the problematic, Imamura conducted extensive field research, talent scouting, and location shooting. His "realism" (Imamura 2010b: 127) became a vehicle to challenge the United States.

In the years after *Pigs and Battleships,* Imamura continued to confront the United States by injecting this "realism" in his fictional work, but also by turning to documentary filmmaking. In 1970, the director returned to Yokosuka to shoot *Nippon sengoshi: Madam Onboro no seikatsu/History of Postwar Japan as Told by a Bar Hostess* (1970, hereafter *Madam Onboro*), which teased out the paradoxical coexistence of American exploitation and Japanese empowerment through an investigation of a resilient Japanese woman. In uncovering the entwined politics of US-Japanese relations during the final years of the Vietnam War, Imamura underscored the perpetuation of US influence in the long postwar or *sengo* era. Confronting the United States, then, was one of Imamura's main career agendas.[2] Much of this began with his 1961 landmark film.

An "Anti-American" Production

Pigs and Battleships was made at a moment when Japanese cinema was enjoying the fruits of its "second golden age." Thanks to a rapidly growing economy, an expanding middle class, and a soaring demand for popular entertainment, Japanese filmmakers, in the 1950s, overcame the woes of war and defeat and churned out hundreds of feature films each year. In the absence of state-controlled censorship, which plagued studios during the war as well as the occupation era, the content of the films diversified. Throughout much of the decade, filmmakers in Japan manufactured a wide variety of narratives and genres. These included literary adaptations, modern melodramas, sword-slashing period films, war films, and monster flicks (Sato Tadao 1995).

Imamura's rise to prominence began during this vibrant time. Born in a middle-class household in Tokyo, he initially cultivated a strong interest in theater and playwriting, but decided to join Shochiku in 1951 in search for artistic and creative opportunities. After working with the likes of Yasujiro Ozu, Hideo Oba, and Yuzo Kawashima as an assistant director, Imamura moved to Nikkatsu, a studio that he found "much easier to work in" than Shochiku because "it was peopled with folks who did not want to form factions" (Izawa et al. 1959: 66). After a few stints as an assistant director, the company allowed him to debut as a director with *Nusumareta yokujō/Stolen Desire* (1958), which gathered critical acclaim and a Blue Ribbon Award. The company, then, tasked him to feature singer-actor Frank Nagai in *Nishi Ginza ekimae/ Nishi Ginza Station* (1959) before allowing him to shoot *Hateshinaki yokubō/ Endless Desire* (1959). His next film was *Nianchan/My Second Brother* (1959), an unusually upbeat film in Imamura's oeuvre. Depicting the vitality of children and *zainichi* Koreans in a mining town, the film not only became a commercial hit, but also won the coveted Education Minister's Award.

Pigs and Battleships was Imamura's fifth film. The project began, rather casually, as a "small story" that involved "yakuza on bases" (Imamura 1971: 66). But through extensive conversations with co-screenwriter Hisashi Yamanouchi, the director decided to expand the scope of the project to showcase "the trampling of Japan by the US" (Imamura 2010a: 80).[3] The issue was a timely one. In the 1950s, the extended presence of the US military had angered local residents and triggered fierce anti-base protests (Miller 2014). Filmmakers reacted to the budding controversy. In 1953, only a year after the occupation, Toho released *Akasen kichi/Red Light Base*, which depicted a repatriated war veteran who discovers that his sister is fraternizing with an American GI and his family is forced to cope with social stigma (Nakamura 2014: 87–118). Independent filmmakers produced a body of "base films" (*kichi mono*) that problematized the seemingly ubiquitous presence of the US forces. Perhaps most famous was left-wing director Fumio Kamei's trilogy of documentaries on protests at Sunagawa, located nearby the Tachikawa Air Base on the outskirts of Tokyo: *Sunagawa no hitobito: kichi hantai tōsō no kiroku/The People of Sunagawa* (1955), *Sunagawa no hitobito: mugi shinazu/Wheat Will Never Fall* (1955), and *Ryūketsu no kiroku: Sunagawa/ Record of Blood: Sunagawa* (1956).

Unlike as in these earlier works, Imamura and Yamanouchi chose to dramatize the base problem at Yokosuka. A historic port city that once thrived as a hub of the Japanese imperial navy, Yokosuka became a strategic outpost for the US Seventh Fleet after World War II. Though not as well known as Sunagawa or Okinawa, this modest-sized city in Kanagawa prefecture had witnessed a rising grassroots movement that opposed the US military's expropriation of local farmlands (Niikura 2016: 18–41). Imamura chose not to focus on property disputes but turned to the city's "night culture," as Yokosuka was, according to a contemporary observer, "the worst base in the country from an educational standpoint, as 4,000 to 6,000 women of the night are swarming across the entire city" (Osada 1953). Imamura was convinced that Yokosuka deserved wider attention. He once described the city as a "meat market that was odd and full of danger" (Imamura 2010b, 223).

In order to dramatize the problems that plagued the militarized port city, Imamura attempted to pursue the course of "realism" to the extent possible (Imamura 2010b: 127). This led him to defy his studio's mode of production, for instance, by taking his time to make the film. Whereas Nikkatsu filmmakers typically turned out a feature film in a matter of weeks, Imamura devoted months to conduct field research and complete the screenplay. The director also resisted the use of company talent. While forced to work with Nikkatsu's contract players, he insisted on using an outsider for the role of Haruko, the female protagonist. Imamura's team conducted a two-month search at schools, factories, and the theater stage. After auditioning over five hundred candidates, the director, according to *Yomiuri shinbun*, built a set at the studio just to test the eight finalists ("Setto o tatete hiroin tesuto" 1960). In the end, Imamura decided to enlist Jitsuko Yoshimura, a high school student who seemed to possess "strength and sexiness in her facial expression" (Imamura 2010a: 78).

Furthermore, Imamura decided to shoot the film on location. Instead of relying on the company's newly built, fully air-conditioned production studio (in Chofu) that, to borrow the words of studio head Kyusaku Hori, was built and managed in an "American style," the director insisted on utilizing actual sites in Yokosuka, such as the train station, the hilly farmland, and "Ditch Plank Street" (*Dobuita dōri*, hereafter Dobuita Street)—a seamy commercial district filled with bars, brothels, and souvenir shops (Nikkatsu kabushiki kaisha 1962: 68). In order to assure that the shooting could be held in rowdy neighborhoods, Imamura not only befriended local yakuza men, but also reached out to the US military for cooperation (though he was flatly rejected) ("Buta to gunkan sōdōki" 1960). Determined to capture the image of actual aircraft carriers as they came in, he kept the camera crew on standby for weeks ("Yokosuka o butai ni 'jūkigeki'" 1960).

Not surprisingly, *Pigs and Battleships* was quickly labeled an "anti-American" project. Imamura recalls that that production schedule was delayed multiple times due to political pressure (Imamura 2010a: 79). Thus, even though the film was originally slated for release in August 1960, the shooting of the film did not begin until September 26 ("Engi mo honban dōri ni" 1960; "Menmitsu na Imamura kantoku" 1960). To add further, the costs for the production quickly exceeded the intended budget. Not only did Nikkatsu balk at the idea of providing additional funds for the project; in the aftermath of the production, Imamura's team was forced to submit a "written apology" (*shimatsusho*) to the company (Imamura 2001: 40). When the film was finally released on January 20, 1961, posters and ads generated hype by treating it as an "unconventional

[and] controversial film" (Nikkatsu kabushiki kaisha, 1961). Even though Imamura was able to gain a "sense of achievement," he was unable to direct a film for three years thereafter (Imamura 2010a: 83).

Exposing American Power

This "controversial film" opens with a shot in which the camera, pulling back from a close-up of an American flag, pans to capture Yokosuka from land to harbor. The following shots bring the viewer to the ground level, on Dobuita Street. Using a long take, the camera slowly tracks backward to capture the shops and bars along the road, as US sailors, the Military Police, storeowners, and young women stroll, chat, bargain, and fraternize with one another. Though the captions claim that *Pigs and Battleships* is "an entirely fictional story," the images invoke the unflattering reality of everyday life in an actual base city. Akira Iwasaki maintains that the film's beginning moments underscore the "colonized, extremely degenerated, customs [*fūzoku*] that would embarrass any Japanese" (Iwasaki 1981: 222).

Imamura's goal, however, was not to end the story with Japanese humiliation, but to dramatize life in the base city as a "heavy comedy" (*jukigeki*), which was meant to invoke "serious [*omoi*] laughter that would hit one's gut" by bringing out "the truth of human beings" (Imamura 2010a: 63). The director sought to draw this effect by presenting the Japanese as "pigs," though the motif did not begin or end with *Pigs and Battleships*. In *Endless Desire*, for example, the director presents a band of shady individuals who endeavor to recoup a bundle of morphine bottles that were secretly buried underground at the end of the war. Drawn together by greed, the conspirators dig furiously—literally like animals—in the hope of striking it rich. One of them, a school teacher, expresses delight in being able to "say what I really think" in front of "you pigs." In *Paraji: kamigami no butabuta/Paraji*, a little-known 1962 play that served as a foundation for *Kamigami no fukaki yokubō/Profound Desire of the Gods* (1968), Imamura presented an extended family originating from a fictitious southern island shaped by incest. In scenes that involve sex, the director inserted photographic slides of pigs cuddling together (Sato Tadao 1980: 82). *Nippon konchūki/The Insect Woman* (1963), a story that chronicles the life story of a poor Tohoku woman, includes a scene in which the female protagonist's parents are regarded "just like a piglet" for having had premarital sex. When the heroine becomes a sex worker in Tokyo, the cunning madam reminds her that she is being "domesticated" (*kawareteiru*).

In *Pigs and Battleships*, the Japanese "pigs" are juxtaposed against US "battleships." This contrast is established in the opening credits, which showcases a string of trucks advancing on a bumpy road along the harbor, where American naval vessels are eerily visible in the background. The formidable gunboats suggest the omnipresence of US power in Japan, nearly a decade after the occupation. The Japanese, by contrast, are represented by Kinta (Hiroyuki Nagato), a petty hoodlum who cuddles with a load of pigs on the back of a truck. Wearing a *sukajan* jacket (a Yokosuka trademark) and a smirk in his face, Kinta works as a henchman for the Himori gang. In a stark contrast to the gun-wielding, no-nonsense *yakuza* men who thrive in the Nikkatsu action film, Imamura's hero is a "weak" male whose masculinity is of no match against the men around him, to say nothing of US military men (his gang "brothers" repeatedly encourage him to "be a man").[4] Kinta's vulnerability also shows in his relationship with Haruko (Jitsuko Yoshimura). Even though she is deeply in love with Kinta—so much so that she agrees to abort their child—the couple repeatedly clashes over Haruko's suggested relationship with US sailors. While seeking to live an honest living, the young heroine is drawn to America's "good life" symbolized by green-grass lawns and Coca-Cola mixers.

For much of the narrative, Imamura stresses the hardships of the Japanese in the face of US influence. In the beginning, Kinta, for instance, is tasked by the Himori gang to run a hog farm with leftovers diverted from the US military. But when Sakiyama (Akira Yamauchi), the nefarious Japanese-American broker, demands a larger cut, Kinta and his fellow hoodlums have no choice but to extort money from local citizens. The Himori gang is left with a boatload of debt when Sakiyama abruptly disappears from sight. Trapped in this "base economy," Kinta and his senior "brothers" feast on a roasted pig that had consumed a yakuza man who had been eliminated upon Himori's orders. After spotting a false human tooth in the cooked meat, the grossed-out crowd in this humorous scene starts to vomit. This indirect cannibalism not only portrays the petty gangsters as animalistic beings, but also points to the perpetuation of social displacement in the shadow of US empire.

The United States also wields influence over women, many of whom work at bars and brothels that cater to the US Navy. This includes Haruko's co-worker Katsuyo (Yoko Minamida), who gets arrested for running the brothel that caters to military clients. Haruko's mother, an admirer of US fighter jets over Japan's Self-Defence Forces, believes that the only way to lift her family from poverty is to have her daughters marry American men. She not only endorses the oldest sister Hiromi (Sanae Nakahara) to become an *onrii*—a lover committed to a single American man—but also encourages Haruko to do the same with a man named Gordon. Following a quarrel with Kinta, the heroine parties with three US servicemen, who rape her in a hotel room. In the aftermath, she steals a pile of cash from a GI and gets arrested by the police.

Like the men around her, Haruko, together with her family and friends, are stuck in a vicious cycle.

Imamura stresses the "the trampling of Japan by the US" by offering a dramatic, if humorous, climax. Kinta tells Haruko that he would quit being a gangster, but he is subsequently caught by Himori (Masao Mishima) for attempting to secretly sell off the hogs. Pressured to take the blame on behalf of the gang, Kinta points a machine gun against his elderly brothers, but perhaps because he is not enough of a "man," the weapon goes off only after he accidentally drops it on the ground. Subsequently, he is shot and dies miserably, with his head dipped in a toilet bowl. Kinta's death, however, does not salvage the gang. While cornered by Himori's men, Kinta unleashes the pigs on the streets. With the merchandise fleeing the gang's hands, the hog business collapses. In the end, the pigs, 500 or so in number according to assistant director Kirio Urayama, ironically run over the fleeing Himori gang (Urayama 1971: 110). The greedy Japanese "pigs," who are ironically crushed by the actual animals, fail to survive in Yokosuka's base economy.

After devoting the bulk of the narrative to highlight America's towering influence over Japan, Imamura offers a glimmer of hope in Haruko, who is presented as a resilient and determined young woman who takes a stand against US power (see later discussion). Not only does she overcome her hardships, she also rejects Gordon and departs from Yokosuka, where she had spent much of her life. In the final scene, Haruko walks against a torrent of young female streetwalkers who wave to a crowd of US servicemen and heads to the train station, presumably to Kawasaki where she wishes to find a steady job. Yet in spite of her rejection of Yokosuka, her fate is far from triumphant. The film ends ambiguously—with a long shot that captures the Yokosuka train station—without offering any promise for success in Kawasaki, which has historically been a site of crime, poverty, pollution, and overall urban blight.[5] Nor does Haruko's departure do anything to change the cultural politics of the port city, which continues to draw female prostitutes and fraternizers as new aircraft carriers enter the harbour. If anything, the base economy remains intact, and the "lowly" women and men in town have no real influence on the larger sinews of power that appear to control them.

Rising from the Black Market

Pigs and Battleships underscores the power of the United States by portraying the extending presence of the US military. Imamura also does this by associating Yokosuka with the black market, or *yamiichi*. During the years immediately after World War II, war-burned fields, dingy street corners, and narrow alleys in almost every city turned into sites of lively—often illegal—commercial activity involving injured war veterans, petty merchants, *pan pan* prostitutes, orphans, and ordinary civilians (Matsudaira 1995). Although these seedy urban spaces, such as in parts of Tokyo, are said to have dissolved by the end of the Korean War, the "feel" of the black market persisted in many neighborhoods. When Imamura visited Yokosuka nearly a decade after General Douglas MacArthur had left Japan, he was immediately struck by the city's resemblance to "the chaotic and vulgar atmosphere of the postwar black market" (Imamura 2010a: 79).

For many Japanese, the *yamiichi* was a symbol of shame and humiliation. It was a site of confusion where the scars of war were painfully visible. But to Imamura, those dingy spaces were sites of liberation. During World War II, Imamura, who claims to have "disdained the military" and "ignored national authority," was unhappy with the "stiffened" (*kōchoku shita*) climate in which "no one spoke their true feelings" (Imamura 1995; "Mukashi shōnen ima shōjo" 1995). The black market was devoid of such constraints. Despite the fact that "every possible vice may be swarming around," it was an oasis-like space of "freedom in the middle of the dark" (Imamura 1995). Yet Imamura relished the black market, I argue, not just because it was devoid of wartime oppression, but also because its "free market" atmosphere was largely indifferent to the "heralded programs of 'democratization'" that the US occupiers were instilling across Japan (Dower 1999: 144). To Imamura, the *yamiichi* was a space of self-assertion. It was a place where he invented his own sense of freedom apart from larger forces, including those of the United States.

This conviction inspired Imamura to spend much of his time in the black market. In the weeks and months following the war, Imamura read and wrote plays in the shady quarters of Shinjuku and Ikebukuro. It was in this climate that Imamura read novelist Ango Sakaguchi's "On Decadence" ("Daraku ron"), which criticized the "facade" of Japanese politics and militarism while calling for a rediscovery of one's human self through "degeneration" and "decadence" (Sakaguchi 1946). The succinct essay provided "great stimulation" and inspired Imamura to fully embrace the "haven of freedom" in the *yamiichi*, which seemed to encourage "all human beings to expose their lust for life and live without any constraints" (Imamura 1995; Imamura 2010a: 47).

The black market also rewarded Imamura with a life-changing encounter: that with Akira Kurosawa's *Yoidore tenshi/Drunken Angel*. Released in 1948, this iconic film pits an alcoholic doctor (Takashi Shimura) against an impulsive gangster (Toshiro Mifune), who eventually loses his life after a "beastly" fight with his former boss (as described in the screenplay) (Toho Company 1947: 2). Imamura enjoyed the film as a whole but was particularly moved by Mifune's performance. In contrast to the typically "handsome" (*nimaime*) male leads (such as Ken Uehara and Shuji Sano) who appeared to be nothing more than "fake" (*usokusai*) (Imamura 1995), the young Toho star displayed the energy of a "beast" that "jumped straight out from the smelly *yamiichi*." While lacking smoothness or savvy, Mifune exhibited a "powerful larger-than-life presence" that carried an "allure of the real" (Imamura 1995; Imamura 2010a: 48). While an undoubtedly fictional narrative, *Drunken Angel* appeared to the young Imamura as a "high-grade documentary." The encounter with this Kurosawa film drove him to become a filmmaker (Imamura 1995).

The ambience of the black market pervades Imamura's works. One can see this, for instance, in the impoverished lives of the theatrical troupe in *Stolen Desire*, the money-hungry war veterans in *Endless Desire*, and the heroine's sex life and prostitution in *The Insect Woman*. In *Pigs and Battleships*, Imamura plays up the *yamiichi* motif by interjecting heavy drinking, filthy toilets, sex work, romantic heartbreak, and underground bartering—all of which he personally witnessed and experienced in the rowdy quarters of Tokyo (Imamura 1995). He paints the "lowly" hoodlums with rich character emotions. In contrast to Kurosawa's *Drunken Angel* and *Nora inu/Stray Dog* (1949), which depicts the underworld as a disease-infested, morally corrupt space, Imamura, as Osabe Hideo argues, saw the black market as a place where one could start life anew (Osabe 1971: 234). While admitting that the yakuza in Yokosuka were "greedy and capable of every dirty trick in the book," the director maintained that these low-life individuals "had their own kind of pride and enjoyed a kind of freedom all their own" (Nakata 1999: 114–15).

Pigs and Battleships also inserts ethnically marginalized characters, most notably the Chinese who are defined on the screenplay as "third-country nationals [*sangoku jin*]," a derogatory term used during the occupation era (Imamura 1964: 69). According to Michael Molasky, the *yamiichi* was a fluctuating space in which "those who were marginalized for a long time were able to demonstrate their power, and [even] built the foundation of economic success and social emergence" (Molasky 2015: 314). *Pigs and Battleships* presents this inverted social climate by inserting a Chinese broker named Chen (Taiji Tonoyama), who agrees to offer a loan for Himori to pay its debt. Wang (Hideo Kidokoro), a second Chinese character, bartends during the day but works as a hitman at night. When Tetsuji (Tetsuro Tanba), Kinta's "big brother" (and another "weak" male figure), is convinced that he will die shortly of stomach cancer, he hires Wang to relieve him of his misery. After realizing that his disease is easily curable (an ulcer), Tetsuji cowardly flees from Wang, even though the assassin was not going for the kill, as he had discovered that Tetsuji paid him with counterfeit money.

Above all, Imamura utilizes the *yamiichi* climate to underscore the resilience of women. In contrast to Kurosawa's black market films, which largely relegates prostitutes, singers, and other women to supporting and marginal roles, Imamura not only interjects stubborn and feisty female characters, but, more important, imparts them with strength and tenacity in the face of seemingly insurmountable difficulties. This is true with Katsuyo, who barks back at the US military police (and kicks one in the groin) when the sex workers are rounded up. More important is the heroine Haruko, who is not only a moral influence over men like Kinta but also is "determined" (*ishiteki*) to the core (Imamura 2001: 37).

Haruko's resilience shows especially through her rape by three American men—presented in a shot crafted with a revolving camera capturing the violent act in the hotel bedroom. Scenes like these, according to Imamura, symbolized a "Japan that was raped by the United States" (Imamura 1995). This devastating moment, however, is also used to accentuate Haruko's determined effort to maintain control over her life. In the wake of her horrifying experience, the heroine decides to ditch Gordon for good. In the famous final scene in which the defiant heroine walks along the harbor toward the train station, Imamura utilizes a telephoto lens to capture Haruko wiping off her lipstick—a rejection of her relationship with Gordon. This shot underscores a recurring theme in Imamura's films: women "discover that their core down deep is never violated even if their bodies are on the surface" (Imamura 1995). It also presents a Japanese individual taking a stand against US power, as Haruko decides to abandon Yokosuka's base economy by heading toward Kawasaki. Shigeomi Sato goes so far as to say that the telephoto shot symbolically represents Haruko's "awakening" to "recover[ing] the 'pride' of the Japanese" (Sato Shigeomi 1961: 93).

Yokosuka, Take Two

Pigs and Battleships exemplified Imamura's energy and audacity to challenge the hegemonic presence of US power in Japan. While presenting the story as a heavy comedy, he strove to present a live and actual issue that seemed to demand greater attention. His intervention in contemporary politics was noted by critics such as Shinbi Ogura, who praised the film for having "portrayed the reality of Japan" and especially for depicting "today's prosperity as forged by becoming an *onrii* of the United States" (Ogawa 1961: 74). Yet if *Pigs and Battleships* succeeded as a political and social commentary, it still left Imamura with more to do. Three months after the release of the film, the director, on *Kinema junpō*, argued that filmmakers ought to encourage "human beings, manipulated in the system, to step into a new direction" by wielding a kind of "energy" that would "deny [and] destroy authority." However, given the persistence of US exploitation and Japanese poverty, he was unsure if *Pigs and Battleships* fully achieved this objective (Imamura 1961).

In the years that followed, Imamura continued to engage the problematic of US hard power in Japan. He did this in part by portraying the lives around US bases in fictional works like *The Insect Woman*, but he also decided to utilize the medium of documentary filmmaking—a means of "drawing out social contradictions" by capturing "genuine people who live lives" (Imamura 2010b: 135; Imamura 2001: 236). In November 1970, Imamura, now an independent producer, visited Yokosuka to seek material for his next film. There, in a gathering of local bar hostesses, Imamura heard of a woman with a colorful life story (Imamura 1971: 86–87). This led to the production of a new feature film: *Madam Onboro*.

Imamura claimed that the purpose of *Madam Onboro* was to illustrate the "collapse of the Japanese home [*ie*]" (Imamura 1970). Its statement of purpose vowed to expose "the various problems embodied by the family, especially . . . the relationship between parent and child as well as [that of] husband and wife" (Imamura 2001: 64). *Pigs and Battleships* already presented this theme by portraying Kinta's father, Kan'ichi (Eijiro Tono), a former Navy man who ekes out a living as a woodchip seller, as a failed patriarch, and by dramatizing the infiltration of American men in Haruko's household. *Madam Onboro* plays up the latter phenomenon by highlighting the romantic and sexual life of Emiko Akaza. Early on, Imamura offers shots of Emiko walking down the streets to reenter the doors of Onboro, her bar (closed for two years) located off Dobuita Street. In the interviews conducted there, Imamura establishes the fact that Emiko, whose father lives as a butcher, is a marginalized *buraku* person raised in western Japan. She stops attending school after being bullied and uses her sexuality to gain power. After failed relationships with Japanese men (including a marriage), she moves to Yokosuka and runs Bar Onboro from 1958. In the years that followed, Emiko confesses to have had romantic and sexual relationships with "over ten" US soldiers, including Harry, a twenty-three-old sailor whom she has married.

Imamura is not just interested in uncovering the most private and intimate dimensions of Emiko's life. He also tries to tease out her views on "Japan's postwar history," as the title of the film indicates. Through a screening of newsreel footage at Bar Onboro, Imamura tries to draw Emiko's reactions to famous historic events, though to his disappointment, she "showed no interest whatsoever" in them (Imamura 1970). Yet her commentaries function to generate a rift between her and official historical knowledge. For instance, in response to the footage of Emperor Hirohito's radio announcement to accept surrender, Emiko challenges conventional wisdom by noting that few people around her actually cried or mourned. More than anything else, they were relieved and happy, she says. After viewing the wedding ceremonials of Michiko Shimoda and Crown Prince Akihito, the madam of Bar Onboro charges that the Imperial family is an "ornament of Japan" and that the construction of a New Palace with tax money was a "waste" (*mottainai*). In introducing Emiko's comments, the narrative questions the unity of the Japanese under Imperial system—a larger metaphor of the "Japanese home" (Imamura 1970).

Imamura, not surprisingly, believes that the history of postwar Japan is inseparable from US military power. To this end, he provokes Emiko to elicit her view on the US conquerors, though her replies counter the director's inclinations to treat the United States in a critical light. For example, after showing footage of Douglas MacArthur and the occupation forces, the director asks about the fear that her family and friends initially may have had toward the new conquerors. Emiko, then, remarks that the Americans were actually "gentlemanly." Shots of demonstrators protesting the entry of the *USS Enterprise* in Sasebo are presented together with Emiko's elaboration of her three-year relationship with an American man named Joe. In an outdoor scene shot on the rooftop, Imamura hands her a volume of the *Asahi Graph* magazine, which includes disturbing photographs of the My Lai massacre. Imamura sets up the scene by opening the film with a juxtaposition of US military atrocities with the brutal processing of cattle in a slaughterhouse—one that is presumably run by Emiko's father. The montage seeks to establish the idea that America's military efforts were a form of animalistic slaughter. But Emiko, seemingly resisting Imamura's agenda, refuses to accept the *Asahi Graph's* imagery.

If these unexpected reactions counter the perception that the Americans are brutal conquerors, the film showcases footage from Yokosuka to underscore the continuing influence of US militarization on the ground. Although the harbor city in the 1970s had lost some of its flourish, the existence of US forces, Imamura later wrote, continued to fuel the business of bars, brothels, and shops of different kinds (Imamura 2001: 225). To illustrate the persistence of the wider base economy and its *yamiichi*-esque climate, Imamura juxtaposes shots of US aircraft carriers, fighter jets, and the military police with glittering neon signs and prostitutes seducing US sailors on the night-time streets. Toward the end of the film, Imamura includes a scene in which Emiko responds to Imamura's interview at the harbor. As the conversation progresses, the camera blurs Emiko's face and shifts its focus to a US submarine that passes in the background. In addition to underscoring the looming presence of American hard power, the shot alludes to the opening credits of *Pigs and Battleships*, in which formidable US gunboats loom in the harbour as Kinta—a lowly

Japanese individual—appears in the foreground. Imamura shows how the dialectic of the "pigs" and "battleships" continues to shape Japanese life.

* * *

Imamura once claimed that "authors" (*sakusha*) needed to pursue their creative endeavours in a "consistently anti-establishment direction" (Imamura 1961). *Pigs and Battleships* was a defining work that expressed this intention. In the film, the director boldly took issue with US military policy by dramatizing the real-life struggles of everyday citizens living under the gaze of American "battleships." He also sympathized with the down-and-out Japanese by illustrating their emotions, desires, motivations in the form of a heavy comedy. To Imamura, the energy of the oppressed Japanese emerged from the liberated climate of the black market—a milieu that seemed to persevere beyond the early postwar years. Yokosuka became a site for him to grapple with Japan's struggle to live and thrive years after a devastating war.

Pigs and Battleships also confirmed that the expansive presence of the United States was a long-term concern. This led him to shoot *Madam Onboro* nine years after his first Yokosuka film. By scrutinizing the "animalistic" life story of a strong, marginalized bar hostess, and by juxtaposing it with the larger historical events of the era, the director illustrated the fracturing of the "Japanese home" while teasing out the continuing influence of the US military. Imamura later noted that he had developed a "deep relationship" (*in'nen ga fukai*) with Yokosuka (Imamura 2001: 65). *Pigs and Battleships* helped inaugurate the director's efforts to make sense of America's transpacific presence in the postwar decades.

Notes

1. See, for example, David Desser, *Eros plus Massacre: An Introduction to the Japanese New Wave Cinema* (Bloomington: Indiana University Press, 1988); Yuriko Furuhata, *Cinema of Actuality: Japanese Avant-Garde Filmmaking in the Season of Image Politics* (Durham, NC: Duke University Press, 2013); Isolde Standish, *Politics, Porn and Protest: Japanese Avant-Garde Cinema in the 1960s and 1970s* (New York: Continuum, 2011); Maureen Turim, *The Films of Oshima Nagisa: Images of a Japanese Iconoclast* (Berkeley: University of California Press, 1988); Yomota, Inuhiko, *Oshima Nagisa to Nihon* (Tokyo: Chikuma shobō, 2010).
2. In addition to *Pigs and Battleships* and *Madam Onboro*, Imamura shot a TV documentary on Yokosuka entitled "Dobuita Street" (*Dobuita yokochō*) in 1980. Due to spatial constraints, this chapter does not discuss this program (Imamura 2010b: 222).
3. Although Yamanouchi is the only person credited for the film's screenplay, Imamura was heavily involved in preparing the script.

4. On the Nikkatsu action film, see Mark Schilling, *No Borders No Limits: Nikkatsu Action Cinema* (Godalming: FAB Press, 2007).
5. For an illuminating and disturbing account of Kawasaki today, see Isobe, Ryō, *Rupo: Kawasaki* (Tokyo: Cyzo, 2017).

Works Cited

"Buta to gunkan sōdōki" (1960). *Asahi shinbun*, evening ed., July 17, 1960, 4.

Desser, David (1988). *Eros plus Massacre: An Introduction to the Japanese New Wave Cinema*. Bloomington: Indiana University Press.

Dower, John W. (1999). *Embracing Defeat: Japan in the Wake of World War II*. New York: W. W. Norton and the New Press.

"Engi mo honban dōri ni" (1960). *Yomiuri shinbun*, evening ed., August 17, 1960, 5.

Furuhata, Yuriko (2013). *Cinema of Actuality: Japanese Avant-Garde Filmmaking in the Season of Image Politics*. Durham, NC: Duke University Press, 2013.

Imamura Shohei (1961). "Hitotsu no kokoro gamae." *Kinema junpō*, April 1961, 66.

Imamura Shohei (1964). *Nippon konchūki*. Tokyo: San'ichi shobō.

Imamura Shohei (1970). *"Nippon sengoshi* o megutte no moromoro." *Kinema junpō*, July 15, 1970, 27.

Imamura Shohei (1971). "Imamura Shohei zen jisaku o kataru." In *Sekai no eiga sakka 8*, ed. Imamura Shohei and Urayama Kirio, 62–92. Tokyo: Kinema junpō sha.

Imamura Shohei (1995). "Ango to watashi to seishun." In *Imamura Shohei no sekai*, ed. Sato Tadao. Tokyo Teatoru sinjuku, n.p.

Imamura Shohei (2001). *Toru: Kannu kara yamiichi e*. Tokyo: Kōsaku sha.

Imamura Shohei (2010a). *Imamura Shohei: Eiga ha kyōki no tabi dearu*. Tokyo: Nihon tosho sentā.

Imamura Shohei (2010b). *Kyōikusha Imamura Shohei*. Ed. Sato Tadao. Tokyo: Kinema junpō sha.

Isobe Ryō (2017). *Rupo: Kawasaki*. Tokyo: Cyzo.

Iwasaki Akira (1981). *Eiga no maesetsu*. Tokyo: Gōdō shuppan.

Izawa Jun, et al. (1959). "Shinjin ishiki afureru Nikkatsu eiga o." *Kinema junpō*. November 15, 1959, 66.

Matsudaira Makoto (1995). *Yamiichi: Maboroshi no gaido bukku*. Tokyo: Chikuma shobo.

"Menmitsu na Imamura kantoku" (1960). *Yomiuri shinbun*, evening ed., November 10, 1960, 5.

Miller, Jennifer M. (2014). "Fractured Alliance: Anti-Base Protests and Postwar U.S.-Japanese Relations." *Diplomatic History* 38, no. 5: 953–86.

Molasky, Michael (2015). "Kaisetsu." In *Yamiichi*, ed. Michael Molasky, 287–331. Tokyo: Kosei sha.

"Mukashi shōnen moto shōjo" (1995). *Asahi shinbun*, December 6, 1995, 18.

Nakamura Hideyuki (2014). *Haisha no miburi: posuto senryōki no Nihon eiga*. Tokyo: Iwanami shoten.

Nakata Toichi (1999). "Shohei Imamura interviewed by Toichi Nakata." In *Shohei Imamura*, ed. James Quandt, 107–24. Toronto: Toronto International Film Festival Group.

Niikura Hiroshi (2016). *Yokosuka, Kichi no machi o aruki tsuzukete.* Tokyo: Nanatsu mori shokan.
Nikkatsu kabushiki kaisha (1961). Poster of *Buta to gunkan.*
Nikkatsu kabushiki kaisha (1962). *Nikkatsu 50 nenshi.* Tokyo: Nikkatsu kabushiki kaisha.
Ogawa, Mami (1961). "*Buta to gunkan.*" *Kinema junpō,* February 5, 1961, 74.
Osabe Hideo (1971). "Kaette kita otoko." In *Imamura Shohei no eiga: zen sagyō no kiroku,* 234–42. Tokyo: Haga shoten.
Osada Arata (1953). "Kichi no ko ra o mamore." *Asahi shinbun,* April 10, 1953, 3.
Sakaguchi Ango (1946). "Daraku ron." in Sakaguchi, *Nihon ron,* Tokyo: Kawade shobō shinsha, 1989.
Sato Shigeomi (1961). "Imamura Shohei to *Buta to gunkan.*" *Eiga hyoron,* August 1961, 92–93.
Sato Tadao (1980). *Imamura Shohei no sekai.* Tokyo: Gakuyō shobō.
Sato Tadao (1995). *Nihon eigashi 2: 1941–1959.* Tokyo: Iwanami shoten.
Schilling, Mark (2007). *No Borders No Limits: Nikkatsu Action Cinema.* Godalming: FAB Press.
"Setto o tatete hiroin tesuto" (1960). *Yomiuri shinbun,* evening ed., August 17, 1960, 5.
Standish, Isolde (2011). *Politics, Porn and Protest: Japanese Avant-Garde Cinema in the 1960s and 1970s.* New York: Continuum.
Toho Company (1947). "Yoidore tenshi" revised script, November 13, 1947, 2, Box 5290, Folder 1, Records of the Supreme Commander for the Allied Powers, National Archives and Records Administration, College Park, MD.
Turim, Maureen (1988). *The Films of Oshima Nagisa: Images of a Japanese Iconoclast.* Berkeley: University of California Press.
Urayama Kirio (1971). "Imamura eiga o megutte." In *Sekai no eiga sakka 8,* ed. Imamura Shohei and Urayama Kirio, 93–110. Tokyo: Kinema junpō sha.
"Yokosuka o butai ni 'jukigeki'" (1960). *Yomiuri shinbun,* evening ed., June 14, 1960, 5.
Yomota Inuhiko (2010). *Oshima Nagisa to Nihon,* Tokyo: Chikuma shobō.

Chapter 4

Insect Men and Women: Gender, Conflict, and Problematic Modernity in *Intentions of Murder*

Adam Bingham

It is, perhaps, the defining image of the cinema of Shohei Imamura: a downtrodden, dispossessed, emotionally battered, often physically abused but ultimately resilient, pragmatic, and practical woman. She is a figure whose earthy, sexual, variously available yet often defiled body (the two states closely intertwined) becomes a marker of both selfhood and resistance; frequently she finds selfhood in resistance—to oppression, manipulation, subjugation, exploitation—and it is this prismatic, problematic groping toward subjectivity that orders many of this director's narratives. Gender and corporeal identity are paramount concerns for Imamura, with the social and political (as opposed to the purely biological) construction of the former expressed through the variously libidinal drives of the latter. *The Insect Woman* (*Nippon konchuki*, 1963) remains arguably the most paradigmatic example of this theme—of what James Quandt terms the "raw, primordial sexuality he (Imamura) consistently celebrates as a force that undermines the 'civilization' of official Japan" (1997: 5)—and, further, of this director's method of extrapolating from this vision a discursive engagement with Japanese modernity. However, its most complex expression may be found in *Intentions of Murder* (*Akai satsui*, 1964), a film made immediately following *The Insect Woman* and that expands upon and refracts its forebear's story in order to place its heroine's narrative in bold relief. It does this in order to suggest something of the stratification of gender in Japanese society—the myriad ways in which inequality is institutionalized and normalized—and to probe and question these relations and the roles that they facilitate as a product (or otherwise) of contemporary Japan.

It is through a juxtaposition of these two successive films that the latter can best be understood and elucidated, and that the latter's reframing of Imamura's perennial concerns becomes most visible. This essay traces the complex and intricate interrelationship of gender and modernity in *Intentions of Murder* as a means of assessing its place within Imamura's oeuvre and of considering the ways in which it not only refines but refracts the parameters of what is often understood as a reasonably lucid and coherent picture of gender relations and social agency. It also draws on intertextuality to help clarify its project, and these concepts are placed within the context of both Imamura's cinema and of gender relations and the gendering of desire and agency within Japanese society, which have typically been problematic sites of sociopolitical discourse and sociocultural definition and representation.[1] As a result, the essay also considers the ways in which *Intentions of Murder* may in fact be seen to complicate extant Imamura criticism, and what has by now become received wisdom in the form of assumptions that underlie and invariably color perceptions and readings of his work.

Intentions of Murder concerns a housewife named Sadako who remains at the behest of two different men. She lives in Sendai (north of Tokyo) with her common-law husband Riichi; her relations with her husband consist of a cursory home life in a dilapidated house beside a railway line, one in which she is expected to keep track of the household accounts, look after their often unruly young son, Masaru, and to be readily available for sex whenever it is demanded of her (something she never seems to enjoy but rather to endure). Sadako has a long-standing relationship with Riichi dating back to her formative years working as a maid in his family home, but is viewed with suspicion and contempt by his mother because she is perceived to be part of a curse placed on the household by her grandmother, who was Riichi's father's mistress. Riichi is a librarian engaged in a long-standing affair with a co-worker, Yoshiko, who is throughout the narrative almost always either pleading to or stalking her lover, while Sadako herself becomes the focus of extramarital desire, in her case of a desperate criminal named Hiraoka. While alone she is raped in her home by this man, who follows her after she has seen her husband and son off at the train station. After his initial crimes Hiraoka follows Sadako around professing to love and need her—ultimately pleading with her to run away with him to Tokyo—and the protagonist (who does not tell her husband about her attacker) is increasingly caught between the competing needs of both men, who are perennially desirous and, in various ways, perennially in need. Specifically, they are each sickly and unwell. Riichi is asthmatic, frequently coughing and struggling to breathe; Hiraoka suffers from a weak heart, something that necessitates frequent medication to combat sudden attacks that leave him close to death.[2]

Thus, the landscape of *Intentions of Murder* is replete with weak and physically compromised masculinity. Attendant on this is a foregrounding of a performative subtext to the desire and agency typically associated with men: associated with men but significantly here not wholly reducible to them, as Yoshiko's frank and oft-stated hunger both for Riichi and to break the bonds of his marriage is similarly positioned beyond the realm of men. Significantly, these needs—and the "activity" associated with their assertion (especially the aggressive and excessive sexuality that is repeatedly visited upon a largely passive Sadako)—become over-determined, too emphatic, as though to compensate for the characters' physical lack (literal but also perhaps psychoanalytically figurative); and lack it is that remains paramount throughout as the gulf between a heightened façade and the shallow reality it is designed to conceal. Imamura then uses this to narrativize this film's ambiguities over time and place and to explore its central theme of compromised modernity. These variously subversive desires cannot be channeled in any acceptable way, and as a result they are marked as disruptive forces, ones for which all the characters are summarily punished. Hiraoka dies, as, more significantly, does Yoshiko when she attempts to procure evidence of Sadako and Hiraoka's relationship. She follows these characters out when they take a train trip together, eventually tracking them to a tunnel on a hillside. Here she proceeds to photograph the pair, in so doing appropriating not only the look, the gaze, that usually marks out masculine desire and agency, but also an investigative function in order to bring to light the perceived affair between Sadako and Hiraoka—to demystify their apparent coupling and once again to appropriate the active functionality of the male subject. This is made almost parodically manifest in the two instances when her poor eyesight is underlined, particularly when she drops her spectacles while following Sadako and Hiraoka in the snow (the first instance finds Riichi scolding her for her weak eyes). For these transgressions Yoshiko is summarily punished. Not only does she remain unfulfilled but she is killed when she returns to the city; she is killed in the very act of looking when she carelessly steps out in the road to photograph Sadako following the protagonist's return from her meeting with Hiraoka at which he had died. Riichi, though he lives, is ultimately subject to the punishment of acceding to the role of head of his family home and thus of being placed in the position of patriarch. As such, the freedoms of his erstwhile life and relationships are curtailed as he is now in a position of more overt responsibility with demands placed upon him, and almost nothing of what has been shown suggests that he is equal to such a role (the role itself also being a deeply problematic and corrosive sociopolitical construction—more of which subsequently).

These characters' desires and deaths link them inexorably together and point to a compromised modernity in that, ostensibly at least, the strictures of the (ancestral) family unit are reinforced by the problems variously associated with its debasement over the course of the film. This implicit sense of antiquation is further represented by Sadako's mother-in-law, who is obsessed by the curse supposedly placed on her family by the protagonist's grandmother. She repeatedly harangues her daughter-in-law about her various habits, blaming her in particular for Riichi's weakness and continuing when the two are married to chastise her for her perceived poor mothering and housekeeping abilities. In addition, an early flashback to Sadako's arrival as a teenager at Riichi's family home shows her to be subject to the suspicious, seemingly malicious chants of a group of elderly women whose appearance (like the witches in *Macbeth*) seems both to outline a "narrative" that the protagonist enacts and to presage trouble for her in subsequent years. Thereafter Imamura repeatedly features their inaudible chants on the sound track during those moments when Sadako is most distressed or put upon (such as when Hiraoka threatens to burn her face with an iron), suggesting the extent to which these ancient customs and beliefs encroach on her life. It is as though the fate of this character is to play out a self-fulfilling prophecy pertaining to the way in which she is summarily regarded as a problem or hindrance to many of those around her.

The other women in Sadako's life, her neighbors and friends of her own age, offer a firm, reliable friendship—in other words, in those instances where sex is not an issue or a question—and Sadako herself remains the center of this storm. In point of fact one could contend that there is actually little that is truly innate in Sadako as regards her wishes or desires. Rather, by remaining at the behest of the desires, actions, and perceptions of others, as she often invariably does, her sense of selfhood is shaped and colored by those around her, at least for a majority of the narrative. And it is this aspect of the film that has not been sufficiently explored or elucidated, perhaps even understood as far as gender and desire are concerned. If those men and women who surround Sadako are overtly, excessively desirous, then the protagonist herself remains largely indifferent (her appetites are literal—frequently feeling compelled to eat—rather than figurative). She is, at times, a *tabula rasa*, almost a blank slate: an aspect of *Intentions of Murder* that has not really been touched upon or covered in accounts of the film. From Joan Mellen (1976: 305–310) and Audie Bock (1978: 293–95) in the 1970s to, more recently, James Quandt (1997: 1–6) and Donald Richie (1997: 7–43), Imamura criticism has typically tended to stress the rural, uncultivated, and uncivilized nature of Sadako. Mellen and Bock both argue that the protagonist, given her peasant background and ordinariness, remains somehow in touch with a raw earthiness and eroticism that her extended time with Riichi has blunted, and they liken this innate sexuality to her adolescent lasciviousness and almost primal sexuality, something expressed most overtly in the image of her letting a silkworm crawl along her thigh. This erotic dimension, they suggest, simply requires a reawakening, which happens when she is raped by Hiraoka; the fact that the image of the protagonist and the silkworm is repeated at the very end of the film (in its final shot) when she returns to the country would appear to reinforce this view. That is, it seems to allude to a rekindling of sexuality on Sadako's part—to the "unholy desire" that has at times been presented as the alternate English language title of the film—and that has lain dormant in the protagonist while living in the city.

Yet if one looks more closely at the images and narrative—at their, for Imamura, idiosyncratic subjectivity—and if one moves away from the strictures of received wisdom regarding Imamura criticism (especially Mellen's work), then one finds not a film about desire and sexuality rekindled but rather one concerned at least as much with sexuality contained or repressed. Specifically, Sadako's return to the countryside is simultaneously a return not only to Riichi but to the seat of his family and its repressive, reactionary domain, which beside the tension between objectivity and its opposite that has already been outlined offers a point of contrast with the city throughout, a prevalent ideological dichotomy. Thus Imamura's theme should instead be expressed as the extent to which sex and traditional gender roles are significant constituents in or determinants on relationships in contemporary Japan. The first image of Sadako with the silkworm crawling up her inner thigh alludes perhaps to a dawning awareness of sex and sensuality (though her expressions bespeak only curiosity rather than sensual excitement), but almost immediately this becomes the point of view of Riichi's mother when she catches and severely scolds her for what she takes to be her sinfulness, her dirtiness of mind and body. This is later redoubled when Riichi's mother perceives Sadako to be inciting the amorous attentions of a young man. Crucially, here, Imamura includes (at two distinct times in the film) the same event but with a different outcome. Initially Sadako recalls that she did not open her window to prompt and facilitate her potential suitor's attention; but subsequently, after running into the same man years later, she remembers opening the window for him and wonders to herself why she had earlier misremembered the incident. This erroneous memory is not especially significant in and of itself; however, given the structure of this film's narrative, its prevalent analepses and subjective ordering of events, it does serve to disturb other aspects of the narrative. Indeed, one feature of the film's sporadic surreal moments (something that has gone unremarked upon by almost everyone writing about *Intentions of Murder*) is to cast doubt on the veracity of those incidents and events that elsewhere seem particularly salient. Sadako's first apparent suicide attempt following her rape is a case in point. Before she attempts to throw herself in front of a train she puts out the washing: a strange enough act, and one underlined by the image of a shirt that flies around by itself before coming to land on a door. The suicide attempt takes place after this moment, and moreover is presented in a very dreamlike way with Sadako (shot in slow motion) preparing to leap under a passing train in an extremely exaggerated manner. Thus the veracity of this incident must at least be questioned, the fact of its having taken place undermined, as the film has moved into a markedly subjective register and seems to be detailed its heroine's troubled psyche, and it is this uncertainty that shapes the meaning and effect of the film.

With this in mind the bracketed images of Sadako and the worms can be elaborated upon, even problematized. The first is explicitly a flashback, which may now be regarded as misleading—especially as this scene includes Sadako being berated by Riichi's mother for her perceived sinfulness, which also occurs following the aforementioned incident with the window and the potential lover outside (in other words, Sadako may be misremembering events)—but even beyond this point of implicit ambiguity there are other aspects of the scene to consider. The flashback here follows the first rape, and this has perhaps fed those accounts of the film that stress the protagonist's primal reawakening in this particular contrast and ordering of events. In contradistinction, though, it could be countered that Sadako here is recoiling from the present into a memory of an anterior time when sex was new and enticing as opposed to forced, violent; or one could contend that she is recalling the sense of dirtiness and shame (about sex as intrinsically pleasurable—away from the institution of the family and the biological process of reproduction) that has been forced upon her by Riichi's mother. Of course, one could argue that she is likening her experience with Hiraoka to that of her dawning adolescent sexuality years before. But this is precisely the point of the film, part of its productive ambiguity; it is not supposed to be clear-cut either way but, like Sadako herself, to be unsure, uncertain.

To more fully adumbrate this feature of the film, it is useful to contrast its narrative and protagonist with those of its immediate forebear in Imamura's oeuvre. He had, just one year before *Intentions of Murder*, made what many now regard as his greatest film in *The Insect Woman*—a study of a rural girl who moves to the city following World War II and ultimately becomes the madame of a brothel before being betrayed and imprisoned and moving again to the country to live with her daughter. Imamura and co-writer Keiji Hasebe had written both these films around the same time following a period of directorial inactivity on the part of the former, so the fact that they may be conceived of as companion pieces is unsurprising, and their companionship can be closely traced. As in *The Insect Woman*, Imamura is at pains to fill in the life of his female protagonist in *Intentions of Murder*. However, the mirror image that the latter offers of the former becomes clear when one considers the respective protagonists, as well as the structure and style, of the two works. Where the former narrative depicts a life lived through history and sociopolitical change and upheaval (with sporadic onscreen text denoting year and month as time moves inexorably onward), the latter is a much more microscopic portrait, a more intimate and claustrophobic narrative in which time and space become constricted, amorphous, subjectively ordered to stress interior temporality rather than the ebb and flow of historical linearity. The earlier film has perennial recourse to key events in twentieth-century Japanese history as experienced by the protagonist—from Emperor Hirohito's historic radio address announcing Japan's surrender at the end of the Pacific war to the presence of US aircraft during the Korean War and ultimately to the widespread social unrest in 1960 over the America/Japan ANPO security pact (presented via documentary footage)—but she remains detached from them throughout. Indeed, the fact that Tome variously misses or is uninterested in or inconvenienced by these events suggests something of the counter-history of Japan that *The Insect Woman* presents: the contrastive image (of resistance, of challenge) that it presents vis-à-vis the tide of official, patriarchal history.

Intentions of Murder takes place in a landscape that, on the surface at least, bespeaks little of specificity regarding time and place; indeed, but for the electrical goods around Sadako's house it is a film that could be set a decade (or more) earlier than 1964. This lack of temporal clarity offers an objective correlative both to the surreality and attendant ambiguity around Sadako: the aforementioned vagueness over her motivations and feelings; it also serves to question her (and the film's) "reality," as well as countering *The Insect Woman's* largely objective style and methodology. Thus where Tome in *The Insect Woman* remains driven, active, a marker of resistance to history as "his story," Sadako figures as a reification of the same by dint of her blankness, the way in which she is positioned (at least for most of the narrative) as a testing ground or indeed a battleground for the various desires, appetites, and personalities of all the men and women around her. Where Tome is assertive, Sadako remains oppressed and unsure of herself, and where Tome's narrative is expansive, Sadako's is constricted and claustrophobic. *The Insect Woman* tends to bifurcate gender relations and ultimately stresses the primacy of female agency, even empowerment (through Tome's daughter who manages to manipulate and procure money from her mother's business partner), and it traces these precepts both alongside and against the (patriarchal) tide of twentieth-century Japanese history. Conversely, *Intentions of Murder* offers a more complex series of mirrored and inverted images that, while centered on and anchored in female subjectivity, in fact places relationships (familial as well as both marital and extramarital) in the spotlight. One may, ostensibly at least, thus regard Sadako as a marker of female suffering and oppression, the more so given the fact that the other three key characters display numerous different traits that pertain to gender and its sociopolitical regulation and stratification. However, there is no Mizoguchi-like cult of victim-hood about Sadako; even Imamura's almost customary contrast of his protagonist with animals—in this case, Masaru's pet mice—sees those creatures killed by their confinement and captivity while Sadako finds a way to survive within the ostensible cage in which she lives.

Emotional and particularly physical desire—both on the part of men and women—are demonstrated by the three characters who surround Sadako, and these characteristics are increasingly compromising and transgressive to the extent that they construct for the protagonist and for themselves an identity that (whether conscious or otherwise) reinforces conservative connotations and assumptions about gender and agency. However, where the men are concerned this is not a simple matter as they are themselves oppressed by the entrenched expectations and demands of a patriarchal culture that has ingrained in them (Riichi in particular) the fact that they are, or should be, the dominant sex. And sex remains the primary means of communication between them (as it variously is in later films like *The Eel* [*Unagi* 1997] or *Warm Water under a Red Bridge* [*Akai hashi no shita nonuruimizu*, 2001]). On numerous occasions both Riichi and Hiraoka force themselves on Sadako when they otherwise seem to be engaged in a discussion; indeed, relations between the different characters in the film are variously defined or delimited by prescriptive, transactional interactions that tend to suffocate rather than liberate Sadako. Hiraoka, after raping and robbing her, almost cursorily leaves money for her, literally paying her for the intercourse they have just finished. We subsequently learn that his mother had been forced into prostitution in order to provide for him as a young boy following the death of his father (another absent and compromised masculine figure), and this ostensibly peripheral moment in fact offers a productive point of departure for the film's litany of relationships. Hiraoka throughout seems to be engaged in an Oedipal trajectory: desiring to reclaim the lost maternal body that has not only been denied him but that he has seen become a commodity, as it were, and thus become defiled. Imamura elsewhere parodies such a drive and relationship both in the literal incest already identified and in the quasi-role playing of Sadako and Riichi, where the former has to call the latter "daddy" during sex. Hiraoka is in fact explicitly contrasted with Masaru in that both verbally attack Sadako with disparaging references to her weight (calling her a "fat cow" and "fatso," respectively, when she admonishes them on two separate occasions), and this particular juxtaposition throws into relief the problematic baggage associated with the sex act throughout the film.

With Hiraoka, Sadako is cast first as a victim, then in the role of furtive lover, even to the extent that she and this man repair to a shabby love hotel like adolescents or an adulterous couple (though Sadako appears not to want to sleep with him). The fact that here, as elsewhere, she does give in to his advances does not necessarily mean, as is commonly argued, that with her rapist she experiences a reawakening of desire on her part. It is true that she appears to experience more fulfilment with Hiraoka than she does with her husband; however, when having sex with her husband she behaves in a particular manner—giving in and feigning pleasure—and this at least raises the possibility that she is behaving likewise with Hiraoka. She is certainly drawn back to this man after appearing to have severed their ties (by literally throwing money at him to leave her alone), and what follows seems to be intercourse that she consents to, even though it could also be argued to be another rape as Imamura elides the beginning, the instigation, of their tryst and thus again foregrounds an ambiguity that undermines any objective veracity associated with this activity. Subsequently, in the scene in which we do see Sadako willingly beginning a physical union with Hiraoka—at the end when the pair have found respite from their climb up the snowy hill—the fact that she clings longingly to him seems to have the ulterior motive of allowing her to hold on to him while he is in the early stages of a heart attack brought on by their lovemaking. In contrast to an earlier moment when he had suffered on a train and she had rushed to help him, Sadako now appears unable to find Hiraoka's medicine, despite his instructions, and thus she appears to let him die. As such, given that she did intend to poison Hiraoka, one may potentially regard the earlier scene of lovemaking as something of a calculated attempt by Sadako to inveigle herself into her attacker's better graces by apparently consummating a relationship with a view to sealing their move away together, during which she plans the aforesaid poisoning (a notion that is further underlined by the beginning of snowfall at precisely the moment when Sadako decides to return to Hiraoka, something that then factors directly into her opportunity to kill him when their train is caught in a blizzard).

Sex, then, is a problematic site of either aggression or performance throughout much of *Intentions of Murder*. This accounts for the fact that Sadako's apparent discovery of sexuality and her body is something she does entirely by herself, and it further underlines her fundamental distance from those around her. Again, this compromises somewhat those views of this film that have by now become ingrained in Imamura criticism. James Quandt, in an essay specifically about *Intentions of Murder*, has discussed Sadako as a clear Imamura heroine, describing her as one among several "amoral, wilful, sexually driven women" that populate his work (2009: 7), while Dennis Lim has implied the same in that he has discussed what he terms the "sisterhood" of all Imamura's heroines (2009: 6). Quandt also explicitly states that Eros, the sex drive, is represented by Sadako, who (and which) "triumphs over civilization" (2009: 5). However, once again these views can all be challenged, or at least qualified. There is certainly a sense in which Sadako stands outside official Japan—particularly as she remains unrecognized in the family register, the *koseki*, which is the chief manifestation of the ideology of *ie*, which supports "a quasi-kinship unit with a patriarchal head" (Sugimoto 2003: 147)—but Imamura complicates this picture. Part of the aforementioned ambiguity pertains to her decision making; she acts from blind panic where Hiraoka is concerned and seems never able to fully commit to or see through an action where he is concerned. Despite her repeated rebuffs of Hiraoka's advances, she ultimately goes to him and gives in to his sexual advances, ironically at precisely the time when she appears to have been successful in dissuading his attentions. Ostensibly, at least (and reading against the aforementioned grain), she cannot kill herself and indeed cannot kill Hiraoka as she plans to toward the end of the narrative; she poisons a drink that she has prepared for him but knocks it from his hand before he can consume it. Moreover, amorality is a term better applied to those around Sadako than to the protagonist herself; Hiraoka is a criminal while both Riichi and Yoshiko seemingly have no compunctions about their affair. Sadako herself remains obdurately wedded to her family, and it is precisely her (misplaced but marked) sense of social and familial duty that propels her in the narrative—or at least her fear of contravening these institutions. Thus, rather than willful she may be said to be perennially indecisive and unsure of herself; or, by way of contrast, one may argue that her willfulness is repeatedly directed in actions that run directly contrary to her best interests. This character's instincts, such as they are, remain for all intents and purposes a problem for her, the tendencies that Imamura critics prize in his heroines—those that present such women as representative of the lower classes and concomitantly of an earthy, uncorrupted vitality—being probed in *Intentions of Murder* as part of its thematic enquiry into determinants on gender agency and identity. Here Imamura questions not so much the gulf between genders but the disparity between individual subjectivity and the gender roles that individuals have prescribed for them in the social milieu in which they live (the distance between Sadako and the perceived iconicity of the archetypical Imamura heroine underlining such a disjunction).

Of course, this applies as much to the men around Sadako as to the protagonist herself. For Riichi and Hiraoka, "love" and violence ultimately amount to one and the same thing; the latter's increasingly vehement protestations of love and desperate attempts to coerce Sadako into running away with him become ever more stringent and vociferous and appear to impinge upon Sadako's life more and more overtly. From this point of view Hiraoka's raping of Sadako during their first encounter becomes a particularly significant image, in some ways a thematic ground zero for the narrative. Physical intimacy and violence become inextricably intertwined, enmeshed within one another. Emotional and bodily desire are transmuted into aggression and coercion, and the fact that emotions become perennially corrupted in expression in this film refracts those questions about the extent to which Sadako actually acts in any preordained manner. If there is a pronounced tension between what is said and what is done, what is meant and what is carried out (the Japanese title of *Intentions of Murder* translates directly as *Red Murderous Intent*), then it is the slippage between these two often disjunctive and opposing poles that helps to underpin the juxtaposition of reality and surreality, objectivity and subjectivity, that defines this film's formal and stylistic organization. Surrealism in the context of the postwar Japan and the Japanese New Wave's direct engagement with questions of gender and representation has in fact been a subject of some enquiry. Chigusa Kimura-Steven has argued that in such works as Hiroshi Teshigahara's *Woman in the Dunes* (*Suna no onna*, 1964)—released the same year as *Intentions of Murder*—there is an emphasis on "real and fantastic elements" (2003: 156). She quotes a prominent critic (Sawa Kozo) in noting that the use of Kagawa Kyoko's body is almost entirely as an *objet*, an object that is perennially available for erotic and for aesthetic consumption. This literal objectification—something highlighted most overtly in the image of the woman sleeping naked with a towel covering her head, making her *just* a body—had significant ramifications for representations of the female body across subsequent work in Japan, and to this end it is interesting to contrast this woman's form with Sadako's body in *Intentions of Murder*.

Sadako's body is sporadically displayed throughout the film, usually as her clothes are hungrily torn off by either Riichi or Hiraoka. However, Imamura's camera perennially refuses the kind of distance or aesthetic contemplation that tends to enhance objectification. Where Teshigahara repeatedly composes his shots in order to enhance (and comment upon) hetero-normative interpellation, Imamura's often handheld camera is disorienting; it undermines any stable point of view from which to observe (and thus eroticize) Sadako, something compounded by a complementary series of compositions that frame scenes of intercourse from an oblique perspective. In this the camera tends to move and react in response to Sadako's distress rather than controlling the gaze cast on her body. Furthermore, this body is ostensibly unsightly (overweight) and thus a potential point of resistance to subject positioning, even as it is purely a means of sexual fulfillment for the characters who, as male subjects, might otherwise be the narrative focalizers. As such, Imamura presents a resistance to objectification even as Sadako is objectified within the diegesis, and in so doing opens up a liminal space between seeing and being seen, a gulf redolent of the dichotomy between life and death in which Sadako's trajectory is framed. It is not that her conventionally unappealing appearance, as it were, delimits sexual attraction; rather, the film dramatizes through this character's corporeality (and the reasons behind it) the distance between herself and those around her, as well as the corrosive rather than the liberating force of sexuality. Imamura stresses Sadako as visible throughout *Intentions of Murder*, and concomitantly this seems to mean that she is attainable or available to those around her. From the moment Hiraoka sees her at the train station at the beginning of the narrative, unbeknownst to her, she is fixed as an object, petrified, caught within the nexus of competing gazes of those around her. This sexual objectification then becomes a kind of death, but one from which Sadako is ultimately reborn when she becomes a part of Riichi's family as his officially sanctioned and recognized wife. And rather than sex it is this concept that is represented by the silkworm—its cycle of transfiguration, of physical change, figurative death and rebirth. The sexual connotations of the image are secondary here. Imamura's camera slowly moves up Sadako's body in the film's final shot—from the worm on her inner thigh to a close-up of her face (something it did not do in the earlier flashback)—and the expression on her face is not one of pleasure. It is pensive, ruminative, as though she were thinking about her youth and perhaps the gulf between then and now, past and present, as opposed to a reawakening of desire and sexual pleasure.

The fact that social and domestic spaces in the film become transfigured as sites of sex and death, Eros and Thanatos, underlines this feature of the film. External specificity (of time and place) is almost perennially overwritten, and the comparative prevalence of narrative ambiguity in *Intentions of Murder* bespeaks the extent to which Imamura places his characters (and their relationships) in a context whose indeterminate timeframe suggests something of the ongoing problems pertaining to gender inequality in Japan: to the fact that this is an issue that is by no means specific to a postwar context. Indeed, the Japan that Imamura was drawn to and wished to represent—his "unofficial Japan"—was one that predated the country's insularity during the rule of the Tokugawa Shogunate throughout the seventeenth and eighteenth centuries and on until 1868. With regard to *Intentions of Murder* it is striking how the director embeds a series of ostensibly antiquated signs and symbols as an index of a past within the present. The aforementioned recourse to subjective aural recapitulations of the cackling old women presents one facet of this ambiguity. The perceptions of these women appear to be related to the curse apparently placed on Riichi's family, and this bespeaks the tangible presence of antiquation—a lineage of irrational belief and superstition—that stands on the periphery of the narrative. The connotations present in these characters represent a picture of the irrationality so prized in Imamura's work; but here it is less a thorn in the side of contemporary Japan than it is an impingement on Sadako's life and identity. Indeed, it is something that is distinct from, and intrusively fostered upon, her throughout. Discussions of the film argue for (or simply assume) Sadako's rural peasantry; however, an early flashback shows her to be relocating to Riichi's family home from Tokyo, and stresses her displeasure at the move, making her (unlike Tome in *The Insect Woman*) as much an urban as a rural girl. She is separate from the perceptions and beliefs that form the foundation of the identities of those ingrained in life away from new urban centers. If Tome becomes representative of Japan's agrarian past, and as such remains a potential marker of what has been lost in the drive toward westernization and modernization, then Sadako offers a contrast to such ancient rural customs and belief systems: those that in films such as *The Profound Desire of the Gods* (*Kamigami no fufukaki yokubo*, 1968), *The Ballad of Narayama* (*Narayama bushi-ko*, 1983), and *Warm Water ua Red Bridge* have formed an integral part of Imamura's cinema as a vivifying force, a counterpoint or corrective to the official face of his country.

From this point of view one can posit a temporal ambiguity in *Intentions of Murder* wherein the contemporary landscape becomes a site of ambiguity. Indeed, there is an arresting of time in the film—what Dennis Washburn (writing about Imamura's *Vengeance Is Mine* [*Fukushu suru wa, ware ni ari*, 1979]) calls a "mythic transgression" of human time (2001: 318–41)—that is attendant on its nonlinear structure. The pressing need on Riichi's mother's part for Sadako to provide a healthy male heir to her son underlines this aspect of the film. The already antiquated social practice of patriarchal succession as connected to Riichi and his family home—the desperate need for an ongoing male bloodline—stands for one such problematic past awkwardly located in the present. The classical design of the family home is also a repository of tradition and the past, and Sadako's shack located beside a railway line is explicitly presented as a mirror image of the rural family home. The latter features cultivated grounds and an interior modeled after an old, pre-Meiji government official's residence. Sadako's unkempt and dilapidated house repeats this in dilapidated fashion, even down to the shoji screens that are defiled both by Masaru (who draws on them with his crayons) and by Hiraoka when he first breaks into the house and destroys one after violently throwing Sadako around the living room.

Elsewhere in the narrative, Imamura anticipates Juzo Itami's *The Funeral* (*Ososhiki*, 1984) and mocks the traditional ceremonial rites associated with characters' deaths. On two occasions very formal ceremonies are shown, and the director cuts to both in *medias res*, as though the full service were too boring or protracted to contemplate. Imamura even shoots one with an ungainly frontal composition and an extreme wide-angle lens that exaggerates the field of view to suggest the distorted values or priorities of this family who are wedded to a corrosive tradition that valorizes their past over the concerns of the present. Moreover, in this particular shot both the director's static composition and the seemingly attendant pro-filmic stasis means that attention on the ceremonial practices has to compete with that on the fidgety young Masaru as he begins to play with his grandfather's false teeth.

The juxtaposition here between staid formality and youthful exuberance—between, in effect, the dichotomy between life and death suggested earlier—offers a correlative to the film's amorphous treatment of historical temporality, its ambiguous signifiers of time and place. In particular, the prevalence of trains further offers a reinforcement of this fractious modernity—this tension between contemporary and traditional Japan—and indeed, in the repeated imagery pertaining to trains one finds an intertextual link to a director who had frequent recourse to such public transport and whose work is generally thought to represent everything to which Imamura stands in opposition: Yasujiro Ozu. In Ozu's work the train, as a practical feature of modern Japan, functions along the lines suggested by Alan Tansman wherein they largely represent a "social linkage and cohesion" (suburban living while working in the city as seen in, say, *Late Spring* [*Banshun*, 1949]), something linked to Takeda Nobuaki's concept of unification and constricted national space (2001: 157). Moreover, 1964 was the apex year with regard to Japan's modernization and emergence on the world stage, a development that culminated with the Tokyo Olympics. One of the preeminent markers of this modernization was the *Shinkansen*, the bullet train, which was presented as its symbol, its centerpiece, and which thereafter became redolent of all that Japan was to become during its miracle economic growth.

In *Intentions of Murder* the trains that repeatedly pass by Sadako's home are not bullet trains; rather, they are fairly antiquated machines, steam engines perennially belching smoke into the air and bespeaking a living past, a mirror image of contemporary Japan and a marker of the repressed of the country's modernity. Tansman and Takeda also highlight the potential connection between the development of train travel and interpersonal alienation (2001: 157), and here the trains' constant traversing of the frame on their way from one place to another underlines the nowhere-space that is this particular house. Furthermore, the appearances of these trains (whether visual or aural) often seem to prefigure or presage a problem for Sadako—an invasion into her home and life. Indeed, they may be seen to be connected specifically to the men around the protagonist. The first sound heard in the film, over the Nikkatsu studios logo (and thus serving as a nondiegetic score), is the shrill, piercing whistle of a train that is subsequently, in the opening shot, shown from a high angle as it passes by Sadako's house. The camera pans to follow the train before a freeze frame suspends the action, though not the sound, following which the train is heard over a proliferation of still shots taken in and around the (empty) home. The train is at once both connected to this domestic space and divorced from it, something that subtly connects it to the men who each seem to be variously drawn to the house only to find themselves repelled or pulled away. For instance, there is constant pressure on Riichi throughout the film to move back to his mother's house to live—to retreat in time, as it were—while one particular scene sees Riichi on board one of the trains that passes by as Sadako remains fixed, waving to him from her garden.

After this opening scene, trains tend to figure not as a practical aspect of life for the characters but as an index of surreality and gendered subjectivity. On two distinct occasions when Hiraoka has attacked Sadako, the film cuts away midscene to a dreamlike, slow-motion image of a train. In one, it increasingly fills the frame as it approaches the camera; in the next the camera frames its wheels in close-up and pans left to right to follow it as it breaks. These apparently subjective interjections reinforce the masculine gendering of these hulking, invasive, antiquated vehicles, reinforcing the fact that the sound of a train can be heard whenever men enter Sadako's house. Furthermore, Sadako and Hiraoka's visit to the love hotel is interrupted when a train passing below causes smoke to fill the room and to almost choke Sadako, and even when the protagonist does use the train her journey is compromised by Hiraoka following her and accosting her during the journey. In addition, one of Sadako's most disturbing dreams occurs when she imagines herself and Hiraoka on a train, one from which she falls into an abyss or a void. Only at the end of the film, when train travel is explicitly frustrated (by snowfall), is Sadako unperturbed, indeed is aided, by trains. This not only reinforces the implicit connection between these vehicles and the men in Sadako's life but further underlines the film's consideration of gender conflict at the confluence of sociohistorical and sociopolitical modernity, progress or reform.

This feature of the film is mirrored in Sadako's home life. The fact that Japan in 1964 was entering into a period of unparalleled economic prosperity, national wealth, and technological advancement becomes an ironic backdrop, or more properly a dramatic counterpoint, to the repeated talk of household goods and consumer durables: from the television set that Sadako is perennially accused of spending all day watching to the sewing machine that she is badgered about buying by her neighbor, the vacuum cleaner that Riichi buys for her, and the fridge that Riichi demands must be unplugged to save on electricity costs. There is even a Douglas Sirk or Rainer Werner Fassbinder–like moment when, following Hiraoka's return to Sadako's house and repeated attempt to inveigle himself into her affections, he responds to her refusals violently and, while she is lying on the floor, picks up her iron and threatens to attack her with it. As he attempts to burn Sadako, her face is reflected in the implement, a melodramatic moment that Imamura frames as central in a dramatic low-angle shot that emphasizes both the iron and the reflection pressing down on the protagonist. This reflection is repeated later in the narrative when Riichi forces himself on Sadako and she glances beside her at the iron and once again sees herself wrought in supplication and distress—a further connection between Riichi and Hiraoka and their relations with Sadako.

A stronger series of Ozu intertexts can also be felt here with regard to consumerism. In *Intentions of Murder* the family home is constantly subject to invasion, disruption, and surveillance. On two occasions either Sadako's neighbors burst into her home or Riichi bursts into his neighbors', and the physical proximity of these families forces Riichi to restate the spatial boundaries demarcating his land from theirs. These latter moments usually occur when Sadako is hanging out washing, and the fact that clothes drying outdoors is one of the (relatively few) recurrent pillow shots in Ozu's cinema helps place Imamura's film in a dialogic relationship to his work in general. Moreover, the aforementioned discourse on contemporary household and consumer goods suggests a mirror of *Good Morning* (*Ohayo*, 1959). Ozu's light and lively film revolves around conflict over television ownership—where ultimately the acquisition of said item both causes tension in and lubricates the wheels of intergenerational relations—as well as a new washing machine that facilitates rumors of misappropriation of group funds and the sad lot of a traveling salesman. *Good Morning* is also similarly set in and around a small community where everyone knows everyone else: where they all appear to live on top of one another and where small talk and gossip provide an almost metronomic rhythm to everyday relations and interactions. It also prefigures Imamura's film in being set just below an elevated bank along which people are perpetually passing back and forth: in Ozu's case this is a walking path, whereas in *Intentions of Murder* it is the aforementioned railway line.

Imamura's wintry black and white *mise-en-scène*, long takes, and handheld mobile camera offer a mirror of *Good Morning's* bright color scheme, typically dense editing, and rigidly immobile cinematography. Furthermore, *Intentions of Murder* extends the focus on the fractious yet ultimately receptive relationship to consumer goods—and by extension by Japan's very specific contemporary sociopolitical modernity—to make of them a constant burden to Sadako and a status symbol to Riichi (who is constantly concerned with a promotion at work). As such, this particular intertext is especially pertinent here as it becomes suggestive of the New Wave director's consideration of the repressed of both Ozu and of modern Japan, its messy underbelly, by foregrounding the fractious violence beneath an ostensibly placid, prosperous surface; and such a dialogic dichotomy with this particular forebear serves to animate the ambiguity over past and present as it informs the treatment of gender and sociopolitical selfhood. That is, between the ordered and becalmed face of Ozu and the oft-commented-upon messiness (formal and thematic) of Imamura lies the ambiguity that festers at the center of *Intentions of Murder*, and that points up both the opaque actions and intentions of Sadako in particular and the film's representation of time, space, and anxious modernity in general.

If *Intentions of Murder* exists at the dialectical intersection of numerous narrative and textual tensions and disturbances, then it is precisely these tensions—between realism and surrealism, memory and selfhood, oppression and liberation, action and intention, the modern and the antiquated—that both propel and focus Imamura's thematic. It is in fact the fissures or slippages between these poles that define in particular this film's engagement not only with gender relations but with the roles and implied narratives pertaining to how men and women in Japan are constructed as social subjects. Given that the very title implicitly alludes to a disparity between interior and exterior precepts, this is a film about the extent to which subjectivity is shaped both by interpersonal and wider sociopolitical circumstances. To this end it reframes several of Imamura's perceived perennial concerns; Sadako certainly has some traits of the typical Imamura heroine, but the fact that she remains problematically situated within a traditional, rural belief system undermines perceptions of her own status as a paradigm of earthy antiquation, while her investment in sex is at best ambiguous. In point of fact, an overt desire for sex better characterizes the men around Sadako; it is Riichi (in the library where he works) who is seen with a copy of Herbert Marcuse's 1955 book *Eros and Civilization*—a quasi-Marxist text that was formed in opposition to Freud and that argues that the release rather than the repression of libidinal drives and instincts is in the best interests of individuals within society—and his unbridled lust is repeatedly a problem for Sadako (something that, as often as not, is mirrored in Hiraoka's behavior as regards his sexual needs).

The relationships between Sadako and both Riichi and Hiraoka are delimited by the perennial subterfuge of transactions; that is, by viewing and interacting with each other in prescriptive ways based on their sociopolitical enculturation, they both reinforce traditional gender roles and power structures and help expose them as such. Ultimately, Sadako's impending status as an official member of her family at the film's end offers a means not to exacerbate her oppression as it seems on the surface but rather in a way to legitimize it—or at least those aspects of her marriage that might continue to be an affront (particularly to Riichi's mother). In other words, she wants to define herself conservatively as a wife and mother (and apparently renounce rather than release her sensuality and libidinous drives) in order to make herself visible, perhaps to embody the curse on her mother-in-law's home. And the fact that this is being seen as predicated on an invisibility (on Riichi being unaware that it is Sadako in Yoshiko's photographs) cements a reversal of the earlier liminal gap between seeing and being seen and stresses Sadako's change and development. David Desser has argued that on the one hand women are less free than men in Imamura's work, but on the other that they remain more "resilient" (1988: 127), and from this perspective Sadako in *Intentions of Murder* is most certainly a key figure in his cinema.

Notes

1. See, for instance, Yoshio Sugimoto's discussion of patriarchy, gender inequality, and family registration in *An Introduction to Japanese Society* (Cambridge: Cambridge University Press, 2003), 146–82.
2. In addition, Masaru is the product of a quasi-incestuous relationship (Riichi and Sadako are related, as she is the granddaughter of his grandfather's mistress) and is consequently frail.

Works Cited

Bock, Audie (1979). *Japanese Film Directors*. San Francisco: Kodansha International Ltd.
Desser, David (1988). *Eros plus Massacre: An Introduction to the Japanese New Wave Cinema*. Bloomington: Indiana University Press.
Kimura-Steven, Chigusa (2003). "The Otherness of Women in the Avant-Garde Film *Woman in the Dunes*." In *Gender and Power in the Japanese Visual Field*, ed. Joshua S. Mostow, Norman Bryson, and Maribeth Graybill. Honolulu: University of Hawai'i Press, 155–78.
Lim, Dennis (2009). "Learning to Crawl." *The Insect Woman* [DVD]. Criterion Collection, supplementary essay.
Mellen, Joan (1976). *The Waves at Genji's Door: Japan through Its Cinema*. New York: Pantheon Books.

Quandt, James (1997). "Pigs, Pimps and Pornographers: A Brief Introduction to the Films of Shohei Imamura." In *Shohei Imamura*, ed. James Quandt. Toronto: Toronto International Film Festival Group, 1–6.

Quandt, James (2009). "Eros and Civilization." *Intentions of Murder* [DVD]. Criterion Collection, supplementary essay.

Richie, Donald (1997). "Notes for a Study on Shohei Imamura." In *Shohei Imamura*, ed. James Quandt. Toronto: Toronto International Film Festival Group–, 7–44.

Sugimoto, Yoshio (2003). *An Introduction to Japanese Society*. Cambridge: Cambridge University Press.

Tansman, Alan (2001). "Where's Mama: The Sobbing Yakuza of Hasegawa Shin." In *Word and Image in Japanese Cinema*, ed. Dennis Washburn and Carole Cavanaugh. Cambridge: Cambridge University Press, 149–73.

Washburn, Dennis (2001). "The Arrest of Time: The Mythic Transgressions of *Vengeance Is Mine*." In *Word and Image in Japanese Cinema*, ed. Dennis Washburn and Carole Cavanaugh. Cambridge: Cambridge University Press, 318–41.

Chapter 5

Hidden in Plain Sight: The False Leads and True Mysteries of *Vengeance Is Mine*

John Berra

A strict adherence to the chronology of events is a hallmark of the majority of screen serial-killer narratives with a series of violent acts prompting a police investigation that eventually results in the arrest of the perpetrator. However, Shohei Imamura's true crime saga *Fukushû suru wa ware ni ari/Vengeance IIs Mine* (1979) immediately disregards this format by beginning with the epilogue to a nightmare. On the night of June 4, 1964, a police convoy crosses provincial countryside terrain in heavy snow to bring captured criminal Iwao Enokizu (Ken Ogata) to the nearest police station for interrogation, marking the culmination of a seventy-eight-day manhunt. This, however, is where the true mystery begins, for Imamura is fascinated less by the chase than its central enigma.

Enokizu is based on the real-life serial killer Akira Nishiguchi, referred to as "the Black Gold Medalist in killing" by the prosecutor assigned to his case. Born into a Catholic family, Nishiguchi committed a series of violent crimes throughout 1963 and early 1964, eluding the authorities for months despite his face being plastered around the country on more than half a million wanted posters. Although he was hanged in 1970, Nishiguchi's sustained rampage still cries out for explanation. If, as Donald Richie (1982: 188) observed, Imamura's films are rife with "a completely amoral, vital, and overflowing rejection of Japanese collective beliefs," then the protagonist in *Vengeance Is Mine* is arguably the director's most extreme subject in a fearlessly sordid canon of social miscreants.

The flashback structure adopted by Imamura initially appears to be a means of pinpointing relevant details of the killer's life to establish the motivating factors behind his monstrous behavior. Jean Murley has argued that "the serial killer has become the container and symbol for a contemporary understanding of evil in popular culture, one that posits evil as hidden, persistent, and spectacularly gruesome" (2008: 5). Imamura seems to be taking this holistic approach with episodes in his elliptical case study, considering such factors as familial dysfunction, social stratum, and the spiritual disillusionment brought about by an increasingly Westernized society. Elana Gomel considers the task of explaining a killer's actions to be the primary concern of the serial-killer narrative, an overriding concern that leads to an emphasis on details that will serve to isolate the root cause of such behavior. These narratives are all driven by the necessity to "explain" the serial killer in terms that assimilate the corporeal particularity of violence to some abstract modality of meaning. This explanation generally takes the form of some narrative of origin. Gomel (2013: 35) asserts that "such narratives, freely exchanged between literature and science, treat violence as a symptom or an outer manifestation of a hidden truth, an oblique symptom of an intelligible cause."

Given that the consumer of any true-crime narrative already knows the identity of the killer and the outcome of the events, it is understandable that the creative parties must forgo the mystery element of the procedural and focus instead on the reason why the murders are being committed. This emphasis on explaining evil gives their "ripped from the headlines" project a point of interest that has not been interrogated in the abundant media coverage. By the time Imamura embarked on *Vengeance Is Mine*, a cinematic template for the genre had been internationally established by such case histories of varying accuracy as *Psycho* (Alfred Hitchcock, 1960), *In Cold Blood* (Richard Brooks, 1967), *The Boston Strangler* (Richard Fleischer, 1968), *The Honeymoon Killers* (Leonard Kastle, 1969), *10 Rillington Place* (Richard Fleischer, 1971), and the television movie *Helter Skelter* (Tom Gries, 1976). *Vengeance Is Mine* follows suit in foregrounding the true-crime concern of motive, but only so that Imamura can cynically toy with it as a means of forcing the audience to question their assumptions about the reasons for human depravity, many of which have been formed through the consumption of narratives that contrive explanations for an internal psychological condition from external circumstances or key events. Imamura provides flashbacks to incidents in the life of his protagonist that may have planted the seeds of his uncontainable rage, but never fully commits to, or pulls together, a set of possibly related reasons that could also be interpreted as mere speculation or even red herrings. Rather, the director seeks to underscore the incomprehensible nature of evil through close observation of a social anomaly while demonstrating the inherently unreliable nature of media reconstruction in identifying the triggers for fiercely anti-social urges.

The Aesthetics of Absence

It has been widely argued that *Vengeance Is Mine* is documentary-like in its presentation (Balmain 2010: 244; Cardullo 2015: 147; Dillard 2014; Sharp and Mes 2005: 31), and it is tempting to subscribe to this argument based on its position in Imamura's filmography. The film marked a return to narrative following an artistically fruitful but financially debilitating detour into documentary that had lasted much of the 1970s. Following the box office disappointment of his 1968 anthropological epic *Kamigami no Fukaki Yokubō/The Profound Desires of the Gods*, Imamura preferred to operate more nimbly by shooting real-life subjects for Japanese television. This way, he was able to continue his examination of Japanese postwar society from the perspective of those on the lower rung of the ladder, providing alternative takes on a resurgent nation with a propensity for oppression. Yet he had begun to question whether documentary was the best mode of expression given the medium's invasive nature. As Imamura recalled in an interview with Toichi Nakata,

> I came to realize the presence of the camera could materially change people's lives. Did I have the right to effect such changes? Was I playing God in trying to control the lives of others? I'm no sentimental humanist, but thoughts like these scared me and made me acutely aware of the limitations of documentary filmmaking. (Nakata 1997: 120)

The source material for *Vengeance Is Mine* was a best-selling account of the Nishiguchi case by Ryûzô Saki. Imamura collaborated with screenwriter Masuru Baba for several years, even undertaking additional research into the Nishiguchi case, which resulted in the discovery of information that had been overlooked by Saki and the police (Cardullo 2015: 145). This approach suggested that he was aiming for a documentary-like reconstruction, but the resulting film instead takes copious liberties with the facts and calls attention to the limits of documentary in ascertaining knowledge about human beings.[1] Imamura certainly utilizes a range of nonfiction practices—most notable are the hand-held camerawork that keeps the actors at a distance, natural lighting, and the frequent use of onscreen text. The crime scene in Chikuhashi City is shown in the style of a television news report and the depictions of the murders in the ensuing flashback are dramatized through extended takes that are all the more shocking for the observational framing that emphasizes the stomach churning messiness of taking human life, suggesting that the camera will serve as a detached observer of events. Previous documentary projects such as the two-part *Mikikanhei o Otte/In Search of Unreturned Soldiers* (1970/1971) had found Imamura looking for people who had gone missing under specific political circumstances, thereby creating troubling absences in Japan's social fabric, but in *Vengeance Is Mine* he would focus on a subject who physically is very much present yet has an inner absence that is better illustrated through dramatization than a straight-forward chronicle of the facts.

Imamura's refusal to facilitate a direct line of psychological access to his subject is evident from the opening frames. Alastair Phillips (2007: 232) notes how our initial, blurred introduction to Enokizu through the window of a vehicle traveling in poor weather conditions "heightens the sense of the scrutiny of a secondary visual surface within the texture of the film that is demonstrably resistant to clear explanation." This resistance to a steady focus is also established by the manner in which the police car carrying Enokizu darts around the screen during the opening credits sequence, with Tamás Pólya (2007: 257) observing that "its lights resemble erratic red brush marks left on the pitch-black canvas of the night." It's an expressionistic credits sequence that, with the car barely visible in a tunnel of darkness, can be read as a signal that Imamura is taking us into the psyche of his subject, but also as a warning that its subject will refuse to be contained and resist a fixed way of looking. The crowd of enraged citizens who greet the police vehicle on its arrival at the station are cast as audience surrogates—they try to get close to the car to get a look at the monster, loudly demanding an explanation, but their chance of catching a glimpse of Enokizu is limited by the adverse weather conditions.

In his DVD commentary, Tony Rayns (2005) describes the film's disjointed narrative approach as a way of replicating "the way that our minds flit from one topic to another, or here one incident or one event triggers a memory or association with another event." This is the process of reintegration whereby the free association of related memories facilitates a reconstruction of past experience (Coon and Mitterer 2008: 239). Rayns goes on to assert that the flashbacks provide information on a "need to know" basis, supporting this assertion with the examples of how police interrogation scenes cut back to the discovery of the corpses of Enokizu's initial victims and to an argument between Enokizu and his mistress, Chiyoko Hata (Moeko Ezawa), to explain how he acquired the stiletto knife that was used for his first murder. While answering certain questions, this method of reconstruction also raises the issue of reliability as these accounts of Enokizu's troubled history come from various perspectives in order to demonstrate the inherently unreliable nature of constructing a definitive narrative from a multiple sources: sometimes we are seeing Enokizu as he sees himself, and sometimes we are seeing him as he is recalled by others, with memories and impressions further muddied by individual anxieties, experiences, and belief systems.

This is the case in what is set up as the film's most important flashback, with his father, Shizuo Enokizu (Rentaro Mikuni), recalling his humiliation at the hands of a Japanese naval officer in the summer of 1938 while living in Gotō in Nagasaki Prefecture. It's a conventionally structured scene, almost self-consciously clichéd in its coverage of events. It starts with a wide shot of Gotō that establishes the island environment but also prominently frames the Christian church that represents the faith worshipped by Enokizu's family, along with rest of the community. An indignant Enokizu (played at a young age by Daisuke Sano) attacks the officer and is then restrained by his Shizuo, who now has no choice but to agree to the official request for his boats; a disgusted Enokizu pulls away from his father's protective embrace, turning his back on the family's faith as he walks toward a nearby cliff where he will stubbornly sit until after nightfall. As we see the family relocate to Beppu, we learn that Enokizu was never able to reconcile with his father.[2] The melodramatic simplicity of this flashback reveals less about Enokizu than it does about his father, who, in accordance with his faith, sees the world in the clearly defined terms of devout righteousness and sinful disobedience.

Documentary-style camerawork is often used to create a sense of intimacy but is really just one component of a complex visual design. Imamura's frequent cinematographer Shinsaku Himeda often reprises the voyeuristic style of *Erogotoshi-tachi yori: Jinruigaku nyûmon/The Pornographers* (1966), with many scenes being shot through windows or doors. After being released on parole in 1960, Enokizu returns to the family home and there is a tense scene in which he taunts his estranged wife, Kazuko (Mitsuko Baishô), with his suspicion that she has slept with another man while he has been behind bars. At first, the scene is shot with a handheld camera witnessing the conversation through the doorway, but as the drama escalates, the camera moves inside the room with compositions becoming more formalized. Later, when Enokizu confronts both his father and wife, the scene begins with the camera looking in at a low angle to capture the expressions of Shizuo and Kazuko, who are sitting on the floor as Enokizu paces around the room, assuming what he sees as his rightful roles as judge, jury and, potentially, executioner. As the argument plays out, though, the participants go outside and the coverage becomes more conventional, although a voyeuristic perspective is maintained by having Enokizu's mother, Kayo (Miyako Chocho), witness her son's vindictive display from inside the house. In confrontations such as these, Imamura seems to be calling attention to the power of reconstruction, specifically how embellishment can give rise to interpretations of events that may be correct but could also be overly convenient and simplistic in their assumptions, such as Enokizu's crime spree being in part motivated by his hatred of his father.

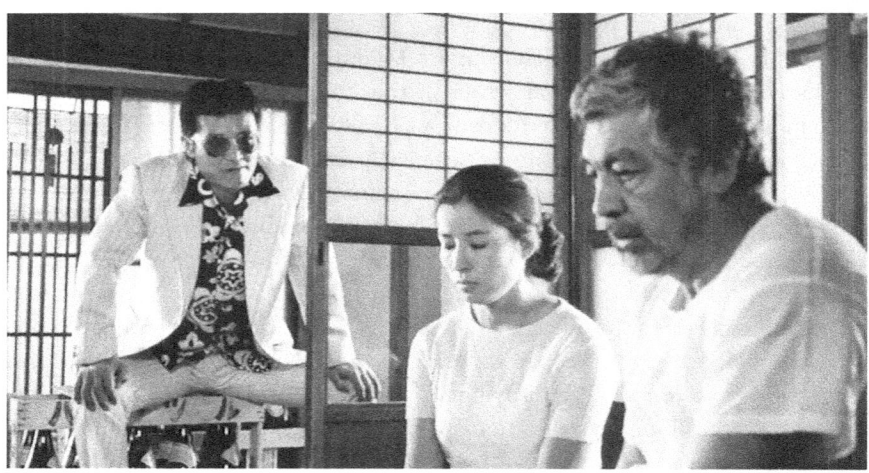

Figure 5.1 The power of reconstruction and the potential for interpretation.

Imamura also blends documentary practices with genre tropes. When Enokizu arrives in Hamamatsu, Imamura uses an extended hand-held tracking shot to follow him out of the train station and into a taxi, and then pans around to show the everyday activity around the station after the vehicle has driven away. Yet the propulsive score by Shinichirô Ikebe is more influenced by Western crime cinema or 1970s US television police drama, with its mounting rhythm adding a palpable sense of desperation and urgency. Imamura then cuts to Enokizu being dropped off near the Asano Inn. It's a matter-of-fact sequence with Enokizu receiving directions from the taxi driver before walking up the alley, but the tight camerawork here accentuates the narrowness of the alley to suggest his options are increasingly limited. Such hybridity is occasionally used for sly misdirection. When a subtitle announces "December 12 Chiba District Court" over a medium close-up of Enokizu sitting in the courtroom, the viewer may assume that he has been apprehended based on this framing. But as the judge asks the accused to stand up, Imamura cuts to a wide shot of the courtroom and a young man rises to his feet, thereby confounding expectations based on the initial composition. Enokizu is actually still at large and about to impersonate an attorney on order to swindle an elderly woman out of the 100,000 yen intended for her grandson's bail.

The Limits of Social Control and the Side Effects of Modernization

Dennis Washburn (2001: 331) insists that the protagonist of *Vengeance Is Mine* has clear antecedents in Imamura's earlier works, such as the prostitute in

Nippon konchūki/The Insect Woman (1963), the oppressed housewife in *Akai Satsui/Intentions of Murder* (1964), and the Adult filmmaker in *The Pornographers*. However, while these characters in Imamura's previous films certainly exist on the periphery of society, they still maintain tenuous relationships with the everyday order via membership in their respective marginal groups and therefore constitute a section of Japan's social fabric. In contrast, Enokizu is actually the architect of his situation, having nihilistically thrown away a number of chances to lead a life of moderate comfort and stability, whether ruining his military career by stealing a jeep, refusing to fully commit to his marriage, or not applying his intelligence to a legal enterprise. Such circumstances would be envied by Imamura's usual protagonists, who represent the truly downtrodden members of Japan's sub-proletariat, but Enokizu nonetheless loathes the hand that he has been dealt. Despite the vindictive bravado of the film's title, which is taken from Romans 12:19 in the New Testament, who or what exactly Enokizu is taking revenge against is never specified.[3] If the explanation that Enokizu is rebelling against his Catholic father is sidelined as a red herring, then one could consider Michael Atkinson's (2014) argument that revenge is being taken at national level "for the very indignity of being born and confronted with life in Japan" or Colette Balmain's (2008: 158) interpretation of Enokizu as a pathological symptom of Japanese modernity. The fact that the amounts of money he gains from his crimes are relatively paltry in relation to the risks he is taking could be read as Imamura's wider indictment of the economic falsehood of Japan's modernization, with two of his victims being employees of a large corporation and another a lawyer specializing in real estate.

The events of *Vengeance Is Mine* take place against the backdrop of the build-up to the 1964 Tokyo Olympics, an international event now synonymous with the widespread modernization of Japan. It becomes clear that Westernization has not only given rise to Enokizu's violence but further enabled it. For instance, Japan's extensive railway system affords Enokizu considerable mobility despite his fugitive status, and Rayns (2005) remarks on the varied topography of *Vengeance Is Mine* as Ezoku travels the length and breadth of the country with relative ease. Enokizu's shakedown of Yasuda (Kikuoto Kanauchi), who has slept with Kazuko during his prison stretch, takes place at the Beppu train station where the latter is employed. A train arrives at and departs from the platform during a heated exchange, which culminates in Enokizu almost strangling Yasuda. With the sound of the departing train, Imamura makes a direct link between modernization and Enokizu's grievances. His crimes and cover-ups are facilitated in part by the increased convenience of obtaining the necessary tools from shops in a society that is steadily developing its own version of consumerism. Clayton Dillard (2014) observes that Enokizu's "undiscerning spaces of commerce," such as the shop where he buys a knife to kill the second driver, adheres to the core national value of frugality by his asking for the cheapest option. Utilizing the strategies and actions of Nishiguchi for social commentary, Imamura later shows Enokizu purchasing a radio to monitor media reports of his case and, when in Tokyo, picking up a hammer and thirty short nails in order to conceal the body of Kyohei Kawashima (Yoshi Katô) in a cabinet so he can temporarily reside in the attorney's apartment.

If Enokizu's crimes are taken as reactions against recent social developments, then mention must be made of how Japan's low crime rate since World War II is often attributed to informal social control mechanisms whereby potential offenders are deterred from committing deviant acts because they are wary of being shunned by family, friends, and colleagues if accused of breaking the law (Smith 1983: 127–28; Hughes 1998: 145). From a sociological perspective, any desire for individuality borne out of a resistance to this group structure is considered as a potential cause of aggression, while homogeneity is tacitly encouraged in order to promote and preserve a sense of honor, thereby curtailing a range of issues from litigious disputes to physical altercations (Roberts and LaFree 2004: 179–80). This promotion of a "meritocracy" leads to a strong sense of familial responsibility and loyalty to social groups, with membership of such institutions being seen as an essential part of postwar life, thereby limiting crime through fear of ostracization from the group. Gordon Hughes (1998: 145) points out that this "high-trust" social model utilizes *haji no bunka* (shame culture) rather than guilt as a prevention method in that the possibility of bringing shame to their family is of greater concern to the individual than any sense of guilt that they may anticipate feeling regarding criminal action. Still, Eric W. Hickey (2015: 398) asserts that even such a restrictive climate "cannot preclude the emergence of societal anomalies that can take root and defy community solidarity." In this respect, Enokizu is defying the structures of a group-oriented society that Harumi Befu (1980: 170–171) sees as comprising members who are focused on working toward the collective goal and remain firmly loyal to its cause.[4]

Playing Society against Itself

Using his flair for role playing, Enokizu is able to exploit the sense of comfort that Japanese citizens have come to feel when in the company of someone who can be readily identified as a member of their group. After cadging a lift from two employees of the Government Tobacco Monopoly Corporation, Tanejirô Shibata (Taiji Tonoyama) and Daihachi Baba (Gorô Tarumi), Enokizu uses light banter to learn that they have only three collections left to make from retailers, ascertaining that they must be carrying a substantial amount of money. The employees are unguarded in his presence because they take him to be a member of their group based on his job, uniform, and working-class demeanor. Leo Goldsmith (2006) notes that it is Enokizu's refusal to be contained in a specific tier of Japan's class system that "allows him to meditate between different levels of society at will." Throughout the course of his crime spree, Enokizu takes on the roles of laborer, university professor, and lawyer, proving at ease in the company of the working class as he is within the formal environment of Japan's court system. While impersonating a lawyer, he even dares to wave at a real attorney to suggest that he knows the man and further the impression that he belongs there, demonstrating the audacity of a natural performer as well as the shrewdness of an actor who understands the importance of casual details in creating a credible portrayal.

This series of identities constitutes what Rayns (2005) terms "a dance of upward mobility," as each killing represents a fabricated advance in social status and income level. These personas can also be seen as Imamura's commentary on the well-intentioned but fundamentally dysfunctional nature of Japan's social fabric in the 1960s as citizens attempt to negotiate group roles that are rooted in tradition but must now strive for new economic standards that are befitting of a resurgent nation. Conveying these personas through Keiichi Uraoka's jagged editing, with new identities appearing without any sense of transition, furthers the impression that Imamura sees Enokizu as being emblematic of growing ideological tensions.

When we first see Ogata in the role, Enokizu is working as a translator for the American military, exuding a burly authority in his smart uniform. On release from prison in 1960, he adopts the appearance of a low-level yakuza, complete with dark Hawaiian-style shirt, striped white suit, and New York Yankees cap, and then proceeds to behave in a particularly boorish manner throughout this

Figure 5.2 Achieving upward mobility by adopting an academic persona.

flashback. He then becomes a working-class truck driver, but it is the roles of a professor of microanalysis at Kyoto University and a criminal lawyer that prove a natural fit; although he lacks a proper education, his detached perspective on the world lends him an air of intelligence.[5]

As Washburn (2001: 335) notes, it is by assuming the identity of a college professor that Enokizu makes himself so desirable to Haru (Mayumi Ogawa), the proprietress of the seedy Asano Inn where the criminal resides while hiding out in Hamamatsu. As part of the film's social satire, Haru sees in Enokizu a way of advancing her standing by achieving domestic respectability. A victim of "shame culture" since her eccentric mother Hisano (Nijiko Kiyokawa) was jailed for fifteen years for the crime of murdering her employer following a period of mistreatment, Haru lacks financial independence as the inn she runs is actually owned by Mr. Ideiki (Kazuo Kitamura), a textile merchant who keeps Haru as his mistress, making her susceptible to Enokizu's cultivated façade.

An Honest Fraud in a Hypocritical World

Bert Cardullo (2015: 147) insists that Enokizu is "a man without a visible shred of humanity," yet Imamura perversely casts his protagonist as a hero or sorts, a rare member of society who is honest in flaunting his transgressive nature and is capable of virtuous behavior when he encounters someone who may be a kindred spirit, qualities that he quickly recognizes in Haru and her mother. He has a capacity for generosity, for instance, sending money to Haru, although this may be a further manipulation and a means of solidifying his assumed identity as, in the note that accompanies the money, he bemoans the lowly salaries afforded to scholars. Still, he seems genuinely at ease in Haru's company and the environs of the Asano Inn where he indulges his sexual appetite with an unreserved abandon that seems atypical of the kind of supposedly buttoned-down professor of microanalysis he is impersonating, at least in part revealing his true nature at the possible expense of his false identity. With its uninhibited sexual atmosphere, Haru's establishment offers an alternative to the Gotō Inn, his father's traditional guesthouse where he spent much of his youth. Haru learns of Enokizu's true identity when visiting her lover in Tokyo: the lovers go to the cinema and Enokizu's case is prominently featured in a cinema newsreel. However, she decides to continue her relationship with him, perhaps because she is further aroused by his rebellious stance toward a society that has seen fit to oppress her or, as Washburn (2001: 335) suggests, she finally accepts that a woman of her standing can only attract a partner who is also an outcast.

Imamura extolls Enokizu's virtues through his passionate relationship with the promiscuous Haru, who has three partners during the film—Enokizu,

Ideiki, and Jun, a regular at her mahjong games. However, Enokizu is the only one who shows her respect and satisfies her sexually with his insatiable appetite for lovemaking that stems as much from a desire to satisfy her as it does from his own need for sexual gratification. Jun asks Haru for money but later marries a woman from a "good family," while a bedroom scene between Haru and Ideiki is all about the adulterer's requirements and concerns. Ideiki desires sex but gets a cramp in his foot, so also asks for a massage; Haru asks when he will transfer ownership of the inn to her, only for Ideiki to respond that he would prefer to hold on to it because he expects the upcoming Olympic Games to bring more business. Later, he will callously break the news of Jun's impending marriage to her, revealing in her dependency on him. Although he has no intention of marrying Haru, the possessive Ideiki pays Hisano to spy on her daughter to make sure that she is not cheating on him. Toward the end of the film, Ideiki forces himself on Haru and Enokizu almost takes action: Imamura frames him tightly next to a rack of knives when, just as Enokizu goes to grab the handle of one of the blades and leap to her defense in what would be his only crime of chivalry, he is stopped by Hisano, who by this point knows what their guest is capable of.

Enokizu will eventually murder both mother and daughter. In the case of Haru, the act is a way for Enokizu to partially fulfill a wish that she had expressed earlier to die together. He is aware from the news reports that the manhunt is closing in and that they will be unable to enter the traditional union that she yearns for. Even taking Haru on the run with him would only postpone his inevitable capture and execution as the mobility that he enjoyed earlier in his crime spree is now restricted. Although her rural background and profession have much in common with Tome (Sachiko Hidari), the determined heroine of *The Insect Woman*, Haru is more of a fantasist than her antecedent and settles into a domestic arrangement with this fugitive out of a yearning for a semblance of normalcy that she has otherwise been denied. As such, his killing of Haru is a crime committed out of an acknowledgment of it, rather than rage or financial necessity. The act occurs while she is making pickles in a homely fashion, with Enokizu beginning to strangle his lover, then lessening his grip as if to give her a choice about her fate, only for Haru to ask him to go all the way. He even utters "thank you" to Haru after she has died, an acknowledgment that she has shared his frustration with an oppressive culture and provided an unconditional respite. Crucially, the only murders that occur onscreen are the killings of the members of the Government Tobacco Monopoly Corporation and Haru, with Imamura providing roughly equal balance in his depictions of Enokizu's extreme expression of hate and love, even if the latter is fulfilled in the most perverse way possible. The men killed in Chikuhashi City represent the capitalist society that he so despises, whereas Haru, despite her lower-level standing on the economic ladder and her attempts at betterment, embodies a traditional, earthy spirit that he wants Japan to return to, hence his propensity for violence being triggered by the sight of her smearing pepper paste on vegetables.

The amount of time that Enokizu spends on the run before effectively being trapped in the Asano Inn could certainly be curtailed if not for a climate of self-interest. As the train hurtles toward Hamamatsu, Enokizu leans toward the newspaper that the passenger sitting opposite him is reading, presumably having spotted an article related to his case, or even a photograph of himself. In a satirical swipe at social norms, the other passenger, who is dressed like Enokizu in a business suit, reacts in a slight yet notable way that implies he feels his personal space is being invaded, and Enokizu instead looks out the window. Although Enokizu is risking being identified, the other passenger is too concerned with Enokizu's inappropriate etiquette to notice that he is sitting in close proximity to a murderer.

In Hamamatsu, Enokizu passes the day at a pachinko parlor where his wanted poster in on display, but the other players are fixated on winning prizes so do not recognize him. Even when Imamura implies national panic with a montage of wanted posters, newspapers, and television news, he shows relatively few people actually looking at these materials, as if everyone is too immersed in the goals of their groups to pay attention to a wider problem. When a prostitute from Club Shiragiku, the business that provides prostitutes to the guests at the Asano Inn, actually recognizes Enokizu as "the professor" who had procured her services, another prostitute opportunistically suggests that they could receive a reward for turning him in, only for the madam to insist that it would not be worth the trouble since they are operating in an illegal industry and therefore need to maintain a low profile.[6] Imamura ultimately has Enokizu being apprehended because the prostitute risks drawing attention to her illegal professional activities by reporting his whereabouts to the police after seeing him get into the pawnshop van, but the filmmaker generally finds moral fiber to be in perilously short supply in the Japan of 1963–1964, a stance indicated by his choice of a serial killer to navigate the self-interested socioeconomic landscape of the period.

A Final Statement from Beyond the Diegesis

Vengeance Is Mine is drenched in a sense of the inevitable. Not only does Imamura begin the film with the epilogue, but he constantly foreshadows Enokizu's eventual hanging (which occurs offscreen) through visual symbolism, alluding to a sense of fatalistic destiny on the part of his protagonist. After committing his initial murders, Enokizu returns to a room that he has rented and turns on the light by pulling a chord. As he sits down to count the money, the camera tilts down and the chord for the light sways back and forth in front of Enokizu's face, suggesting a noose. Later, while squatting at the attorney's apartment, he goes into an inebriated rage when he cannot find a can opener and theatrically mimes hanging himself with the dead man's scarf out of frustration. At the eel farm, an expressionistic image of a noose and pair of hanging boots appears suddenly, bathed in garish yellow lighting that is at odds with the naturalistic lighting scheme of most of the film. Punishment and retribution are twofold with Enokizu lashing out at society, only for its accepted order to strike back in the judgment of his actions by the legal system. Locating the Asano Inn near a cemetery further positions Enokizu not only as a harbinger of death, but as one whose transgressions will cause his own demise.

Murley (2008: 3) observes that the end of most true crime stories finds the guilty party being incarcerated or executed, thereby providing a "good old-fashioned reordering of the chaos wrought by crime." Imamura's foreshadowing of Enokizu's hanging seems to be building toward such a reordering, but in the film's final and most audacious act of misdirection—one that merges naturalism, surrealism, and the breaking of the fourth wall—the director shows that he believes nothing of the sort by focusing on two lesser characters who are still trying to come to terms with their relationship to the killer. After the execution of Enokizu, his father and wife take a cable car to the top of a mountain in order to scatter his remains. It is a compromise of sorts for Shizuo, who is unable to bury Enokizu in the family plot following his excommunication, but he still wants to give his son a spiritual send-off. Washburn (2001: 338) notes that this must be a sacred place as we see a cable car full of religious pilgrims descending in the background as Shizuo and Kazuko ascend to the peak, while Rayns (2005) takes it as a surreal touch since there are so many pilgrims in the descending cable car that this background detail must have been designed to draw attention to itself. The location of this climactic scene has been identified as Mount Tsurumi, which has a view of Beppu and the sea (Muzuhashi 2015). However, this is one of the few places in the film that is not identified by a subtitle so, although the conversation between Shizuo and Kazuko is played naturalistically, Imamura is now surrendering any pretense of documentary objectivity. During the ride, Shizuo and Kazuko talk about Enokizu and their respective futures: Kazuko tells Shizuo that she received a final letter from Enokizu instructing her not to have another man, which causes them to laugh about Enokizu's controlling nature. But what occurs at the top of the mountain will make them realize Enokizu's legacy is no laughing matter.

Figure 5.3 Breaking the rules to visualize the presence of the restless spirit.

At the observation platform, their attempt to return Enokizu's bones to the earth is thwarted as Imamura uses a freeze-frame technique—executed in an archaic manner that draws attention to itself as a basic special effect—to leave the remains suspended in mid-air, stubbornly refusing to fall. To return briefly to "shame culture," Enokizu's vile legacy will forever hang over the family, who will possibly be subjected to social rejection or verbal abuse regardless of whatever rituals they perform to excommunicate or expunge his spirit. At the eel farm, Hisano remarks to Enokizu, "You haven't killed the ones you really want to." "Maybe not," he replies. Enokizu's hatred for his father is articulated in its penultimate scene that Washburn (2001: 321) considers to constitute an "emotional and intellectual climax," as it finds Shizuo visiting his son in prison while he awaits execution. When pressed by his father as to his criminal motives, Enokizu explains that he wanted to be "free" but eventually snaps and states, "I want to kill you." His lingering presence through notoriety, though, can be seen as his vengeance on his devout father, whom he regards as a hypocrite for harboring desires for Kazuko but not acting on them. However, making this point through the blatant use of a special effect, which makes a sudden and potentially disruptive late break from film's otherwise largely orthodox recreation of events, is surely intended to do more than restate the Oedipal tension that Immaura's use of more conventional film language has marked out as the most convenient explanation for Enokizu's crimes.

The final frames of *Vengeance Is Mine* violate a supposed rule of narrative cinema—just as the viewer is not usually looked at, fictionalized characters are not usually privy to the techniques that are used to tell their stories, at least not in films that do not announce their postmodern sensibilities at the outset. The shot in which Shizuo and Kazuko look directly at the camera in a state of shock could be interpreted as Enokizu looking back at them in defiance. Washburn (2001: 337) considers it to constitute an "arrest of time" as Enokizu refuses to allow the world to further progress now that he is no longer in it, echoing his complaints to the police detectives in the opening scene that they will outlive him. There are a number of moments in the film when Enokizu comes close to making eye contact with the audience—looking out of the window during his police interrogation and glancing over his shoulder when approaching the Asano Inn—thereby making the spectator complicit in his actions. In this final scene, however, his restless spirit transcends not only the limits of society and Japan's justice system, but also all the cinematic methods that Imamura has employed to box him in. After spending over two hours trying to achieve understanding of this aberration, the audience has been unwittingly lured into Enokizu's perspective on a hypocritical society, as represented by the unconsummated desire between Shizuo and Kazuko, leaving the viewer still uncertain about the exact reason for his transgressions, but in no doubt that his rage will reverberate for all eternity.

Notes

1. Imamura reorganizes the chronology on the real case as Enokizu murdered the women at the inn in Hamamatsu before the lawyer in Tokyo. Also, the apprehension of Akira Nishiguchi actually came about after he was spotted by an eleven-year-old girl, not a prostitute whose services he had procured.
2. The city of Beppu lies at the base of a slope of volcanic debris, making it an all-too-appropriate childhood home of a man who will erupt with devastating rage.
3. The Japanese title of the film, *Fukushû suru wa ware ni ari*, translates literally as "I Shall Have Vengeance." However, both the Japanese and international titles correspond to common translations of the same biblical verse, Romans 12:19.
4. *Vengeance Is Mine* highlights unpleasant hierarchies within this collectivism that should be noted. For instance, those who have turned to the Catholic faith are victimized, while the reaction of the two women who discover the corpse of Enokizu's first victim while tending to an allotment garden is casually racist as they almost overlook the crime because they assume the body to be a drunken Korean.
5. The casting of Ken Ogata in what would be his star-making role exemplifies the license that Imamura took with the Nishiguchi case, as he has a more ruggedly imposing presence than his real-life counterpart, at least based on the unassum-

ing look of Nishiguchi in a photograph that is available online (Headsman 2011). Many other cast members are theater actors who were unfamiliar to mainstream cinema audiences so as not to prove fleetingly distracting. However, they are experienced performers and not the nonprofessionals that are cast by directors aiming for a "documentary-like" quality.
6. Prostitution was outlawed in Japan by the Anti-Prostitution Law of 1956, which calls for the punishment of the prostitutes rather than the clients. *Vengeance Is Mine* illustrates how prostitution continued to remain a thriving industry after the closure of its brothels through the opportunism of other enterprises. The Asano Inn provides a space for the prostitutes of Club Shiragiku to entertain their clients, while the taxi driver who takes Enokizu from the Hamamatsu train station to the inn serves as a go-between for the two businesses.

Works Cited

Atkinson, Michael (2014). "Vengeance Is Mine: Civilization and Its Discontents." Criterion Collection. August 26. https://www.criterion.com/current/posts/479-vengeance-is-mine-civilization-and-its-discontents. Accessed January 18, 2016.
Balmain, Colette (2008). *Introduction to Japanese Horror Film*. Edinburgh: Edinburgh University Press.
Balmain, Colette (2010). "Vengeance Is Mine." In *Directory of World Cinema: Japan*, ed. John Berra, 244–55. Bristol: Intellect.
Befu, Harumi (1980). "The Group Model of Japanese Society and an Alternative." *Rice Institute Pamphlet - Rice University Studies* 66, no. 1: 169–87.
Cardullo, Bert (2015). *Film Analysis: A Casebook*. New York: Wiley-Blackwell.
Coon, Dennis, and Mitterer, John O. (2008). *Introduction to Psychology: Gateways to Mind and Behavior*. Belmont CA: Cengage Learning/Wadsworth.
Dillard, Clayton (2014). "Vengeance Is Mine." *Slant Magazine*, August 24. http://www.slantmagazine.com/dvd/review/vengeance-is-mine. Accessed January 16, 2016).
Goldsmith, Leo (2005). "Vengeance Is Mine." Notcoming. November 18. http://www.notcoming.com/reviews/vengeanceismine/. Accessed January 20, 2016.
Gomel, Elena (2013). *Bloodscripts: Writing the Violent Subject*. Columbus: Ohio State University Press.
Headsman (2011). "1970: Akira Nishiguchi, 'Vengeance Is Mine' inspiration." Executed Today. December 11, http://www.executedtoday.com/2011/12/11/1970-akira-nishiguchi-vengeance-is-mine. Accessed March 1, 2016.
Hickey, Eric W. (2015). *Serial Murderers and Their Victims*. Boston: Cengage Learning.
Hughes, Gordon (1998). *Understanding Crime Prevention: Social Control, Risk and Late Modernity*. Buckingham: Open University Press.
Mes, Tom, and Jasper Sharp (2005). *The Midnight Eye Guide to New Japanese Film*. Berkeley: Stone Bridge.
Murley, Jean (2008). *The Rise of True Crime: 20th-Century Murder and American Popular Culture*. Westport, CT: Praeger.

Muzuhashi (2015). "Gaijin on a Push Bike - Day 5." Muzuhashi, May 14. http://www.muzuhashi.com/blog-125021252512464/gaijin-on-a-push-bike-day-5. Accessed March 11, 2016.
Nakata, Toichi (1997). "Shohei Imamura Interview." In *Shohei Imamura*, ed. James Quandt. 107–24. Toronto: Toronto International Film Festival Group.
Phillips, Alastair (2007). "Unsettled Visions: Imamura Shôhei's Vengeance Is Mine" (1979). In *Japanese Cinema: Texts and Contexts*, ed. Alastair Phillips and Julian Stringer, 229–39. London: Routledge.
Tamás, Pólya (2007). "Omitting Depth Cues: The Aesthetics of Perceptual Reflexivity." In *Narration and Spectatorship in Moving Images*, ed. Joseph D. Anderson and Barbara Fisher Anderson, 246–59. Cambridge: Cambridge Scholars Publishing.
Rayns, Tony (2005). Commentary track. *Vengeance Is Mine* (DVD). United Kingdom: Masters of Cinema.
Richie, Donald (1982). *The Japanese Movie*. Tokyo: Kodansha International.
Smith, Robert J. (1983). *Japanese Society: Tradition, Self, and the Social Order*. New York: Cambridge University Press.
Washburn, Dennis (2001). "The Arrest of Time: The Mythic Transgressions of *Vengeance Is Mine*." In *Word and Image in Japanese Cinema*, ed. Dennis Washburn and Carole Cavanaugh, 318–41. New York: Cambridge University Press.

Chapter 6
The Eel: Trauma Cinema

David Desser

By the time 1997 rolled around, Shohei Imamura had not made a film since *Black Rain* (1989), an extraordinary achievement, perhaps underrated for its stylistic beauty that contrasts with its appalling theme. Although only sixty-three at the time it was made, his health was poor and his energies were dispersed. As the years passed it is likely that many thought *Black Rain* was to be his final film, a fitting elegy to a splendid career. But the seventy-one-year old director surprised everyone with *Unagi/The Eel* (1997), not only that it was made at all, but that it was both critically and commercially so well received.

Despite its receipt of the Palme d'Or at the Cannes Film Festival and its *Kinema Jumpo* Best One award, very little has been written about *The Eel*, perhaps surprisingly, given its success and accessibility. To take the film seriously beyond its numerous prizes in Japan and the West is to recognize the way the film responds to the near-collapse of the Japanese economy in the 1990s when the country suffered a prolonged recession that followed the bursting of the fabled economic bubble of the 1980s. This stretch of economic stagnation has been called the "lost decade" (*ushinawareta jūnen*). This disastrous situation led to the production of what I call "trauma cinema," a cycle consisting of films that reflect the degree to which Japanese verities had been dismantled. My understanding of this cycle of the 1990s is a *symptomatic* one. I read the films as a response to the trauma of the lost decade. While there are very few films that deal directly with the lost decade as it was happening, there are films that take into account the numerous economic and social changes as they occurred.[1]

I propose that the overwhelming positive reception of *The Eel* is owed to its intense examination of trauma that leads to a (perhaps surprising) happy end—the overcoming of trauma through a budding romance and the formation of community, combined with many moments of overt comedy. This is blended with a film style utilizing the prevailing conventions of the art cinema of the period, such as the use of long takes and a sometimes static or only slightly moving camera that had become the dominant mode of the art cinema under the influence of Taiwan's Hou Hsiao-hsien starting in the late 1980s. Certainly, the art cinema of earlier eras had manifested long takes—Bergman, Fellini, and especially Antonioni favored takes longer than the Hollywood cinema to which they were reacting against. The French New Wave, recalling the films of Jean Renoir and Andre Bazin's influential writings in favor of the long take/deep focus style, often made use of takes of Wellesian proportion. Japanese directors need not have looked too far afield to find long-take virtuosos in their own history, as, for instance, the works of the graceful master of the mode, Kenji Mizoguchi. But under the sway of Hou, the takes become more insistently and consistently longer and, rather than the fluid movements of Renoir and Mizoguchi, the camera is virtually on lockdown. In *The Eel*, takes that range in length from forty to fifty seconds are common—the longest take being three minutes in length. The camera is usually static for all or most of the shot; when it moves, it does so with very subtle pans or tracks. A couple of the most important moments of the film occur within these long takes, but one or two of them are not particularly put to such a use. Rather, the long takes, in their consistency of length and the small camera movements, create a flowing rhythm at odds with the dramatic content of a murder and its aftermath, thus providing both a vision of trauma and the means to its overcoming in the aesthetic material of the film itself.

Trauma and the Lost Decade

In the 1980s Japan was perceived as on its way to world economic domination due to rapid economic growth; growing wealth; large and growing trade surpluses; rapid-asset price appreciation (land and share prices); and rapidly rising stock of Japanese-owned foreign assets. The expansion of the 1980s was fed by low interest rates and government guidance to financial institutions to continue to lend for investment. Optimism and growth were fed by the asset price bubble, which had no technological or economic basis: that is, there was no substantive reason for the bubble (Mendelowitz 2003). These record low interest rates fueled stock market and real estate speculation that sent valuations soaring throughout the 1980s. In fact, property and public company valuations more than tripled to the point where a small area in Tokyo was worth more than the entire state of California. When the Finance Ministry realized that the bubble was unsustainable, it raised interest rates to try and stem the speculation. The move quickly led to a stock market crash and debt crisis, as many debts fueled by the rampant speculation turned out bad. A great deal of economic insecurity resulted, until finally the issues manifested themselves in a banking crisis that led to consolidation and government bailouts (Kuepper 2016).

Japan has been perceived as in economic decline since the 1990s, attributed to the bursting of the asset price bubble, which led to the sharp decline in Tokyo stock and real estate prices that plummeted; the loss of international competitiveness (especially relative to Asian competitors); a banking system plagued with Non-Performing Loans (NPLs) and on the brink of collapse; economic stagnation and recession; rising unemployment; and little opportunity for new entrants into the labor force. Heroic macroeconomic policies failed to stimulate economic recovery, which led to enormous budget deficits and zero interest rate monetary policy and a government weighed down with massive levels of national debt and unfunded social obligations. (Mendelowitz 2003). This came as an enormous shock to the Japanese economy and Japan's sense of optimism and accomplishment. After all, by the late 1980s, Japan ranked first in GNP per capita worldwide. By the 1990s, however,

> its economic expansion halted for more than 10 years. The country experienced low growth and deflation during this time, with its stock market hovering at record lows and its property market never fully returning to its pre-boom levels. Some economists ... blame the lost decade on consumers and companies that saved too much and caused the economy to slow. Others blame the country's aging population demographic and/or its monetary policy for the decline. For instance, the central bank's slow response to intervene in the marketplace may have exacerbated the problem. (Kuepper)

Although the bubble economy ended essentially in 1990, it wasn't until January 29, 1993, that Prime Minister Kiichi Miyazawa acknowledged that the inflated economy had essentially collapsed (McNabb 2016).

The social effects of the bubble economy, followed by its spectacular collapse, took only a few years to appear. One manifestation is described by Megumi Ushikubo in the book *Soshokukei Danshi Ojo-man Ga Nippon wo Kaeru/The Herbivorous Ladylike Men Who Are Changing Japan*. Here the claim is made that about two-thirds of all Japanese men aged 20–34 are now partial or total "grass-eaters" (*soshokukei*). "People who grew up in the bubble era [of the 1980s] really feel like they were let down. They worked so hard and it all came to nothing," says Ushikubo. "So the men who came after them have changed." They are not as competitively minded about their jobs as men in older generations. They are not interested in dating girls, having relationships, or even having sex (choosing from a plethora of "self-help" toys instead). This has spawned a disconnect between genders so pervasive that Japan is experiencing a "social recession" in marriage, births, and even sex, all of which are declining (Otake).

Timothy Iles talks about a "crisis of identity" in recent (post-bubble) Japanese cinema. I am interested here in the notion of "crisis" while Iles is more interested in the notion of "identity." For Iles, Japan has undergone "turmoil" at different times throughout its modern history, such as the Meiji Era and the Occupation period (Iles 2008: 18–21). At these differing times, the Japanese underwent such crises of identity in light of the world-changing social and political circumstances. A third period of turmoil, this one economic, erupts with the bursting of Japan's bubble years. Iles tends to conflate films from the late bubble years with those made in the post-bubble period. My contention is that the turmoil is a function of the enormous shifts in middle-class life that occurred in the 1990s and shows up in cinema as the decade progresses. There is a sense in which the concerns of Iles's fine study overlap with what I am getting at here, though Iles does not at all discuss *The Eel*; nor does he mention any of the other films that I highlight to show how what I am calling the economic trauma and Iles calls the crisis of identity forms a context in which Imamura's film should be seen. Mes and Sharp see both the bubble years and the puncturing of the bubble as having profound effects on Japanese society and cinema. Discussing the early films of Shinji Aoyama, they write, "Too many people had been marginalized in the huge accumulation of wealth of the bubble years. The slow, steady rise of the '80s, followed by its subsequent collapse, effectively left many trapped outside of the system, analogous with the pathetic figures . . . in [Shinji Aoyama's] *Chinpira/Two Punks*" (2005: 215).

Director Shinji Aoyama himself notes that at this time, "Something very strange was happening in Japan which we couldn't quite put our fingers on" (2005: 216). Yet as Adam Bingham notes, 1997 could be marked as a turning point in Japanese cinema. He points to Takeshi Kitano's *Hana-bi*, which won the Golden Lion at the Venice Film Festival; Naomi Kawase's *Moe no suzaku/Suzaku*, which won the Camera d'Or at Cannes, and where Imamura's *The Eel* shared the Palme d'Or (his second such prize); Masayuki Suo's *Shall We Dance?*, which became the highest-grossing Japanese film ever released in the United States; while *Mononoke hime/Princess Mononoke* became the highest-grossing film ever released in Japan, eclipsing *ET* (1982) (Bingham 2015: 4). The *Yomiuri Shinbun*, one of Japan's major daily newspapers, declared 1997 "the year of the Japanese film phoenix" (Bingham 2015: 5). If indeed 1997 was a turning point in Japanese cinema, it is either a coincidental concatenation or the culmination of a roiling cultural and economic contraction. To appreciate Imamura's implication in 1997, we need to look very briefly at a handful of "trauma" films made around this time.

Trauma Films, 1995–1997

If 1997 seemed a renaissance of the Japanese cinema in both domestic and international realms, the year 1995 marks the beginning of a cinematic response to the bursting of the economic bubble and the long journey through the lost decade. Such films include:

- *Love Letter* (Shunji Iwai, 1995). On a whim a young woman whose boyfriend died in a mountain climbing accident writes a letter to him at his rural hometown address, never, of course, expecting a reply. When she gets one, she is shocked.

- *Maborosi* (Hirokazu Kore-eda, 1995). This was the first film of the Renaissance Japanese cinema to make a splash on the international festival circuit. A young husband and father apparently commits suicide both unexpectedly and shockingly. After five years his widow marries a man who lives in a rural fishing village on the Japan Sea. She attempts and eventually does come to an accommodation with her beloved first husband's death. Mes and Sharp note that the film seems consciously modeled on the work of internationally renowned arthouse directors like Theo Angelopoulos and Hou Hsiao-hsien (Mes and Sharp 2005: 211).

- *Ashita* (Nobuhiko Obayashi, 1995). The director of the cult hit *House* releases a film with only a touch of the supernatural in this tale of a varied group of people who receive mysterious messages from loved ones who were killed three months earlier in a shipwreck. Though little known, the film perfectly captures the sense of loss across the society and the regret at not being able to fully process this loss without magical intervention.

- *Okaeri* (Makoto Shinozaki, 1995). A young husband must try to understand and come to terms with his wife's slow decline into schizophrenia. The static, fixed shots combine with the pale lighting and subdued color scheme to present an image of suburban life that is rather downbeat and cold (Mes and Sharp 2005: 203). The economic struggle of the couple—he teaches at a cram school at night, she transcribes interviews on a typewriter—is probably not a factor in the wife's deterioration, but it does provide a grim background to her disease.

- *Helpless* (Shinji Aoyama, 1995). Set in the crucial year of 1989—the end of the long, violent, and ever-shifting Showa era and the beginning of Heisei—"when the collapse of the country's economy brought about a severe recession with wide-reaching ramifications . . . the characters [in the film] represent eras in contemporary Japan, the discord and disconnect between the lost prosperity of the recent post-war past and the enforced hardship of a present." The film features "problematic patriarchal figures" that signify the collapse at the end of Showa (Bingham 2015: 3) and the beginning of the use of the male body as a site of trauma.

- *Shall We Dance?* (Masayuki Suo, 1996). This film is a lighthearted look at the repressed life of Japanese salarymen. A happily-ever-after story amid the far more traumatic deaths and illnesses on view in so many of the other films; yet it should be taken as a metaphor for the dissatisfaction of the life of a salaryman.

- *Hana-bi* (Takeshi Kitano, 1997). One of Kitano's most successful films, especially in the West, *Hana-bi* is the story of a disgraced policeman whose wife is dying of cancer and who takes her on one last trip (courtesy of an ingenious bank robbery) until at the end he shoots both her and himself. Aaron Gerow's fine analysis of this film in his monograph on the director does not relate it to immediate social circumstances. Adam Bingham does relate the film to its immediate social circumstances, claiming that there are repeated mentions of the recession and attendant economic hardship in the dialogue. He thinks the oft-noted highlighting of specifically Japanese landscapes and traditions may very well be a means of negating and overcoming contemporary problems (2015: 6).

- *Tokyo Biyori* (Naoto Takenaka, 1997). This film is based on the true story of the early death of the wife of famed photographer Nobuyoshi Araki. "The film is executed in impeccable taste, it is beautifully shot, slow paced with carefully understated acting, never becoming overly sentimental. Set before us is a collage of incidents wherein the seemingly trivial and 'everyday' in retrospect take on profound significance" (Tooze).

- *Moe no suzaku/Suzaku* (Naomi Kawase, 1997). A lengthy prelude is set fifteen years earlier in which a small community in rural Nara has been depleted by an economic crisis. The community awaits a railroad spur that will revitalize the town, but it never materializes. One day the father wanders off into the night, his fate unknown until the police find his body. The film consists of long takes in a documentary style.

- *Bounce Ko Gals* (Masato Harada, 1997). This is a somewhat hyperbolic but effective look at the real-life phenomenon of *enjo kosai* (compensated dating), where high school girls "date" older men, indulging in anything ranging from conversation to sexual activity. The film wishes to castigate both the rampant consumerism of the girls and, even more, the often-perverse sexual interests of the older men.[2]

Death—by disease, murder, or suicide—illness, profound sadness, and the struggle to overcome these losses link these films as responses to trauma, a symptom of a society at loose ends and suddenly possessed of social dislocation.

The Art of Trauma

Unagi/The Eel was adapted from *Yami ni hirameku/Sparkles in the Darkness* (1997), a novel by Akira Yoshimura, whose main interest was Japan's penal system and its effects on both prisoners and guards. But in the film the eight-year prison sentence served by protagonist Takuro Yamashita (Koji Yakusho) is completely elided. All we learn of his time in prison was that he developed skills as a barber and that he adopted a pet eel. As Nelson Kim describes: "*The Eel* begins as a bloody thriller, turns into a drama of redemption, and finally becomes a knockabout comedy with surrealist touches" (Kim). Lawrence Van Gelder's highly appreciative review in the *New York Times* sees the film's concerns as "the possibilities of redemption, the persistence of hope, the achievement of love and the miracles of rebirth and survival" (Van Gelder 1998). For a film whose first section concludes with the brutal stabbing of a wife by her enraged husband, Imamura must make us work to see how redemption, hope, love, rebirth, and survival can come about. We must appreciate that if *The Eel* is a trauma film, it is one with a large difference from those highlighted above: the trauma is self-inflicted. Disease, death, and suicide all make up the films discussed above. *The Eel* differs in that the loss of the spouse and the lifestyle to which one has become accustomed is due to murder. As much as the protagonist feels betrayed by his wife's infidelity, as much as he is enraged by the fact that she never responded sexually to him as she does to her lover, that is no excuse for murder; what he does is inexcusable. It is not enough to note that this is the great insight of Imamura's cinema—the anthropologist who understands the animal instinct under the veneer of the blue suit.

The film begins in the summer of 1988, when Japan's economy was still strong. If the murder is a symptom, then we need to know of what: what is the disease? Alienation and humiliation. Imamura sketches out this alienation in the first six shots. The film opens with an establishing shot of a high-rise office building, followed by a shot of another building—the bland cityscape of contemporary Japan. Then there is a shot indicating the company name via a building sign. Takuro works for a flour company—unexciting, simply a commodity to be bartered and sold, a thing that in itself is useless, something that must be molded, shaped, into something else. A shot of Takuro in a crowded office is taken from a middle distance so that we see him at work until another office worker sits down between him and the camera. He is not important enough either to merit a close-up or to cut to him straight on. His typicality is then highlighted by a pan of his walking to the train station amid the anonymous crowds as the credits roll. Another pan takes him from the turnstile to the platform and then onto the train. We watch as the train gets more and more crowded. But then this blue-suited salaryman takes out a letter from his suit pocket and begins to read. An over-the-shoulder shot shows us the letter, accompanied by a woman's voiceover claiming that when Takuro goes on his weekly fishing trip, his wife entertains her lover.

The next series of shots tells us all we need to know about what will happen next. In a high-angle shot the camera pans as Takuro walks home through a quiet, rather bucolic neighborhood. He is greeted by a neighbor who notes, "You're home early," indicating that neighbors know everyone's business. The camera cuts from a crane shot down his exterior staircase and tracks with him to his back door and stops in the door frame. The wife's "You're going fishing tonight, right?" takes on an ominous tone, especially as Takuro walks through the house to the bedroom while his wife is on the right side of the frame preparing a lunch for him. This gives us the layout of their small home and will come into play later when Takuro enters his house after spying on his wife's lovemaking. Meanwhile, the wife's preparing sashimi, deftly slicing the fish with a knife, has two functions. The first is to create tension as Takuro watches her wielding a knife, as he will later, grabbing one from a work shed

Figure 6.1 A long-take, deep-focus shot of the layout of the house with kitchen on the right and bedroom in the background.

and using it to slaughter his wife; the second is that later, Keiko, the woman with whom he falls in love, will prepare lunch in the exact same manner, thus connecting the two women—and making clear why Takuro will refuse the lunches that Keiko prepares.

Takuro cuts his fishing trip short and returns home to find his wife with her lover, as he expected. It is typical of reviews to note that as Takuro spies on his wife with her lover, she is much more responsive to this man than she is with him (though we cannot know this at the time; this notion is put forward by Takasaki, his *bête noire*, much later in the film). Yet perhaps this is what sends him into a blind rage—the screen goes red in accord with his feelings. Or perhaps his feelings go deeper into the realm of a fear of female sexuality let loose, of the power of women when their desire is unfettered. He stabs the lover with the knife, but he reserves his true rage for his wife. She looks up at him with an almost unreadable expression, certainly one containing no fear and perhaps a little bit of loathing. He repeatedly and horrifically stabs her, the blood spattering onto the camera lens. Then he reverts to his more placid persona, as he gently covers her nude body with a blanket. Covered in his wife's blood, he calmly rides his bike to the nearest police station and turns himself in. These changes of tone—from rage to placidity—are not only typical of the entire film but reveal the narrative mastery of Imamura's cinema at this point in a lengthy and already respected career.

After he turns himself into the police, the film engages in a major ellipsis, announcing it is eight years later (1996) as Takuro is paroled from prison.[3] We are at the twelve-minute mark when this occurs, the film having daringly and economically introduced us to a typical salaryman who is squeezed into an office and squeezed into a commuter train only to learn that his wife is lustfully cheating on him. Except for the quick nine shots of the murder whose average shot length is five seconds, the rest of this opening sequence has an average shot length of about seventeen seconds. The longest take in the pre-murder sequence is almost one minute in length (fifty-five seconds)—a simple shot of him collecting his fishing rod, giving away the fish he caught (his wife won't be preparing sashimi with them, after all), and saying goodbye to his fellow fishermen. Such a lengthy take (and there are others of thirty and forty seconds in the pre-prison section) shows Imamura's willingness to let things play out in real time. Though it is always tempting to read long takes as symbolic or for other content- or thematic-oriented components, in fact the deployment of long takes should be seen as an aesthetic choice and as part of the art-cinema mode of the time. Although the average shot length for the film is twenty-three seconds—hardly long compared to *A City of Sadness* with its ASL of forty-two seconds and certainly hardly comparable to Hou's *Goodbye South, Goodbye* (1996) with its ASL of 105 seconds—the majority of shots in *The Eel* range between forty and fifty seconds.[4] The film's elliptical narrative, character-driven plot, and long-take style conform to contemporary art-cinema modes.

The credits, which have intermittently run over this entire sequence, finally come to an end with Imamura's directorial credit at the end of the elided eight years in prison, with Takuro's release. It is as if Imamura will take credit for directing the film *after* this point; Imamura is interested in the effects of the trauma and possible recovery. This prologue, so to speak, is virtuoso "pure" cinema, a daring condensation of information and action; and the trauma belongs as much to the audience—shocked by an act as gruesome as anything in the serial-killer narrative that is *Fukushu suru wa ware ni ari/Vengeance Is Mine* (1979)—and the narrative arc of recovery for the protagonist from this early point is similarly an arc of recovery for the shocked viewer who is attempting to find his/her narrative bearings for much of the second act.

Return to the Rural

It is well established that for Imamura, the rural contains the essence of Japan and the real Japan is found among the ordinary people therein. Thus, to return Takuro to some semblance of humanity following his release from prison, he must return to the rural. He is given over to the care of a priest who resides in the town of Sawara. Though only ten miles from Tokyo's Narita International Airport and about fifty miles from Tokyo itself, Sawara will function as the rural with its village atmosphere and collection of comic types who represent the peasants of old Japan. A tourist guide to the area notes, "The streets remain much as they were in the Edo period, providing a terrific sense of nostalgia" (Jnto Japan). The area also has many waterways that provide the opportunity for Takuro to go eel fishing and eventually to release his pet eel. In fact, the first shot of the town is of a small waterway running through. The priest's home is a traditional Japanese-style house that could easily be right out of an Ozu film. Indeed, Imamura employs the typical Ozu tatami-level shot whenever the home's interior is on view. And Takada, Takuro's fishing-pal in Sawara, fishes for eel with a spear from a small boat in another paean to the rural and traditional. Like much of Imamura's cinema as a whole, *The Eel* is a study in contrasts: the explicit sex and violence contrasting with the symbolism and minimalism of the middle stretches contrasting with the violence and slapstick of the third act.

Figure 6.2 The priest's traditional house, with characters sitting on tatami mats, shot from the low level characteristic of Yasujiro Ozu.

In prison Takuro was permitted to keep the eel as a pet. When asked by the priest, "Why an eel?" he replies, "He listens to what I say" and "He doesn't say what I don't want to hear." It is as this point when he gets into the car with the priest that the film's title "Unagi" (in hiragana) appears. When he arrives in Sawara, he notes that his eel does not look well, and he fills the plastic bag in which he carries it with river water. The eel regains his health due to the water of this remnant of rural Japan, just as Takuro will eventually find his selfhood restored. Meanwhile, he will communicate with his pet eel, kept in a large tank in the barbershop that he runs. No one familiar with Imamura's cinema can help but be reminded of the shots of the carp in its tank in *Erogotoshi-tachi yori: Jinruigaku nyumon/The Pornographers* (1966).

The person that will restore Takuro's selfhood is Keiko, who, he claims at one point, "resembles" his wife. The actress who plays his wife and the actress who plays Keiko are not the same—the wife is played by Chiho Terada, while Keiko is played by the much better-known Misa Shimizu. However, we can say that there is a kind of "exchange" in the film between Emiko (his wife) and Keiko. Initially, he seems to have no regrets for killing his wife, that he thinks he did nothing wrong. That is the conclusion of the priest and his wife, Misako (the veteran actress and Imamura-regular Mitsuko Baisho). That he has no remorse may not be entirely true, however, though he is later accused of the same thing by Takasaki, an ex-con who torments him throughout the film for this very reason. Yet he is uneasy when he first spots Keiko walking past his barbershop, though he says nothing. It may indeed be that she resembles his wife, thus his look of unease. Significantly, it is while fishing for eel food that he spots Keiko lying in the grass following her suicide attempt. As he looks at her lying there, the film cuts to the bloodied nude body of his wife. A voiceover reminds him that "while on parole, don't let yourself be drawn into any kind of trouble." Thus, when trying to get help for Keiko there is a possibility of trouble for himself.

In saving Keiko at some peril to himself—in exchanging her life for his wife's, that is (the flashback to his wife's body while he sees Keiko's lying on the ground making this exchange clear)—is the beginning of his redemption. Yet first he bicycles back to the barbershop as if to ignore what he saw. But he thinks better of this and leads a group of men back to the site of the body, also on his bike—the bike being how he went to the police station following the murder. Now the bike is how he saves Keiko. By the same token, his presence at the police station links the murder and the rescue. Indeed, a teenager in the police station, learning that it was a suicide from which the woman will recover, says, "What a bummer. It wasn't a murder."

Keiko is frequently linked with Takuro's pet eel or eels in general. Not only does Takuro find Keiko while fishing for eel food, but when Takada spears an eel while night fishing with Takuro, Takada asks Takuro if he knew the woman that tried to kill herself. This is when Takuro claims that she resembles his wife, from whom he is separated. Takuro is initially (and understandably) loathe to admit to the townspeople that he is an ex-con who was sent away for murdering his wife. Not only does Takuro toss the eel back into the river, but he finds himself unable to try to spear an eel. Music comes up on the sound track at this point, the same leitmotif associated with his pet eel—notes played on an electronic keyboard made to sound almost like a didgeridoo, with strings played behind it. There is something almost traditionally Japanese about the main theme of this motif, reminiscent of the opening music of Mizoguchi's *Ugetsu* (1953). Thus, there is a concatenation of the eel, Keiko, and Japanese tradition in this scene. The links between his wife's murder and the eel are highlighted that night when Takuro dreams of a bloodied eel and then goes out to look at his pet eel in its tank. The musical motif is heard—thus linking the fishing scene with this night-time unease. The opening lines of the letter that Takuro reads in the first scene are also heard in voiceover—a mélange, then, of the eel, the killing of his wife, Takuro's inability to spear an eel, and Keiko's rescue. This is virtually a tour-de-force of cinematic derring-do, an almost uncanny ability to blend narrative, theme, and symbolism. Later, again sitting in front of the eel tank, Takuro will hear the voiceover of the letter, see it in the bottom of the tank, and dive in, at least in his imagination. When he comes out of this fantasy, his arm is plunged into the tank until he realizes there is no letter there. Takuro is not untroubled and unbothered by what he did to his wife.

Keiko's dedication to Takuro's redemption occurs in the very next scene when Misako brings her to the barbershop. Misako, Keiko, and Takuro sit down, the two women on the left, Takuro facing them on the right. The shot lasts for one full minute, a static camera from the time they all sit down. The long take here is part of the pattern of long takes within the barbershop, though the film's longest take, as we will see, occurs on the river where eels will lead to a revelation about Takuro's ex-wife. In the meantime, this introduction of Keiko to Takuro will result in her coming to work at the barbershop. A later scene (one month later) shows us a neat barbershop with two chairs occupied and two men waiting, one of them claiming that Takuro couldn't do without Keiko. This first shot in the shop, taken from behind the waiting customers, lasts forty-four seconds. A cut to the reverse angle shows us how the shop has become not only profitable as a hair-cutting establishment, but also a town center as a teenage boy, the one seen in the police station earlier, comes in to leave tickets for his girlfriend to pick up later. This take, lasting fifty-two seconds, begins as a static shot that is held for thirty-four seconds, then contains two slow pans to the left to follow Takuro across the shop for the duration of the take. Takuro, we learn, is anxious to prevent rumors about the state of his relationship with Keiko.

Yet if there is no sexual relationship between the two, a genial companionability has clearly already set in, as we see in the next scene where Takuro and Keiko eat lunch together in Takuro's small kitchen. Here another static shot is utilized, one taken at a slightly elevated angle of the seated couple and confining them to only the right portion of the frame. The center of the frame is occupied by the kitchen sink in the background. The take lasts fifty-one seconds and although the camera remains static the whole time, the scene ends as both Takuro and Keiko get up from the table and put their dishes by the sink. Just before the scene ends, Keiko asks Takuro why he keeps an eel. He says, "An eel suits me." He certainly cannot tell her that it was allowed him as a pet during his prison term and she doesn't press him further for an answer.

Though most of the long takes in the film either feature a static camera or a slightly panning one, there is the occasional tour-de-force take. In one such example, there is a shot taken in the barbershop with Takuro in the middle ground and the outside background in sharp focus as a garbage truck pulls up in front of the shop. Soon Keiko will enter the shot from the right, occupying the foreground. All three planes, foreground, middle ground, and background, are filmed in deep focus. This composition lasts for thirty-two seconds. Keiko goes outside to guide the truck around the building, moving offscreen right. At the same time, the camera does a fast dolly to the right (the direction from which Keiko initially came) sweeping across the outside of the building until it slows down as Keiko enters the frame (i.e., the camera has been moving at the same time that Keiko has been moving offscreen) and the camera stops as Keiko is centered in the frame, the sanitation men grabbing up the garbage bags and putting them in their truck. This fast dolly and then reentrance of Keiko takes another twenty-six seconds, the whole take, then, lasting fifty-eight seconds. This is the kind of take that has absolutely no discernable symbolic content or thematic weight. It is simply a mini-tour-de-force of deep focus and shifting *mise-en-scène* for its own sake. But if the take has no symbolic or thematic force, the content of the scene does, for it is the case that the older of the two sanitation men recognizes Takuro and vice versa. He tells the priest of this, concerned that the townspeople will learn of his past.

The small boat is another space where long takes predominate. When Takada makes an eel trap, the two men go out at night to try it out. Here, again, eels are linked to the women in Takuro's life. Takada notes that Takuro didn't divorce his wife, but that she died, something he can tell because he lost his wife as well. But Takuro claims at this point, "I've had my fill of women." The take is a static one, lasting almost one minute. The camera is positioned on the water and seems to float along with the row boat it is filming. Another night shot taken on the water, as the two men have caught two large eels in Takada's trap, lasts a little more than thirty seconds. The same positioning of the two men in the boat with the camera floating on the water watching them occurs later, in a daytime shot that is the longest in the film, lasting an impressive three full minutes. Eels, wives, and women are again the subjects of the discourse, though this time the link between eels and women, between the water-dwellers and the land-lubbers, is made more anthropologically apparent.

Figure 6.3   Of eels and women; the longest take in the film.

The shot begins at dawn, the sun casting only a little light on the water. As the boat floats gently on the water, so does the camera, initially panning as the boat floats left to right, but then almost imperceptibly floating in sync with the boat. It is likely that the camera is handheld with a steadicam, the camera operator and perhaps an assistant or two in the shallow water near the riverbank. Takada offers a disquisition on the reproductive cycle of the eel, beginning with the observation that it was once thought there were no female eels. This comment and the subsequent lecture follows Takada's inquiry as to Keiko's absence. This again links Keiko and eels. In fact, this subject of eel reproduction follows a sequence where Keiko learns she is four months pregnant (her absence in Sawara is due to her visit to a gynecologist in Tokyo), which is followed by a flashback scene of her lovemaking with Dojima, her now-estranged boyfriend who has located her in town (discussed below). Human reproduction and eel reproduction are juxtaposed. A pause in the conversation to put the eel trap in the water is followed by Takada's noting that he saw the papers Takasaki had posted on the barbershop window. Takasaki, after trying to rape Keiko, posts a sutra and a notice on the window. The following morning, Takuro discovers them on the ground, the notice reading, "Don't be so smug, you filthy wife-killer." Takada asks Takuro if it is true. We then get the most intense dialogue Takuro delivers in the film, a dramatic moment aided by the camera's slow move in to a closer shot. He says, "I couldn't forgive her . . . because . . . I loved her. I couldn't help myself. I often wondered how I could kill the one I loved so much. I just couldn't forgive her."

Immediately following this three-minute take we are back at the barbershop in front of the eel tank at night. The drama that closes the boat scene continues here as Takuro laments to the eel that "when I killed Emiko, I died along with her. I didn't want . . . I couldn't accept anyone else." This revelation, combined with the previous lament, indicates that he has been plagued all along by his act. There is a strange moment earlier when he is bathing at the priest's house. He sits in the tub and holds his hands in front of his face. Later, he confesses to Keiko that he murdered his wife. He says, "I tried to forget, but these hands can't." Just as importantly, he comes to ponder the letter that incriminated his wife. "That letter . . . I wonder who wrote it?" He then has a vision of being questioned, "What did you do with the letter?" He claims he threw it away. At this moment, he runs backward away from the eel tank, repeats that he threw it away, and then is seen running around the bottom of the eel tank wondering where he threw the letter. And then, most significantly, he thinks that maybe there was no letter. We later learn that there was no letter and that is when we realize that he has come to terms with his actions.

The climactic moment of Takuro's coming to terms occurs at the night-time party held in honor of Keiko's ridding herself of her boyfriend. This is Imamura demonstrating the importance of community, as all the barbershop regulars along with the priest and his wife are in attendance. While Keiko and Misako dance and Yuji plays the guitar, Takuro gets in the boat with his eel and poles out a few yards from shore. He says goodbye to the eel, recalling Takada's disquisition with his own sentiments and claiming that he and the eel are similar. But as he does so, Takasaki appears out of the water, clearly a hallucination. Earlier, the two men had a fight in the barbershop—a fight filmed counterintuitively. Instead of the usual fast-cutting such a scene would typically merit, this one is filmed in only seven shots with an ASL of fifty-three seconds. Takasaki, on the losing end of the fight, claims that Takuro is a "boy scout" when it comes to sex and that Takuro killed his wife out of jealousy when he saw how his wife's lover satisfied her in ways he couldn't. Whether this strikes a chord with Takuro is hard to say. But the hallucination-Takasaki is surely right when he says, "There was no letter. Jealousy made you hallucinate." At that point, Takuro lets the eel go into the river. His acceptance of Keiko's pregnancy and claiming the baby as his though it isn't (see below), and telling Keiko not to have an abortion, are his redemption. He no longer needs the eel for company, and in preventing Keiko from having an abortion he saves another life, now having saved both Keiko and the baby. The community has rallied around him, and at the end Keiko tells him she will wait for him and be there at the barbershop when he gets out of prison.

Money—Trauma—Redemption

Imamura has two redemptions in mind, both Takuro and Keiko. She too must learn to deal with trauma—the events that led up to her suicide attempt. Her trauma is even more directly related to the cultural trauma of the bursting of the bubble economy. This is played out on the ruined relationship between Keiko and Eiji Doujima. Keiko is deeply worried about whether her mother's mental illness is hereditary and deeply angry when she realizes that Doujima wants her mother's money. His need for money gives the film its direct connection to the post-bubble economy. Doujima is a failed financier, a speculator whose attempt to get his hands on the thirty million yen held in a bank account belonging to Etsuko (Keiko's mother) is symbolic of the economy that robs and swindles its way to success until it ultimately fails, as happened in Japan in the 1990s.

Almost exactly halfway through *The Eel*, during a deceptively complex forty-two second-take, the villainous Doujima enters the barbershop. When Keiko

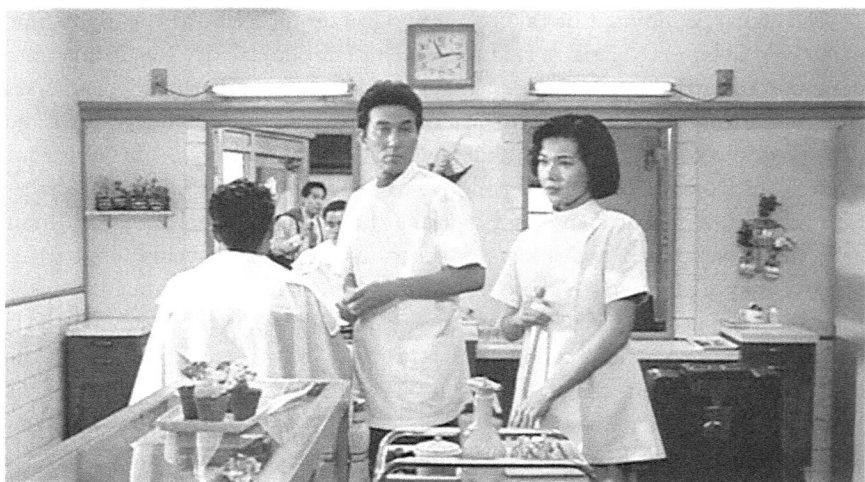

Figure 6.4 It's all done with mirrors: note the entrance of Eiji Dojima in deep focus in the background.

comes in and sees him, we get a flashback to the incidents that led to her suicide attempt. The scenes that begin with the flashback are intended not only to further the links between Keiko and Emiko, but to establish a connection between Keiko and Takuro. The flashback begins with Keiko at a train station, just as we saw Takuro at a station in the first scene. She is bringing her mother back from a rest home in Akita, a northern prefecture, to put her in a mental hospital in Tokyo. The night before they do so, they dine in Doujima's apartment. This is a one-scene-one-shot sequence, lasting one minute and twenty-six seconds. Its importance is clear when Etsuko dons a red scarf and begins an impromptu flamenco dance and claims she is *"Akita no Carmen"* (The Carmen of Akita). The camera watches as she dances around the table and off to the left, a smooth pan following her. When Keiko and Doujima make love later that night (the important connection to Emiko is further established in showing her in the throes of sexual passion just as Emiko was earlier, both explicitly displayed), Keiko sees her mother spying on their lovemaking and wonders whether mental illness is hereditary. Later, Keiko will visit her mother in the Tokyo mental hospital, where she finds her mother leading the entire ward in a flamenco version of Carmen.

In the final fight in the barbershop, when Doujima comes to look for Keiko and the bank book she took from his office, we see the final exchange between Keiko and his wife along with the final link between Keiko and the eel. First, Misako, to get everyone to stop fighting, announces that Keiko is pregnant. Doujima first claims the child is his, but Keiko insists it is not (it is, of course). When Doujima angrily asks if it is Takuro's, Keiko says nothing. After a long pause, Takuro answers that the child is his. It is important to note that Takuro and Keiko have not slept together, though perhaps the whole town thinks they have. When Doujima leaps at Takuro, Keiko—and this is simply too important not to acknowledge—picks up the eel tube and gets into the fray. First, she accidentally hits Takuro with it. Then, going after Doujima, she accidentally breaks the eel tank. Wounding Takuro with the eel tube and releasing the eel from its tank sets Takuro free to finally acknowledge his love for Keiko. This he does in the long-take sequence of one minute and twenty-three seconds, where the two walk and talk with the camera leading them down the road away from the police station. (His freedom from reliance on the eel we see in the river scene discussed above.) Though he must serve about one more year of prison for parole-violation for fighting with Doujima, Keiko says she and the baby will wait for him. She does so as Masaki stands beside her, a symbol of not just the formation of a new family unit but of community. Masaki has all along eagerly waited for UFOs to land in the field across from the barbershop, even using Takuro's barber pole to help attract them. No one in the circle of friends that come to surround Takuro and Keiko ever make fun of him. In fact, one night there is a party in the crop circle they made as they all await a UFO landing. Except for Masaki, they don't necessarily believe a UFO will appear; but they hope one might for Masaki's sake and will do everything to help make that happen. By the same token, they will all await Takuro's release and return as regulars to his barbershop. The rural community has thus redeemed Takuro from being a murderer with only his pet eel for company.

Notes

1. We can look to the Korean cinema as a model for how social affects show up as symptoms. Kate E. Taylor-Jones notes,

    > The cinematic method for the extrapolation of the South Korean past has often been conducted via a violent exposition of the (male) individual in crisis. The male-in-crisis figure can be seen in many of the films to have emerged from South Korea over the last two decades ... [Such films] focus on an individual male subject as the site of tensions and stresses that traverse South Korean society. (2013: 75–76)

    The male body as the site on which the symptoms of trauma play out is seen, for instance, in one of South Korea's most important and powerful films, *Bakha satang/Peppermint Candy* (1999). Unlike most Japanese films, *Peppermint Candy* directly confronts many of the traumas of the recent South Korean past, including

the Gwangju Massacre of 1980 and the 1997 IMF crisis. The Japanese films do not all focus on men, though they largely do, and the violence they inflict on others or upon themselves is symptomatic of the increasing violence and shocks in Japanese society of the period.
2. The finest film to emerge from this cycle, even including *The Eel* and *Hana-bi*, is *Eureka* (Shinji Aoyama, 2000), "a film about reconstruction, about starting anew and finding a way of living when the old way has disappeared forever. The visual beauty, particularly that of the landscape, works as an influence on this process of regeneration" (Mes and Sharp 2005: 227). A bus driver and two children survive the bloody end of a bus hijacking and form a new family unit based on their trauma. The film is nearly silent, as long takes and long shots predominate. (Many critics write that it is "four hours" in length. It is 217 minutes.) The bus driver is played by Koji Yakusho, star of *The Eel*.
3. Although eight years served for murder seems a light sentence, we should realize that Takuro is released on parole and is at the end of the film returned to prison for parole violation. As it happens, the death penalty is rare in Japan and life without parole is not an actual sentence. Instead, what is called *muki chōeki*, imprisonment with labor for an undefined term, is sometimes imposed, but even here murderers may hope for parole after two or three decades. It is likely, given his early parole, that Takuro was sentenced to *chōeki*, imprisonment with labor, usually imposed for a defined term of up to twenty years. *Chōeki* seems to be reserved for morally culpable crimes like murder or theft. Labor as punishment reflects the Japanese emphasis on *kyōsei* (corrections), *kōsei hogo* (rehabilitation and protection), and *shakai fukki* (returning to society). Part of the exercise is thus for *jukeisha* (inmates or, literally, "people receiving punishment") to acquire skills and discipline. Thus, Takuro has learned to be a barber in prison—which stands him in good stead upon his release—and the discipline is seen early on in his release as he marches rather than walks. (See Jones for a discussion of Japanese sentencing and prison laws.)
4. The average shot length and percentage of moving camera shots in Hou's films are taken from Udden (2007). The average shot length and other aspects of style in *The Eel* are my own calculations and observations.

Works Cited

Bingham, Adam (2015). *Contemporary Japanese Cinema since Hana-Bi*. Edinburgh: Edinburgh University Press.

Gerow, Aaron (2007). *Kitano Takeshi*. London: BFI.

Iles, Timothy (2008). *The Crisis of Identity in Contemporary Japanese Film: Personal, Cultural, National*. Leiden: Brill.

Jnto Japan: The Official Guide. Japan National Tourism Organization. https://www.jnto.go.jp/eng/regional/chiba/sawara.html. Accessed December 30, 2017.

Jones, Colin P.A. "Words about Sentences: The Japanese Vocab of Crime and Punishment." *The Japan Times*. n.d. https://www.japantimes.co.jp/life/2016/02/08/language/words-sentences-japanese-vocab-crime-punishment/#.WkrAjWinGUk. Accessed January 1, 2018.

Kim, Nelson. "Shohei Imamura." http://sensesofcinema.com/2003/great-directors/imamura/. Accessed July 27, 2018.

Kuepper, Justin. "Japan's Lost Decade: Brief History and Lessons–What Japan's Lost Decade Could Teach Us about Financial Crises." https://www.thebalance.com/japan-s-lost-decade-brief-history-and-lessons-1979056. Accessed November 28, 2017.

Lynch, Brian. "Hou Hsiao-Hsien Retrospective: *Goodbye South, Goodbye*: An Enigmatic Creeper." http://www.straight.com/movies/400436/hou-hsiao-hsien-retrospective-goodbye-south-goodbye-enigmatic-creeper. Accessed November 28, 2017.

McNabb, David E. (2016). *A Comparative History of Commerce and Industry: Converging Trends and the Future of the Global Market*. Vol. 2. New York: Palgrave Macmillan.

Mendelowitz, Allan I. "After the Bubble: Is Japan's Recent Past America's Future?" http://www.rieti.go.jp/en/events/bbl/03061201.html. Accessed November 28, 2017.

Mes, Tom. Review of *The Eel*. http://www.midnighteye.com/reviews/the-eel/. Accessed November 12, 2017.

Mes, Tom, and Jasper Sharp (2005). *The Midnight Eye Guide to New Japanese Film*. Berkeley: Stone Bridge Press.

Otake, Tomoko. "Blurring the Boundaries: As the Future Facing Japan's Young People Changes Fast, So Too Are Traditional Gender Identities." http://www.japantimes.co.jp/life/2009/05/10/general/blurring-the-boundaries/#.WXZFVulgkdU. Accessed December 3, 2017.

Taylor-Jones, Kate E. (2013). *Rising Sun, Divided Land: Japanese and South Korean Filmmakers*. New York: Wallflower Press.

Tooze, Gary. DVD Beaver. http://www.dvdbeaver.com/film/DVDReview/TokyoBiyori.htm. Accessed November 20, 2017.

Unagi. http://www.jmdb.ne.jp/1997/du001570.htm. Accessed December 30, 2017.

Udden, James (2007). "This Time He Moves! The Deeper Significance of Hou Hsiao-Hsien's Radical Break in *Good Men, Good Women*." In *Cinema Taiwan: Politics, Popularity, and the State of the Arts*, ed. Darrell William Davis and Ru-shou Robert Chen. London: Routledge, 183–202.

Van Gelder, Lawrence (1998). "Film Review: The Passions That Seethe under the Orderly Surface." *New York Times*, August 21. http://www.nytimes.com/movie/review?res=9D07E6DA133DF932A1575BC0A96E958260. Accessed November 20, 2017.

PART II
CLIENTS

Chapter 7

The Insect Woman, or: The Female Art of Failure

Michael Raine

Introduction

The Insect Woman was by far the most financially successful film of Shohei Imamura's career, and a critical triumph, too. Bringing in more than 350 million yen over a record four-week run, it returned at least ten times its production budget. The film was the third-highest-grossing film of 1963, beating all the star vehicles for Nikkatsu's "diamond line" of "dynamite guys," and coming in behind only Akira Kurosawa's *High and Low* and Toei's all-star period film *Seizoroi tōkaidō*. In fact, *The Insect Woman* was among the top twenty-five most successful films of the twenty years after World War II, the only film not headlined by a big star until the most lucrative film on that list, *Tokyo Olympic*, was released in 1965 (Tahara 1977: 204; Iwasaki 2003: 258). Why was Imamura's film, made only reluctantly by the Nikkatsu studio, such a commercial and critical success?

This chapter argues that *The Insect Woman* came at a turning point in the modernization of the Japanese economy, and of the film industry. With the spread of television and the decline of the family audience in cinemas, studios turned to "adult" topics such as cruelty, sexuality, and violence aimed at an increasingly male audience, shot in new ways that relied less on the relatively high production values of earlier studio cinema. At the same time, the defeat of the forces that resisted Japan's subordinate role in its Cold War alliance with the United States, and the enshrinement of "income doubling" and "high economic growth" as national policies, caused some Japanese intellectuals and cultural workers to turn away from the progressive narrative that envisaged Japan as following a Western path to economic and cultural modernity. They emphasized instead indigenous (*dochaku*) aspects of Japanese society, not simply as residual elements but as ongoing and formative in the experience of most Japanese, in the cities as well as in rural areas.

That emphasis was both a refuge and a warning: *The Insect Woman* pits the *shomin* (the common people) against the bourgeois *shimin* (the citizen; the urban, westernized subject of political rights and duties), but in Imamura's hands the *shomin* become the *senmin* (outcasts; the exploited exploiters that make up the lower levels of both rural and urban Japan under high economic growth) (Kanesaka 1964b: 41). Imamura joins a long line of filmmakers who sympathize with female protagonists whose suffering is caused by Japanese modernization, but *The Insect Woman* foregrounds that protagonist's selfishness and materialism, and refuses easy depictions of an untouched, authentic Japan. Although it is often cited as a masterpiece of naturalist filmmaking, from another perspective the film's exaggeration of primitive Japaneseness echoes Yanagita Kunio and Hanada Kiyoteru's strategy of "using the premodern as a negative mediation to overcome modernity," while its mix of documentary footage and grotesque comedy draws on contemporary strategies of distanciation, found in avant-garde theories of documentary and performance, that mark it as a significant moment in the history of the "Japanese New Wave" (Hasebe and Satō 2003: 622; Tsurumi 2008: 175).

The Insect Woman

Imamura said of *The Insect Woman* that he wanted to make "something presented 'just as it is' (*jojiteki*) . . . a flat scenario, just facts and conclusions lined up in a row, with no linkage between one scene and the next" (Imamura 1994: 1279). The film traces the life of Matsuki Tome (Sachiko Hidari) through a series of episodes that span the years 1918 to 1961. We see Tome's birth in an isolated mountain village in Yamagata, in northern Japan, and we see her witness a "primal scene" between her mother and Onogawa, a demobilized soldier who may be her real father. We see her work at her family's landlord's silk mill, where she is raped by the landlord's son and consequently gives birth to a daughter, Nobuko (Jitsuko Yoshimura). We also see Tome's intimate relationship with her intellectually disabled father, Chūji (Kazuo Kitamura), who sucks pus from a boil on her leg and milk from her breasts when Nobuko will not nurse. Further episodes show her patriotic labor in a silk-spinning factory during World War II and her affair with a union foreman there after the war that leads to another betrayal. We then see Tome "emigrate" to Tokyo, where she works for Midori (Masumi Harukawa), the mistress of an American soldier. Midori's daughter is scalded to death when Tome's sexual curiosity causes her to eavesdrop on Midori's lovemaking. To assuage her guilt, Tome attends meetings of a postwar new religion (*shinkō shukyō*), where an officer of the sect is also the madam of an unlicensed brothel. Madam Suma (Tanie Kitabayashi) employs Tome as a maid but tricks her into serving a client, who rapes her. Suma threatens to withhold payment and forces Tome to acknowledge that she is now a prostitute. In the second half of the film, after the madam refuses to pay the hospital bill for an ectopic pregnancy, Tome betrays her to the police and establishes a call-girl ring of her own. However, after a visit home during which she shocks Nobuko by offering her breast to her dying father, Tome is betrayed in turn to the police by her own maid. When she emerges from prison she finds that her lover, Karasawa (Seizaburo Kawazu), has taken Nobuko as a mistress. Abandoned by both lover and daughter, Tome works as a cleaning woman until Nobuko takes Karasawa's money and returns to the model farm that she is developing with her agricultural school comrades. Karasawa commissions Tome to get Nobuko back and the film ends in *media res* as Tome climbs a mountain road toward the farm.

These episodes cannot be understood apart from how they are represented. *The Insect Woman* broke the rules of studio filmmaking: it was the first Nikkatsu film to be shot entirely on location, using long lenses and in long takes, with almost no built sets or post-recorded sound, and limited artificial lighting. The film's images, while typically sharp and carefully composed, often feature areas of darkness or shallow focus, and bodies are cut off by the frame line as they move through the cramped field of view. Wireless microphones and hidden cameras allow for scenes to be taken unawares in public spaces, a setting that, along with the lack of three-point lighting, makes the distinction between protagonist and environment less pronounced than most studio films. Satō Tadao described those raw images, and the performances they reveal, as "a pinnacle of Japanese naturalist realist cinema" (*Nihon no shizenshugi rearizumu eiga no kyokuchi*) (Satō 1980: 71). Whatever the meaning of "naturalist realism," there are other aspects to the film's presentation. Newsreel footage of well-known incidents in postwar Japanese history is cut into the film, from the "bloody May Day" of 1952 and the battles over the expansion of the Tachikawa air base in 1957 to the deadly Typhoon Isewan of 1959 and the struggle against the America-Japan Security Treaty (Anpo) in 1960. That footage is juxtaposed with narrative sequences in which the events take place offscreen, to the indifference or annoyance of the protagonist. Other sequences end in freeze frames, sometimes accompanied by a voiceover, for example of Tome's maudlin diary entries, recited as *waka* poems, while yet more close-up still images are distributed throughout the film.

Figure 7.1 Newsreel footage of the demonstrations against the America–Japan Security Treaty in June 1960, with superimposed text. The placard gives the text of the famous Article 9 of the postwar Japanese constitution, which renounces the right to make war.

Melodrama and Comedy in *The Insect Woman*

The tone of *The Insect Woman* differs from the reverence that characterizes the long history in Japan of social problem melodramas centered on women and directed by male "*feminisuto*" (Satō 1970: 24). As Kanesaka Kenji argues, Mizoguchi, Naruse, and even Kinoshita see women's exploitation from the position of the men in their films, engendering feelings of guilt and longing for forgiveness, or, I would argue more cynically, a kind of male connoisseurship of female suffering in the history of Japanese prestige melodrama (Kanesaka 1964b: 41). However, Imamura focuses on female frustration rather than male guilt, leading to films that present more directly the disordered subjectivity of the women who endure exploitation. Torn from an intimate relation with her father, Tome is exploited at every turn until she becomes both cruel and pathetic: merciless in her exploitation of her fellow prostitutes but "submissive, dominated, and sentimental" in her relations with men (Tessier 1997: 61). As Bill Mihalopoulos writes, "Tome's life is tragic because she desires the very things that dominate and exploit her" (Mihalopoulos 2008: 286). However, the mood of the film is not simply tragic horror and pity. As Satō Tadao writes about the freeze frames of Tome's melodramatic poses: we can't help laughing at the banality of Tome's poetic expression, but the brilliance of the film's comedy is that we're not laughing at her foolishness but admiring the toughness with which she manages her sense of frustration (Satō 1970: 26).

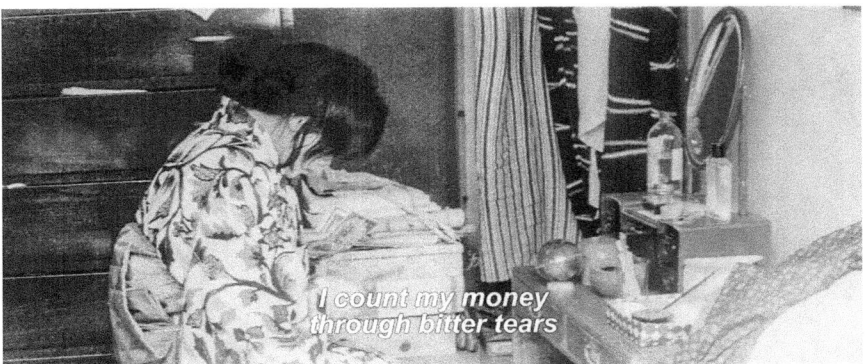

Figure 7.2 Freeze frame of Tome counting her money after she has been tricked into becoming a prostitute. The lament is both heartfelt and absurd in its sentiment and 5-7-5-7-7 *waka*-style intonation.

That robust buoyancy is what differentiates *The Insect Woman* from the woman-centered films of Mizoguchi and others: its dominant tone is comic rather than the melodramatic. Women do not decline gracefully toward the ground as they do in a Mizoguchi film—in the final image, Tome freezes in mid-air as she leaps a puddle, a gesture that reminds Kanesaka of Chaplin (Kanesaka 1964b: 41). Sequences are edited to create visual gags that end the scene, as in the jealous Chūji's wordless looming when Matsunami comes for Tome, or Nobuko's startled reaction when a silk moth lands on her. In a more cynical register, editing creates virtual punchlines that juxtapose the cruel inevitability of exploitation with absurd images of greed, anger, or desire. For example, the freeze frame of Tome counting her money that follows the two-and-a-half-minute take in which Suma coerces her into prostitution. Or the parody of Hideko Takamine's refined Keiko in *When a Woman Ascends the Stairs* (Mikio Naruse, 1960) when Tome returns home to find her maid making side-deals, just as she had in similar circumstances. Outraged that she had paid for Hanako's cosmetic surgery (to compensate for scalding her hand), Tome breaks the vinyl nose she bought her. The scene ends when Nobuko arrives to find Tome at her most embarrassingly deranged.

Comedy is often connected to sex in *The Insect Woman*. From the raucous conversation of the women in the silk factory to Midori's role-playing as a prostitute and comparison of her American and Korean boyfriends, women's rejection of sexual propriety is often played for laughs. After a series of extreme close-up photographs of Karasawa in bed with Nobuko, the longest

Figure 7.3 After having beaten with a piece of firewood the last person to try to take Tome away, Chūji's sudden looming behind Matsunami creates a kind of ironic visual punchline.

take of the film adopts a similar shot scale to follow his hairy hands as he paws and mouths her naked body. But when the old man finally kisses Nobuko on the lips, his false teeth fall out and the disturbing scene is broken up by her helpless laughter. As Matsushita Keiichi quipped, the basis of Japanese comedy is not French "esprit" or American "mechanism," but the "eroticism of the lower level of Japanese culture (*Nihon no kisō bunka*)." Echoing Bakhtin before Bakhtin was widely known in Japan, he argued that "Japanese couldn't survive the tragic exploitation of agrarian society without the comic eroticism of the lower orders" (Matsushita 1971: 22).

Sex and *The Insect Woman*

Why did two million Japanese watch a film without major stars made by a director who had not released a film in almost three years? Like comedy, sex sells. Scriptwriter Keiji Hasebe and Imamura chose to write an "erotic" script after the rejection of their first draft of *Intentions of Murder*, with the intention that this one not be "left on the shelf" (Yasumi 1964: 40). Even a bare plot summary of *The Insect Woman* indicates that it pushed the boundaries of sexual representation in Japanese film. Although there were already films marked for adult audiences only, the reformation of the Japanese industry censorship body, Eirin, after the "Sun Tribe" scandal of 1956 led to the introduction of the term "adult film" (*seijin eiga*) in 1957 (Endō 1973: 206). The term was initially used in a sense close to Barbara Klinger's, to indicate serious films with content unsuitable to general audiences, and saw a similar but more rapid shift to signify pornography (Klinger 1992). Early adult films included *Untamed Woman* (Arakure, Naruse, 1957) and *Bakumatsu taiyōden* (Yūzō

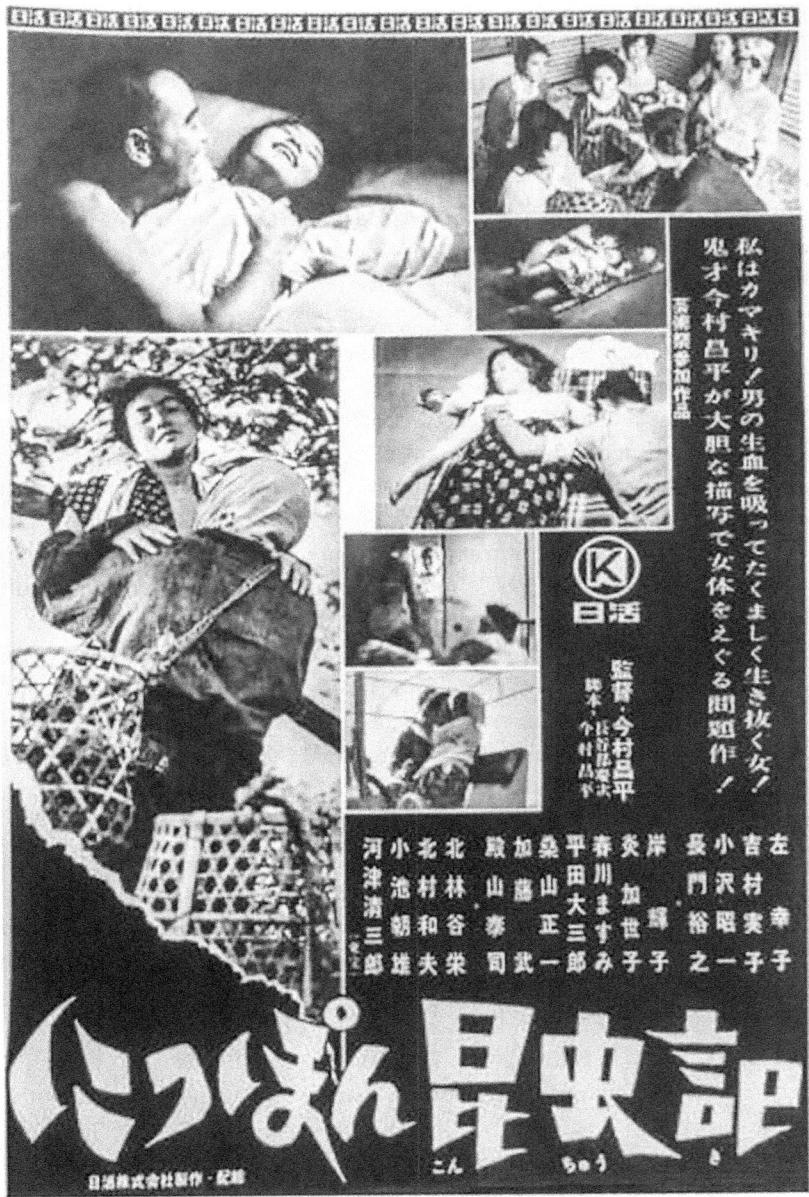

Figure 7.4 *The Insect Woman* press sheet (advertisement, *Kinema junpo*, November 1, 1963, unnumbered photographic front section). Whatever Imamura's intentions, the film was promoted as one of the new "adult films." The text on the right reads: "I am a praying mantis! A woman who stubbornly survives by sucking men's lifeblood! The great Imamura Shohei's bold style exposes the truth of a woman's body in this controversial film!"

Kawashima, 1957), scripted by Imamura, as well as several films by Yasuzō Masumura. Those films were produced by major studios, but with the rise of Okura Eiga and other independents in the early 1960s, "pink films" (soft pornography) overwhelmed the list. There were 19 designated adult films in 1957, 13 in 1958, 5 in 1959, 11 in 1960, 7 in 1961, 5 in 1962, 18 in 1963, and 86 in 1964, when *Daydream* (Hakujitsumu, Tetsuji Takechi) was distributed by Shochiku and caused a scandal. If the 1960s was a "season of politics," it was also, as Ueno Kōshi has noted, an "age of flesh" (*nikutai no jidai*) (Yamane 1992: 128). Unlike Imamura's earlier films, both *The Insect Woman* and *Intentions of Murder* were designated adult films.

Even before *The Insect Woman*, which was advertised with an image of Tome being suckled by her own father, Imamura had a reputation as a "sex monster" (Kanesaka 1964b: 43). His attraction to prostitution was personal, not merely sociological, and when he wanted to put a bar hostess in the film she replied, "Imamura Shōhei? A dirty film like his? No way!" (*anna kitanai eiga yame yo!*) (Katori 2004: 177, 181). Even the president of Nikkatsu, which benefited enormously from the film at a time when cinema audiences were in steep decline, complained that it was "dirty" (Takano 1979: 210). However, although Tsumura Hideo publicly criticized *The Insect Woman* from his position as film critic for the *Asahi* newspaper, describing it as "confused" (*waizatsu*) using a character from the word "obscene" (*waisetsu*), the general critical response was far more positive (Tsumura 1963: 11). In 1965 Masumura defended his own interest in sex and violence as the essential themes of cinema by arguing that the "ero boom" was led not by studios, which worried about limiting the audience, but by young directors such as Shohei Imamura (Masumura 1999: 145–7). Other writers also praised Imamura, comparing him to Ingmar Bergman in international art cinema as introducing a new, more explicit sexuality to Japanese film (Ishidō 1971: 30; Muramatsu 2003: 96). Prize-winning author Yoshiyuki Junnosuke dismissed Tsumura as sounding like a PTA, claiming that though the images were merely "crappy realism" (*kuso rearizumu*), it was precisely Tsumura's confusion that made the film exciting: "in jazz, it would be called 'funky'" (qtd. in Katori 2004: 184). The richness of *The Insect Woman* as a film derives from the confusion between that "crappy realism" and something more avant-garde.

Dochaku, or: What's the Matter with Yamagata?

In his *Asahi* newspaper critique, Tsumura Hideo was outraged by the liberties Imamura took with the relation between Tome and her father, Chūji: "This kind of damp and dirty sexual connection between parent and child does not exist.

This is not healthy eroticism but a step into a grotesque world" (Tsumura 1963: 11). That reaction to Imamura was not uncommon. Yasujiro Ozu, for whom Imamura had worked as assistant director, once asked him, "Why do you always write maggots (*ujimushi*)? Why not write a decent character for a change?" Imamura acknowledged that predilection even before *The Insect Woman* was released: "I tend to want to forcefully marry the problem of the lower half of the human body with the lower level of Japanese culture (*Nihon no kisō bunka*) that stubbornly churns out everyday life (*nichijōsei*)" (Imamura 1994: 1279) This often-repeated quotation is usually translated differently, to make sex seem like the natural mode of expression of the lower classes. But Imamura is quite clear about his own agency in making the connection, and his ambivalence about that lower level, in his films. He also announced that this chronicle of a "human living an inhuman life, thinking only of herself and ignoring her surroundings" would allow him to explore "what it means to be a Japanese" (*Asahi shinbun* 1963a: 9). Imamura continued that line of thought at the press screening, saying that "maybe women will hate this film and think it's a world that has nothing to do with them. But I feel this is a basic model of what it is to be Japanese" (Shioda 1992: 201).

In later years, Imamura recalled that he was motivated by a friend's stories of being sent into the mountains by the Japanese Communist Party to foment a Maoist revolution in 1952. The students in those "Mountain Village Operation Units" (*sanson kōsakutai*) were told that the local people were primed for revolution, but in fact the activists were spurned and soon arrested. Imamura sided with those who criticized Eurocentric cultural politics and critical theory for being out of touch with ordinary Japanese people, whose lives were still informed by indigenous culture and folk beliefs (*dochaku bunka* and *dozoku shinwa*) (Imamura 2001: 40). The search for indigenous modes of life, rooted in the soil (*dochaku*) and prior to Western contact, was common after the failure of the 1960 protests against the renewal of the America-Japan Security Treaty (Anpo). Hirosue Tamotsu wrote a series of books on premodern popular culture that informed the 1960s avant-garde (Goodman 2001: 348–50), and in the early 1960s Yoshimoto Takaaki savagely attacked political theorist Maruyama Masao in the name of "the people" who, he claimed, were ignored by progressive activists (Yoshimoto 2006: 397–400). Although he was involved in theater at Waseda University and knew communist students, Imamura was never very radical himself. As he wryly put it in 2004: "During the season of politics the only thing I was interested in was Yanagita Kunio and folklore studies. How did Japanese create today's society and sense of values? It wasn't the democracy forced on us by America but folk beliefs and rules passed down from ancient times" (Imamura 2004: 105). If we are to understand *The Insect Woman* we must follow, and question, Imamura's own trip into the mountains, taken not in the spirit of abstract political liberation but as part of a keen desire to see, smell, and taste the Japanese soil.

Yanagita Kunio was a Meiji-era bureaucrat who, failing in his attempts to relieve rural poverty, resigned his position and dedicated his life to the study of Japanese folk practices (*minzokugaku*), which he believed retained the true ways of ancient Japan. As Hashimoto Mitsuru argues in a powerful re-reading of his work, Yanagita understood "the geographical distinction between centre and periphery as a temporal distinction between modern and ancient" and "juxtaposed the beliefs he found there with the consciousness of contemporary Japanese, who took distorted modern life for granted and accepted the modern as the best of all possible worlds" (Hashimoto 1998: 137). However, Yanagita abandoned the dream of discovering an authentic Japan on the margins of the new nation-state, since it had already been corrupted by top-down forms of social organization such as national rather than local shrines. He claimed instead that the true Japan lived on, now invisible, in the fragmentary memories of ancient customs on the part of the "common people" (*jōmin*) that only he, Yanagita, could interpret. In Yanagita's "new nativism" (*shin kokugaku*), modernity in Japan was forcefully introduced from outside, so native modes of life were preserved as an invisible layer that must be excavated from underneath superficial modernization (Hashimoto 1998: 142). Imamura adopted from Yanagita a strategy of "investigation" (*chōsa*) by which he filled three notebooks with the life history of a woman from the provinces who had come to Tokyo and run a call-girl ring (Katori 2004: 233; Sato 1980: 72; Hasebe and Imamura 1962). Yet Imamura also learned from Yanagita that "investigation" was not dispassionate but an imaginative recreation of a mode of existence that endured, albeit in fragmentary and disordered ways that required the agency of his reconstruction, in the city as well as the country.

Bill Mihalopoulos adopts Yanagita's early, spatial model of center and periphery, arguing that "*The Insect Woman* constitutes the Japanese village as a topos free from the commands and obligations imposed upon Japanese life by the twin forces of modernization: the nation-state and capital" (Mihalopoulos 2008: 279). However, Imamura's portrait of the village seems less rosy than this "space for the spontaneous enjoyment of life" in which "the Japanese people were transparent to one another" (279). The bond between Tome and Chūji may be innocent (Shimizu Masashi calls it "eros" rather than "incest"), but the village is already subject to the family register system, its land is parcelled among petty landlords, and the farmers are absorbed into a cash economy, selling their silk cocoons to the local spinning mills that were the foundation of Japanese economic modernization in the nineteenth and early twentieth centuries (Shimizu 2001: 132;

Tsurumi 1992). Even inside the farmhouse, the hand loom is operated by the grandmother, whose face is invisible in a shot dominated by the sound of the beater she relentlessly operates, like a machine. Tome and Nobuko may both fantasize a mutual "couple" (*fūfu*) relation to Chūji, but this is not representative of rural life. Tome's intimacy is mocked by Rui and obstructed by her family, who trick her into working for the landlord to pay back their debt. Only Chūji is connected to the hand-powered and filthy past: he whittles offerings to the female mountain god, slogs through chest-deep water, and checks the liquified human manure by tasting it.

Rather than presenting the village as a prelapsarian ideal, *The Insect Woman* shows that there is no outside to capitalism in twentieth-century Japan. Money is constantly foregrounded in the film, as a topic of conversation and as banknotes or handfuls of dirty coins. Tome's family exploits her loyalty just as the state exploits her initial patriotism. Chūji endures as a devalued remainder, but even those beliefs are shown to be corrupted. Tome is delivered with the help of a shaman, but the shaman is played by Tanie Kitabayashi, who also plays Madam Suma. The magic of the mountain gods is replaced by a new prosperity religion in the city, but in both cases superstitions are used to control and console life in the bottom layer of society. The rest of the film is one long round of betrayal. When she is promoted by madam Suma, Tome immediately betrays Take, the only fellow prostitute who had visited her in hospital, as shamelessly as her own family exchanged her body for debt relief and schemed to trick Chūji out of his land. Tome then sells out the madam when she refuses to pay her hospital bill, and goes on to cheat Midori, Miyako, and the other "call girls" of their promised cut even as Karasawa uses her to lubricate a business deal.

Political theorist Matsushita Keiichi wrote one of the most perceptive evaluations of *The Insect Woman* on its release. He points out that Japanese modernization was built on the exploitation of rural women, part of a class that was now migrating to the cities in the period of high economic growth. Matsushita argues that this creates a "dual structure" to urban society and politics: only one-third of the population (the white collar and big factory workers) exhibit "city consciousness" and are addressed by ideologies of economic growth and social progress; the lower orders (*teihen, kisō*) are "fought over by communists, the LDP, and new religions" (Matsushita 1971: 23). Despite the "consumer revolution" and "leisure boom," Matsushita argues, *The Insect Woman* focuses on the two-thirds of Japanese who are not part of that culture, through a formally conscious investigation of the "lower half of the body indigenous to Japan (*Nihon ni dochaku no kahanshin*)" (Matsushita 1971: 24, 21).

That investigation involves sound as well as image. Accent is one of the preeminent markers of difference in Imamura's films, sometimes turning speech into a kind of sound effect that marks the character with a comic alterity. Critic Hasebe Hideo came from northern Japan and thought by her convincing accent that Sachiko Hidari did too (in fact, she was raised in Toyama, some way southwest of Yamagata, where the rural scenes are set). Hasebe describes listening to Tome's stereotypically "hick" regional accent in the cinema: "Laughing along with the audience, at the same time I felt my heart freeze" (Hasebe Hideo 1964: 57). That reaction was not just personal: in a period of mass migration, many people, including artists and critics, came from the provinces to the metropolis. That migration implicates the smooth space of Japanese capitalism that incorporated the hinterlands into a unified system but it was also the ground of a felt inequality, an ambivalent pride and shame central to the work of artists such as Shuji Terayama and Tatsumi Hijikata. There is a tension in *The Insect Woman* between Imamura's social position as the upper-middle-class son of a doctor from Tokyo, graduate of the prestigious Waseda University, where he studied with the leaders of a new generation of *shingeki* theater actors who also appeared in his films, and the marginal position of his films' outlaw protagonists, marked by regional, ethnic, and gender differences. For example, Tanie Kitabayashi and Kazuo Kitamura were members of prestigious *shingeki* theater troupes in Tokyo. Imamura's approach is now regularly described as anthropological or even entomological, but at the time some critics were more skeptical. As Sugiyama Heiichi put it, Imamura "is interested in *dochaku* things like a foreigner, a novelist looking for local colour" (Sugiyama 1971: 29).

Perhaps Hazumi Tsuneo was right that there was no incest in mountain villages. But the question is not one of accuracy but of who speaks, and for whom. Imamura always discussed *The Insect Woman* as if he had written it, but the film was co-authored with Keiji, Hasebe who claimed to have produced the first draft (Yasumi 1964: 41). Hasebe was not simply a native informant. Although he graduated from a Yamagata high school in 1933, he took part in avant-garde theater with his friends who had studied commercial art at a time when Dada, surrealism, and expressionism had a strong influence (Mizutani 1977: 203). Hasebe went on to write scripts for Heinosuke Gosho and Kon Ichikawa, including scripts for *A Billionaire* and *A Full-Up Train* that are masterpieces of absurd humor. He claimed that he was never satisfied until he had included something surreal in his scripts, and that he had invented the montage of newsreel and drama in the film: "When I wrote *The Insect Woman*, I deliberately made it dialectically surrealist" (204). Perhaps Tsumura's "step into a grotesque world" is precisely Imamura and Hasebe's strategy of "grotesque realism" that destabilizes the existing social order by foregrounding the body in "acts of defecation and copulation, conception, pregnancy, and birth" (Bakhtin 1984: 21). It makes Japan seem strange to Japanese audiences, forcing them to reflect on "what it means to be Japanese." That strangeness goes beyond the extreme behavior in the film to the mixed modes of its presentation: documentary and fiction, quotidian naturalism and absurd interruptions, deeply inhabited roles and radical changes of tone.

Documentary and the Avant-garde

With audiences in steep decline, studios in the early 1960s were focused on the bottom line. After Imamura went over budget on *Pigs and Battleships*, and the film was not a hit, Nikkatsu did not allow him to make a film for almost three years. At 33 million yen, the budget for *The Insect Woman* was slightly below average, which supports Imamura's claim that, despite the difficulties it raised, his turn to all-location shooting using wireless mikes and direct sound was justified by its speed and economy (Izawa et al. 1994: 1270; Sekikawa 2002: 216). But, like the French New Wave before him, there were other than budgetary reasons for this turn to a "documentary" aesthetic. Imamura explained to *Kinema junpō* in October 1963 that he was searching for a new style: "We who were trained in the studios have absorbed a certain way of doing things. I want to find a different way. That's why I chose the all-location method and discarded the convenience of working on a set" (Imamura 1994: 1279).

Imamura was two years older than Susumu Hani, who had already made a name for himself as a documentarist before using similar techniques on *Bad Boy*, chosen by *Kinema junpō* as the best film of 1961. Hani made *She and He* with Sachiko Hidari, his then wife, just before *The Insect Woman*, and both films played at the Berlin Film Festival in 1964, where Hidari won the prize for best actress. As Furuhata Yuriko has shown, there was a general concern with the representation of "actuality" in Japan around 1960, a consequence of leftist interest in "reportage," as well as the growth of television news programs and a documentary film industry making commercials for Japan's expanding industrial sector (Furuhata 2013: 3–5). For example, film critics and members of art study circles founded the group Cinema 57 to make *Tokyo 1958* for the Brussels World's Fair (Expo 58), while young filmmakers such as Toshio Matsumoto produced experimental advertising films such as *Ginrin* (1955) and wrote theory in documentary film journals such as *Kiroku eiga*.

The visual style of *The Insect Woman* is strongly affected by Imamura's decision to use equipment and techniques common in the world of documentary filmmaking. Black and white film stock, faster than color, allowed him to shoot in mostly natural light, while the cramped dimensions of real farmhouses and

Figure 7.5 Tome, followed by Nobuko, in the middle ground. Radio microphones pick up their dialogue in the crowd, but they are not recognizable until the end of the shot.

apartments (Imamura made a point of not removing paper screens) forced the camera to remain static or to chase action in shallow focus through pools of shadow. Cinematographer Shinsaku Himeda said they used two cameras with long (150-mm) lenses to further flatten the space (*Asahi shinbun* 1963b: 9). Rather than the centered, highlighted image and closely miked (often post-recorded) speech of the typical studio film, hidden cameras with long lenses and wireless microphones created scenes that must be scanned to find the speaker. Referring to the shot of Tome and Nobuko walking in a crowd of evening shoppers, in 2001 Imamura recalled that he wanted "acting that makes you think 'that's really real'" (*nakanaka shinjitsu da na to iu shibai*) (Imamura 2001: 45). Although such responses to the film are now commonplace, the historical distance and ambivalence of that statement—reality produced through acting, as a feeling rather than epistemology—leaves space to rethink the ways in which *The Insect Woman* is a naturalist film, or a film in the documentary style.

The resemblance to contemporary documentary, for example, was not very deep. *The Insect Woman* lacked the explanatory voiceover of NHK series such as *Nihon no sugao* that introduced Japanese regions to the metropolis, but it also lacked the accusatory voiceover and tight shot scale of more radical films such as Nagisa Oshima's *Forgotten Soldiers* (*Wasurerareta kōgun*) on NTV's *Non-fiction gekijō*, broadcast three months before *The Insect Woman* was released. Although there was a boom in TV geography documentaries between 1961 and 1963 that showed Japanese regions to the nation on multiple TV channels, *The Insect*

Woman lacked the maps and local products that were a feature of even the short film on Yamagata directed by Noriaki Tsuchimoto and shot by Tatsuo Suzuki, part of the *Discover Japan* series on NET, produced by Iwanami Films and sponsored by the Fuji Iron and Steel company.

The Insect Woman is also posed and choreographed in a way that orthodox documentaries did not allow. Performance and blocking was so important to Imamura that he could spend all day in rehearsals without shooting anything (Katori 2004: 31). That planning intensifies scenes of power and cruelty in shots of long duration, like the two minutes we spend watching the prostitutes draw blood from a vein and then from a cat. The lack of fill light in long takes of tense confrontations among family members or prostitutes may seem documentary-like, but the carefully positioned top lights tend to outline the main character and allow slight movements to significantly alter the *mise-en-scène*. In a film with an average shot length of 30 seconds, far longer than most contemporary documentaries, the second longest take in the film (after the shot of Karasawa with Nobuko) consists of a newly forceful Tome persuading the other women at the unlicensed brothel to quit the imprisoned madam Suma and allow Tome to run them as a "call girl" ring. Tome's false openness and Miyako's suspicion are indicated not only by their speech but by slight tilts of their heads, up toward the light and down into shadow. The careful construction and stylistic extremity of *The Insect Woman* speaks to Imamura's search for a "different way" of making dramatic films, more avant-garde than contemporary documentary.

Documentary filmmaker and theorist Toshio Matsumoto's manifesto "A Theory of Avant-Garde Documentary" was published in *Kiroku eiga* in 1958 and was edited and republished in his book *Eizō no hakken* in December 1963. Against the self-effacing orthodoxy of "objective" documentary, Matsumoto insisted on the subjectivity (*shutai*) of the filmmaker in an encounter with an active object (*taishō*), different from mere material (*sozai*). He argued that the goal of avant-garde documentary should be a dialectical confrontation between the objective "thing-in-itself-ness of the exterior world" of naturalism and the subjective "thing-in-itself-ness of the interior world" of surrealism, to "grasp the totality of the conflict and the unity between the exterior world and the interior world, aiming for a synthesis of both" (Matsumoto 2012: 150–51). Matsumoto said he met regularly with Imamura in 1963 and praised *The Insect Woman* as the best film of the year, not for its ethnographic portrait of an underrepresented way of life but for its schematic representation of the blocked possibilities of political change in post-Anpo Japan. Matsumoto argues: "Imamura sees in Tome's consciousness, and the conditions of existence that support it, a structure of self-alienation in which the energy that could revolutionize the existing political situation instead, in a negative sense, gives form to the everydayness of the current state of affairs" (Matsumoto 1967: 83–84). Rather than protest, Tome "desires the very things that dominate and exploit her," repeatedly begging Karasawa for a "stability" (*anteisei*) that echoes the leftist critique of post-Anpo Japan as a period of "relative stabilization" (*sōtaiteki anteisei*) under the LDP-led "1955 system" (Curtis 1999: 22). Matsumoto criticized the "naïve naturalism" of Imamura's documentary methods (Matsumoto 1967: 84) but then goes on to argue that Imamura's "documentary-like rejection of sets, pretty lighting, and after-recording" pushes us close to reality in order to dialectically negate it. Imamura "repeatedly breaks the mood of sympathy with the protagonist of the chronicle film through the relatively high number of cold, objective shots, the limitation of movements and pans, the insertion of still frames and photographs, and the attempts to fix the object in an estranging, frozen gaze (*taishō o ikateki ni gyōshi shiyō*)" (Matsumoto 1967: 85). Kanesaka Kenji also highlights disruptive aspects of *The Insect Woman*, such as Mayuzumi Toshiro's modernist music and the use of the high-reverb microphone in some shots, and likens the film to the contemporary "informel" movement in gestural painting: "I don't understand why the film is overwhelmingly seen as realism" (Kanesaka 1964a: 69).

Imamura and Brecht

Imamura famously called himself a "country farmer" in contrast to Oshima's samurai (Bock 1978: 288), but he was less at home in the provinces, and more of an intellectual, than he let on. He was born and raised in Tokyo to an educated upper-middle-class family, and he recalled his brother taking him to the avant-garde little theater *Tsukiji shōgekijō* (Satō 2003: 386). While at Waseda University he was heavily involved in *shingeki* theater, which became the main conduit for introducing Brecht to postwar Japan through Senda Koreya and others. A translation of Brecht's drama theory was published in 1954, and after Brecht's death in 1955 several articles per year on Epic Theatre, *Verfremdung*, and other aspects of his dramaturgy were published in journals that Imamura or his close college friends and *shingeki* actors Shōichi Ozawa and Kazuo Kitamura would have known (Tanigawa and Akiba 1986: 163–87). *Mother Courage* was performed in Kyoto in the mid-1950s, and the top *shingeki* troupe *Haiyūza* performed *The Good Person of Setzuan* in 1960 and *The Threepenny Opera* in 1962. Those major productions were accompanied by a spate of Brecht's easy-to-stage documentary-style *lehrstücke* from smaller companies at the time Imamura was engaged in a production of his *shingeki* play *Paraji* (1962), which contained many of the themes he and Hasebe had first elaborated in the scripts for *Intentions of Murder* and *The Insect Woman* (Iwabuchi 1982: 111–29).

Derived in part from Japanese classical theater, Brecht's Epic Theatre emphasized "clear description and reporting" as well as "choruses and projections as a means of commentary" to disrupt the unthinking emotional identification with the character in dramatic theater and to "portray social processes as seen in their causal relationships" (Brecht 2014: 176). *The Insect Woman* presents a grotesque everyday world in a long-take style with relatively little camera movement, into which it introduces disruptive textual effects, from the sudden inclusion of newsreel footage to freeze frames and voiceovers that, Hasebe Hideo argued, create a gap between "objective" image and "subjective" sound and elicit audience reflection (Hasebe Hideo 1964: 57). There is a diagrammatic quality, too, to the historical newsreels that interrupt Tome's life. The events interrogate Tome's ignorance but also, dialectically, the gap between what progressive intellectuals saw as the major punctuation marks of twentieth-century Japan and the lives of people living at the bottom of that society. Imamura waited days to film the scene at Cathy's grave in order to include the American military airplanes landing, but the relation between foreground and background remains ambiguous (Muramatsu 2003: 88). As Saitō Ryūhō argues, "People talk about the historical events in the film while ignoring land reform, and talk about Tome's disinterest in politics without talking about how politics rejects the participation of people like her" (Saitō 1971: 17).

In a Brechtian frame, the "forceful" (*muriyari*) aspect of Imamura's "I tend to want to forcefully marry the problem of the lower half of the human body with the lower level of Japanese culture that stubbornly churns out everyday life" comes to the fore as a mark of the active, subjective engagement with the material world that Matsumoto championed. The "just as it is" (*jojiteki*) of Imamura's description of the scenario as "something presented 'just as it is' . . . a flat scenario, just facts and conclusions lined up in a row" seems less straightforward when we consider that Brecht's Epic Theatre, with its "clear description and reporting," is known in Japanese as *jojiteki engeki*. And Matsumoto's claim that the film's project is to "fix the object in an estranging (*ikateki*), frozen gaze" is a direct reference to *ikateki kōka*, the Japanese translation of Brecht's *Verfremdung* (cognitive estrangement). In a sense, *The Insect Woman* is a remake of Brecht's *Mother Courage*. As Kanesaka Kenji points out, circularity and repetition structure the film: like Mother Courage, "Tome learns along the way to be an exploiter but in the end is back at square one" (Kanesaka 1964b: 38).

Matsumoto criticized Imamura for putting "a lot of weight on realistic (*hakushinteki*) acting" because "he cannot overcome his faith in realisticness (*shinjitsurashisa*)" (Matsumoto 1967: 85). Though deglamourized, without makeup and spotlights, perhaps realism is not the best description of Sachiko Hidari's tour-de-force performance, and Imamura's relationship with his actors was more contentious than Matsumoto allows. There is something gestural about Imamura's realism, from the funny accents of his theater actors to the typage of dancer-turned-actress Harukawa Masumi (Midori), whose stage nickname was "daruma-chan," after the rotund doll. Katori Shunsuke claims that Imamura chose Sachiko Hidari over Junko Ikeuchi and Kyōko Kishida for her earthiness but also, astonishingly, that he had asked superstar Hibari Misora to play the lead, which would have produced a completely different film (Katori 2004: 176, 183). Although reviews of *The Insect Woman* praised Hidari's acting as "superb," critics were divided on whether Imamura identified with Tome, sympathetically or as self-critique (Ogawa 1965: 152; Katori 2004: 66; Kanesaka 1964b: 41). According to Hidari, Imamura despaired of her performance, claiming that he wanted her to play a "four-sided" role but she insisted on playing it in a "three-sided" way (Muramatsu 2003: 81). The director would bully the pregnant Hidari on the set, promising that the infamous breast-sucking scene would be done quickly and then insisting on multiple takes, or pulling open her legs for the gynecological examination that Tome undergoes. Although Hidari shared the "anger" of Imamura's postwar generation, she also regarded him as a male chauvinist (Muramatsu 2003: 86). Hidari saw herself in Tome, a rural woman with similar wartime experiences (Muramatsu 2003: 81), but the film reveals a tension between identification and alienation. Hidari's powerful performance shifts rapidly from innocent to submissive to exploitative and then resigned, each tone layered with moments of absurdity. Brecht's "cognitive estrangement" (*Verfremdung*), "a technique of taking the human social incidents to be portrayed and labelling them as something striking, something that calls for explanation" (Brecht 2014: 180), informs repeated scenes of Tome's unrequited sexual desire that leads her to eavesdrop on Midori and roll on her bed, or the orality of sucking and tasting that is such a prominent feature of the film. In short, Imamura acted like a bully and a pervert to draw out the contradictions in Tome's situation: perhaps, like Brecht and Mother Courage, it was not Imamura who empathized with Tome but Sachiko Hidari, or her audience.

Imamura eclipsed Oshima as the representative New Wave filmmaker in the early 1960s. Even before French critics praised *The Insect Woman* for its

"Brechtian" qualities at the Berlin Film Festival in 1964 (Yamada 1994: 1532), Sekine Hiroshi had called the newsreel footage in the film historical "shocks" that interrogate Tome's *shomin* consciousness, and compared it to the "detached representation" (*tsukihanashita byōsha*) of the film that brought Brecht's ideas into cinema—Godard's Vivre sa vie (1962, released in Japan three days after *The Insect Woman*, in November 1963) (Sekine 1964: 29; Thompson and Bordwell 2009: 521). That same year, Izawa Jun enumerated three postwar generations of Japanese filmmakers, headed by Akira Kurosawa, Kon Ichikawa, and Shohei Imamura (Izawa 1964: 24). *The Insect Woman* was voted best film of the year by critics at the mainstream journal *Kinema junpō* and at the more vanguard *Eiga hyōron*, which gave top place to each of Imamura's films from 1961 to 1968 (Satō and Kishikawa 2003: 824–32). In Katori Shunsuke's words, "Students in the 1960s would no more miss a new Oshima or Imamura film than they would skip reading Sartre or Dostoyevsky" (Katori 2004: 63). To complete the circle, when Godard came to Japan in 1966, he named Hani and Imamura as filmmakers engaged in similar projects, and praised *The Insect Woman* when it was screened for him (Shibata and Shirai 1994: 1643).

Conclusion

The turn to indigenous (*dochaku*) culture in early 1960s Japan was a symptom of high economic growth. While conservatives increasingly trumpeted Japan's cultural difference, anti-capitalist intellectuals struggling with a post-Anpo sense of defeat (*zasetsukan*) employed those local resources to "overcome modernity using the premodern as a negative mediation" (*zenkindai o hiteiteki baikai to shite no kindai no chōkoku*) (Hasebe and Satō 2003: 622; Tsurumi 2008: 175). Artists also looked to Brecht and other theorists for ways to break the fetters of a naturalism that quickly became a chronicle of despair (Goodman 2001: 350). *The Insect Woman* is caught between a rationalist, ethnographic view of Japanese underdevelopment and those dark forces that animated the avant-garde. Toshio Matsumoto recognized Tome as a woman whose "*shomin*-like indigenous lifestyle consciousness (*dochakuteki na seikatsu ishiki*) is ingrained in her body" such that she is motivated by an "instinctual logic of eat, do, sleep; she thinks only of what is directly in front of her" (Matsumoto 1967: 84). Tsumura Hideo objects to the gratuitous scene of Tome pausing to urinate in a mulberry field as her father lies dying, but for Imamaura this *shomin* is not simply the warm-hearted communitarian of more conventional films but an outcast (*senmin*), or even an animal (Tsumura 1963: 11). That grotesquery, and the artificiality of its representation—the field was planted for the film, with a farmhouse drawn on sheets of paper, in order that Imamura could include the mountain range in

Figure 7.6 Tome urinates in a mulberry field. Imamura had the field planted, and one of the farmhouses drawn on paper, so that he could get this shot against the mountain range.

the shot—estranges this depiction of "what it means to be Japanese" (Iwamoto 2001: 181; *Asahi shinbun* 1963a: 9).

Imamura's treatment of regional, ethnic, and sexual difference raises questions about his role in representing marginalized Japan. Mockery is not far from the surface of the film, which played to predominantly male audiences in Nikkatsu cinemas, nor of a 1960s criticism that reveled in descriptions of sexual and other transgressions. Nevertheless, some critics were sensitive to Imamura's balance of sympathy and critique. Kanesaka Kenji argues that female characters are sexually humiliated again and again in Imamura's films, but he sees the women's ability to endure their own humiliation not as a weakness but as a strength greater than men's (Kanesaka 1964b: 41–42). That "female art of failure," characterized by exploitation and illegitimacy but also endurance, distinguishes *The Insect Woman* from typical Japanese melodramas. The film's sexualized imagery and grotesque comedy, presented in the mixed modes of contemporary art cinema, with hints from avant-garde forms of documentary and theatre, put into question both a narrative of economic and political modernization and a conservative nostalgia for indigenous Japan.

In 1964, in an astonishing metaphor Matsukawa Yasuo likened *The Insect Woman*'s still images to the photographs in albums of ancestors that brides brought with them when they married in Japan's patriarchal family system, albums that spread across Japan like "fungus" or "phlegm," or an "atomic cloud" that "wraps us up, protecting us from all suffering" (Matsukawa 1964: 30). He writes that he had always enjoyed those photographs, but after seeing *The*

Insect Woman his ancestors in the albums seemed like "bunraku puppets with mouths split from ear to ear" (30). In Imamura's Brechtian critique, Japanese modernization, and the patriarchal family system that supports it, is cognitively estranged from the Japanese audience:

> When this female lineage of mother and daughter is superimposed on the genealogy of the family (*ie*) the inhumanity of that family system is manifested, and when it is superimposed on May Day and Anpo, for example, the extraordinary flimsiness of the history of Japan constructed by men is cast in a different light. Men, excluded from this female lineage, exhibit a dispirited and sorry pose.

Rather than Satō's masterpiece of "naturalist realism," Matsukawa argued precisely the opposite, praising *The Insect Woman* as a "wonderful abstract film—perhaps the first in a Japanese cinema obsessed with naturalism (*shizenshugi banzai*)" (Matsukawa 1964: 31). The film established Imamura as the leading light of new Japanese cinema in the mid-1960s, but its abstractions paled before the disjunctive political modernism of the "hard to understand" (*nankai*) films of the "art theatre tribe" shown at ATG cinemas from 1968 (Kurahashi 1971: 37). Hasebe and Imamura's script won a prize in a 1962 anthology of best scenarios, but in 1967 Toshio Matsumoto mocked Imamura's *A Man Vanishes* and criticized the clear structure of his films, claiming that their linkages are "strikingly rationalist. All the images link to the total meaning, with no waste . . . We should turn to what till now seemed wasteful: the untaken subject, the discarded film, the connection that doesn't connect" (Matsumoto 1967: 100). Displaced from the cutting edge of the Japanese New Wave, critics (and Imamura) fell back on an undialectical sense of *The Insect Woman's* representation of indigenous Japanese culture. Yet on its release the film was most perspicuously praised not for its nativist nostalgia but for its negative dialectic that questioned the society of high economic growth. As Kanesaka Kenji put it, "In this age in which we are surrounded by a new culture based on the control of objects, Imamura's primitive society based on a vision of the gods is the strongest resistance we have" (Kanesaka 1964b: 45).

Works Cited

Asahi Shimbun (1963a). "Ijō na onna o egaku." *Asahi Shimbun*, May 12.
Asahi Shimbun (1963b). "Nippon konchūki roke susumu: Jibun katte ni ikiru onna: honmono no 'kichi no onna' no ie de satsuei." *Asahi Shimbun*, September 14.
Bakhtin, Mikhail (1984). *Rabelais and His World*. Bloomington: Indiana University Press.

Bock, Audie (1978). *Japanese Film Directors*. New York: Kodansha.
Brecht, Bertolt (2014). "The Street Scene: A Basic Model for an Epic Theatre." *Brecht on Theatre*. 3rd ed.) London: Methuen.
Curtis, Gerald (1999). *The Logic of Japanese Politics*. New York: Columbia University Press.
Endo Tatsuo (1973). *Eirin: rekishi to jiken*. Tokyo: Perikansha.
Furuhata, Yuriko (2013). *Cinema of Actuality: Japanese Avant-Garde Filmmaking in the Season of Image Politics*. Durham, NC: Duke University Press.
Goodman, David (2001). "Concerned Theatre Japan Thirty Years Later: A Personal Account." In *Japanese Theatre and the International Stage*, ed. Stanca Scholz-Cionca and Samuel L. Leiter, 343–56. Leiden: Brill.
Hasebe Hideo (1964). "Imamura Shōhei." *Eiga hyōron*. September.
Hasebe Hideo and Satō Jushin (2003). "Imahei densetsu o kiru: Imamura Shōhei no giwakujutsu." In *Eiga hyōron no jidai*, ed. Satō Tadao and Kishikawa Shin. Tokyo: Katarogu hausu.
Hasebe Keiji and Imamura Shōhei (1963). "Chōsa to fikkushon." *Terebi dorama*. May.
Hashimoto, Mitsuru (1998). "Chiho: Yanagita Kunio's 'Japan.'" *Mirror of Modernity: Invented Traditions of Modern Japan*, ed. Stephen Vlastos. Berkeley: University of California Press.
Imamura Shōhei (1994). "Jisaku o kataru." In *Besuto obu Kinema junpō, 1950–1966*. Tokyo: Kinema junpōsha.
Imamura Shōhei (2001). *Toru*. Tokyo: Kōsakusha.
Imamura Shōhei (2004). *Eiga wa kyōki no tabi de aru*. Tokyo: Nihon keizai shinbunsha.
Ishido Toshiro (1971). "Watashi tachi wa doshitsu ka ishitsu ka: Bergman=Imamura 'kakū' taidan." In *Gendai Nihon eigaron taikei*, vol. 4, ed. Ogawa Tōru et al. Tokyo: Tōjusha.
Iwabuchi, Tatsuji (1982). "Brecht Reception in Japan: The Perspective of Theatrical Practice." In *Brecht and East Asian Theatre: The Proceedings of a Conference on Brecht in East Asian Theatre*, ed. Anthony Tatlow and Tak-Wai Wong. Hong Kong: Hong Kong University Press.
Iwamoto Kenji et al., eds. (2001). *Eiga bijutsu ni kaketa otoko*. Tokyo: Sōshisha.
Iwasaki Akira (2003). *Eiga wa sukueru ka*. Tokyo: Sakuhinsha.
Izawa Jun, et al. (1994). "Nihon eiga keiei kaizō." *Besuto obu Kinema junpō, 1950–1966*. Tokyo: Kinema junpōsha.
Izawa Jun (1964). "Sengo Nihon eiga sannin no kantoku." *Kinema junpō*, October.
Kanesaka Kenji (1964a). "Eiga sakka to Nihon dasshutsu: Ichikawa, Kurahara, Teshigawara, Imamura no baai." *Eiga geijutsu*, April.
Kanesaka Kenji (1964b). "Imamura Shōhei ron." *Eiga Hyōron*, September.
Katori Shunsuke (2004). *Imamura Shōhei densetsu*. Tokyo: Kawade shobō shinsha.
Klinger, Barbara (1994). "'Local' Genres: The Hollywood Adult Film in the 1950s." In *Melodrama: Stage Picture Screen*, ed. J. S. Bratton, Jim Cook, and Christine Gledhill, London: BFI.
Masumura Yasuzō (1999). "Eiga hihyōka to wa nani ka." In *Masumura Yasuzo no sekai*, ed. Fujii Hiroaki. Tokyo: Waizu shuppan.

Matsukawa Yasuo (1964). "*Nippon konchūki* ni tsuite no danseiteki hansei." *Kiroku eiga*, January.
Matsumoto Toshio (1967). "Honnō to gaikai no setten." *Hyōgen no Sekai*. Tokyo: San'ichi shobō.
Matsumoto Toshio (2012). "A Theory of Avant-Garde Documentary." Trans. Michael Raine. *Cinema Journal* 51, no. 4: 148–54.
Matsushita Keiichi (1971). "*Nippon konchūki* to Nihon seiji." In *Gendai Nihon eigaron taikei* vol. 4, ed. Ogawa Tōru et al. Tokyo: Tōjusha.
Mihalopoulos, Bill (2008). "Becoming Insects: Imamura Shōhei and the Entomology of Modernity." In *The Power of Memory in Modern Japan*, ed. Sven Saaler and Wolfgang Schwentker, 277–90. Folkestone: Brill.
Mizutani Kenji (1977). *Eiga kantoku Gosho Heinosuke*. Tokyo: Nagata shobō.
Muramatsu Tomomi (2003). *Imahei hankachō: Imamura Shōhei to wa nani ka*. Tokyo: Nihon hōsō shuppan kyōkai.
Ogawa Tōru (1965). "Ura kara yonda *Akai satsui* ron: Imamura Shōhei no shisō." *Gendai Nihon sakka ron*. Tokyo: San'ichi shobō.
Saitō Ryūhō (1971). "Boku no *Nippon konchuki* ron'*Gendai Nihon eigaron taikei*." Vol. 4, ed. Ogawa Tōru et al. Tokyo: Tōjusha.
Satō Tadao (1970). *Nihon eiga shisō shi*. Tokyo: San'ichi shobō.
Satō Tadao (1980). *Imamura Shōhei no sekai*. Expanded ed. Tokyo: Gakuyō shobō.
Satō Tadao (2003). *Waga eiga hihyō no gojūnen: Satō Tadao hyōronsen*. Tokyo: Heibonsha.
Sekikawa Natsuo (2002). *Shōwa ga akurakatta koro*. Tokyo: Bungei shunjū.
Sekine Hiroshi (1964). "Umarekawaru jōkyō: Imamura Shōhei sakuhin o mite." *Kiroku eiga*, January.
Shibata Hayao and Shirai Yoshio (1994). "Godāru kantoku no Nihon no tōkakan." *Besuto obu Kinema junpō, 1950–1966*. Tokyo: Kinema junpōsha.
Shimizu Masashi (2001). *Imamura Shōhei o yomu: bosei to kaosu no bigaku*. Tokyo: Chōeisha.
Shioda Nagakazu (1992). *Nihon eiga gojūnenshi*. Tokyo: Fujiwara shoten.
Sugiyama Heiichi (1971). "Imamura Shōhei ron." *Sekai no eiga sakka 8: Imamura Shōhei*, Tokyo: Kinema junpōsha.
Tahara Katsuhiro (1977). *Nihon eiga no ronri*. Tokyo: San'ichi shobō.
Takano Etsuko, ed. (1979). *Eiga de miru Nihon bungakushi*. Tokyo: Iwanami Hōru.
Tanigawa Michiko, and Akiba Yusuke (1986). "Nihon ni okeru Berutoruto Burehito no juyō 2." *Doitsu bungaku* 76.
Tessier, Max (1997). "Shōhei Imamura Interview." In *Imamura Shōhei*. ed. James Quandt, 1–6. Toronto: Toronto International Film Festival Group.
Thompson, Kristin, and David Bordwell (2009). *Film History: An Introduction*. New York: McGraw-Hill.
Tsumura Hideo (1963). "*Nippon konchūki* no mondai: shakaiteki setsudo ushinau." *Asahi shinbun*. December 15.
Tsurumi, Patricia (1992). *Factory Girls: Women in the Thread Mills of Meiji Japan*. Princeton, NJ: Princeton University Press.
Tsurumi Tarō (2008). *Yanagita Kunio nyūmon*. Tokyo: Kadokawa gakugei shuppan.

Yamada Kōichi (1994). "Furansu eiga no shin'ei to Nihon eiga." *Besuto obu Kinema junpō, 1950–1966.* Tokyo: Kinema junpōsha.

Yamane Sadao (1992). *Masumura Yasuzō: Ishi to shite no eros.* Tokyo: Chikuma shobō.

Yasumi Toshio, et al. (1964). "Ima koso bōken no jidai! Shinario raitā wa hatsugen suru." *Kinema junpō,* October.

Yoshimoto, Takaaki (2006). "The End of a Fictitious System." *Sources of Japanese Tradition, Abridged: Part 2: 1868–2000.* New York: Columbia University Press.

Chapter 8

The Obscene in the Everyday: *The Pornographers*

Lindsay Coleman

Shohei Imamura's fascination with the abject, social undesirables and with taboo relationships permeates much of his work. Even what is arguably one of his warmer, more sentimental narratives, *The Eel*, features as its central character a mournful cuckold and killer. When he fully embraces the darker side of life, as in *Vengeance Is Mine*, Imamura is pitiless, unflinching, incisive in both his imagery and characterizations. What audience could forget the sight of the serial killer Iwao Enokizu urinating on his hands to wash off the blood of his latest victim? This casual moment in the film, free of editorial or cinematographic accent, shot in a wide master, is emblematic of Imamura's gift for a style both shocking and unflinching in its clear-eyed observation of life's true misfits and its painful or transcendent moments. Of necessity, such a style, observational in its willingness to capture or convey the layered psychic and social influences on a scene, is atypical when compared to many of the norms of cinema. Imamura depicts the actor Ken Ogata head to toe, full frame. He crosses the frame harried, adrenalized. He notices his hands, sees the blood, makes a split-second decision. He removes his penis from his trousers, urinates a quick stream to rinse his hands, then crosses offscreen left. There is no insert from his point of view, no Hitchcockian realization of the incriminating blood. Rather, there is the human animal in the foreground, the nondescript, unmoved Japanese countryside in the background. Ogata's physicality is the scene's central focus, but also Imamura's choice to film at a remove, to frame this addled killer in a nondescript space, is central to his message. Enokizu's murder of his fellow tobacco company employee finds meaning in its social moment, in the fact that this conman has been forced to execute a peer who like him occupies the periphery of Japanese society. The observation of the killer, in his context, the style of its presentation, is central to Imamura's thesis.

The shocking scene described in *Vengeance Is Mine* is symptomatic of Imamura's approach. However, while that film is radical in its structure and timeline, it lacks the wild stylistic flourishes of his earlier film *The Pornographers*, perhaps a more indicative work of Imamura's stylistic range. The marginalized context of the characters could not be clearer. This film offers up a compelling portrait of Japanese society as permissive, profligate, and absurdly commercialized. Characters are poor, with few options, in work or in love. The low-rent, industrialized processes of the film's title characters, all in an effort to feed the never-ending appetite for pornographic content, speak to such qualities within a society. In turn, they create a thematic filter wherein sentiment, desire, ardor, and passion are all calibrated by the invasive presence of smut. However, paradoxically, sexuality and sexual desire are presented not as commodified in the film, but rather as a shocking, and ungovernable, quantity. Their presence within the narrative triggers, conversely, the bemusement of the film's protagonists and an increasing stylistic incisiveness on the part of Imamura himself in his role as director. This chapter analyzes the means, via lighting, editing, composition, and the sequence of scenes, by which Imamura established a unique directorial approach to allow for the interrogation of taboos such as incest, sexual attraction toward minors, and indeed the manner in which sexuality may pervade a wide range of social and economic activities. For this approach to be better understood, contextual writing on pornography in modern society is analyzed. To further understand how a precision in style allows for the exhaustive sociological analysis to which Imamura aspires, the chapter also analogizes the work of Imamura to that of another famed observer of society, the novelist Marcel Proust. Both seek to place his varied subjects beneath an inquisitive stylistic lens that is expository, analytical, and observational. In doing so Imamura may engage more fulsomely with the specifics of the social moment of his subjects, the immediate context that defines their thoughts, emotions, and responses as human animals, very much like the cinematic observations of a naturalist of human beings. This is, finally, contrasted with filmmakers detailing similar scenarios, specifically Sam Mendes and Alfred Hitchcock. The ultimate purpose of this chapter is to place Imamura's stylistic and narrative ambitions within a broader cinematic and novelistic tradition, wherein through style the author of the work aspires to the status of social scientist as much as storyteller.

Shohei Imamura is a self-designated naturalist of those upon the margins. He shies from no taboo interaction, no forbidden word or moment of human impulse, be it judged evil or pure. His characters are murderers, cuckolds, serial killers, prostitutes, low-rent criminals, and rapists. They may also be victims, wives, landladies, callow youths, or brusque everymen. Intriguingly, in this respect he resembles a grand novelist in the nineteenth-century tradition, prizing his God's eye view, and in so doing designating himself an ironic moralist. In one interview, Imamura declared that he considered human beings and animals similar, and his work was about attempting to make the distinction: "I ask myself what differentiates humans from other animals. What is a human being? I look for the answer by continuing to make films" (Laprevotte). Indeed, there we could trace a consistent inclination to drawing parallels between animals and humans throughout his filmography, which always implies more than a visual metaphor and a moral analogy.

In our present cultural moment this may be more difficult to easily appreciate. We live in the era of reality television where a constant stream of images of all levels of social interaction fills our viewing hours. We have become accustomed to viewing the human animal in every kind of social setting. We can watch the British Royal family go about their codified social duties or marvel at the shamelessness of the *nouveau riche* in the *Real Housewives* franchise. We may access almost any social scenario, from the upper class at leisure to prostitutes selling their wares. The notion of watching for the purpose of vicarious thrills, as extracted from documentary, reality television, and narrative film, has traveled beyond cliché. However, Imamura's impulse was distinct from this. First, his oeuvre evolved during a period in which such content was scandalous at best, banned at worst. Second, shock value and the documentation of life, not titillation, were Imamura's stated aims. He sought, like a journalist imbedded in a war zone, to depict the marginalized and lower classes from their own perspective. To what was this in aid? Other than a narrative and thematic egalitarianism, Imamura strongly believed in the need for a comprehensive cataloguing of the psychic, physical, and sexual realities of the underclass. To do this he sought as complete an absorption of their paradigm as might narrative cinema permit, and in turn his documentary work complemented that which would not easily fit the more rigid dramaturgy of his theatrical features. If, in short, there were the commercial cinematic equivalent of a social scientist in mid-century Japanese cinema, Imamura was that man.

An easy analogy to this enterprise would be the work of the great early twentieth-century novelist Marcel Proust, whose great project was cataloguing life in late nineteenth- and early twentieth-century Paris. Proust believed in the possibility of art and style to capture the dynamics that fueled a given social moment. Proust was a master technician as a writer, as capable of exploring the psychologies of the French upper class as was Imamura capable of analyzing the Japanese underclass. His immersion in characterization was so great that he could transcend his own psychology through his work, taking objectivity to its most reasonable extreme. Sections of his book explore the antisemitic views of his elite class in French society during the late nineteenth century, specifically in relation to the Dreyfus Affair. A tortured court case surrounding the wrongful conviction of a Jewish soldier, and the scandal revealed deep antisemitism in elite French society. Ironically, Proust himself was Jewish, yet he articulates the whims and prejudices of his class without obvious bias or moralistic comment. In doing so, he engaged with the issues of his time in a manner in which it appeared that partisan issues had themselves hijacked his narratives. In *The Guermantes Way*, the Dreyfus Affair, a major scandal of the Third Republic of France, courses through the novel. Effectively, the discourse, the voice of said aristocrats, came in the mind of his readers and friends to dominate the work, taking on its own life separate from Proust's pro-Dreyfus stance as a Jewish man. The manner in which Proust achieved this supposed position was by design, however. Proust was able to use his stylistic gifts to place his characters in a world seemingly unimpeded by his own editorializing, a world that made explicit their sexual, ethical, and emotional peccadillos. During the years of the Dreyfus controversies Proust sought to develop himself as an artist by turning his literary gifts, previously focusing primarily on his own psyche, and that of his narrator, to the larger issues animating the society, of which the Dreyfus Affair exemplified so many. He honed his

> sense of observation and his literary craftsmanship ... detecting nuances of approbation or approval, undulations in social status, discreet or open barbs and witticisms, double entendres, tacit boundaries of acceptable social behaviour and hints of illicit behaviour, the spectacle of "polite" conversation as a battle field—in other words, elements essential to his distinctive style. (Ebert 1993: 199)

By passing through this era, effectively as a pure observer and cataloguer of his times, Proust created a record of sufficient objectivity to be regarded a vital social document for future generations. He had painted "the immense and detailed fresco of the social life of France of his time that became his great contribution to literature and to history" (Ebert 1993: 199).

Proust's narrator, Marcel, observes the social phenomena of his society as might a naturalist. While Proust himself catalogued the ethical and moral quirks and hypocrisies of his society, he did the same for its sexual life. The playwright Samuel Beckett notes of Proust's writing of homosexuals: "This preoccupation accompanies very naturally his complete indifference to moral values and human justices. Flower and plant have no conscious will. They are shameless" (Bloom 1987: 34). As such, in describing humans in a manner allusive to plants, Beckett observes, Proust may attain the status of a naturalist, collecting and classifying the behavior of his human subjects as he might a creature or plant, exempt of a moralizing stance. The narrator is sensitive, perceptive, and ultimately a great confidante and chronicler of the experience of what was known in Proust's period as "inversion" (Ellis 2004: 1). Through Beckett's likening the homosexual to a plant in Proust's writing, a style is created that legitimately seeks to explain the experience of the homosexual from a supra-social position. Rather than being repulsed or unnerved by homosexual behavior, as might have been the social conditioning of the period, he instead responds with dispassionate analysis.

To review, then: in the search for balance, Proust the writer/artist hopes to evoke the spiritual struggles of the individual and those of the outer society. What this may inevitably lead to is the taboo, the point at which the individual struggles against society's barriers. By applying no self-censorship, either political, moral, or sexual, Proust inevitably revealed a society whose upper echelon frequently engaged in covert sexuality, closeted bigotry, and willful character assassination. In the case of Proust this is found in his observations of "inversion" and antisemitism in the seemingly cosmopolitan salons of Paris (Ellis 2004, 1). Proust likewise affected a studied neutrality and was thus enabled to catch a greater glimpse of the heart of human nature than might an ordinary person. As with his observations of inversion, rooted in his naturalist persona, he attempts to observe, with a scientist's method, and indeed scientific language, the passions and quirks of behavior he sees in those around him. In short, he hopes to find a connection between elements of intuition, natural human behavior, and scientific method. He apprehends his subjects' psychology, engages in rigorous observation, and follows scientific, seemingly objective, criteria in documenting their behavior, exempt of the usual social niceties; or, if inclusive of such niceties, he is always eager to contextualize them in the broader scope of the individual's daily activities, good or ill as judged by the larger society. In doing so it is hoped that he will, through unexpected connections, provide some greater and intuitive insight on the nature of the phenomena he encounters (Kristeva 1993: 290). To do this he, as both writer and through his narrator, affects an opaque, ambivalent persona whose true motives, and indeed identity, are unclear to those he encounters in social interactions. He is, in short, much like a detached naturalist, exploring humanity as though it were some alien species, and he its detached cataloguer (Bloom 1987: 34).

An example of how Proust utilizes style, in the form of thematic analogy, and the precision of his characterization, to examine the taboo might be found in the manner in which his work analogizes the bigoted belief in his society that the act of being a homosexual passing as a heterosexual is equivalent to being a Jew passing as a gentile. Large descriptions are found of the manner in which a Jew might hope to pass as "normal," just as might a homosexual:

> Marcel also wishes to claim that Dreyfusism is easier to conceal than inversion, which, in Charlus's case, is evident despite his considerable efforts to hide it. Marcel asserts that the signs of Charlus's effeminacy emerge directly and, as it were, irresistibly from the secret of his homosexuality, whereas the secret of one's political opinions may, in his view, be kept concealed. (Carlston 2002)

Proust's willing analogy, one formed on the subject of the twin taboos of Jewishness and homosexuality, effectively allows his narrator to look longer, and more intently, than decorum would seem to permit, at the tiny quirks of behavior that reveal the social stain—by the standards of his era—which these conditions represent.

What these elements in the construction of Proust's masterwork *In Search of Lost Time* represent are complex shifts in perspective and in the narrative framing of events. While Proust himself rejected the notion that his writing found an easy corollary with the cinema, it is arguable that this focus on perspective and the framing of events and characters from a complex authorial perspective is a method that fits comparison to the similarly anthropological and naturalist designs of Imamura.

Imamura's style in *The Pornographers* is visual rather than novelistic, but his unusual framing choices, counterintuitive uses of screen space and blocking, radical point-of-view shots, and master shots create a world in which the behavior of his characters may be more easily scrutinized. To process the film's visual storytelling involves navigating this unusual style, one sufficiently striking that it forces the viewer to watch more intently in order to appreciate fully what the film is revealing. Equally, the narrative focus on pornography, in its production, consumption, and influence on sexual and social attitudes, gives permission to look for longer than propriety might permit. In fact, more than to look, the film gives permission to actually study.

Imamura, too, is an anthropologist, a naturalist, both cataloguing Japaneseness and reducing his subjects to the human animals they are, transfixed like experimental subjects through his stylistic gifts of framing, lighting, editing, and eliciting performances entirely sui generis to Imamura's sociological and narrative milieu. In preparing for his films, Imamura does extensive anthropological research. Imamura "wants to engage in filmmaking itself as an instance of anthropological research" (Quandt 1997: 96). Hence morality does not censor or intervene in his aestheticizing of human experience. Imamura is neither an exploiter of smut nor a high moralist. All acts are observed and catalogued, no detail too graphic to prompt his recusing himself. When they are captured, however, Imamura's editing choices, and framing, are key to the explicit nature of the scene being thematic rather than visually effusive. Imamura does not shy away from the profession of his title characters, the film populated with their shooting, watching, and editing their work—pornography—often speaking in direct terms of the money they will make, colleagues too jaded in their cynical cash grabs to pretend their work is anything other than pure commerce. Equally, Imamura's choice to focus on the behind-the-scenes nature of the film is explicit from the start, the men loading multiple cameras—so they can get multiple copies of the same sex act—in the first scene's foreground, while bored adult performers lounge in the background. Very much like the nondescript country setting of *Vengeance Is Mine*, so key to the context of the frazzled killer in the foreground, here the urgent loading of film is the director's focus, and with it his explicit intent to frame his thesis: These pornographers may be men on the margins, but they are the most willing flesh-peddlers, turning every frame of their creations into a stream of money. No cameras, no sex, no pay. The performers, and the nondescript, urban park setting, are the essential context that allows for Imamura's expert observation. This may be nothing more than a porn shoot, but the protagonists of the film are as serious and driven as they might possibly be in their professions. This carried over into Imamura's editorial choices, framing the men's reaction shots to the porn loops they have assembled, their concentration and professionalism the ironic focus of the scene. Yet, once again, context is everything, and through these loop-cutting scenes the audience is persistently reminded, through the dialogue and sound of the projector, that the men are pornographers watching their creations. Yet, like any good naturalist, Imamura treats this as not a behavior to be ashamed of, but one of a number of activities the men engage in.

But, the question must be asked, is this really so significant? Is Imamura's act of editorially making the focus of the first scene on the point of view of the pornographers, his favoring the worker bees of the scene, such an unusual departure? Yes. Godard's famous saying that all that is needed for cinema is a girl and a gun is essentially disavowed, as Imamura is stating that the act of the making of the film, the balance of commerce, personality, technology, and the grinding reality of logistics, is what his camera and cutting focus on. The "girl" in this case, the presumably attractive adult performers, seen in the background as a slender, youthful woman and a tall, athletic young man, is to Imamura the context wherein these more pressing concerns are brought into literal focus, with them in turn relegated to the contextualizing frame of the business at hand.

The visual metaphor established, that of the business of the shooting of sex in the background, the harried producers of the pornography in the foreground, allows us to take the necessary steps to conceive of the place of pornography in the 1960s of Japan. In the pornified era in which we live it is difficult to conceive of the status of pornography through much of the twentieth century. In a world where males peek at hardcore sex scenes on their iPhones while on public transport, or perhaps on their computers at work, only shielded by their cubicles, the notion of pornography as a subset of prostitution seems bizarre. But indeed it was, and Imamura's *The Pornographers* is the depiction of a man who is both a pornographer and a pimp. Imamura's naturalist eye allowed him, in the mid-1960s, to survey this and other burgeoning taboo trends in modern, urban, postwar Japan. But other than it being an expression of his willingness to reduce humans to anthropological/naturalist specimens, the inevitable question would become "Why pornography?"

What is most surprising about the debates that surround pornography is how much the various sides agree upon. Pornography is banal, predictable, convoluted, and fundamentally impoverished intellectually. By and large it requires little talent, as many of the performers themselves admit. The goal of pornography is to temporarily relieve the consumer of the pornography of their sexual desire. The desire will return, and with it the need to consume even more. Catharine MacKinnon's definition of pornography, that as a discourse it is invested in the exploitation of women and depictions of violence against women, certainly holds true for much of the content found. She goes so far as to state that the roots of this mistreatment, of which pornography is symptomatic, are found in the patriarchal nature of our society:

> Women and men are divided by gender, made into the sexes as we know them, by the requirements of its dominant form, heterosexuality, which institutionalizes male sexual dominance and female sexual submission. If this is true, sexuality is the linchpin of gender inequality. (1989)

This is certainly a dominant feature of many of Imamura's films, and *The Pornographers* is no exception. Caught in the glare of male entitlement, Imamura's females suffer sexually, but do so with a knowingness of the give-and-take of sexual politics and dominance that never allows them to become true victims. The very notion of sexual congress, and its depiction, effectively places women in a position of subservience. Gail Dines reinforces this idea, in turn repudiating the idea that any other interpretation of pornography's role or influence other than to reinforce white male hegemony is moot. "While [pro-sex] research sheds light on the various sectors of the industry, it cannot stand in for a critical macro-level approach that explores how capitalism, patriarchy, racism and first-world economic domination provides the economic and cultural space for international, mass-scale pornography production" (1998: 62). This in turn is very much in line with Imamura's chosen depiction of the business of the film's title characters. Men who compulsively objectify women, in both their business and private lives, are adept pornographers because the mechanism of its production is a simple extension of their patriarchal psyches. Yet, to stop there would be to undersell the extent of Imamura's inquiry. Sexual desire is a crucible the men must endure, their facility with their own libidos eventually enslaving them, like masturbating primates fascinated by their own genitals. In short, the experience of capturing the production of pornography gives Imamura not only access to the sexual selves of his characters, but also to their primal psyches.

Such a notion is not unprecedented. Marxist critiques on gender have long maintained that the study of an individual's sexual practices and peccadillos will also lead to the heart of their political identity:

> In spite of the elaborate discourses and analyses devoted to it, and the continual stress on its centrality to human reality, this modern concept of sexuality remains difficult to define ... what the ideologists of sexuality describe, in fact, are only the supposed spheres of its operation: gender, reproduction, the family, and socialization; love and intercourse. (Parker and Aggleton 2007: 18)

Collectively, these define sexuality's place in society and, in turn, clearly describe a vast array of components of our modern life. Imamura's cinema is of course concerned with this broadly and expressly. "Imamura shows how people relate to their surroundings, how they relate to the other ... to desire ... In doing so he reveals a chain of connections, a series of links, between human beings and things within or beyond their grasp" (Quandt 1997: cx). In the case of *The Pornographers*, this concern allows for a stylistic and thematic focus on the minutiae of life, simultaneously a panopticon generated through the unique lens of the enveloping, biological paradigm pornography addresses, the need to procreate and copulate.

Imamura told critic Koichi Yamada that he was most interested "in the relationship of the lower part of the human body and the lower part of the social structure" because this is where "the reality of daily Japanese life supports itself." (Richie 1997: 17). Just as the genitals are the basis of the person, so the "lower classes" are the makers of the nation. And, as the genitals and their functions are hidden, so are these classes of society ignored. This represents the social, economic location of the narrative of Imamura's film. Adapted in 1966 from Akiyuki Nozaka's prizewinning bestseller, the film *The Pornographers* is set in Osaka. The central figure is Subuyan Ogata, a producer/distributor of 8-mm porn films. Ogata believes that he and his fellow pornographers perform a useful social function: to provide solace for the lonely. It is also worth noting that he is a part-time pimp. In creating a central narrative figure with few inhibitions, and a taste for the transgressive, it makes thematic and narrative sense that Ogata enjoy a vivid, unconventional sex life and sexual fantasies. The maestro—as he is pretentiously known by his assistants—lives with the widowed Haru. His prime interaction with her, and she with him, is indeed characterized by "the genitals." His seduction of her is seen in flashback, a spontaneous act of absurdist lust, the loved-up pair sinking below the frame to do who knows what. Imamura is in full command of his frame, blocking the scene for maximum objectivity in a wide master. Ogata's gesticulations, accompanying his ardent confession of desire, seem desperate, frenzied, the man's exhortations theatrical in Imamura's wide proscenium. These observations are not unique. Donald Richie observes the manner in which the characterization and framing in Imamura's films commingle:

> Imamura's people inhabit a world so filled with vitality that their energy is visible—everything in the scene (and outside it) belongs to them. The Imamura view is packed with movement, the screen is so full that parts of the people are cut off. This exclusion of part (tops of heads, sides of bodies) is important. It implies a burgeoning, something growing outside what the director is showing. (2009: 48)

In short, in the psychology of the moment is found the manner in which Imamura makes the viewer acutely aware of the scene's blocking with respect to the camera, and the explicit movement of his characters' bodies into and out of what would be the conventional frame. Just as her suitor's ardor is rendered theatrically, thus bringing to the audience's attention the scene's unique blocking, Haru's response is coy but also frazzled. She is doubtless already aware of her suitor's interest, but the wider frame reveals her being overwhelmed, comically flustered, as his gesticulations are complemented by her flinches. The two ending in a sweaty mess below the bottom of the frame is Imamura's great "button" on the sequence, allowing for the sleaze of the scenario, the awkwardness of the physicality, and naturalist's remove found in the wide, somewhat eccentric framing, to create offscreen carnality entirely specific to the film's milieu, style, and expository nature. It is also a style highly aware of the relative response of female to male in a sexual situation, eager to highlight the *bodily* experience of the characters, and further emphasized by how their bodies are supremely autonomous, eagerly diving beneath the frame of the proscenium. This choice is very much in line with Imamura's thematic preoccupations, symbolically and literally.

Ogata and Haru seduce one another and make love on the floor because their social paradigm allows for it. There is little in Ogata's background to suggest decorum would forbid him from such a spontaneous expression of desire, particularly given the conditioning of his work. Equally, Haru, as the kind of woman Imamura is so expert at portraying, is sufficiently libidinous:

> Imamura once described the real Japanese woman he intended to portray. "Medium height and weight, light coloring, smooth skin. Maternal . . . good genitals. Juicy." The sexual emphasis is strong. Her genitals are in good working order (juicy) and at the same time she is described as maternal. (Richie 2009: 46)

In being libidinous she is both receptive to Ogata's admission of lust that is so disruptive to the established social paradigm of their landlady-tenant relationship, as well as capable of normalizing such desire with her innately maternal nature. But, greater than any of this, based on Imamura's anthropological bent, is the acquiescence of the scene to both their mutual animal nature/attraction as well as the sacrifice of need for significant decorum when occupying the nether regions of the Japanese social order. "The inference is that in such a natural situation it is only the female who, despite her undignified position, enjoys herself. Further, any dignity or lack of it is far from her thoughts. Sex and its various positions are natural to her—natural to us all, would but men realize it" (Richie 2009: 46). Haru accepts Ogata and accepts the awkwardness of his lust. In turn, Imamura's audience accepts it, in its own edifying way.

Imamura's scenario allows for such a comic, absurd, sex-centric scene. The setup is both clichéd, the stuff of cheap pornographic fantasies, and the broader necessities of farce. His characters are predetermined in their erotic collision by social factors such as age, personal history, and philosophical predisposition. Finally, his style bolsters such a specific model of flaying social observation. Their desire is pathetic, but it is fitting of their social context, and Imamura's scientific remove spares them the condescension of his obvious editorializing. But one thing is certain, both Haru and Ogata cannot govern their unruly libidos. This quirk of biology in turn allows Imamura to reveal the simplicity, the ironic harmony of their coupling, and the specific social *cul-de-sac* that facilitates it.

Ogata is used to looking at sex and is an orchestrator of scenarios involving cheap seduction. His choice of the same with his landlady is appropriately pushed to the level of farce. The proximity of pornography, and the kinds of attitudes expressed by MacKinnon and Dines, coupled with the farce, allows this most awkward of seductions to be stylistically appropriate to the sexualized world Imamura has created. His framing, an epic of negative space at the scene's end, with sex happening beneath the camera, is his directorial hand directing us, through the striking, atypical nature of the framing and blocking, not to look away from the embarrassing middle-age copulation which is the scene's *raison d'être*.

This same approach allows us to see many other images that most cameras, and directors, would shy away from. We spy, from Ogata's sideways point of view from his hiding place, Keiko, Haru's teenage daughter, in her underwear. We, the audience, know that this chosen point of view means that the act is forbidden, that he is seeing her in sexual terms. Yet the striking nature of the composition, arguably, does not allow us to look away. Our surprise at Imamura's boldness holds our attention for the editorial duration of this forbidden moment. The style holds our gaze, and allows us, for a moment, to identify with the taboo desire of a middle-aged man for what is effectively his step-daughter.

The specific shot echoes one found in Alfred Hitchcock's *Psycho*. There the shot is essentially an iris. Here is it is a double frame, a double proscenium, as Ogata stares through a door frame, and in turn within this "frame within a frame" the rice paper screens are parted such that they symmetrically form another frame within the parted doors. This composition is so striking as

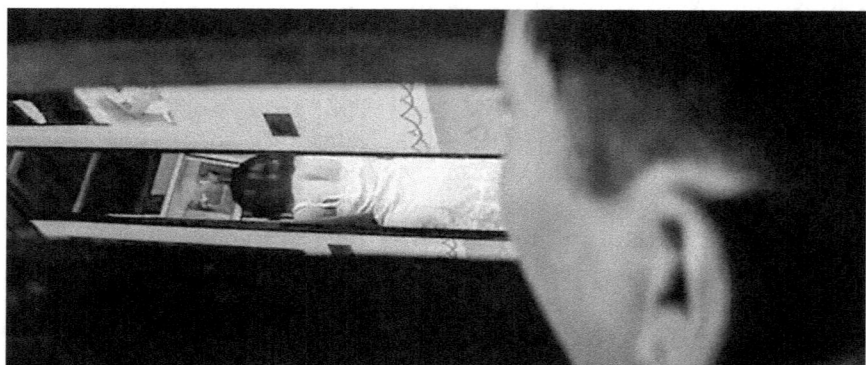

Figure 8.1 Ogata spies on Keiko through multiple frames-within-frames. Due to the inclusion of his head within the frame, we stare with him at the teen girl.

The Obscene in the Everyday   151

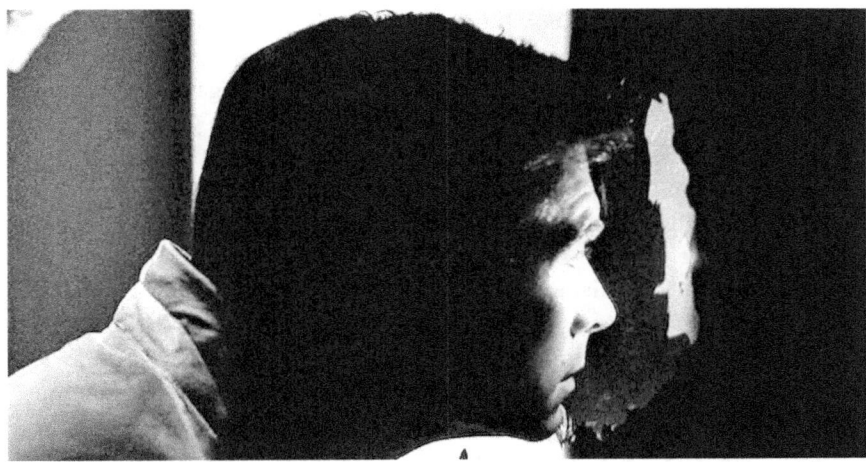

Figure 8.2   In a similar "peeping tom" shot from *Psycho*, we first engage with the taboo of voyeurism in an establishing shot of star Anthony Perkins, as the character Norman Bates. The audience effectively catches him in the act and is not implicated in the act.

Figure 8.3   Following this less invasive introduction to a character engaging in voyeurism, Hitchcock then allows the camera to adopt the perspective of Norman as we now spy on an undressing Janet Leigh/Marion Crane.

to center the audience's gaze on the near-nude Keiko, and in doing so acknowledge Ogata's taboo, near-incestuous lust.

Desire apart, sex acts are often carefully framed to engage the audience's imagination. In an early scene the camera is resting beside Ogata and Haru's bed as he attempts to engage her in morning sex. The camera then moves ninety degrees to the head of the bed as the screen doors open and Haru's adult son piles into the bed with them. The "subjective" camera created by the framing emphasizes their surprise and shock to be interrupted, mid-congress, by the young man who is behaving as might a young child. Ogata twists his body around, away from the son, in this moment, as the adult son squeezes between them. The implication is clear. He does not wish for his erection to be obvious to Haru's son. Nothing is shown, but the scene, via framing and specific cuts, emphasizes the sex act occurring beneath the covers, and the attendant social shame found in its discovery. In a later scene Haru shaves her lover. He repeatedly fondles her throughout, and yet it is via the careful framing of a barber's chair such that it obscures his ambling arm that the audience is both spared and invited to imagine his wandering hands. To classify Imamura's style as "suggestive" would be a disservice. He is hiding nothing, more occluding actions, intentions, desires, such that we, as the viewer, may feel permitted to keep looking. Our own shame is spared by his mature, clinical style.

This style was not only the result of discretion on the part of Imamura. It was also a stringent factor in the screen culture of Japan at the time, involving the laws regarding the portrayal of sex in the mass media of Japan where it was illegal (and still pretty much is) to depict or show genitalia. This was true in the 1960s in terms of movies, TV, photographs, anime, and manga. While certain aspects have changed from the 1960s, Imamura could not have shown hardcore sex even if he had wanted to. Nudity entered Japanese cinema with Satoru Kobayashi's independent production *Flesh Market* (Nikutai no Ichiba, 1962). This film is considered the first pink film (Weisser 1998: 21). Thus, the "discreet" portrayal of sex, things left to our imagination, was also a matter of law, not just style. The Japanese film ethics board Eirin has long enforced a specific ban: genitals would not be displayed, nor would pubic hair. Donald Richie noted that this meant that filmmakers went to extremes to avoid displaying the "working parts" of their actors (1987: 156). Japanese directors often positioned props in such a way that they would obscure the genitals, or any activity surrounding the genitals. In this period director Tetsuji Takechi made the earliest mainstream "pink films" (along with Seijun Suzuki's *Gate of Flesh/Nikutai no mon*, made at Nikkatstu which helped produce *The Pornographers*). *Daydreams/Hakujitsumu* and *Black Snow/Kuroi yuki* were both controversial and the subject of government lawsuits and forced censorship—the former tried to show pubic hair, but ended up with a "cloud" over the area. Imamura's films, in their implicit depiction of raw sexuality, are found at the inception of the "pink films" era, and in context his depictions of sex are very much prototypical of that period, be it in mainstream film or independents by the likes of Koji Wakamatsu.

Style is a tool in Imamura's brand of naturalism. It is an instrument in service of elemental thematic concerns. There are two major scenes in which Imamura's vision of a world as permissive as that of porn production, coupled with his incisive style, allows for a truly unflinching glimpse of the human animal. Let us examine the first. In a scene in which Keiko seduces Ogata, she offers to let him kiss her. Like his earlier frenzied seduction of Haru, this scene sees Ogata in a state of fevered and confused desire. Yet, in the earlier scene he is aware of how there is some degree to which a sexual union with Haru would be socially sanctioned. She is a widow, of his age, of his class. In sociological terms the seduction makes sense. In the later scene Keiko offers to let him kiss her. There is a counterintuitive cut from a two-shot of the two of them crouched on the floor to a wider, higher shot peeking through the windows of the apartment at the scene. In this wider shot, Ogata and his desire are dwarfed, and it is in this shot that he resolves to act on his desire. However, by shooting from outside of the apartment, so far back, Imamura ensures that this pivotal moment in which the protagonist of the film will act on his desire is framed in the wider context of the world and society they inhabit, the audience placed like the world peeking in on this transgressive moment.

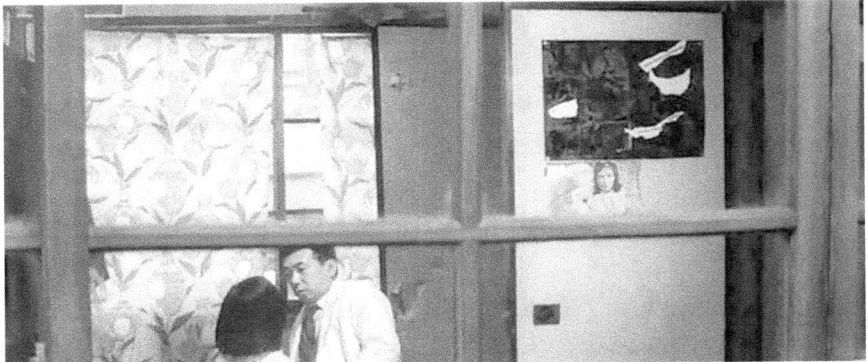

Figure 8.4 Ogata is briefly tempted by young Keiko. Imamura's choice to frame this moment from that of the outside world looking in, utilizing a long lens and a high angle, pushing his desperate characters down to the bottom of the frame, highlights the extreme sensitivity of Ogata to his predicament.

True to form, Imamura interrupts this transgressive cinch with a knock on the door from a visitor, the police arriving to arrest Ogata for another infraction relating to his work, symbolic of the world intruding on this illicit moment. Consider similar scenes in the Oscar-winning Best Picture of 2000, *American Beauty*. This a similar tale of forbidden middle-aged lust for a teen visitor to the hero's house, but here the hero's lust is rendered pure fantasy for the first three-quarters of the film.

The director, Sam Mendes, is even cited as evoking the framing of classic westerns in the hero's final seduction of his teenage dream girl (DVD commentary, 2000). Such an approach is antithetical to Imamura's and speaks to the entirely oppositional priorities of the Mendes film. In *American Beauty* fantasy is the desired destination, the final seduction of the teen girl a complete inversion of Imamura's Keiko. In Mendes' film the attraction is mutual. The audience is never forced to deal with the uncomfortable possibility Lester might be a lecherous patsy, as is Ogata. There is little of sociological value in this film. We acknowledge Lester Burnham's desire as pathetic, but also lyrical, and by the film's end the audience is presumably seduced by the fantasy, urged on by the film's famed cinematography, to will this child and middle-aged man

Figure 8.5 Thirty years later director Sam Mendes approached the same taboo from a completely different aesthetic point of view in his film *American Beauty*. Kevin Spacey's Lester Burnham invests in a complex erotic fantasy life, peopled only by himself and the object of his desire, Mena Suvari's Angela Hayes.

The Obscene in the Everyday 155

Figure 8.6 Angela is eroticized not only for Burnham in this image, but also for the audience. She faces the camera boldly and directly, the gloss of the Hollywood aestheticization of taboo desire inviting us to gaze at Angela's youthful erotic charms.

Figure 8.7 The final seeming consummation of Burnham's desire is framed classically and romantically. Angela attempts to surrender her virginity to him in a moment of emotional vulnerability, a far cry from Keiko's casual attempt at seduction in *The Pornographers*.

to have sex. Imamura places the desire mid-frame, in the middle of a dingy, poor flat, in a claustrophobic society where strangers can and do barge in at a moment's notice. Ogata never has the wherewithal to make his fantasy a reality, specifically because Imamura as a filmmaker denies him this.

The second scene is undeniably the most disturbing of the film. In the preceding scene the pornographers have discovered, mid-shoot, that a male performer is in fact the father of a seemingly mentally impaired daughter. The scene is shot from alternately low and high angles, their combination emphasizing the cramped, awkward nature of the shoot, and the guilty discovery of the incestuous father, shot from an incriminating low angle, his face lit harshly. In a brilliant cut the father of the girl attempts to calm her due to her being manic, in doing so referring to himself as "Daddy." In a flash he realizes his mistake, as a look of guilt, wariness, and a sickening double-take passes across his face.

All this occurs in a matter of seconds, and then Imamura executes a time shift. On a zoom lens, we see the pornographers through the windows of a spa, relaxing. The sound is synced to their immediate proximity, but we, the audience, are dozens of yards away from them, again perceiving them though a widow, the society looking in. Remarkably, with Imamura's frame, he reemphasizes the presence of humanity with the left corner of the frame capturing the foot traffic on a nearby street. The conversation of the pornographers is entirely seen in its wider social context, the surge of humanity literally and figuratively sitting on their shoulder. Then, while we cannot see their faces clearly we listen to what is a wholly transgressive conversation in which the men speak in nonjudgmental,

Figure 8.8 A father's incestuous relationship with his own biological (and mentally challenged) daughter is discovered in a blackly comic moment in *The Pornographers*.

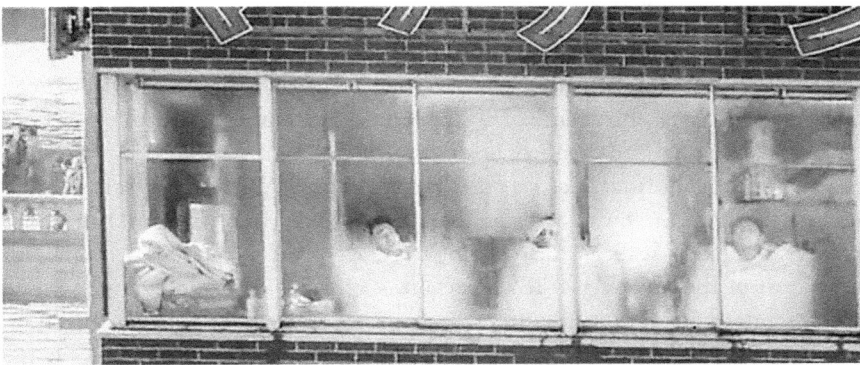

Figure 8.9 The titular characters engage in a semi-absurd, and again blackly comic, exchange on the relative virtues of incest. Very much like the scene in which Ogata's desire for Keiko is nakedly revealed, this candid exchange on the ultimate taboo is framed utilizing a long lens and, juxtaposed, the hustle and bustle of urban life at the margins of the frame.

justifying terms about the impulse of incest, going so far as to speak of how such events were common at the dawn of humanity. The only protest is raised when one of the men points out that in their modern era such customs have been abandoned. The conversation is expressly about sex. The pornographers, given their work, perceive the shocking nature of what they have seen in animal and social terms. Similarly, Imamura's framing, and collusive cut to the scene, place this appalling conversation in its wider social context. Imamura wants his audience to be aware that the words, these attitudes, this seemingly obvious transgression of social and sexual norms, are a part of the persistent fabric of society, and the possessors of these opinions, the titular pornographers, incorporate it into their worldview such that they might debate it while engaging in something as banal as a spa treatment.

Imamura offers a vision of society wherein the taboo is as much a part of the fabric of society as any other element, such as families, the law, the intelligentsia, the working classes. Imamura does not revel in smut, does not seek to shock his audience. Nor does he precisely normalize what he depicts. The work of the title characters of *The Pornographers* is not "normal," and Imamura the scenarist is constantly reminding us of this fact. Yet in this scene I have discussed, and those previous to it, Imamura's approach to style is such that these forbidden or subversive moments cannot exist outside the experience of the film. They are not asymptomatic of its overall style. Equally, they are not demarcated fantasy. They exist within the fabric of everyday life for his characters, and represent the obstacles of economics and class, plus the lodestone of desire, that his characters must contend with in their daily dealings within both their personal lives and their work. Like Proust, Imamura successfully conflates the socially stigmatized practices of a minority (Jews, pornographers) with their sexual peccadillos (inversion, incest/pornification/hypersexuality), and in so doing permits a window to open on the wider society. His stylistic lens of choice for this window is sufficiently arresting to produce audience identification with a portrait of the underclass. To be certain, such a project is bold, and it would be rare indeed for a single film to realize such an ambitious project, but in fragmentary snatches of narrative and imagery Imamura achieves his goal of being a naturalist of the human animal.

Works Cited

Beckett, Samuel (1987). "Memory, Habit, Time." In *Proust.* ed. Harold Bloom. New York: Chelsea House, 17–36.

Dines, Gail (1998). "*Playboy* Magazine and the Mainstreaming of Pornography." In *Pornography: The Production and Consumption of Inequality*, ed. Gail Dines, Robert Jensen, and Ann Russo, 37–64. London: Routledge.

Ebert, Isabelle M. (1993). "Le Premiere Dreyfusard: Jewishness in Marcel Proust." *French Review* 67, no. 2: 196–217.

Ellis, Havelock (2004). *Studies in the Psychology of Sex*, vol. 2. N.p.: Plain Label Books.

Kristeva, Julia (1993). *Proust and the Sense of Time*. Trans. S. Bann. London: Faber and Faber.

MacKinnon, Catharine A. (1989). *Toward a Feminist Theory of the State*. Cambridge, MA: Harvard University Press, 179.

Parker, Robert, and Peter Aggleton, eds. (2007). *Culture, Society and Sexuality: A Reader*. London: Routledge.

Quandt, James, ed. (1997). *Shohei Imamura*. Toronto: Toronto International Film Festival Group.

Richie, Donald (1987). "The Japanese Eroduction." In *A Lateral View: Essays on Culture and Style in Contemporary Japan*, 156. Berkeley: Stone Bridge Press.

Richie, Donald (1997). "Notes for a Study of Shohei Imamura." In *Shohei Imamura*, ed. James Quandt, 7–44. Toronto: Toronto International Film Festival Group.

Richie, Donald (2009). "Imamura Revisited." *Film Quarterly* 63, no. 1: 44–49.

Chapter 9

Shohei Imamura's Profound Desire for Japan's Cultural Roots: Critical Approaches to *Profound Desires of the Gods*

Mats Karlsson

Introduction

An intense, whitish sun rises above the clouds on a bright orange sky. With no establishing shot in between, there is a sudden cut to a tracking shot following a snake swimming in crystal clear water over bright sand. Next, close-ups from above of a sea cucumber, shellfish, fish, and an extreme frontal close-up of another fish puffing its cheeks. The style appears documentary—despite the haunting nondiegetic music on the sound track—somehow foreshadowing that the film to ensue will be deploying the same kind of observational mode; that it will subject humans to the same intense objective scrutiny. With the next

Figure 9.1 Star Rentaro Mikuni as an islander with his own ideas in *The Profound Desires of the Gods*.

cut to a young man struggling to pull a straw basket laden with stones toward a beach, the music gives way to diegetic sound. The man catches an octopus that he happens to spot and starts to suck at a live fish caught together with it. Next, there is a cut to a tracking shot following a young woman from behind. She is carrying an earthenware pot of water on her head, which she hands over to an old man who uses it to water the small plot that he is tilling. We are still in an observational, documentary mode that matches the atmosphere of the introduction.

Yet the next few shots suddenly undermine the initial impression, indicating that the film about to unfold will be a narrative film after all. The woman catches a rat with her bare hand and proudly holds it up for the old man to see. There is a rack-focus shift to a couple of huts and a huge rock in the background. The ensuing shot from above features another man who is toiling hard in a pool of water that has gathered in a deep hole next to the rock. The man, who is fettered to a tree with a chain, dives underwater to remove rocks from the bottom of the pool. The young man we saw earlier returns with his straw basket to hoist up the stones with a winch. This had been his task, to transport the stones to the seashore. Even without any prior knowledge of the plot of the film, the association with Sisyphean labor is immediately evoked in the viewer. Furthermore, the sheer absurdity of the situation indicates that the unfolding film should not be read within a realistic paradigm after all.

The setting is Kurage, a fictitious island in the Okinawa archipelago. The *mise-en-scène*, dominated by the magnificent natural setting, is vividly captured by the cinematography in bright, crisp tones. Constantly sweating characters in the glaring sunlight accompanied by the omnipresent sound of cicadas signal

Figure 9.2 Nekichi's Sisyphean labor.

the tropical south. Early on in the film the crippled village storyteller introduces what is to become a kind of theme song of the film. Facing a circle of small children in the shade of a Malayan banyan tree, he recites the island's foundational myth while playing a simple tune on his snakeskin samisen:

> Long, long ago, very long ago there came to the Kurage Sea a brother and a sister, a god and a goddess. Together, they created an island, this is their tale. The tale of how the island began . . .

In the leafy shade of the tree, the silhouette of his face suddenly takes on a clear green hue. There is a cut to a frontal close-up of him looking straight into the camera while repeating the refrain of the tune. The left side of his face turns reddish, reflecting the sunlight, whilst the right side keeps its green tone. There is a new cut displaying the silhouette of his face, now against the setting sun. As he finishes his tale the haunting, nondiegetic score returns while the title and credits appear against the sun. Through the exaggerated color scheme the viewer is yet again cued to expect something beyond realism from the film. This weaving together of believable realism and blatantly unrealistic features—concerning both style and story—will turn out to be the defining mode of the film.[1] Moreover, its fictitious setting—a unique feature in Imamura's oeuvre—signals a leap from his trademark realism.

Incest and Taboos

Whether they embrace it or not, most critics tend to agree that *The Profound Desires of the Gods* is a problematic, troublesome film. Yet, as it is arguably Imamura's most ambitious project in terms of scope of themes, an examination of these various critical perspectives will contribute to a deeper appreciation of his art in general.[2] Yūkichi Shinada, for instance, in his review for *Kinema junpō*—the most influential film journal in Japan, which awarded the film its prestigious Best One award—touched on these problematic features even though he considered it the most rewarding Japanese film premiering in 1968. From its release *Profound Desires* had been discussed in terms of a compilation (*shūtaisei*) of all of Imamura's art so far, but according to Shinada this characterization was not really to the point. In his view, the film does not amount to an answer or conclusion to "Imamura folklore" as a total system. Lacking the consistence or coherence (*matomari*) of a compilation, it thematically overflows and spreads out in various directions, rendering it difficult to grasp the film's contours (Shinada 1969: 128).

Another commentator, Masashi Shimizu, who to my knowledge has conducted the closest reading of the film yet, doubts whether *Profound Desires* succeeds in its attempt to blend reality and mythology. The problem is not the blending as such, but that the two paradigms do not engage with each other appropriately (Shimizu 2001: 462). Shimizu deconstructs the plot of the film at great length to show his point. In his reading, it is Imamura's ambivalent treatment of the theme of sin versus punishment that takes precedence.

Early in the film, Yamamori (Kanjūrō Arashi), the family patriarch and village elder, gives a synopsis of the narrative background in the form of a prayer in front of the *kamidana* home altar:

> We, the Futori family, are the oldest family on the island. In recent years, our transgressions have caused trouble on the island, therefore, I now promise the gods, that the Futori family will never go out to sea, and I will keep Nekichi in shackles. We will topple the rock and restore the paddy fields of the gods. Once we have made good our promises, please let us associate with the islanders again, please let us go out to sea again, and please let us participate in the Dongama Festival. Please let us restore the way things were.

Both Nekichi (Rentarō Mikuni), the protagonist, and his younger sister Uma (Yasuko Matsui) have been conceived as the result of incest between Yamamori and his biological daughter. Shimizu, however, observes that Yamamori counts neither his own nor his offspring's incestuous acts among the disgraceful deeds to atone for, but restricts these to Nekichi's betrayal of the islanders' code of behavior after returning from the war. So why did the rock appear in the first place, Shimizu asks. A tsunami big enough to carry a rock like that would surely have swallowed the whole island, people and all. This would be the realistic way of reasoning. The fact that the rock appeared in the paddy field is in itself an unrealistic contrivance. Consequently, the film incorporates the unreal (*higenjitsu*) from its very inception: the film's setup is unrealistic in itself. Therefore, in order to bestow reality onto the unreal there is a necessity to convince the audience about the cause of the appearance of the rock. Shimizu argues that the inevitability of the arrival of the rock is weak. If its appearance is due to divine retribution, then there must be a sin that corresponds to that punishment. In that case, what kind of sin is it that members of the Futori family have committed? Remember that incest is not recognized as a sin by either Yamamori or Nekichi. The only other thinkable sins are the various transgressions perpetrated by Nekichi, although these do not feel grave enough to warrant divine retribution (Shimizu 2001: 436).[3]

Likewise, the film would have had to convince the spectator of the reason why Nekichi had to be slain toward the end of the film by establishing inherent inevitability. More specifically, why is it that Nekichi, who fiercely resists the modernization of the community, must be killed in the name of the antimodern indigenous gods (Shimizu 2001: 475)?

Shimizu goes on to deconstruct various story elements in response to their perceived lack of persuasiveness. Indeed, there seems to be something about the film that makes it susceptible to various (perhaps irrelevant) types of objections. Ryūzō Saki, for instance, in his review of *Profound Desires* on its release, points to an ambivalence in Imamura's treatment of the incest theme.[4] Since Imamura purposely raises incest—which is not such an exceptional phenomenon that it would necessarily warrant thematic treatment—you would expect him to deliver some kind of new anthropological discovery on the topic, he argues. He cites the Chikuhō zone of abandoned mines in Kyushu where inhabitants unreservedly have testified to incest becoming more prevalent as their communities became alienated from the rest of society. In *Profound Desires*, though, we are dealing with the opposite scenario: the Futori family has become estranged *because* they are suspected of inbreeding within the family. Saki's argument runs as follows:

> Nekichi fondles Uma's breasts. Kametarō covers Toriko [both being Nekichi's offspring] with his body. Imamura is telling us "these males and females are siblings, this amounts to incest!" But, watching the screen, what come across are only beautiful love scenes. Is this a feat or due to a slip on Imamura's part? The drama unfolds without the audience being able to tell how this point should be understood. (Saki 1969: 218)

Tadao Satō, the doyen of Japanese film criticism, also finds the incest theme problematic. As he explains, the tourism development plans of the island can only go ahead over the dead bodies of the members of the Futori family of undesirables, who refuse to sell their land. Nekichi's persistence in digging the hole year after year is also a display of intent to sink their roots even deeper in the ancestral land. Interpreting incest is, however, problematic according to Satō. From the anthropological perspective, which holds that even the most primitive tribes have a taboo against incest, this theme intends to emphasize the backwardness of the island. However, the case of Nekichi and Uma is different. Satō tentatively understands their incestuous relationship as something caused by their persecuted and isolated circumstances: it is the abnormal form that their resistance takes against the dismantling of the family structure required by modernization (Satō 1997: 126).

Although the "intentional fallacy" should perhaps be avoided, it is interesting to note how Imamura has commented on the role of incest in the film:

> The idea came from *Kojiki* [the foundational history, *A Record of Ancient Matters*, c. 700], one of the oldest surviving texts in Japan. It's a collection of creation myths and legends, and one of the stories is about incestuous gods, a brother and sister. It's cited directly in the film, when the old disabled man teaches the children about the island's legends. The point is that incest is bad—in fact, immoral—because it's something that only the gods are supposed to do. Before I made the film, I had the impression that incest might be common on such isolated islands. But when I did my research and travelled around the southern islands, I came across only one account of incest. It turned out that geographical isolation doesn't engender incest; it's seen as a taboo, even on these islands. Interestingly, there are more cases of incest in a big city like Tokyo, where individuals are emotionally stressed and sometimes feel repressed by society. (Imamura 2011: 37–38)

Imamura's point of view is made clear in a dialogue between Nekichi and his son Kametarō (Chōichirō Kawarasaki). When Kametarō asks Nekichi if the rumors of him repeating the incestuous sins of Yamamori are true and that he and Uma are a pair, the father vehemently retorts: "Human beings aren't allowed to do such things. Man must not imitate the gods." The point might be that incest is immoral, something reserved for the gods, but Imamura is not a filmmaker prone to subject his characters to moral judgement.[5] Shimizu concludes his long treatment of the film on this theme. He argues that all main characters in the film have something incomplete, something ambivalent about them, but that Imamura does not adopt a position of passing severe judgment on them. Accordingly, he is not inquiring into sin and retribution in the Christian sense of these terms. On the contrary, his gaze observes and unconditionally accepts all petty humans carrying on their ambivalent lives; it accepts them in their entirety, with all that involves in terms of meanness, pettiness, deceit, and treachery (Shimizu 2001: 480).

The Tale of How the Island Ended

Saki reads *Profound Desires* in a sociocultural vein as a critique of the concurrent phenomena of modernization and rationalization. In his review he lays stress on a line from film studio Nikkatsu's promotional leaflet for the film: "The culmination of Imamura's art, a film uncovering the roots of the Japanese through a fight by islanders against the wave of modernisation unfolding in the setting of a solitary island in the southern sea still steeped in mythical tradition." As he points out, the setting with its sugar cane fields covering the island is an unambiguous sign of modernization. Conflict is introduced when Kariya (Kazuo Kitamura), son-in-law of the owner of the Tokyo-based sugar company and its chief engineer, comes to the island on a mission to rationalize the sugar cane enterprise and to secure a fresh water source for the factory. The irrational villagers sabotage his efforts to find water, spurred on by their superstitious beliefs. He finally discovers a well only to learn that it is situated in a grove dedicated to the gods and therefore off-limits for the company. This merely confirms for him the view of the island head and sugar factory manager Ryū Ryūgen (Yoshi Katō) that the island lags fifty years behind the mainland. Kariya, whose very demeanor—to borrow a phrase from Saki—personifies rationalization, is initially appalled by the backwardness of the place. But he soon shows signs of following in the footsteps of his predecessor, the previously dispatched engineer, who has adopted the islanders' lifestyle, married one of their widows, and ceased reporting back to the head office. Steadfast to his ethical principles, Kariya initially rebuffs attempts at seduction by the nymphomaniac half-wit Toriko (Kazuko Okiyama), but gradually relents to end up making love on the beach in a pivotal scene. Tempted by Toriko and the lure of a life more in harmony with nature, Kariya thereafter sets his inhibited natural impulses free and "goes native."

While repairing thatched roofs ripped off in a storm, Yamamori has accidently slipped and fallen to his death. In another pivotal scene, the head shaman-priestess Uma invokes Yamamori's spirit from the other world. Appearing

Figure 9.3   Kariya goes native.

Figure 9.4 The Rock appears to budge.

as a huge phantom illusion, Yamamori uses Toriko as a medium to admonish his family: "Everyone on Kurage is kin with each other, do not break apart!" However, as Saki pertinently observes of this scene, Kurage is already breaking apart: Ryūgen has moved the sacred grove in order to develop its water resource, while the apathetic-looking youngsters put their energies into the only thing they know well: "night crawling" (*yobai*, or sneaking into a woman's bed under cover of darkness). When Nekichi finally succeeds in burying the rock to restore the sacred paddy field, it is too late. Ryūgen is scheming to acquire the plot to turn it into an airfield. For this purpose, he coaxes Uma into appealing to Nekichi to let go of the ancestral land. It is at this point, Saki argues, that it becomes clear to the audience that the island god is none other than Ryūgen himself, who answers to mainland capital as a god of superior rank. In his reading the film turns out to be, in a sense, "The tale of how the island ended," in ironic contrast to the foundational myth that is featured as a sort of theme song for the film. His summing up of the film's message runs in a metaphorical vein: "We Japanese are unmistakably islanders even if we happen to live in Tokyo or Fukuoka. But the reality is that we have exerted ourselves willingly, one hundred million people with one mind, to destroy the island within us" (Saki 1969: 219–20).

Messages and Interpretations

Other critics have also struggled with explicating the film's multiple meanings. On the day of its Dongama festival—a combination of coming-of-age festival for the young men on the island and a festival to pray for a rich harvest—Ryūgen

Figure 9.5   The masked villagers closing in for the kill.

dies in the act of making love to Uma. Nekichi, who is secretly witnessing the scene, is spotted by Ryūgen's wife, who mistakenly believes he has killed her husband. With Ryūgen dead, Nekichi and Uma can reunite freely after an interval of twenty years. Reminiscent of the story of Noah's ark—as pointed out by Satō, Saki, and others—Nekichi and Uma set out in search of the new promised land in a small boat loaded with pigs and hens and other necessities for starting a new life all on their own on the uninhabited Western Island. Meanwhile, Ryūgen's wife has alerted the villagers to Ryūgen's death and the young men taking part in the festival, including Kametarō, set out in pursuit of the pair in long canoes. They finally catch up with Nekichi and Uma toward dusk after an engine failure. The young men don their festival masks as disguise and attack Nekichi with their oars. Nekichi dives into the water but, bleeding profusely from the head, immediately attracts sharks that complete the killing.[6] The pursuers leave the boat to the mercy of the waves after tying Uma to the mast.

For Satō this slaughter sequence, combined with the feverish coloration of the subtropical sea and sky at sunset, comes across with an almost mythical forcefulness and cruelty laden with symbolic meaning. The orange luminance of the sunset clouds over the blue ocean, in his reading, alludes to mankind's forbidden and suppressed original desire. So what is this original human desire? The film appears to hint that it is total freedom to live an unrestrained life, according to Satō.[7] In an act that repeats the island's foundational myth, brother and sister flee the existing community that has come to shackle them in search of a new world where the two of them can live in total freedom. Within the myth the image of this basic human desire is tolerated, but civilization does not sanction such selfish individual behavior. The Dongama festival masks that Nekichi's slayers don, by way of allusion to Greek tragedy and Noh theater—theatrical forms with strong mythical implications where fate plays an important role—have them embody a community bound together by a common fate that transcends the individual, in Satō's reading.

In the film's epilogue, set five years later, an airplane with a load of tourists lands on the airstrip now built on the island. Among the passengers are Kariya the engineer and his wife. Kametarō, who has been positioned as a character longing to escape the backwardness and superstition of the island in favour of modernity on the mainland, has returned from working for the company in Tokyo. He is now the engine driver of the narrow-gauge train that used to transport sugar cane and now carries tourists. As they set off, Toriko (who has died in the intervening period) appears to Kametarō as a vision, running on the track ahead of the steam engine. When he shouts out her name she laughingly stops to face the train. Kametarō pulls on the brakes but too late, he fears. He jumps down to look for her body beneath the engine, but she is no longer anywhere to be found. He apologizes to his passengers for having created the commotion and sets the train in motion again. There is a cut to an extreme long shot taken from the air of Nekichi and Uma's boat with its red sail set against the blue ocean. As the nondiegetic music builds up, the three-hour film abruptly ends. To return to Satō, he reads the red sail still lingering on the ocean five years after the event as a symbolic expression, the apparition of the primitive spirit that modern Japanese have expelled from their consciousness.[8]

What is it, then, that *Profound Desires* communicates to us in the final analysis? Satō argues that while the film brings us intense images and strong impressions, like myths their meanings are elusive. Is the film trying to convey the kind of passionate love, faith, and simple spirit that the Japanese have lost in the process of modernization? Yes, but that is probably not all. The film has the power of myth, but not its simplicity. Rather, through its analytical way of grappling with social structure, the film presents highly intellectual scientific observations. So is it trying to make us reflect on the distortions and imbalances brought about by sudden modernization? No, the film contains too strong a tragic passion for it to encourage intellectual self-examination. Just as with myths, the film is a riddle, Satō concludes. Its true appeal is that—presenting a powerful riddle—it sets the audience on a quest for the meaning of that riddle (Satō 1997: 134–35).

Myths and Allegories

Satō's reflection that *Profound Desires* presents intellectual observations based on an analytical approach to social structure leads on, in a wider sense, to a feature of the film that in my view amounts to a certain ambiguity that can be seen as contributing to what many critics identify as the "problematic" nature of the film. In this context, there is merit in turning to Hiroshi Teshigahara's *Suna no onna/Woman in the Dunes* (1964) for comparison. Thematically, the two films have many points in common—Sisyphean labor and attachment to one's community, for instance—but those are not of immediate concern here. What attracts our attention is the way in which *Woman in the Dunes* invites symbolic or metaphorical interpretations regarding its "meaning." To be sure, there is no need to switch on the interpretive faculties to enjoy it. Still, the film invites analytical speculation as it quickly becomes obvious that one cannot read it within a realistic paradigm. In other words, from early on the film appears as some sort of allegory or metaphor. Moreover, to the very end the film does not deviate from this narrative mode. As such, it is a film that can easily bear the weight of various types of interpretations, philosophical ones included. Niki Junpei, the protagonist, could for instance be understood as an embodiment of Albert Camus' "absurd man," and the argument can be fashioned so that the film logically holds up to such a reading. It is obvious that the plot of *Woman in the Dunes* signifies something beyond what it depicts. It begs to be interpreted figuratively.

When it comes to *Profound Desires* the situation is arguably different. The film does seem to signify something wider than what it tells. But in this case it somehow does not hold up as a coherent system of significations that makes sense.[9] Not only is it a difficult task to pinpoint exactly what is signified, as argued by Satō above, it is also hard to come up with any particular reading that is sustained by the various elements of the plot.[10] Perhaps this problem could be brushed aside with a claim that *Profound Desires* is a more open film than *Woman in the Dunes* and that it lacks closure. But that does not appear to be the point here. What is essential is rather that Imamura's film incorporates both literal story elements (though in a fictional context) and other elements that carry metaphorical implications as opposed to purely narrative ones. The subplot surrounding the rock in the paddy field, for instance, is obviously a story element not to be taken at its face value. The audience is not likely to ask themselves whether they would have continued digging the hole for twenty years if they were put in Nekichi's situation. But Kariya, the engineer, does arrive on the scene literally, dispatched to the island from the Tokyo head office. The audience can identify with him and ask themselves how they would have acted if they were suddenly thrust into a totally new environment.[11] Would they be likely to set professional and marital obligations aside and go native like the engineer? The subplot of the development of the island for tourism is another narrative thread meant to be read literally. Conversely, when Niki Junpei arrives at the dunes and is hoisted down to the woman in the sand pit, we are already in the realm of allegory. We are prone to ask what the filmic situation has to say allegorically or metaphorically about the condition of modern man, or some such question. The question of what we would have done in Niki's situation does not occur to us because the situation is too absurd to begin with. Hence the two films trigger different readerly responses. While *Woman in the Dunes* sticks to its mode throughout, *Profound Desires* in this respect appears more as a hybrid creature, featuring different layers of signification.

Interestingly, Imamura himself has touched on this dual aspect of the film in a journal article:

> Even reflecting on it now, from my point of view, it's a film that does not really relate enough of what I feel . . . Watching it a second time, which is unusual for me with my own films, I don't necessarily think it's a successful work . . . I doubt how thoroughly my intention with the film was realised, the intention to invite the audience to a temporal and spatial borderline site between an everyday feel of human life and mythology understood as our racial sub-consciousness, and to plunge them into a state where they can't really tell whether any of this really happened or not. (qtd. in Katori 2004: 246)

Imamura has made several elucidative comments elsewhere on his treatment of mythology in relation to *Profound Desires*. For instance, he stresses that we should not mistake allegory (*gūwa*) for mythology, that mythology in his understanding is something that displays in a refined form one of a people's orientations, in other words the subconscious of a whole race.[12] If we want to know what a member of a certain race really aspires to, there is nowhere better to look than in the myths of that race, he has said. Moreover, since the state and the race are closely aligned in the case of the Yamato race, his intention was to treat mythology as an amalgam of the state, the emperor system, and the orientation of the race all linked together (qtd. in Imamura 1971: n.p.; Katori 2004: 245–46). In response to an assessment that he had abandoned the city in favor of the countryside in the film, he has commented: "If we understand the myths of a certain race as the craving for freedom that lies dormant within a race, in that case *Profound Desires* relates myths, it is not an allegory. The wish to recount mythology with a certain sense of reality probably made me turn to the countryside" (Imamura and Baba 1969: 20).

In his review of the film for *Eiga hyōron*, Hideo Osabe attempts a largely metaphorical reading. From the final sequence he thus reads an antimodern stance on the part of the filmmaker. Here, it appears as though nature itself on Kurage is at any moment going to swallow the small toy-like train running through the cane fields. Osabe understands this from Imamura's cynical gaze, which implies that, in the final analysis, all the rationality acquired by mankind amounts to nothing more than this toy train. For Osabe, the epilogue constitutes a highly elucidative sequence in an otherwise somewhat impenetrable film. But this does not prevent him from speculating, for instance, about the pit that Nekichi is digging, whose water is said to be connected to the ocean via its bottom. In Osabe's reading this becomes a metaphor for Imamura's belief that if you keep digging away at the irrational bedrock you will all of a sudden strike through and catch sight of the horizon of rational enlightenment. The motif also recalls for him the notion that it is only by descending to the bottom of nationalism that you will be able to glimpse the wide horizon of internationalism (Osabe 1969: 38–39). Yet at other times he also applies a literal reading in a way that illustrates my point about the film's dual aspect. Referencing certain villages in a mountainous region in northeast Japan where marriage between blood relatives is still (in 1969) being practiced, he wonders when incest became a taboo on Okinawa. He remonstrates with Imamura for having permitted the rationalist within him, his modern consciousness, to interfere with his judgment. If there were no taboo against incest somewhere deep down in the consciousness of Kurage villagers, then Imamura would only be tilting at windmills like another Don Quixote (Osabe 1969: 40). Osabe is here evincing a literal reading of the incest theme, in contrast with for instance Satō's reading, mentioned above, where incest in the film signifies something wider, perhaps some errant resistance against modernization.

In a 1977 lecture Imamura explicated his underlying motivations for *Profound Desires*. What prompted him to make the film in the first place was a desire to locate the features in which the fundamental origins of Japanese culture were to be found. But he felt that relying on historical sources would not suit his purpose, as those could not provide the gut feeling needed to start the creative process. Instead, he realized that he needed to embrace the corporeal history of the Japanese people found in the repetitive pattern of the common person's existence. His original intention with the film was thus to search for the cultural archetypes of the naked Japanese, stripped of their fashionable surface (Imamura 2010a: 140). As he argues, religious beliefs (*shinkō*) linger on in the daily life of the Japanese, as an afterimage of ancient times within their consciousness. In general, he concludes, he is striving to use the human heart (*kokoro*) still present as a remnant in traditional Japanese communities as a resource in the creative process of his filmmaking (Imamura 2010a: 148, 151).[13] Even though, as we have seen, *Profound Desires* is a problematic film in terms of interpretation, Imamura's basic stance, as related in this lecture, appears to have struck a chord with the reviewer for *Kinema junpō*, who likened the film to a persistent excavation of the structure of the Japanese people's consciousness. He defined the film's basic idea—an idea that runs through Imamura's whole production—as a way to understand gods as real, workable entities in daily life for the Japanese. The gods are a means of maintaining communal order; they are believed in, respected, and then utilized (Shinada 1969: 128).

Conclusion

Imamura's comments at the above occasion tie in well with Tony Rayns' observation that *Profound Desires* "stands as a major testament to his [Imamura's] belief that the fundamental truths of Japanese life are found not in modern society but in pre-civilised, 'primitive' attitudes and behaviour"; and that Imamura moreover argued through his films for the primitive "as a truthful state of being. For Imamura, *nostalgie de la boue* was a positive, virtually a necessity." In agreement with Imamura's own manifesto, Rayns identifies that search for the primitive in terms of creative method: "Imamura's determination to dig out 'primitive' roots licensed him to confront pre-civilized behavior in the raw, as the material for naked, visceral drama, and he was quite ready to embrace irrationality if that was what emerged" (Rayns 2010: 5, 7, 18). Imamura himself has referred to *Profound Desires* as a story about irrationality (Imamura 2011: 36). It is perhaps this feature of the film that best explains the divergence of its narrative mode from an allegory like *Woman in the Dunes*. To continue with Rayns, "The film's approach is anything but scientific. Imamura's basic strategy is to plunge the viewer into a miasma of seemingly irrational behaviour and incomprehensible relationships" (Rayns 2010: 13).

As regards approaches to appreciating Imamura's filmmaking, Rayns touches on something essential with his observation that Imamura's excavation of primitive roots licensed him to confront pre-civilized behavior as the material for *visceral drama*. One is reminded of Siegfried Kracauer's dichotomy of reasoning versus sense impressions. In a discussion of film's impact on the senses, Kracauer argues that film "can be expected to influence the spectator in a manner denied to other media." He proposes that, "unlike the other types of pictures, film images affect primarily the spectator's senses, engaging him physiologically before he is in a position to respond intellectually." For him this assumption finds support in, for instance, the argument that film not only records physical reality but also reveals otherwise hidden provinces of it:

The salient point here is that these discoveries mean an increased demand on the spectator's physiological make-up. The unknown shapes he encounters involve not so much his power of reasoning as his visceral faculties. Arousing his innate curiosity, they lure him into dimensions where sense impressions are all-important. (Kracauer 1997: 157–59)[14]

Although Kracauer is here interested in the characteristics of the film medium in general, his arguments lend themselves as a manifesto for Imamura's particular art of filmmaking. Even though, as we have seen, *Profound Desires of the Gods* has given rise to considerable intellectual speculation, not least by Imamura himself, it appears as though the film does not respond well to such approaches. Therefore, it is when we subject it to rational intellectual analysis that the film's "problematic" aspects appear. Might it not be the case that the film is intended to be enjoyed viscerally, first and foremost, before we pull it apart logically?

Notes

1. Tony Rayns has noted that "any Japanese viewer will immediately recognize Kurage as both real and unreal," and that "the unreal element springs from Imamura's conceit that Kurage represents an older, messier Japan—a Japan still in touch with its own creation myths," with a further conceit being that the Futori family behaves very much like the mythical gods did (Rayns 2010: 12). Conceit or not, Shunsuke Katori has pointed out that Imamura reached the understanding that the most basic parts of the Japanese remained in their most pronounced form on Okinawa and the Southwest Islands while doing folklore fieldwork in the region (Katori 2004: 243). Aaron Gerow has suggested that *Profound Desires* offered a critique of Japan's pursuit of high economic growth, "yet treated Okinawa as the primitive object of an ethnographic gaze." He continues: "Imamura's ethnographic perspective on Okinawa . . . is reminiscent of that of prewar ethnologists like Yanagita Kunio and Origuchi Shinobu who located Okinawa at the beginning of a narrative of Japanese origins. This cultural nostalgia always posed the danger of rendering Okinawa in a Japanese version of an Orientalist palette, and in Imamura's case, the Okinawan self is rendered more natural, more original than the Japan of the high-economic growth era, often in order to imagine a Japanese self in opposition to Western modernity" (Gerow 2013: 277). Interestingly, this point of critical perspective is totally lacking in the contemporary reviews and later discourse on the film discussed in this essay. Indeed, Gerow's valid point is probably more in line with more recent trends of sociocultural academic critique. On the other hand, Imamura recalled how the project was met with a protest campaign from a local newspaper on the grounds that the script for the film contained insulting portrayals that emphasized the primitiveness of the

island, such as incest and half-naked islanders. In this context Imamura is clear about applying the ethnology of the abovementioned Yanagita Kunio to investigate Japan in the film (Imamura 2010b: 109).
2. In 1969 Imamura elaborated on his motivations for making the film: "I wanted to try to fix my gaze on the pantheistic climate of Japan just as it is. It felt like something would emerge from there. In this sense, since several years back this film was the one I just had to make no matter what. Perhaps you can call it the final settlement of accounts of all the films I've made until now" (qtd. in Imamura 2001: 57).
3. Shunsuke Katori, for his part, argues that there are many parts of the film that are difficult to understand because too much has been left out in terms of providing motivation to the characters and that there is therefore a tendency for authorial intentions not to come across as strongly compelling to the audience (Katori 2004: 245). In fact, some plot elements explained in the official leaflet for the film cannot be discerned from the film alone.
4. Ryūzō Saki is the author of *Vengeance Is Mine* (*Fukushū suru wa ware ni ari*, 1976), the novel on which Imamura based his film of that title.
5. In his review of *Profound Desires* for *Eiga hyōron*, Hideo Osabe claims that Imamura is someone who interprets the world but does not really attempt to change it; moreover, that his stance is to not deny anything. On the contrary, he accepts everything. Osabe is, however, looking forward to a film from Imamura that will not only deny the modern and affirm the primitive but affirm unconditionally a present Japan of indeterminate form where the premodern, the modern, and the contemporary coexist in a disorderly fashion (Osabe 1969: 41).
6. Early in the film—in a scene that appears sudden and gratuitous to the plot—a pig falls off a ferryboat leaving the island and is devoured by sharks.
7. This reading would seem to be endorsed by Imamura, who has spoken of the film in terms of a myth that relates the orientation of a race, a wish that courses down the riverbed of that race to live freely (Imamura and Baba 1969: 26).
8. Imamura has explained the epilogue of the film, including the sailboat with its red sail, in terms of a narrative device—the threshold between myth and present—with the function of elevating the preceding story to a myth-like five years past (Imamura and Baba 1969: 26).
9. Tony Rayns has observed that "the film doesn't feel at all like a political allegory," in response to Tadao Satō's idea that the island kingpin Ryū Ryūgen should be read as an emperor figure (Rayns 2011: 12–13). To this I would add that it doesn't feel like an allegory of any kind, but somehow must be taken for real.
10. This feature of the film has not prevented commentators from interpreting various story elements in terms of their significations. Shunsuke Katori, for instance, argues that the fictitious Kurage represents an essence of Japanese society that is very much alive in various contemporary Japanese settings. Even if you will not literally be tortured to death, as Nekichi and Uma are at the end of the film, the way in which people who break the social code are excluded according to group logic is reminiscent of situations often observed among salarymen (Katori 2004: 243).

For a roundtable talk that presents a veritable plethora of suggestive readings and interpretations of a whole range of themes and motifs from the film, see Ishidō (1969).

11. The poet Shiroyasu Suzuki asked himself this very question in a long musing about the film for the journal *Shinario* (Suzuki 1969: 34). This is a rare article in that it tries to explicate the film's implications for the daily lives of contemporary Japanese, even though he concedes it is a difficult task to read the implied meanings of the images into the milieus of our everyday life (Suzuki 1969: 29).
12. Imamura uses the word *minzoku* throughout, a word variously translated as race, people, or nation.
13. For an article that treats the film in relation to the anthropology of Okinawa, see the 1969 discussion between the anthropologist Kin'ichi Ōgo and Keiji Hasebe, Imamura's co-scriptwriter for *Profound Desires*.
14. Kracauer restricts his argument to films that conform to what he calls the "cinematic approach," which he argues materializes in all films that follow the realistic tendency: "Creative efforts are in keeping with the cinematic approach as long as they benefit, in some way or other, the medium's substantive concern with our visible world" (Kracauer 1997: 39).

Works Cited

Gerow, Aaron (2003). "From the National Gaze to Multiple Gazes: Representations of Okinawa in Recent Japanese Cinema." In *Islands of Discontent: Okinawan Responses to Japanese and American Power*, ed. Laura Hein and Mark Selden. Lanham, MD: Rowman & Littlefield.
Imamura, Shōhei (1971). *Imamura Shōhei no eiga: zensagyō no kiroku*. Tokyo: Haga shoten.
Imamura, Shōhei (2001). *Toru: Kannu kara yamiichi e*. Tokyo: Kōsakusha.
Imamura, Shōhei (2010a). *Kyōikusha: Imamura Shōhei*. Tokyo: Kinema junposha.
Imamura, Shōhei (2010b). *Imamura Shōhei: eiga wa kyōki no tabi de aru*. Tokyo: Nihon tosho sentā.
Imamura, Shōhei (2011). "Imamura Shōhei at the Edinburgh International Film Festival, 1994." In *Profound Desires of the Gods*, Eureka Entertainment, Masters of Cinema series no. 10, 31–40.
Imamura, Shōhei, and Baba Masaru (1969). "Shinwa to machi no aida: 'Kamigami no fukaki yokubō' o megutte." *Shinario*, March: 12–27.
Ishidō, Toshirō, et al. (1969). "Imamura Shōhei no uchinaru kokyō wa doko ka: 'Kamigami no fukaki yokubō' ni shōchō sareta Nihonjin genzō." *Eiga geijutsu*, January: 69–73.
Katori, Shunsuke (2004). *Imamura Shōhei densetsu*. Tokyo: Kawade shobo shinsha.
Kracauer, Siegfried (1997 [1960]). *Theory of Film: The Redemption of Physical Reality*. Princeton, NJ: Princeton University Press.
Nikkatsu (1968). "Puresu shīto: *Kamigami no fukaki yokubō*." Unpublished.
Ōgo, Kin'ichi, and Hasebe Keiji (1969). "Mikai no shikō: 'Kamigami no fukaki yokubō' ni itaru bunka jinruigakuteki shikō." *Shinario*, January: 30–38.

Osabe, Hideo (1969). "Hatashite iwa wa ochita no ka: Imamura Shōhei no 'Kamigami no fukaki yokubō.'" *Eiga hyōron*, January: 38–41.

Rayns, Tony (2010). "Gods, Humans, and Profound Desires." In *Profound Desires of the Gods*, Eureka Entertainment, Masters of Cinema series, no. 10, 5–18.

Saki, Ryūzō (1969). "Shima no owari no monogatari." *Bungei*, January: 218–20.

Satō, Tadao (1997). *Imamura Shōhei no sekai* (enlarged ed.). Tokyo: Gakuyo shobo.

Shimizu, Masashi (2001). *Imamura Shōhei o yomu*. Tokyo: Choeisha.

Shinada, Yūkichi (1969). "Nihon eiga hihyō: *Kamigami no fukaki yokubō*." *Kinema junpō*, February (jōjun): 128–29.

Suzuki, Shirōyasu (1969). "'Kamigami no fukaki yokubō' o koete, gokushiteki heisagoe." *Shinario*, March: 28–40.

Tayama, Rikiya (1971). "Imamura Shōhei den." In *Sekai no eiga sakka* 8. Tokyo: Kinema junposha.

Chapter 10

"Products of Japan": *Karayuki-san, The Making of a Prostitute*

Joan Mellen

"About two years ago," a man says matter-of-factly in voiceover, "I went to Malaysia." He is on a boat plowing through dirty, grey-blue water. "By chance," the nameless man continues, he met some *karayuki-san*.[1] "I had always wanted to hear their story," he adds. These women were the "untold story of the common people's history." His tone is that of a professional journalist, even as his subject bespeaks high emotion, the Japanese state's exploitation of young women sold into slavery as prostitutes and taken by force or guile into the far-flung corners of Asia, the outer limits of Japan's "Greater East Asia Co-Prosperity Sphere." The speaker is soon replaced by a fellow narrator, a woman. "I am seventy-three years old," she says. "I was the youngest of eight children."

You would not know that this pudgy man in a short-sleeved blue shirt with white stripes and gray pants is an accomplished Japanese film director named Shohei Imamura, because he has the gift of making himself seem invisible. He is an ordinary-looking man in horn-rimmed sunglasses, in his late forties, with a small mustache and black hair. We are entering a nondescript harbor somewhere east of Suez. Imamura's personality is muted. Clutching a microphone, he is recording the words of his subject, an elderly *karayuki-san* named Kikuyo Zendo who had worked in Malaya, today's Malaysia.

When I interviewed Imamura at his studio in the outskirts of Tokyo in 1975, the first thing he said to me was, "Do you know what 'satori' means?"[2] He was referring to the Zen ideal of sudden spiritual awareness, the enlightenment that in the case of cinema arises from the confluence of images and sound. His films illuminate and penetrate truths too uncomfortable for mainstream dramatic films to express.

Imamura's focus is simultaneously spiritual and historical and his perspective clear: Japan's historical and cultural identity is best dramatized by focusing on its victims. The story of the thousands of Japanese women forced into prostitution unfolds through Imamura's gentle probing of his protagonist. She is a small, shrunken, elderly woman who is missing a number of teeth. Her skin is leathery and wrinkled, her smile ready.

Entering Waseda University at the end of World War II, Imamura majored in Western History, although his quintessential subject is Japan. He is an artist uneasy with the perspective of the official culture with which Ozu, his first teacher, was so strong a proponent. Donald Richie claimed that Imamura told him that Ozu was "one of the two strongest influences on his work" (Richie 1997: 39). Imamura said elsewhere, "Ozu barely acknowledged my existence." "I got into filmmaking because I wanted to be like Kurosawa," he told Toichi Nakata (1997: 115).

This seems more plausible since Imamura shares with Kurosawa an abiding opposition to injustice. Like Kurosawa, in his youth Imamura was involved with the Communist movement (Nakata 1997: 111). Of Kurosawa, Imamura said, "This is someone I idolized" (Phillips 2000). Imamura has recounted that he found Ozu, for whom he worked as "fifth assistant" on three films, cold and unapproachable (Nakata 1997: 112). On the day of his mother's funeral—while they were working on *Tokyo Story*—Ozu, who rarely spoke to Imamura, suddenly addressed him during a chance meeting in the urinal. "Mr. Imamura, is that what a cerebral hemorrhage looks like? Have I got it right?" Ozu said. The question chilled Imamura. He had gone to work at the Ofuna studio of Shochiku only because the year he applied to enter the film industry, Toho, Kurosawa's studio, was on strike and had suspended its entrance examinations.

At the age of thirty, Imamura became interested in social anthropology. All his films spring from a documentary impulse, the dramatic films no less than the formal documentaries. He even termed *Eijanaika* (1981), his recreation of the fall of the Tokugawa shogunate, a "documentary period film." His characters are people who spring from the landscape of their circumstances. He was interested not in the conventional middle-class Japanese of the Ozu pantheon, but in working people, "strong, greedy, humorous, deceitful people who are very human in their quality and their failings." He focuses on women, uneducated, vulgar, lusty, strongly affectionate and heroic when confronting their suffering (Nakata 1997: 117).

Imamura became acquainted with such people in the aftermath of World War II when, alone as a college student in Tokyo, his parents not yet repatriated from Hokkaido, he survived by participating in the black market (Nakata 1997: 111). In the chaos of the postwar moment, son of a doctor though he was, Imamura sold liquor and cigarettes to his professors at Waseda University, commodities he bought from soldiers of the American occupation. Meanwhile, as a student who had strongly leftist views, he opposed the Imperial system and debated with classmates the extent of Emperor Hirohito's personal responsibility for the war.

People exploited and undervalued by official Japanese society, those whose survival is always in question and with no one to support or speak for them, are Imamura's subjects. Imamura has recounted how a scriptwriter friend once said to him, "Oh, you are still writing about beggars and all those dropouts from the mainstream of society" (Phillips 2000). In fact, the values of the mainstream, buttressing the Imperial system and nourishing Japan's march to conquest in the 1930s, held no charm for Imamura. Of his characters, he said, "They are human beings and even though they may be at the bottom of society, what they say is true ... I want to enter the character's heart" (Imamura 1997a: 126).

Feeling like as an outsider himself, not offered employment by the big studios, he turned away, vowing to "only write about oppressed people all my life." His people may not be rational or prosperous, but they are robust with a strong capacity for survival. He treats them as equals, no matter that they were not "successful" in a conventional sense.

"There are few films made today," Imamura said in the year 2000, "which indicate that their directors have a strong grip on the situation facing ordinary people. They don't seem to be able to look squarely at the real situation." He made his films not to entertain but to convey these harsh realities. "I have always insisted that I would never tell lies in my movies, to only tell the truth. This is a big principle for me." Further: "It's a lot easier to be obedient and stay within the establishment," he has said. "But this is not my way of life. I always try to change society with my films. Of course, filmmaking is not like catch. You can throw the ball but there is no guarantee that it will be caught" (Phillips).

Among the truths Imamura penetrates in *Eijanaika* is that the amulets falling from heaven at the moment of the demise of the *bakumatsu* were in fact planted by a group of lesser samurai grappling for power with others. Their aim was to throw the populace into disarray, as the mobs cried, "Isn't it good!" (*eija nai ka*). They are all too willing to embrace the turbulence of this moment of profound change in Japanese history as common people were seduced into dissipating their energy in support of a new establishment that would replace the Shogunate. The memorable scenes of carnival energy in this film are heartrending.

In *Karayuki-san,* Imamura is personally present throughout the film; he appears as a character to encourage his people, and to make it clear that that he is no different from them. His very presence conveys sympathy, a reassurance to the former *karayuki-san* that however Japan may have abandoned them, they are not alone. He does not condescend to his characters; that would amount to a sentimentality that would be an affront to the quiet magnificence of their capacity to endure.

Karayuki-san was not the first of Imamura's documentaries about women abandoned by Japan in its rush toward prosperity. It forms a companion to A *History of Postwar Japan as Told by a Bar Hostess* (1970) (*Nippon Sengoshi: Madame Onboro No Seikatsu*) (1970), a film Imamura called "semi-fiction," and the actual story of a woman very much like Kikuyo Zendo (Imamura 130). Both Etsuko Akaza, proprietress of the Onboro bar in Yokosuka, site of an American base, and Kikuyo Zendo were born *burakumin*, or *eta*, people whose families were in the business of slaughtering animals, outcasts from respectable Japanese society.

By birth, both women were rendered lifetime victims of discrimination and hardship, outcasts unlikely to marry respectable Japanese men. With resources of energy and fortitude, Etsuko works in a brothel catering to Americans; she saves up enough to open her own bar frequented by American sailors, marries one of them, and moves to America. Kikuyo survives in the outposts of Japanese imperialism amid the red light districts of Malaysia and Singapore.

Like all the woman in Imamura's documentaries, Etsuko and Kikuyo welcome him, perceiving his affection for them. "I love all the characters in my films, even the loutish and frivolous ones. I want every one of my shots to express this love", he has declared (Imamura 1997a: 126). He is on their side, unforgiving of those who caused them pain, whether callous individual men or Japan as a culture and a society. "I don't want you to look at my characters and say they are all oppressed or that they are at the bottom of society." His abiding premise is opposition to "the way these people have been treated" (Phillips 2000).

"Onboro" paved the way for *Karayuki-san: The Making of a Prostitute (1975)*, the culmination of Shohei Imamura's nine-year excursion into documentary filmmaking. The direct link between these two films is that neither woman can forge a satisfactory life in Japan. Both films offer unforgettable characters in the course of the director's investigation into Japanese history. *Karayuki-san* is more poignant. Through Kikuyo, and then through several other *karayuki-san* whom he and Kikuyo meet and interview together, Imamura presents the horrific story of women he has called the "shock troops" of Japan's ascension to power and military predominance, Japan's foray into imperialism. Kikuyo becomes Imamura's assistant, reassuring the elderly broken former *karayuki-san* that it is safe to tell him their story. She asks them the same questions that earlier he had put to her. With Imamura's guidance, she has become the author of her own life, free to express herself in a way she never has experienced, embodying the ideal of freedom that Imamura described as the foundation of his filmmaking.

By the 1930s, Japan was bent on establishing a political, economic, and cultural union in greater East Asia in the service of a Japanese empire. Its slogan was "The eight corners of the world beneath one roof," its project a holy war of Japanese aggression. Annexing the weaker countries of Asia, from China and Korea to Borneo, Japan considered itself their natural ruler by virtue of its more developed industrial base. Japan's rulers contended that there was a common racial and religious affinity between Japan, Korea, and China in particular that justified Japanese expansion and the appropriation of their resources (OSS).

An important component of this crusade, the Greater East-Asia Co-Prosperity Sphere, was blotting out the influence of Anglo-American culture in East Asia, thereby acting for the good of all Asians (OSS). Western notions of individualism would be dispelled as Japan, in a symbiotic relationship with the other countries of Asia, would pursue its "world historical mission." There would be "co-prosperity" between the countries in question, mutual cooperative development, solidarity, and coexistence. Western values, individualism in particular, would dissipate.

In reality, its economy stretched thin, Japan enslaved local populations into forced labor and starved the workers mercilessly (see, for instance, Masaki Kobayashi's *Ningen no Joken,1959–1961*, a three-part film released in English as *The Human Condition*). Japan promised countries under colonial domination, like Indochina, that they would grant them their independence, which never occurred. There was little effort to develop local economies.

As it geared up for war, Japan sought essential natural resources, such as oil and rubber, which were unavailable in the homeland. There was oil to be had in the Dutch East Indies, iron and coal in Manchuria and rubber in French Indochina. The situation was exacerbated when the United States embargoed oil and steel shipments to Japan. All these economies soon came under the sway of Japan.

In the service of the "Greater East Asia Co-Prosperity Sphere," Japan treated its most vulnerable citizens as expendable. In a culture that had always devalued and exploited women and that had institutionalized prostitution, the concept of "karayuki-san" was not unthinkable. The term itself meant "going to Kara," which first referred to China, and was later extended to include all of Southeast Asia.

The system of *karayuki-san* or "comfort women" actually began in 1868 with the fall of the Tokugawa dynasty when Chinese merchants in Japan sent their Japanese house servants to China. The first two decades of the twentieth century saw thousands of young women leaving Japan for lives as prostitutes in neighboring Asian countries. With the Japanese invasion of China in the early 1930s, *karayuki-san* were sent to the far-flung corners of the "Co-Prosperity sphere" that came to include Korea, Thailand, Indonesia, Borneo, Malaysia, Burma, French

Indochina, New Guinea, and the Philippines. There had been such frequent rape of local women by Japanese soldiers that *karayuki-san* were enlisted to tamper the frustration and discontent of the soldiers that the authorities feared might otherwise precipitate revolt. As Japanese historian Yoshiaki Yoshimi put it, "The Japanese Imperial Army feared most that the simmering discontentment of the soldiers could explode into a riot and revolt" (Yoshimi 2000).

Sometimes a woman's parents, or siblings, sold her to brokers who ranged over Japan in search of poor women with no resources. Sometimes girls as young as nine and ten years old were carried off to ships without knowing where they were going. Sometimes the pimp promised the woman a respectable job in a factory or a restaurant, or as a maid, and the woman did not discover until it was too late that her fate was to be a prostitute. Always she was treated as a virtual slave and was told that to escape she would have to pay off a considerable debt.

Thousands of women were herded into military brothels. Members of the Japanese military were instructed on how to manage comfort stations, including how to determine the actuarial "durability or perishability of the women we procure." Army doctors ostensibly conducted tests for venereal disease. Lacking microscopes, they used "simple visual checks." There was an instrument inserted into the vagina that made it pop open so you could see inside.

Well into the millennium the Japanese government denied that the institutionalized sexual enslavement of thousands of Japanese women had taken place. Yet there were between 300,000 and 400,000 women and girls impressed into this service. Later there were apologies issued by officials; in 1994, the Japanese prime minister Tomiichi Murayama apologized "to all the women who underwent immeasurable and painful experiences and suffered incurable physical and psychological wounds as comfort women." In July 1995, Prime Minister Murayama repeated: "I offer my profound apology to all those who, as wartime comfort women, suffered emotional and physical wounds that can never be closed."

Yet in 2007 Prime Minister Shinzo Abe declared, "There was no evidence that the Japanese government had kept sex slaves." The *Yomiuri Shimbun* newspaper insisted that the women voluntarily provided "comfort" to the frontline troops and accused the rival *Asahi Shimbun* of helping to fuel anti-Japan sentiment in South Korea and "misperception of Japan throughout the world." The flurry of apologies and denials were referred to as Japan's "apology diplomacy" for its wartime misdeeds. Coming twenty years earlier, Imamura's film deepened the political debate. *Karayuki-san* is a historical act as much as it is a work of art.

"I want to make really human, Japanese, unsettling films," Imamura told poet and film critic Heiichi Sugiyama (Richie 1997: 31). There could be no more "unsettling" subject than the war-time *karayuki-san*, a subject perfectly suited to a director who in all his films challenged official Japan, from the *bakumatsu* to the Japanese war of the thirties and forties to the postwar moment where little had changed for those outside the burgeoning economy. Into the twenty-first century, Imamura depicted people who remained as expendable as they always had been throughout Japan's history.

For Imamura these are the people who built Japan, contributing their energy to the struggle for progress. "I am interested in the relationship of the lower part of the human body and the lower part of the social structure on which the reality of daily Japanese life supports itself," he told critic Koichi Yamada (Richie 1997: 17). Whatever vitality Japan has found, it is through such people.

Kikuyo Zendo, the central character of *Karayuki-san*, is a prime example. She responds to Imamura's appreciation of her; he has called her "a gentle old lady of seventy" who was "tolerant" of his crew. She laughs at some of Imamura's questions, particularly whether she enjoyed the sex, not out of embarrassment, but recognizing the irony. He was the one who was uneasy: "I was less and less sure that I could justify asking her such questions as how many men she had to sleep with every night" or "Did you enjoy sex with your clients?" (Nakata 1997: 120).

"I had to ask myself," Imamura added, "whether or not I was exploiting her, whether or not I had good enough reasons to expose her past in public, and whether or not I really understood her feelings." He also asked himself whether documentary was "really the best way to approach these matters," aware as he was that the very presence of the camera "could materially change people's lives."

All the "old ladies" he interviews try to help him understand what had happened to them, perceiving that his aim is to render the truth of their lives. For him, they are willing to remember their pain, the hardships and the loneliness. Unaccustomed to being looked at for themselves, unaccustomed to being taken seriously, in exchange for the respect Imamura offers, they are willing to tell their stories. Imaginative and lucid, they help him to create the illusion that we are actually viewing them at the time of their lives as *karayuki-san*, lives for which, of course, no footage exists. Yet, whenever possible, Imamura intercuts rare photographs of the *karayuki-san* in their innocent youth, posing stiffly in kimono. Their expressions are stoical, bereft of false hope. Most of the women were illiterate. Kikuyo went up to the fourth grade.

"I understood," Imamura told Toichi Nakata, interviewing him in Edinburgh in 1994, "that my filmmaking would only be truly international if it was derived from a Japanese cultural and ideological struggle" (Imamura 1997b: 129). Like all his films, *Karayuki-san*, he has said, is "like myself, very Japanese" (Imamura 1997b: 129). His films appeal to Western audiences precisely because they are rooted in Japanese values, modes of perceiving, and historical understanding.

Kikuyo Zendo attempts to piece together her past, as Imamura unfolds the realities of twentieth-century Japanese history, of which Kikuyo is an emblem. "Tricked" by a woman named Tomiko, who worked with Kikuyo's sister weaving straw mats, at the age of nineteen (she is not certain whether she was born in 1898 or 1899) Kikuyo was promised that she would be working at a hotel in Kobe. Instead, she was kidnapped and hidden at the bottom of a dilapidated boat, where in darkness and in space so tight the five or six girls imprisoned there could scarcely move; they were then sent to Kelang, the shabby outpost of civilization in Malaysia where she and Imamura have traveled together to make this film.

It must have been a Japanese boat since they were brought Japanese meals, Kikuyo reflects. Imamura intercuts old photographs of the harbor at the time she arrived, a shabby impoverished port studded with industrial refuse. There are no shots of blue sea exoticism, the vulgarities of orientalism. The streets of Kelang are filled with the poor and the idle, with leering male passersby staring at Imamura and at this elderly woman in a brown and gold patterned house dress, who pointedly ignores them. Later Imamura remarks, "One of these men around here might have known you from back then." Kikuyo laughs out loud, the first of many such moments, all coming as a surprise. She finds the ironies of her life, the absurdities, a source of humor. All the former *karayuki-san* are beyond anger.

When women appear in the *mise-en-scène* of the present, they are middle-aged prostitutes, sitting around waiting for customers. Their tight, revealing shorts and low-cut tops make them seem desperate and unappealing. These images suggest that the situation of poor Asian women has not altered substantially over the past century.

The odd couple, Imamura and Kikuyo Zendo, climb a set of rickety very steep stairs to the wharf. A shaky hand-held camera records their movements, reflecting the precariousness of what would be Kikuyo's future. Imamura carries the microphone, its cord awkwardly trailing behind, bending down to her level. "Couldn't you have refused?" he asks. "I see how hopeless you were, but couldn't you have fought with him more?" This seems callous. It isn't. Imamura has offered Kikuyo the opportunity to recount how trapped she was. "Once you're in that kind of situation, you're helpless," she explains, without emotion. She tells how she had agreed to appear at a court to "register" to work. "I had to lie and say I was over twenty," she explains. Imamura's sympathy is expressed in voiceover as he murmurs, "The heat was so intense it made me dizzy." It was into a debilitating climate that the young Kikuyo was thrust.

Imamura wants to know about her first client, who was a policeman. He wants to know how much she charged. He learns that she preferred the "short timers," who paid only two dollars, because they would be gone fast.

When Imamura asks why a woman like Tomiko would bully her, Kikuyo laughs. "Was she pretty?" Imamura wants to know. When she remarks that Tomiko was a beauty, Imamura says, "You must have been a beauty too." Kikuyo laughs and contradicts the filmmaker in whose project, offscreen, she has already enlisted whole-heartedly. "I was always like this," she says firmly. Every detail of her life is important. "It didn't help if we fought or cried," she explains. "They wouldn't let us go home."

When Imamura asks whether it is true that women can't forget their first, Kikuyo laughs again. They laugh together, fellow Japanese, collaborating.

The first half of the film is shot in half-darkness as Kikuyo tells her story; even the exteriors are devoid of illumination. The place was not lit during the day, and so the shots reflect this darkness. Imamura remarks that Kelang "must have changed," but Kikuyo, her face in shadow, corrects him here too. The camera situates itself on the ground floor looking up at Imamura and Kikuyo, it pans and moves attempting to discover the world in which she was once enslaved, a world almost unchanged, now populated by half-dressed idle prostitutes.

That in the first part of the film Kikuyo's face is in darkness provides a kind of privacy as Kikuyo reveals the secrets of her history. The takes are long because everything she says is worth pondering, as she considers the motives of the woman who betrayed her. Maybe "money."

Nothing has changed, even as Japan has not made amends for its brutality, and the number "20" is just as it was the day she arrived fifty years earlier, high on the wall. Did the place have a name? She explains that "20 Malay Street" was quite famous. Imamura requests that Kikuyo recount her daily routine, "we put on our makeup and got to work," because she is important to him. When she explains that she worked during the day as well as at night, Imamura protests: "but it is so hot." Kikuyo laughs. The heat was the least of it.

It is part of Imamura's determination to impart dignity to the *karayuki-san* that Kikuyo never complains, not about the heat, and not about how many men she serviced (on her worst day, thirty). On busy days, there were seven or eight clients. She was forbidden by the "master" to write letters back to Japan. Marriage did not work out for her. As for the sex, she doesn't hesitate. "You hated it?" he asks. "Yes, I hated it," she says.

Kikuyo has no particular memories of the Japanese war, and so Imamura uses voiceover narration at intervals to introduce historical facts of Japan's pursuit of the Greater East Asia Co-Prosperity Sphere. After World War I the light manufacturing industries of China and Japan were in competition; *karayuki-san* were shunned as "Japanese products." They became an embarrassment at a time Japan was suffering great poverty because they earned foreign currency. After Japan sent its military into Asia, all Japanese products were burned.

These women were now expected to contribute to the economy of the homeland, as was the case with O-Saki in a book by Tomoko Yamazaki originally published in 1972 (and which appeared in English in 1999) about the *karayuki-san* called *Sandakan Brothel No.8*.[3] The main character is "Yamakawa Saki," or "O-Saki," the pseudonym for a woman who was shipped to North Borneo at the age of ten. Abandoned by her mother, she agreed to remain abroad to earn money so that her brother might buy farmland, build a house, and secure a wife. When O-Saki returns home to Amakusa as an old woman, she is shunned by her family because it was shameful to have been a *karayuki-san*.

As the late Donald Richie elegantly noted, Imamura foregoes "the consolations of plot." He wants nothing to do with the "well-made film." His films are sometimes "messy," Imamura admitted, and *Karayuki-san* proceeds by the accretion of episodes. There is no rising action, no climactic moment. There is, instead, an accumulation of information. So we are told the system was enforced by "ex-convict abductors." A sepia photograph of a very rough character is interpolated. These enforcers told the women it was "their duty" to send money home. In the first-person plural, Imamura assumes full responsibility for Japan: "Our homeland sucked up their profits."

Awkwardly, Imamura suddenly says, "Let's go back to Kikuyo's story." He lights a cigarette for his subject (they are both heavy smokers), and the narrative resumes. Kikuyo too, we learn, sent currency back to Japan when her sister sent letters begging for money. She sent what she could, Kikuyo says without bitterness. She talks about how she had a regular client, who came on a ship that she went to the harbor to meet. "You were like a local wife?" Imamura says, and Kikuyo laughs, laughter not out of mirth but in acknowledgment of the absurd. She never enjoyed the rights and privileges of a wife.

"Did you ever fall in love?" Imamura wants to know. Kikuyo suggests that she did, with Tadokoro, the manager of a rubber plantation, whose wife had died and who wanted to marry her. "I just couldn't," she says. "I had no education so I could not marry him." She was a woman who never put herself first, and who expressed a natural solidarity with others suffering the same plight. The pathos of her story accelerates.

"I wanted to marry him, but I said no to him and he went back to Japan," she reveals. It was the turning point of her life when she said farewell to Tadokoro at the Miyako Hotel. Did you cry when you said goodbye to him? Imamura wants to know. Kikuyo laughs out loud, then replies: "No, I didn't cry, but I was sad." She is laughing, this time, at the pointlessness of tears.

As a staunch documentary filmmaker, Imamura tries to locate the Miyako Hotel, so critical a location for Kikuyo's story. It was a place where auctions of *karayuki-san* were held, the location of a slave trade. The building is gone. He finds only old sepia photographs showing a sea of self-satisfied men, "masters" and "pimps" with a few karayuki-*san* sprinkled among them. One girl's face is twisted in agony as a man clutches her arm.

There are other old photographs. "This is me," Kikuyo says simply, glancing at an old photograph of herself in her youth, a plain woman in an unembellished kimono. The photos were taken when she took up with an Indian who worked in a photo studio. She married him, but he quit his job and became a dry cleaner. "I didn't like his decision, so I left him," she says, without emotion, that commodity no *karayuki-san* can afford.

Kikuyo married a man who worked on the railroads and had a son, now a doctor, but he visits only occasionally and only then gives her money. All their money went for his medical training, and so when her husband died she sold the house and paid the debts of his son's education. The life of this woman who became Imamura's subject "by chance" was without luck, and was so grim that to survive she chose to accept everything that happened to her as her "fate."

When the Second World War began, she was placed in a prison camp run by Indians. Imamura interviews a man who was a Singapore newspaper editor at the time, and so learns that the interned Japanese hung pictures of the emperor and empress. Imamura offers no comment. There were two types of Japanese there, those who supported the war and those who didn't, even as for these outcasts whether Japan won or lost the war made no difference to their lives. The Indians shot one *karayuki-san* who refused to believe that Japan had lost the war.

There is a freeze-frame of Kikuyo, a signature Imamura technique, a punctuation mark on her story and its brutality, its finality. The action resumes as she begins to talk. Does she miss Japan? Imamura asks. She says that she would like to visit once. As the camera picks her up through a barred window, we see how Kikuyo lives, as a servant doing chores from sunrise to sundown for her son's mother-in-law. "I don't just live here doing nothing," she remarks. "They don't have a maid so I do everything for them." Imamura films a typical day in Kikuyo's life. We observe her servitude in horror even as Kikuyo says, "As long as I can smoke my cigarettes, I'm fine."

What would await her in Japan is revealed when, abruptly, Imamura intercuts a visit he made to Japan. In one scene he interviews Mrs. Nishimura, the wife of a Sumitomo Company businessman for whom Kikuyo worked as a maid for six months in Singapore. "She lives with her in-laws, whom she loathes," Mrs. Nishimura reveals. Her grandchildren say terrible things to her every day. She does not ask for money, and is paid for her work only in cigarettes and soap.

"I'm impressed by her," Mrs. Nishimura says. After fifty years of hardship, she never insists on any rights, never asks for anything for herself, and is resolved to help others. (Kikuyo has written to Imamura that she is worried about his film, troubled that she hasn't provided enough documentation.) All that suffering must have made her what she is: tough, strong, and resilient. Only from Mrs. Nishimura do we learn that Kikuyo, more than once, has had to beg her son's in-laws to allow her to stay.

"I was moved by her generosity," Mrs. Nishimura says. In Kikuyo Zendo, Imamura has discovered an essential Japanese spirit, rural in its origins, free of material desires, free of bitterness, without guile. She may be uneducated, he reveals, but she is intelligent. Kikuyo requested as her farewell gift from Mrs. Nishimura a kimono to be spread over her when she died, and we see her in this kimono—it's purple with flowers—in the penultimate scene when she places flowers on the graves of the *karayuki-san*.

On Imamura's visit to Kikuyo's ancestral village near Hiroshima he gathers information that Kikuyo has not revealed. He locates two elders and when he shows them old photos, they remember her from grade school. "Was this a *buraku* village?" Imamura asks. The elementary school went up only to the fourth grade, after which many of the children went to work at a spinning mill. Her family owned no land and were hired as day laborers. Not all were *burakumin*, but those who were left the village. The camera is placed high, looking down on these poor, powerless people as two men describe Kikuyo's brother Tsuichi as "a nice gentle person" who was picked on and harassed; he sold fish and bean curd from a cart and because he had a disability in his right hand, the villagers in their rural cruelty demanded that he not touch the food he was selling, but to use chopsticks. Kikuyo had grown up in a house with one room and a small kitchen.

They describe how a local girl was rejected by her boyfriend's parents and was "so devastated that she killed herself." Injustice and cruelty remain embedded in the fabric of Japanese culture. Imamura and his subjects share this view. Has that changed now? Imamura persists. "It still exists," the elder says, as "marital discrimination." This happened only two years earlier.

"Poor thing," one of the elderly men says, speaking of Kikuyo. "I think she should come home once before she dies." Now Imamura does interpolate his own feelings: "I was deeply affected by the gentle words of the discriminated (people), taken advantage of by Japan's prosperity." In voiceover he explains that he now knows why their opinion about the war, about Japan, was so negative. "The bruises on their hearts are profound," he notes.

It remains only for Imamura, back in South Asia, to interview other aged *karayuki-san*, the better to reveal that the life experiences of all these women followed a similar pattern. Kikuyo is now part of Imamura's crew. "This man wants to interview us about when we were working in the houses in Malaya," she says, encouraging other *karayuki-san*. Imamura places himself first on the left, three-quarters out of frame, and then on the right. He is inconsequential to their stories. Tora, born in Shimabara, came to Kelang at sixteen and married a Chinese policeman a year later so he might help find her sister. He failed. Yae was sold off by her mother, "tricked." "I cried all the time at first, but I had to go on living," she explains. As for going back to Japan, she says, "What would I do there?" There was no place in Japan for her as a young woman and there is none now.

When Yae brings out her photo album, we see that the opening pages are occupied by photographs of the emperor and the empress. The imperial system is embedded in this culture, as much in its victims as in those who prospered. Another *karayuki-san*, a very weak old lady, her face ravaged and wrinkled, tells Imamura that her parents "sold her." Imamura interpolates a shot of an unidentified young girl, perhaps a grandchild, listening to the tale in horror.

The last of the *karayuki-san* resides at the National Nursing Home in Kuala Lumpur. There is a long line of shabby cots. *Konnichiwa*, hello, Imamura says shyly to Matsu. He notes in voiceover that Matsu and Kikuyo seem like old friends, although they have just met. This *karayuki-san* from Amakusa, the home of many *karayuki-san*, is deeply bent over and walks with a stick, as she tells the same story. "I had no choice." There was no food in Japan back then, she says. The director sits on the edge of a bed observing a circle of four *karayuki-san*. "I see what you mean," he says, and then he listens while Kikuyo questions Matsu, as once Imamura questioned her. Where are you from? What kind of ship? Were the men Japanese? For a final time Imamura intercuts more shots of the middle-aged prostitutes in Kelang's darkened rooms and stairwells, waiting for men. The connection is thematic, the technique "messy," but by now we have been converted to Imamura's aesthetic (Imamura 1997b: 129). Each of the elderly women says the same thing: they felt nothing for the men who deceived them and purchased their services, not even hatred. Does Matsu hate Mr. Iwata? Imamura presses. "I don't feel anything for him," she says, and Imamura and Kikuyo laugh. As they depart, Kikuyo remarks, "I hope I die before I have to live here. It'll be a lot easier to die early."

At a cemetery, dressed in her best purple-flowered kimono, Kikuyo pauses at the grave of a young woman who died for one yen. "Poor thing," she says, echoing her neighbor's words for her. Many graves have no names, only numbers, no stones, only blocks of wood. The music is Japanese, the samisen respectful as silently Kikuyo places a large flower on as many graves as she can. The sky is blue and the palm trees sway in the breeze in sharp contrast to the misfortunes depicted in this narrative.

Most of the women died in the first two decades of the twentieth century. These were Japan's first troops, Imamura says, paving the way for tens of thousands of women to follow. When author Tomoko Yamazaki visited the cemetery of the *karayuki-san* in Borneo, she noticed that all the graves faced in one direction, away from Japan. It is a sentiment with which Imamura would concur. Imamura underlines that Japan's forays into Asia have not ceased, that the most recent Japanese cast out into the world, latter-day *karayuki-san*, male and female, are sent by corporations.

From the tranquility of the cemetery, Imamura overlaps the roar of a jet plane, then cuts abruptly to a bustling airport, where Kikuyo has arrived back in Japan, hosted by the Burakumin League against Discrimination. Mrs. Nishimura is at her elbow. There is a date, May 23, 1973. Kikuyo does not utter another word in the film.

Imamura sums up: the *karayuki-san* were the front-line troops to build the economy. The shaky, hand-held camera records, by way of comment, Kikuyo's facial expressions, startled, confused, distracted, bewildered at having been thrust into an alien world, half-smiling. In voiceover, Imamura adds that this is her chance to see whether Japan has changed, even as everything he has shown points to nothing having improved. Japanese women of the lower class remain victims of Japan's thirst for wealth, *burakumin* the objects of discrimination and abuse.

Karayuki-san ends abruptly, as if Imamura has run out of film. Having remarked that it's not a simple story, Imamura departs with the implication that Kikuyo, in her seventies, is being exploited by the Burakumin League just as she had been by her family, by the slave traders who sold her, by the men who used her—and by Japan.

His voice is as gruff and unemotional as it was at the moment the film began. This is a documentary and he is here to state facts, the images sufficing for interpretation. His goal has been to make the spectator feel deeply for these abandoned women and their ruined lives, and that purpose has been accomplished triumphantly.

Notes

1. *Karayuki-san* is the form, in the Japanese mode, for both the singular and the plural.
2. I interviewed Imamura at his studios in a suburb of Tokyo. He was the only director of the many I interviewed who had me sit on the *tatami* across from him. He also invited me back to view his documentaries, and so one evening I found myself in a very unfamiliar part of Tokyo watching *Karayuki-san* for the first time.
3. The novel was adapted into a successful film by Kei Kumai in 1974.

Works Cited

Imamura, Shohei (1997a). "My Approach to Filmmaking." In *Shohei Imamura*, ed. James Quandt, 125–28. Ontario: Cinematheque Ontario, 125–28.

Imamura, Shohei (1997b). "Traditions and Influences." In *Shohei Imamura*, ed. James Quandt, 129–32. Ontario: Cinematheque Ontario.

Nakata, Toichi (1997). "Shohei Imamura Interview." In *Shohei Imamura*, ed. James Quandt, 107–24. Ontario: Cinematheque Ontario.

OSS (1945). Current Intelligence Study Number 35. Office of Strategic Services. Research and Analysis Branch. R& A 3337S. August 10.

Phillips, Richard (2000). "Japanese Film Director Shohei Imamura Speaks to the World Socialist Web Site." http://www.wsws.org/en/articles/2000/09/imam-s19.html. Accessed April 27, 2016.

Quandt, James, ed. (1997). *Shohei Imamura*. Ontario: Cinematheque Ontario.

Richie, Donald (1997). "Notes for a Study on Shohei Imamura." In *Shohei Imamura*, ed. James Quandt, 7–44. Ontario: Cinematheque Ontario.

Yoshimi, Yoshiaki (2000). *Comfort Women: Sexual Slavery in the Japanese Military during World War II*. Trans. Suzanne O'Brien. New York: Columbia University Press.

Chapter 11

The Female Body as Transgressor of National Boundaries: *The History of Postwar Japan as Told by a Bar Hostess*

Bianca Briciu

Imamura's films are famous for capturing the irrational, bodily aspects of human existence giving a voice to people marginalized or excluded from official discourses. While his fiction films have received a lot of critical attention, his documentaries made in a transition period of his career in the 1970s are less well known, but they nevertheless epitomize, through a self-reflexive cinematic style, Imamura's concern with marginal experiences. Two of his documentaries, *Nippon sengoshi: Madamu Onboro no seikatsu/The History of Postwar Japan as Told by a Bar Hostess* (1970) and *Karayuki-san, The Making of a Prostitute* (1975), describe the embodied experiences of low-status women, unpacking gender and class-power relations. Both films critique the nation-state discourse that erases and abjects subordinate groups, and they suggest an ironic parallel between women's experiences and Japan-US relations situating the female body as the symbolic sexual boundary of the nation. Isolde Standish suggested that "these films center on a dialectic in which historiography is juxtaposed to the physical embodiment of history through consciousness" (2011: 116). Both documentaries explore a marginalized version of history inscribed on the female body. This essay analyzes the points of contrast and convergence between female embodied history and Japan's postwar official history in *The History of Postwar Japan as Told by a Bar Hostess*. My central questions are concerned with the relationship between national official discourse and female-embodied experience and the documentary-style articulation of the personal-as-political in a manner close to feminist oral history.

The History of Postwar Japan traces the course of Etsuko Akaza's (Madame Onboro) life in terms of Japan's experiences of defeat and occupation, critiquing her oppression as a woman and a *burakumin*.[1] Her testimony reconstitutes her own experiences of Japan's modernization, defeat, and occupation, revealing the intricate connections between the nation and the female body. Japanese national identity has been constructed through the close policing of female bodies, while the bodies of low-class prostitutes have been marginalized serving at the end of World War II as buffer zones between the occupied nation and the occupiers. These low-class prostitutes came to symbolize the sexual boundary of the nation, and many intellectuals in the post-defeat period used the representation of prostitutes catering to Americans as metaphors for a feminized, sexualized Japan.

The film is an interventional documentary structured like a *cinema verité* interview. Imamura parallels the national discourse presented through newsreel footage with Etsuko Akaza's embodied presence, creating an ironic contrast between voice and images. He deconstructs official discourses through the ironic juxtaposition of sets of binaries: national versus individual, the male disembodied national discourse versus female embodied experience, Japan versus US, image versus voice.

Official discourse is portrayed in the film through newsreels, pictures, and Imamura's own commentary. Newsreels are visible both for us as spectators and for Akaza, while other documentary inserts are only made available to us as spectators. She is a tireless interlocutor, with a passion for speaking and an excellent memory. She mediates spectators' viewing of news footage as she appears next to the images in the frame, and instead of confirming them in the manner a traditional voice-of-god commentary would do, she interrogates and defies them. As Standish points out, "The voice of a *burakumin* woman throws into uncertainty the tones of authority that a male voice over would do" (2011: 128). Her marginal position in society in terms of her gender and class places her at the boundary of the nation, where she ironically finds empowerment through Japan's defeat and disempowerment. National discourse contains female sexuality within the marriage system and abjects the body of the prostitute, but Akaza is a survivor who learned how to use her sexual body to claim her own place in the world by transgressing national boundaries.

Akaza (or Madame Onboro) used to be the owner of a bar catering to Americans. At the time of Imamura's interviews, she is getting ready to move to the United States with her American lover. Imamura discovered her in Yokosuka and made her the character of his film in an effort to understand her rejection of Japanese identity. Her *burakumin* family managed to rise above the poverty level through illegal dealings on the black market. She was married to a Japanese policeman, but as their relationship grew stale due to his violence and infidelities, she started working in a brothel serving Americans. After earning some money, she opened her own bar and started having affairs with her American clients. The film describes her life experiences against the backdrop of Japan's tumultuous postwar events, such as the US occupation, the repatriation of Japanese soldiers, the Vietnam War, and public protests.

Cinematic Ironies: *Kokutai* and *Nikutai* Discourses

The film employs Eisensteinian montage techniques, proposing many subtle meanings from the juxtaposition of newsreel footage with Akaza's commentary. Joan Mellen observes that Imamura does not judge Akaza but uses instead "cinematic ironies" that contrast her experience with that of the nation (1976: 236). The film critiques both Akaza's perspective limited to the body and the national discourse limited to ideology. The newsreel footage represents national events whereas Akaza's discourse represents embodied experience. While the newsreels show how Japanese people suffer because of the Occupation, Akaza states that Americans gave her a sense of freedom. As she flips through pictures of atrocities from the war in Vietnam, she states that Americans are not like that; they have been good to her. The ironic montage invites spectators to question the notion of historical truth that is fragmented and at times contradictory. It shows that Akaza's limitation to personal bodily experiences makes her fail to grasp the larger cultural implications of American occupation and the influence of various policies upon her own life. She prefers American men because their presence freed her from the racism and poverty she experienced among her own people, as well as the violence of her two former Japanese partners. Alternately, national discourse, although claiming to represent the truth through the visual weight of newsreels and the voice-of-god commentary, proves to be fragmentary, contradictory and favoring certain perspectives. I analyze more closely three scenes that punctuate with irony the gap between Akaza's personal experiences of embodied encounter with American GIs and Japan's experience of defeat. The newsreel footage shows the occupation as the source of national shame and suffering whereas for Akaza it represents opportunity. A closer analysis of these scenes reveals the relationship between the nation and the female body; in other words, between *kokutai* and *nikutai*.

Douglas Slaymaker offers an interesting etymological analysis of the differences between *kokutai* and *nikutai* (2004: 8). He explains the *kokutai* as the national body close to a state religion with the emperor at its apex and the people as part of a body space. While this concept was used in the wartime years for establishing Japanese uniqueness and masculine domination, after defeat Japan was feminized and turned into a colonial Other (Igarashi 2000: 35). To

Female Body as Transgressor 195

Figure 11.1 Akaza and her daughter are walking arm in arm with GIs, a ubiquitous scene in the occupation years but nevertheless one that provoked a great deal of national anxiety.

what extent is national discourse a *kokutai* discourse and what are the connections between *kokutai* (collective, public, national) and *nikutai* (personal, private, material)? *Kokutai* ideology disappeared only to return from repression as the feminized body of the nation. This metaphoric expression of the nation as an ideological body subordinated the will of individuals to the larger will of the nation in the wartime period, sublimating the materiality of *nikutai*. It is for this reason, Slaymaker argues, that there was a strong preoccupation in the post-defeat years with the material body, the *nikutai*, as a form of liberation from the constraints imposed by the wartime regime (2004: 11). The body liberated from state ideology starts to be defined through its instinctual drives: survival and sexuality. Many Japanese writers and filmmakers in the postwar period celebrated sexuality as a strong mark of the liberated body, as a material energy that defies the ideology of state control.

The film juxtaposes the breaching, the wounding of the national body by the arrival of occupation forces with Akaza's celebration of the pleasures of the flesh. The female body and the national body come together metaphorically under the sign of US military politics and strategies in Asia. The national body is now in the female position of subordination and lack of agency while the female body marginalized from *kokutai* discourse is now empowered through sexual pleasure and direct access to the power of the occupiers. For Japanese women of lower caste, Americans offer the promise (no matter how illusory) of a better life. Their gender and class marginality allow them to embrace

Figure 11.2 Newsreel footage shows General MacArthur descending from a plane and occupation troops marching on Japanese soil.

the Occupation, transgressing national boundaries. They do not experience the shame and humiliation of Japan's defeat because they did not partake of national ideology in the first place. They were preoccupied with immediate bodily survival at a time when the national ideology was strong, and they are preoccupied with immediate bodily survival when that ideology crumbles. Their marginalization makes it easier to transgress national boundaries becoming emotionally and sexually involved with "the enemy."

To a certain extent Akaza's words echo the vision of occupation that Americans themselves had, as a form of gentlemanly liberation. "They were all kind and gentlemanly . . . They brought soap and chocolate. There was nothing to worry about. People calmed down." While she and her mother talk about their social position as *burakumin*, newsreel images of poverty and suffering are inserted. "The conquered Japan suffers," the commentator says against images of the homeless, vagabonds, orphans, and bodies sprayed with DDT. Madam Onboro's relationship with GIs structures her response to occupation in general, as she has vicarious access to America's idealized power and bounty as many impoverished Japanese saw it, including Akaza. She is free from the national ideology that makes Japanese men experience defeat in shame and suffering. Through her sexual body and emotional availability she enters a world of apparent freedom through consumerism.[2] Unlike the underlying meaning of US occupation as subjugation for Japan, for Akaza it means freedom and agency.[3] Imamura shows newsreel footage of massive protests against the presence of US bases and the trespassing of the Sunagawa

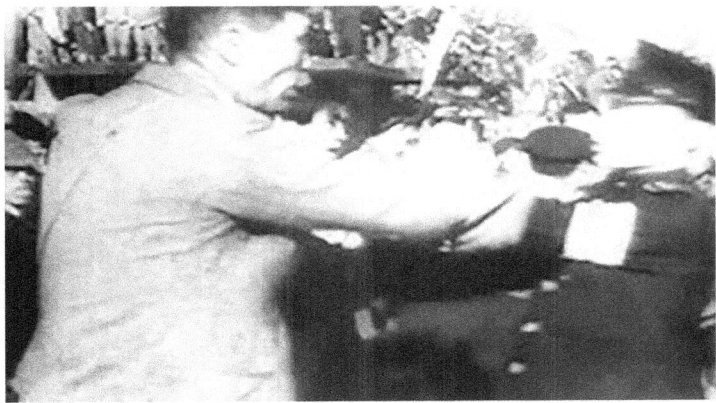

Figure 11.3 Newsreels of violent protests show the divided nation and the public opposition to occupation in contrast to the discourse of peaceful democratization.

military base while the voiceover of the newsreel comments that farmers in Japan regarded the pillars used to demarcate the bases as "planted in their hearts." The despair and suffering of the nation as seen in newsreels is contrasted with Akaza's commentary about the opportunities she had once the Americans set foot in Japan.

The newsreels of the large demonstration at Yokosuka base on May 30, 1966, show the embittered protests against the docking of a nuclear submarine. In contrast to these images of national subjugation and the suppression of dissent, Akaza muses that she relied on the presence of GIs for her livelihood. The protests of Japanese people against occupation and especially against the renewed Anpo treaty are futile due to the nation's subordinated position. In contrast, Akaza finds agency by catering to GIs. The first level of her agency is economic, her ability to make her own money instead of relying on an abusive husband. The second level of agency happens when she becomes a bar owner and has the emotional freedom to start affairs with Americans instead of the transactional act of prostitution. Her transgressive body marks the volatile boundaries of an imagined nation.

The second contrasting editing occurs when Imamura asks about her experience of occupation. The newsreels show ordered rows of people listening to the emperor's announcement of defeat, some of them crying. Akaza retorts that in her experience nobody cried, but, on the contrary, they were all relieved. They didn't say anything out of fear but deep down in their hearts they were relieved. Mellen reads Akaza's reaction as an example of

Figure 11.4 Akaza is watching documentary footage showing people's reaction to the emperor's announcement of defeat.

how the Japanese really felt, a demystification of defeat (1976: 237). What I see in this scene is not an example of the real experience pitted against a myth, but rather the presence of the fractured nation into groups with various experiences. The ideology of *kokutai* crashes down with the experience of defeat, revealing its fragmented, contradictory nature. The male ideology that shored up *kokutai* is destroyed, placing Japanese men in an effeminized position. The only truth that remains after defeat is the pragmatic nature of immediate bodily survival and sexuality, a truth that women have also experienced under *kokutai*.

Another ironic juxtaposition is the newsreel showing the wedding of the Crown Prince with Princess Michiko edited together with images of poor, starving Japanese citizens. Akaza laments the *mottainai*, the waste of huge amounts of money, spent for the wedding and the reconstruction of the Imperial palace, arguing that with all that money they could have built an orphanage. Her egalitarian views offer a powerful critique of the Imperial system, a critique paralleled visually by the newsreel where a bystander throws a stone at the royal couple. As Imamura stated, "I thought I should describe from Madam Onboro's perspective the collapse of the Japanese family and its connection with the collapse of the Emperor system" (Imamura 2004, 63–64). As the newsreels show, the emperor system continues, raising doubts about the official discourse of occupation as a democratizing process. Akaza's voice echoes the frustration of marginal people with the inequalities and unfair structure of the nation based in ideologies that support domination.

Figure 11.5 In contrast to the images of the sumptuous wedding of the crown prince, Akaza tells how she explained to her American lovers that the imperial family are not gods: "They're Japan's shop window decorations."

The last scene of cinematic irony highlighting the gap between female embodied experience and transnational politics is the moment Imamura shows Akaza pictures of atrocities committed by American soldiers in Vietnam. The pictures are enlarged as close-up images of mutilated corpses while Akaza verbally defends the Americans. "Maybe this is a *mise-en-scène*. I know the Americans. They are nice and gentle. I believe in what I see and what I touch." This immediacy of perception limited to embodied experience puts under question the notion of historical truth. What is relevant about this scene is the coexistence of radically different perspectives, both of them equally valid. Akaza did experience American men who were gentler with her than Japanese men, but also the American men were US soldiers, embodiments of America's colonial domination. This scene epitomizes a collision of perspectives where Imamura himself regards American soldiers as representatives of imperialist domination, whereas for Akaza they are representatives of a better life and free sexuality.

These instances of irony not only deconstruct documentary as a cinematic mode that reveals the truth about historical subjects, but they also work in the way suggested by feminist historian Chizuko Ueno (2004) to critique the documenting of history itself. Official history was documented through the exclusion of embodied, sensual, and sexual experiences. As Mellen notes, "Madame Onboro remains unaware that through the newsreels Imamura

Figure 11.6 Imamura shows her pictures of atrocities committed by the Americans in the Vietnam War, but she denies their reality, stating that the Americans she knows are not evil.

is contrasting her praise of Americans with the harsh realities of Korea and Vietnam" (1976: 236). Is the purpose of the irony to criticize Akaza and her experientially limited view that overlooks the realities of the American imperial involvement in Asia? The irony works on multiple levels. Akaza's bodily immersion in her sexual adventures, her cheerful amorality and lack of any interest in politics, all suggest a limited view dominated by immediate, sensual bodily experiences. National discourse and the failure of democracy are also criticized through the pragmatic policies implemented by the Japanese government in collaboration with US imperialist expansion. US imperialism is criticized through the contrast between war atrocities, unscrupulous policies of intervention that change according to the shifting interests in Asia, and the official discourse of US as a marker of democracy and freedom. Imamura's irony saves him from taking sides with any of these partial truths, instead presenting them as a detached observer.

If the cinematic ironies highlight the contrast between newsreel as national discourse and Akaza's embodied experiences, visual metaphors and freeze-frames bring them together. Akaza's survival strategies and her reliance on foreigners are used to parallel the Japanese nation that adopts the same strategies. For David Desser the metaphor of Akaza-as-nation is a critique of loss of values. "Her reliance on American soldiers is a loss of moral values just as Japan's reliance on US is a loss of something deep within the Japanese spirit"

(1998: 126). The film highlights the fact that disempowered people have no moral values because their identity was not formed through affiliation with national identity. Lack of principles and survival through subjection and consumerism bring the nation and Akaza together in a metaphor that haunts many Japanese postwar films.

In the post-defeat years Japan as a nation experiences for the first time the embodied female condition marked by control by an outside power. Isolde Standish observes that Imamura focuses on prostitutes to critique "the economic recovery based on Japan's seemingly subservient role as provider of logistics support to American military campaigns in Asia" (2011: 129). The *kokutai* is now experiencing the subordinate position of female *nikutai*. Newsreel footage of red purges and the crackdown on communist factions in Japan are edited together with US bombing in Korea and with Akaza's experiences, suggesting that the enormous political unrest in Japan is the result of transnational politics of military strategy. The parallel between the nation and the female body is interesting for Imamura and for other Japanese New Wave filmmakers, who pursue the politicized relationship between bodies and a subordinate, disempowered nation. Akaza regards the American soldiers as a source of freedom from all the oppressive elements in Japanese society: racism, abusive husbands, poverty, marginalization. However, America is ultimately not turning Japan into a peaceful, democratic country, a bitter realization of the 1960s and a tremendous source of social unrest. After the militaristic period Japanese citizens realized they were being again used for imperialist purposes, a second crisis of truth that crushed the hopes for democratic freedom. The film ends with Akaza joining her husband in the US, so we do not have the opportunity to see whether her hopes for liberation became a reality or not.

The freeze-frames used three times in the film highlight Akaza's role as witness of historical events. The camera freezes on a bystander of a train wreck or a demonstrator and then zooms in on Akaza's face, thus visually linking her presence to the making of Japan's history. What is important for this visual compression of time and space is the suggestion that Akaza is not an agent of historical change but is nevertheless a witness that interprets events from a double marginal perspective as a *burakumin* woman. The documentary shows that historical change impacts people of different social positions differently. The ironic montage and the contrast between images of newsreel as national, official history and Akaza's voice testifying to her experiences performs a double critique—of national, homogenizing history and its authority to express truth as well as of the female embodied experience unaware of the extent of the political construction of the personal.

The film deconstructs the ability of the documentary to represent historical truth visually by introducing conflicting perspectives. It highlights the conflict between the value of images as objective, indexical recordings of historical truth and the female voice that reconstructs personal memories at times in conflict with the images. The thematic dichotomy the film enacts between national historical discourse and female embodied experience is replicated at a cinematic level by the dichotomy between the official authority of images and the female voice. The same problem has been raised by feminist historians in Japan. Ueno has shown that "the greatest challenge facing women's history is finding ways to allow the silenced voices to speak. This is why women's history turned to oral history" (2004: 123). Imamura's documentaries open up the space for women's voices that reconstitute their embodied experience of history.

However, the writing of women's history as oral history is not without problems, as Ueno points out. Testimonies are characterized by lapses of memory, selective memory, inconsistencies, and the intervention of the present in the narratives about the past (Ueno 2004: 123–24). The subjective version of history filtered through the emotional consciousness of women raises questions of objectivity, value, and truth that are also valid for national discourses. The truth about Japan's postwar years is a highly contested terrain divided along subjective views. In that sense, the film does not necessarily confer authority to the woman's voice as being the representative of truth, but rather it deconstructs the highly contested notion of historical truth. Although the movie is a predominantly visual representation of a woman's testimony, the focus is more on the sound track and the oral reconstitution of experience. Kaja Silverman has related the sound track to the preoccupation with authenticity and interiority (1998: 42). The voice is always connected to the expression of inner feelings or thoughts, and it is anchored in its embodied source. As Robert Stam has argued, when attention moves from predominantly visual expression to a space of the vocal, it becomes a way of restoring voice to the voiceless. He suggests that the voice is a metaphor of seepage across boundaries, in contrast with the "visual with its limits and boundaries and border police" (1994: 214). Akaza's voice reveals female embodiment as the blind spot of history in contrast to official national discourse. The female voice challenges both the power of the nation-state and the power of visual images, performing a critique of historical truth and of visual representation.

Freeze-frames and metaphoric suggestions bring together the female body and the body of the nation under the sign of American domination manifested through military strategies and the embodied presence of GIs on Japanese soil. In the following part I analyze the racial and sexual politics that place Akaza as transgressor of national boundaries.

Madame Onboro's Body: Performing Sexual and Racial Politics

Madame Onboro's resilience is the result of her ability to use her sexual body in order to enter the world of pleasure and consumption offered by the Americans. She started as a sex worker catering to their pleasure but as she rose in status she started experiencing sexual agency through more involved relationships with Americans in which she claimed her own pleasure. Her body stands at the borderline between prostitution and female sexual freedom. As Moira Gatens has pointed out, "The body politic was established through the exclusion of women" (1996: 49). The policing of national boundaries was closely related to the policing of the female body (Pettman 2005: 132). Women's bodies signified the reproduction of the family unit (the good women) or the abjected experience of sexuality (the bad women). The body politic in the wartime era was constructed through the close policing of female sexuality as the respectable norm of domestic reproduction and its opposite, the deviant marginalized body of the prostitute. Japan's experience of defeat in World War II shows the dismantling of the body politic and the emergence of the carnal body ruled by norms of survival and pleasure rather than state ideology. Akaza found sexual agency, thus moving away from the survival mode of many low-class prostitutes, by accessing the world of pleasure.

Slaymaker observes how in the post-defeat context, "sex workers (especially *pan-pan*)[4] obtained singular representational power as a locus of possibility and autonomy in the despair that characterized postwar society. They marked a site for protest against the preceding militaristic era" (2004: 40). Many writers of the so-called "flesh school" (*nikutai-ha*) celebrated the physical carnality of these women as a site of freedom and excess. Not only writers but filmmakers too were fascinated by these women's bodies, most famously Mizoguchi and Imamura. Prostitutes sexualized the American experience of occupation since they entered bodily relationships with Americans. At the end of the war the Japanese government invited lower-class Japanese women to work as prostitutes serving American soldiers in the belief that this would reduce the incidence of rape of "respectable" women. In her work on prostitution in postwar Japan, Yuki Fujime (2006) has shown that its legal status lasted only one year, from the end of the war to 1946 when the occupation forces abolished it because of the widespread STD cases among Americans. Women could still sell sexual services on their own, but this system exposed them to mistreatment by American customers and by police. Lower-class women marginalized by the nation found it easier to enter the world that America signified. Imamura explicitly stated that he wanted to interview people abandoned by their country but became interested in Madame Onboro because she abandoned hers. As he did in *Karayuki-san*, Imamura explores how the nation marginalizes low-status women. Kikuyo Zendo, the trafficked woman he interviews in *Karayuki-san*, lived her life in loneliness and isolation whereas Akaza finds agency through that abandonment. Imamura mentioned that he was fascinated by "the strong, dark feeling of someone who abandoned her village and was about to abandon Japan (*Nihon wo suteru*)" (Imamura 2004: 118). He tries to understand Akaza's lack of commitment to Japanese identity. In contrast to the artistic fascination, national discourses projected these women as a threat to national respectability and to the pure Japanese body, further marginalizing and stigmatizing them (Koikari 1999: 328). The bodies of women involved with American soldiers were the objects of conflicting discourses of fascination and abjection. Writers and filmmakers see the prostitutes' bodies as markers of sexual freedom, whereas they are a threat and a source of shame for official discourses. They are a threat to the idea of racial and ethnic purity, embodying the perils of miscegenation. Although women involved with American soldiers depended on them financially, they also had the opportunity to experience sensual pleasure and the pleasures of consumerism in a time of scarcity and despair.

Akaza's body is excessive both in her sexual presence and in her vitality. Her body shown in medium close-up with a slightly erotic cleavage is beaming with sensuality while her voice is tirelessly recounting personal experiences in vivid details. Her sexual body is both an object and a subject since she started taking lovers among the Americans once she became the owner of the bar and her favors were not paid directly in money. She embodies the ambiguous border between prostitution and free love. After her experiences with two abusive Japanese partners, Akaza has a series of American lovers. She marries one of them, Harry, who is considerably younger than her and travels to America with him, planning to open a bar there in case he deserts her.

While the occupation was hailed for the introduction of women into the public sphere through the new constitution, occupation policies were complicated by conflicting sexual policies. Mire Koikari has shown in her interesting article that the liberation of women from "Oriental male chauvinism" has been a central project in Japan's "reorientation" (1999: 313). This rhetoric projected gender relations in the US as equal in order to claim superiority over the repressive sexual politics in Japan. While the *pan-pans* were vulnerable to both sexual and legal violence, hostesses managed to have a certain degree of agency by choosing whom they bedded. The film shows newsreels representing the prohibition of prostitution and the rounding up of streetwalkers together with the comments of women themselves. As many scholars have shown, the sexual politics of the occupation were just as contradictory as the strategies of involving Japan in imperial war in Asia. "The meaning assigned to Japanese women's bodies was fundamentally linked to the sexual, racial, class and ultimately nationalistic politics developing between the two countries" (Koikari 1999: 326).

The occupation actively repressed manifestations of "masculinity," robbing Japanese men not only of their warrior identity but also problematizing their access to women. The *pan-pan* was a fascinating figure, but also a sore spot on Japanese male identity. Her body marks the boundaries of the nation that have now been transgressed. Akaza's body finds agency through the transgression of national boundaries in a manner different from the *pan-pan*. She is a performer of sexuality, taking advantage of transnational politics and she is aware of the power of her female body to survive through changing circumstances. She uses her sexuality to secure the emotional and financial commitment of her American lovers rather than experiencing the more abjected bodily transaction of a disempowered prostitute.

The film shows how agency was possible for Akaza in the postwar years. Her family benefited from the meat trade in the black market, which allowed them to rise above the poverty level and allowed her to buy a club. She manifests her agency by using other women's bodies for prostitution and she thus participates in their marginalization. The first shots of the film use a disturbing montage of the slaughtering of cows edited together with shots of the horrors in the Vietnam War. The montage is Eisensteinian, creating powerful metaphors. Standish argues that it creates the link between butchering and war (2011: 117). It also shows the link between violence and power through the management of death and of bodies. The slaughtering of cows shows the empowerment of Akaza's family, while the atrocities in Vietnam are the marker of US imperialism causing death in order to achieve political and economic power. The film portrays a vision of a dog-eat-dog world in which people survive using and abusing others. Marginalized people are not more innocent than their oppressors, a vision Imamura returned to again and again in many of his films, refusing to sentimentalize people on the fringes of society.

Akaza is aware of the potential of her sexual female body to secure a place for herself in the context of occupation. Although the occupation was a source of national humiliation and American military strategies in Asia subjected Japan to unwanted policies, she was able to perform successfully the sexual politics of interracial relationships. She is in a doubly inferior position in relation to her American lovers, as a woman and as representative of a defeated nation, but at least for her American lovers she is not an abjected *burakumin*. Her financial independence allows her to have a certain level of self-expression and choice. Whereas *pan-pan* women bore the brunt of abjection both on American and on Japanese side, her sexuality is an instrument of status change. Emotional involvement in the unequal sexual transaction between Japanese women and Americans becomes possible only in a context of relative financial independence.

The Ethic versus the Erotic Image

Documentary codes and conventions are essential for understanding the politics of embodied representations. There are two formal aspects of the film that create an ethically engaged representation of women's reality. The first aspect is the visual embodied presence of the filmmaker, a taboo of the cinematic apparatus in fiction film (unless the filmmaker is an actor). The embodied presence of the director brings together the structure of the face-to-face interview with the distancing presence of the camera, successfully combining the gaze as a form of power and the look as mutual negotiation and dialogue. The second aspect is the interplay between the visual power of images as markers of verisimilitude and the sound of the female voice as testimony of personal experiences. The film performs a critique of the predominance of the visual as part of the dominant national discourse.

Paraphrasing Mulvey's argument that through the manipulation of space and time fiction film produces "an illusion cut to the measure of desire," Nichols argues that the documentary produces "an argument cut to ethical, political and ideological measure" (Nichols 1991: 77). While fiction films produce an eroticism (regardless of the presence or absence of erotic images per se) of the image meant to give pleasure to spectators, documentaries aim to produce knowledge about the historical world. The desire to know is far from innocent, being just as anchored in power relations as eroticism. However, in the dichotomy outlined above, documentaries represent the desire to understand reality and to grasp difference, negotiating and even abdicating power. Imamura's political and ethical agenda is to offer a counter-narrative to Japan's official discourses of history by recording a doubly marginalized discourse: that of women and of bodily experiences that have been long absent from the rational discourse of official history.

The visual construction of the movie juxtaposes classic interview scenes with newsreel footage accompanied by the sound track of Akaza's voice or Imamura's own commentary. Returning to Nichols's paraphrase, the film involves ethical and ideological commitment rather than the desire to offer visual pleasure. Imamura tries to represent women's real lives without imposing a certain meaning on them and he critiques the homogenizing concept of the nation. I start with an analysis of ethical representation since it is essential for grasping the gendered relationships between the male director and the filmed woman.

E. Ann Kaplan formulates a definition of ethics as an intersubjective relation not governed by power. She highlights the difference between the look and the gaze. The look is governed by curiosity about the other, by closeness and intimacy, while the gaze is a one-way subjective vision governed by anxiety or desire and constructed as "an attempt not to know, to deny even" (1997: xvi). For Nichols, "Ethics can be said to be an ideological mechanism by which those with power propose to regulate their own conduct" (1991: 103). The film was made with private funding, an aspect that reveals the director's personal commitment. As he states in an interview with Nakata Toichi, "Documentary seemed a better vehicle for my unending desire to get close to people's true natures" (1997: 119). Rather than portraying how people interact with society as in his fiction films, he is trying to understand how women lived their own lives through the constraints imposed on them by social systems. In other words, there is a time lag of life experiences that can only be described from memory. This aspect of documentaries raises a series of questions about the effort to structure the absence of women's real embodied experiences through personal memories. Unlike important historical and social events that were registered in official documents or the visual images of the newsreels, women's personal, intimate events could only be reconstituted from personal memories. The reconstitution shows that even the most intimate aspects of their lives for these women were implicated in larger, social events. Through the recall of events as memories, the film articulates material, real bodies into a "literal embodiment of social practices," revealing the constructed nature of embodied subjectivity (Nichols 1991: 255). Both definitions suggest an equal dimension of encounter and communication of open subjectivities not articulated through power.

Imamura was aware of the power of the camera to control the subjects within its gaze. This awareness of his power position lies at the center of his documentaries, taking us back to Nichols's definition of ethics as a mechanism through which those in power are ready to regulate their power. Although the documentary did not in any way empower Imamura since it was not funded by an institution and did not bring him financial or artistic success, the very fact that he is the one holding the camera and formulating the questions structures his dialogue with Akaza in a problematic way. The filmmaker's intention to construct the film as a dialogue governed by the look is accompanied by the presence of the technological apparatus that structures his ethical intentions in terms of gaze. Imamura turned the gaze of the camera into a scientific object for exploring women's reality, while the look entailed by the film is one of openness and respect. The director negotiates his power position versus women with his desire to open a space for their own experiences. The documentary is an expression of the negotiation among the objective gaze of the camera, the male gaze, and the look. Nichols has pointed out the dual dimension of camera, as a machine that produces indexical images and as an anthropomorphic extension of the operator's worldview and values. All films are haunted by this duality, but few of them problematize it in their diegesis like this documentary. Imamura's own presence entails a look at the woman, curiosity about her life, and the desire to open a space for her marginalized subjectivity, while the presence of the camera entails a gaze, a one-dimensional mode of knowledge close to Foucault's notion of the confessional. The gaze of the camera "supports an epistemology based on scientific principles of mechanical reproduction" counterbalanced by Imamura's empathetic approach that abandons the conditions of distance and unidirectionality through his embodied presence (Foucault 1977: 89). As a male embodied presence he has a form of authority over Akaza close to the male gaze, but he negotiates it through his desire to let her represent herself. The documentary performs a double function: it critiques the homogenizing official discourse of the nation and it creates a space that represents how the most intimate bodily aspects of women's experiences were related to larger social transformations.

Conclusion

I have argued that the film reconstitutes the history of postwar Japan through the embodied experience of a marginalized *burakumin* woman. Akaza's marginal position as a woman and as a *burakumin* made possible her postwar experience of freedom through the transgression of national boundaries. The disempowerment of a defeated nation ironically made possible the empowerment of women marginalized from national discourse. The marginalized, low-caste female body celebrates the world of consumerism signified by the United States, finding agency through sexual expression.

Through its representation of embodied experience, the film offers a critique of historical discourse, ironically juxtaposing conflicting discourses about national suffering and unrest, American occupation, and interracial sexual encounters. The radical reality of the body freed from ideological constraints is survival and sensual pleasure, an aspect that fascinates Imamura in many of his fiction films. Akaza signifies the vitality of the body free from national ideology and moral principles but nonetheless caught in the process of historical change. The film also problematizes the power of visual representation to contain and subordinate the female body through its self-reflexive style that pits images of official historical representation against the authority of the female voice. The documentary style constructs a representation of female-embodied experience close to feminist oral history bringing to the forefront the experiences of a low-caste woman. Through the presence of conflicting views, the contrast between image and voice, between newsreel events and personal memories, national discourse and the female body, the film articulates the definition of historical truth as perspectival and contingent. At the same time, it creates a space for representing experiences marginalized from history, politicizing the body.

Notes

1. Member of the low caste in Japan.
2. I am not arguing that she is free but that she experiences her relationships with American soldiers as liberation. It could be argued that she exits one power regime (Japanese national ideology) and enters another.
3. Her agency is problematic because it is based on her exploitation of other women who work as prostitutes catering to American soldiers.
4. *Pan-pan* was a generic name given to prostitutes who served Americans.

Works Cited

Desser, David (1988). *Eros plus Massacre*. Bloomington: Indiana University Press.
Foucault, Michel (1977). *History of Sexuality*. 3 vols. Trans. Robert Hurley. New York: Vintage.
Fujime, Yuki (2006). "Japanese Feminism and Commercialized Sex." *Social Science Japan Journal* 9, no. 1: 33–50.
Gatens, Moira (1996). *Imaginary Bodies: Ethics, Power, and Corporeality*. London: Routledge.
Igarashi, Yoshikuni (2000). *Bodies of Memory: Narratives of War in Postwar Japanese Culture*. Princeton, NJ: Princeton University Press.
Iles, Timothy (2008). *The Crisis of Identity in Contemporary Japanese Film*. Boston: Brill.
Imamura, Shōhei (2004). *Eiga wa kyōki no tabi de aru: watashi no rekishi-sho*. [Film Is a Journey into Madness: A Personal History]. Tokyo: Nihon keisai shinbun-sha.
Kaplan, E. Ann (1997). *Looking for the Other: Feminism, Film, and the Imperial Gaze*. New York: Routledge.
Koikari. Mire (1999). "Rethinking Gender and Power in the US Occupation of Japan, 1945–1952." *Gender & History* (July): 313–35.
Mellen, Joan (1976). *The Waves at Genji's Door: Japan through Its Cinema*. New York: Pantheon.
Nakata, Toichi (1997). "Shōhei Imamura Interview." *Shōhei Imamura*, ed. James Quandt, 107–25. Toronto: Toronto International Film Festival Group.
Nichols, Bill (1991). *Representing Reality: Issues and Concepts in Documentary*. Bloomington: Indiana University Press.

Pettman, Jan Jindi (2005). "Boundary Politics: Women, Nationalism and Danger." *New Frontiers in Women's Studies: Knowledge, Identity and Nationalism*, ed. Mary Maynard and June Purvis, 187–203. London: Taylor and Francis.

Quandt, James, ed. (1997). *Shōhei Imamura*. Toronto: Toronto International Film Festival Group.

Silverman, Kaja (1988). *The Acoustic Mirror: The Female Voice in Psychoanalysis and Cinema*. Bloomington: Indiana University Press.

Slaymaker, Douglas (2004). *The Body in Postwar Japanese Fiction*. London: Routledge Curzon.

Stam, Robert, and Ella Shohat (1994). *Unthinking Eurocentrism: Multiculturalism and the Media*. London: Routledge.

Standish, Isolde (2011). *Politics, Porn and Protest: Japanese Avant-garde Cinema in the 1960s and 1970s*. New York: Continuum.

Ueno, Chizuko (2004). *Nationalism and Gender*. Trans. Beverly Yamamoto. Melbourne: Trans Pacific Press.

PART III
KINDRED SPIRITS

Chapter 12

Better Off Being Bacteria: Adaptation and Allegory in *Dr. Akagi*

Lauri Kitsnik

Towards the end of the Pacific War, there's an old doctor nicknamed Kanzo Sensei who diagnoses everyone suffering from hepatitis. The Japanese army accuses him of squandering precious resources when he prescribes glucose injections for all his patients, believing all of them to be malnourished. It tells the story of his exploits in those chaotic months when Japan was losing the war. (Nakata and Imamura 1997: 123)

This is how the director Shohei Imamura succinctly describes his penultimate (and what he thought at the time to be his last) feature film, *Kanzō sensei/Dr. Akagi* (1998). There seems to be a consensus that after the somewhat sedate *Unagi/Eel* (1997), *Dr. Akagi* was a welcome return to the more typically Imamurian "messy" filmmaking, despite the film being arguably less consistent in artistic terms and failing to garner the critical acclaim of its immediate predecessor. However, prompted by *Eel*'s success there the year before, *Dr. Akagi* was screened (out of competition) at the Cannes Film Festival and domestically placed at the fourth position in the *Kinema junpō* annual critics' poll.[1]

This chapter looks at how certain alterations and shifts in emphases to the short story by Ango Sakaguchi (1906–1955) on which *Dr. Akagi* is based shaped it into a film dealing with a number of issues that Imamura has made central to his oeuvre. Looking at the production process and the main themes and motifs of this adaptation enables us to detect allusions both public and private, with the depiction of a war-torn rural community extending to Imamura's own family and professional background. By presenting allegories of state-induced violence and perseverance of common people, *Dr. Akagi* readily relates to a number of concerns that permeate his work while quite deliberately adding finishing touches to a long career in filmmaking.

Adaptation

Adapting literary works to the screen commonly causes grievances vis-à-vis fidelity to its source, especially in the case of filmmakers with a distinctive cinematic style and established aesthetic or ideological agenda. It might seem surprising, then, that Imamura's version of Masuji Ibuse's (1898–1993) novel *Kuroi Ame/Black Rain* (1989) has conversely been criticized for being excessively faithful to its source and uncharacteristically conventional in cinematic style. Audie Bock suggests that this might have been

> a case of being overwhelmed by the original story, one that many a first-rate director before him had wanted to adapt for the screen, Naruse and Kurosawa among them. Moreover, the author of the original . . . was still alive to approve or disapprove. (Bock 1997: 153)

In comparison, *Dr. Liver* (Kanzō sensei),[2] a little-known short story by the long-deceased Ango Sakaguchi, seems by default more suitable for Imamura's vision and working mode that tends to prefer loosely connected scenes to an overarching plot (Richie 1997: 31). First published in the monthly *Bungakukai* (Literary World) in January 1950,[3] *Dr. Liver* is markedly fragmentary and merges different modes of writing by the inclusion of a frame story and a free-verse poem that concludes it. Ango,[4] best known for his polemical essay *Discourse on Decadence* (*Darakuron*, 1946), is often aligned with Osamu Dazai (1909–1948) and Sakunosuke Oda (1913–1947), and, as such, a notable proponent of the Burai-ha (Decadent School), a notorious group of writers who shared certain stylistic preoccupations and philosophical concerns that were audaciously played out against the backdrop of the immediate postwar confusion and search for new societal values. However, it could be precisely this fragmentary and essayistic character of Ango's work that has all but kept it away from the silver screen: before *Dr. Akagi* there had been only three film adaptations.[5]

Imamura has admitted to having read and liked Ango's story when it first came out just before his joining the Shōchiku studios as an assistant in 1951. However, it was only after winning at Cannes with *Eel* that sufficient funds suddenly became available to realize this "material long warmed" (*nagaku atatamete ita sozai*) by the director (Katori 2004: 463). Unlike the bestselling *Black Rain*, this somewhat obscure piece by an author whose work has only rarely been adapted at once refuted the danger of being inundated by its earlier reception, arguably allowing the filmmaker to treat it with considerable freedom.[6]

Ango's *Dr. Liver* employs an extended frame story that takes up about one-third of its entire length. The narrator is invited by a sculptor friend to visit a fishing town in the Izu Peninsula where he meets a local fisherman called Ika Tora (Squid Tiger) who then proceeds to tell the story of the life and death of the eponymous doctor. In the denouement, the narrator composes a poem commissioned to be etched into a liver-shaped stone sculpture for his commemoration. The frame story describes local life and people; the physical appearance of the fishermen is given in terms of their well-developed upper bodies in contrast to the regressed lower ones (Ango 1990: 331). Such an emphasis on portraying rural communities is something also closely associated with Imamura (bearing in mind his infamous claim about the relationship between the lower half of the body and the lower strata of Japanese society). All villagers seem to have nicknames that derive from particular marine species with a place in their respective family histories in fishing; it is within this context of nicknaming that Fuū Akagi becomes Doctor Liver for the villagers due to his penchant for diagnosing all his patients with hepatitis.[7]

In the film adaptation, the time of main action remains unaltered, while the location has been moved from Izu to a fishing village in Okayama Prefecture by the Inland Sea. Notably, though, Imamura has discarded the frame story and the layers of narrators. The setup of the story is instead attained by the first scene in the skies with a group of American pilots talking to each other over radio. This sequence is reminiscent of so many awkward depictions of seemingly dim-witted foreigners in Japanese cinema, in this case complete with gesturing a Hitler mustache to indicate Germany's recent defeat, which effectively functions to set the story in the final months of the war. Meanwhile, by a rundown shack in a village below, a boy is trying to make love to a girl (later revealed to be the female lead). They are interrupted by a middle-aged man in a white suit running frantically about the village roads. Rising from their embrace, the boy explains to the girl about the doctor and his nickname. After this (s)exposition, the tired and sweating doctor sits down by a field, plucks a huge white radish out of the ground, and greedily munches it down.

This comic tone set in the very beginning of the film is taken further by the introduction of an array of additional characters, all profoundly flawed in their particular ways. The doctor himself, as we shall later see, incessantly navigates between truth and delusion. Then there is a Buddhist priest Umemoto (Jūrō Kara), with a serious drinking problem whose fourth and current wife, Tomiko (Keiko Matsuzaka), is a former prostitute. A notable addition from another story by Ango, *Drifting Clouds, Flowing Water* (*Kōun ryūsui*, 1949), is Sonoko (the newcomer Kumiko Asō), a teenage village whore turned into the doctor's assistant and housekeeper (her dying father's last wish). In a flashback set in a

Figure 12.1   Dr. Akagi (Akira Emoto) running through streets to meet another patient.

red-light district, both hilarious and disturbing, her prostitute mother instructs young Sonoko never to give away *tadaman* (an abbreviation of *tada manko*, literally: free vagina), except to one's true love. It is only when a mother of a conscripted youth comes to beg Sonoko to make love to her son that she strays from this path. In the final scene of the film, Sonoko states her willingness to do the same for the doctor, allowing (or forcing) the film to develop something of a perverse romantic plotline.

Donald Richie has noted that

> Imamura's characters certainly do not admire each other or the state in which they find themselves. It is their creator, their director who admires them. He does not feel himself to be one of them and here Imamura resembles an intellectual looking at the unlettered masses and envying them. He admires, precisely, their wholeness—for it is this which gives them their strength and ambition, saves them from the fragmentation that the intellectual (being intelligent) often suffers. That Imamura does not himself experience this wholeness is perhaps one of the reasons for his interest and consequently his films. It is also perhaps the reason for the distance from which he views his characters. He is never one of them. (Richie 1997: 20)

In the doctor who takes on a very creator-like stance as a sympathetic and benevolent albeit deeply troubled overseer, Imamura might finally have found a character to whom he might have been tempted to relate to. Admittedly, Imamura's own role as film director and the ambiguity of being a self-proclaimed observer has been displayed in his earlier works and characters such as himself in *A Man Vanishes* (*Ningen jōhatsu*, 1967) and engineer Mr Kariya in *The Profound Desire of the Gods* (*Kamigami no fukaki yokubō*, 1968). However, in the case of *Dr. Akagi*, Imamura's identification with the protagonist even affected the production process and the tone of its outcome.

Kazuo Kitamura (1927–2007) was Imamura's first choice to play the doctor but had to bow out due to having to undergo an operation. His initial replacement was another Imamura regular, Rentarō Mikuni (1923–2013). However, a week into shooting Mikuni, too, stepped down and Akira Emoto (b. 1948), who had initially been cast in a smaller role, was promoted to the lead. The exact reason for this reshuffling has remained unclear. Imamura claimed that Mikuni could not memorize his lines while the actor himself complained about the pain in his knees that made it impossible to depict a doctor who is "all feet," always on the run from one patient to another (Muramatsu 2003: 244–45). It seems more likely, though, that there were artistic disagreements about which course the film should take. Thinking back to his involvement, Mikuni has noted that

> it is true that my knees got bad but there was this weird homage inside [the character]. [Imamura] was obsessed with an homage to his own blood relative. I couldn't help but to notice this. He'd have the portrait of his own father hanging on the set. I first thought of quitting when Imamura said that "My father's didn't do things like that.'" I felt that this was not an act I could go through with. (Katori 2004: 466)

Mikuni who had already played father figures in Imamura's films before, notably in *Vengeance Is Mine* (*Fukushū suru wa ware ni are*, 1979), had enough of the director's excessive identification of the character with his own father who had been a general practitioner. Interestingly, Kitamura, first cast in the role, had actually suggested that Imamura himself should play the part (Katori 2004: 464).

In his review of the film, Hide Murakawa has speculated whether a version starring Mikuni would have been more energetic as comedy (Murakawa 1998: 100). Indeed, by eventually casting the much younger Emoto, *Dr. Akagi* arguably became a film different from how it was originally conceived. The result lacks certain dynamics and immediacy that would have emerged from a contrast of a septuagenarian endlessly on move despite his advanced age. It is also the final scene of the film (discussed below), which, due to the (relatively) reduced age gap between the doctor and Sonoko, comes through not quite as grotesque as it might have been intended and fails to provide a parallel to the infamous apple tree scene in *The Insect Woman* (*Nippon konchūki*, 1963), in which the young protagonist offers her breast to a senile old man.[8]

In addition to creating an homage to his own doctor father, something he has emphasized in subsequent interviews (Kakii and Imamura 1998: 95), Imamura's adaptation of Ango (itself an example of anxiety of influence) is imbued with several layers of father-son relationships.[9] As we shall see, there is an additional character, Akagi's son, also a doctor, who is forced to take an altogether different path in his medical career during the war. Last but not least, the story was adapted by none other than Imamura's own son, screenwriter and director Daisuke Tengan (born Daisuke Imamura in 1959). He is also responsible for co-writing *Eel* and Imamura's final film, *Warm Water under a Red Bridge* (*Akai hashi no shita no nurui mizu*, 2001), as well as the Maiku Hama trilogy directed by Kaizō Hayashi (b. 1957)[10] and Takashi Miike's (b. 1960) notorious *Audition* (*Ōdishon*, 1999). This web of homosocial relationships might come as a surprise within the context of Imamura's oeuvre, which is commonly celebrated for its masterful portrayal of strong female (and weak male) characters. Conversely, *Dr. Akagi* takes place in a markedly masculine world, with Japan's failing war effort serving as an inextricable backdrop to this allegorical story.

Allegories

Donald Richie has noted that "allegory, the narrative description of a subject under the guise of another suggestively similar, is never obvious in the Imamura film, but neither is it ever entirely absent" (Richie 1997: 29). In the case of *Dr. Akagi*, such themes rather seem to be worn on the sleeve: it is all too apparent to which phenomenon the widespread malaise is alluding to. The same could be said about Ango's story on which it is based. In a scene where the doctor goes to Tokyo to attend a banquet to celebrate his mentor's birthday he delivers a speech where he addresses his medical colleagues by presenting the preliminary results of his research on the liver disease that he got his nickname from.

> Following the Manchurian Incident in 1932 [sic], there were a few patients of jaundice in whom hypertrophy of the liver was noted. Back then I only thought of it as a little strange and didn't pay much attention. However, since about 1937 seeing such patients became more frequent very rapidly... I have treated two thousand or more and concluding from this I suggest that the

Better Off Being Bacteria 219

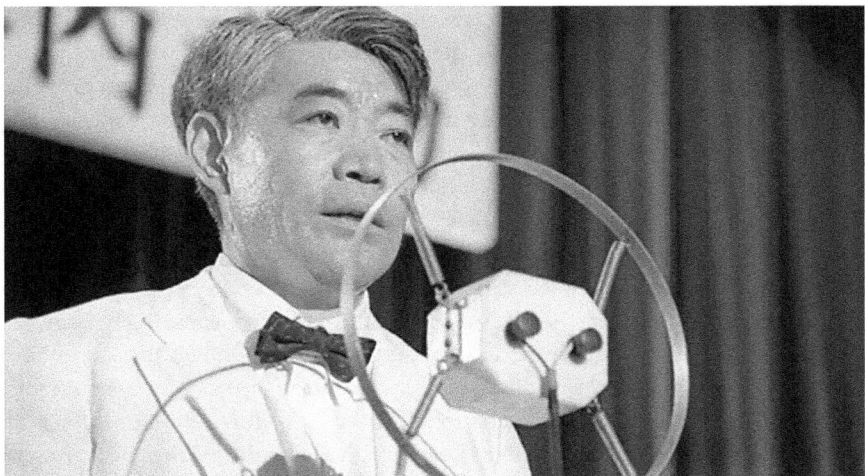

Figure 12.2 Dr. Akagi presenting the results of his research on liver disease.

disease should be called epidemic inflammation of the liver [*ryukōsei kanzōen*] or influenzic hepatitis [*ryūkansei kanzōen*]. I think that this might be related to the flu brought back from the Chinese continent [*Shina tairiku*]. (Ango 1990: 343–44)

The same dates appear over and over again in the story as the doctor keeps pondering over the cause of the disease. He makes parallels both to syphilis-causing spirochete brought from the Americas by Columbus, which reached Japan last due to its isolation from the rest of the world, and Spanish Flu that killed millions at the end of the First World War. Akagi even gives it a nickname, *tairiku kaze* (Continental Flu), according to its speculated source (Ango 1990: 337).

Such precise temporal and geographical coordinates leave little doubt about what this allegory of a disease that has gradually overwhelmed Japan is targeting. First detected around 1931 and substantially spread since 1937, this version of hepatitis neatly parallels Japan's military campaign in China. The hitherto-secluded country that has come to embrace colonial aspirations is suddenly contaminated by something that originates back to the Asian mainland. On the one hand, this is the vengeance of a microorganism, a terrifying and invisible Other (by way of analogy, syphilis has been thought of being precisely that for the European invaders of the Americas). On the other hand, Japanese militarism itself was something akin to the wind (*kaze*, a homonym of flu in Japanese) sweeping the continent. Either way, the allegory of a national malady that fails to find official recognition functions as a critique of Japan's military adventures and atrocities and, by extension, people's state of mind.

In the film, upon his return from the banquet, the doctor finds out that Sonoko, his assistant, is hiding a wounded Dutch soldier, Piet, in his house. The Dutchman has been wrongly accused of being a spy and subsequently has managed to escape. The doctor decides against returning him to the military authorities and instead treats his wounds. The two quickly establish a bond, speaking in German (lingua franca of the Japanese medical profession), and when Piet turns out to be a film projectionist by trade he offers his help for setting up relevant instruments for the doctor's study of the bacteria in question. Unfortunately, after a turn of events they are discovered and Piet is beaten to death by the soldiers. It is shortly before expiring that he shouts to his murderers that they must have hepatitis of the brain. This presents another example of how the disease has become synonymous to military thinking. War is the symptom, ideology the illness.

While helping an enemy soldier could be seen as part of the Hippocratic Oath, the doctor's attitude toward military authorities and the state is mostly that of distrust. After all, it is his successive confrontations with the army that first get the narrative going and then contribute to its conclusion. In the beginning of the film, the doctor makes a visit to a brothel frequented by soldiers that has been closed by the authorities due to an outburst of typhus; unsurprisingly, he gives a diagnosis of hepatitis instead. In the course of the film, there is a deepening conflict with the army that accuses him of overusing the limited stock of glycose for treating his patients. On the other hand, when Akagi talks with a fellow doctor critically about the war, he still brings up the need to protect Asia from the West, a familiar argument in militarist rhetoric. Tellingly, after this outburst he halts and falls silent as if lost in belief, realizing the futility of it all.

In a way, *Dr. Akagi* is also a story of how his professional oath and loyalty to the state are becoming increasingly incompatible. Even when toward the end of the film he suddenly rushes to the town hall to announce his wish to be sent to the front in the name of the emperor, this is just a disguise, coming as it does at the moment when he finally realizes what being a doctor is all about: helping anyone in need—not the war effort, but people. This unabashedly idealistic portrayal is also contrasted with that of his own son. Ichirō (Minoru Tanaka), one of the characters added to the film adaptation, is a doctor stationed in Manchuria. While he helps his father by sending further evidence about the disease, we see in a brief dream sequence how he has been

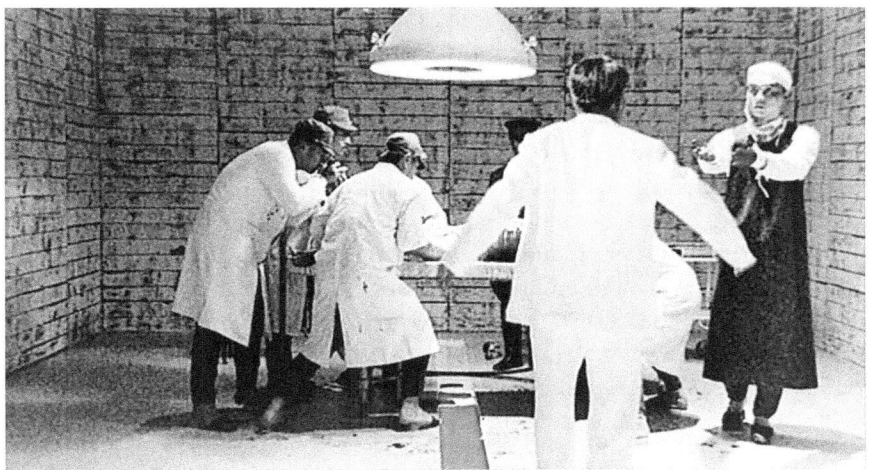

Figure 12.3 A dream sequence about Dr. Akagi's son in Unit 731.

involved in more than dubious activities. This is an allusion to the infamous Unit 731 of the Imperial Japanese Army based in Harbin, which conducted medical human experimentation on war prisoners.[11]

While the doings of Unit 731 certainly represent the most radical violation of the medical code imaginable, the doctor's dilemma in *Dr. Akagi* could also be considered within the context of Imamura's self-proclaimed observationist filmmaking. Parallels could be drawn between Dr. Akagi and Mr Kariya in *The Profound Desire of the Gods*, both coming from the city and outsiders to the local community. While the stance of an anthropologist as detached observer is ambiguous to say the least, it is the doctor, constantly obliged to intervene with people's very existence, who appears to be effectively shut out from being a mere observer. At best, he is a selfless, benevolent, God-like presence who descends to help and educate the amorphous masses, viewing them with a clinically detached eye, not even as humans but rather as vessels of disease.

Aside from the malady that is a militaristic mindset, there is also a positive side to the same image of the widespread disease in *Dr. Akagi*. This part of the allegory is closely associated (and perhaps equated) with Sonoko, the female protagonist of the film, who at one point tells the doctor that "people are better off being bacteria," a declaration that seems to strike at the heart of what Imamura must have seen as the main motif of the film. On a number of occasions, it is bacteria that becomes a metaphor for common people who survive the societal calamities despite (or precisely because of) their general ignorance. This is an image of people as irrepressible as bacteria, hard to see by the naked eye but no less potent, always persevering and spreading. Tadao Satō has noted that it is through female characters that Imamura tends to display the condition of the masses (Sato 1982: 81–82), and it is highly informative that in a film untypically (for Imamura) male-centered, it is still a woman who gets the final word.

Employing bacteria as an image for common people, both miserable and persistent, Imamura stays true but at the same time falls back on some of his more recognizable tropes on human existence and identity of the Japanese in particular. What adds a certain freshness to this is the fact that it is played out against the backdrop of a rural community at wartime with an implied question of the people's exact role in and attitude toward the state that Japan had drifted into since the outset of its expansionist policies. However, ridding the people of critical faculties by comparing them to swarming single-cell organisms simply suggests masses who were not even in a position to know or care. At any rate, Imamura's arc of allegories seems to have moved from insects to include bacteria toward the very end of his career. In effect, an anthropologist-as-entomologist now becomes microbiologist, taking human existence to the cellular level.

The doctor's own stance as the locus of reason amid the swarming masses also relates to the quest for unattainable truth, another persistent motif of Imamura's. However, this time the "truth" has a decidedly pragmatic dimension: to alleviate the suffering of people while turning a critical eye toward the official truth. This is turn seems to make such an effort appear not quite as vain as in many other films. While Akagi fights the ignorance of superstitious common people and the army in equal measure, he paradoxically mystifies the disease that perhaps does not even exist apart from his wish to help his patients by however meager means. This quixotic quest for bacteria, invisible to the eye much like the imaginary giants (windmills) for its most famous antecedent, poses a question about a man whose heart might be in the right place, but his mind is no longer there. Perhaps what Imamura suggests is that at such desperate times, madness is the last retreat to sustain humanity.

In a metatextual twist, cinema itself has a part in this search for truth. In his ambition to study the hepatitis bacteria more closely, the doctor obtains a microscope that he then augments with a light source taken from the local cinema's projection room. The film running at the time is *Kato's Falcon Fighters* (*Katō hayabusa sentōtai*, 1944, Kajirō Yamamoto), a biopic of a pilot killed in combat two years earlier. This seems to suggest that now that films are only good for propaganda purposes, the projection light can be put to better use. In

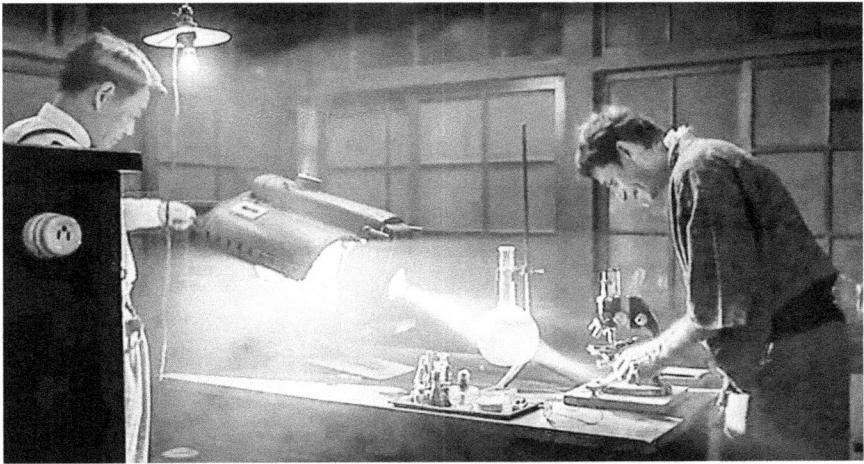

Figure 12.4 Dr. Akagi and war prisoner Piet (Jacques Gamblin) setting up research equipment.

other words, it takes an apparatus from cinema and a foreign projectionist to have a shot at truth, or at least enlightenment.

Endings and Conclusions

While themes such as the resilience of common people are not difficult to detect in *Dr. Akagi*, Imamura has created more links that tie it with both his own oeuvre and that of others. In this context, it is significant that Imamura considered and approached this, rather than the subsequent *Warm Water under a Red Bridge*, as his final film (Quandt 1997: 1). In September 1998, a month before the release of *Dr. Akagi*, Akira Kurosawa (1910–1998) passed away. In his last feature, *Madadayo* (1993), based on the later years of the writer Hyakken Uchida (1889–1971), a notable sequence takes place during the Allied air strikes on Tokyo in the final months of the war, with Hyakken's house burning down and him moving into a shack. Imamura's decision to adapt a story about another old man facing the end of the war is only one thread that connects the two directors. Imamura has admitted that it was only after being greatly impressed by Kurosawa's *Drunken Angel* (*Yoidorl tenshi*, 1948) that he first thought of entering filmmaking; he had initially aspired to become an assistant to Kurosawa but ended up at Shōchiku instead, working with Yasujirō Ozu (1903–1963), whose style he soon came to detest (Nakata and Imamura 1997: 111). *Dr. Akagi*, which seems to operate in a mode more nostalgic than is common to Imamura, also harks back to his beginnings as a filmmaker.

This private dimension is further underlined by the inclusion in the adaptation of Akagi's friend and colleague, an anesthesiologist. He also happens to be a morphine addict and unwittingly meets his end during an attack on an army warehouse where he hopes to obtain another shot. His final words ring: "Life is but farewell!" (*Sayonara dake ga jinsei da*). Those more familiar with Imamura will instantly recognize an allusion to his mentor, the director Yūzō Kawashima (1918–1963), who had a notorious drinking problem that contributed to his early death.[12] Kawashima liked this phrase from a Chinese poem translated by Masuji Ibuse so much that he included it in several of his films.[13] In *Dr. Akagi*, which is partly homage to his general practitioner father, Imamura has also made sure to include a nod to his father-figure in cinema. Further attesting to this attempt of tying ends together, one should recall that in Imamura's third feature, *Hateshi naki yokubō/Endless Desire* (1958), all characters meet their early demise due to pursuing a hidden stack of morphine.

This sense of an ending, not only because the film depicts an end of an era, relating as it does to the last days of the war, is also part of the gesture of making one last picture and a quest for one final image that might encapsulate one's entire career. The doctor's final assignment is to a faraway island, taking Sonoko along. On the way back, they notice a whale swimming nearby. It is then that Sonoko remembers her promise to hunt one for the doctor (there is a family legend that her father had singlehandedly caught one) from an earlier scene where she first confessed her love. She harpoons the creature and jumps out of the boat only to be dragged under water at the end of the rope, losing most of her clothes in the process. In the ensuing confusion, the doctor, too, falls out of the boat and ends up in water.

In Ango's story, this is when the doctor drowns, followed by the narrator composing a poem that retells the whole story in different form, a tale reminiscent of the end of Kafū Nagai's (1879–1959) *A Strange Story from East of the River* (*Bokutō kidan*, 1937). Imamura lets him live, fished out by Sonoko. Emoto, who played the doctor, has noted that he in fact considered this outcome of surviving beyond Japan's and his own defeat far crueler than death (Kanazawa and Emoto 1998: 99). The lead actor also mentions that it was in this particular late work by Imamura that the director's *sakkasei* (auteurship) had once more become visible. As if to emphasize this, there is a link to the element of water that often concludes Imamura's films, with the characters meeting their destiny on water (*Endless Desire*, *The Pornographers*, *The Profound Desire of the Gods*). In comparison to these earlier works, the denouement of *Dr. Akagi* seems more life-affirming but no less ironic.

Figure 12.5 Witnessing the end of the war.

Saved from their certain death in the waves, the half-naked Sonoko stands up and proclaims: "I am bacteria. Doctor, please spank me." As the two embrace, a sudden flash in the distance is reflected on their faces. It now makes sense that in the beginning of the scene the date was marked as August 6 as a mushroom cloud starts forming in the sky over the sea. Akagi, once again seeing nothing but hypertrophied liver in its shape, comments that this might be the ire of a man whose body they had exhumed for experiments, or then maybe the wrath of all people tired and disgusted of war.[14] The fact that the doctor survives, cruel as it may be, can also be seen in a moralistic contrast to the demise of his own son who strayed from the path of medical professionalism. This final scene, filled with hope and irony, hints at the ambiguities of postwar, so well displayed in both Ango's and Imamura's work, that were soon to follow.

Notes

1. The distributor of the film, Tōhō, made Imamura cut it down substantially into a more audience-friendly length of 129 minutes; the director claims that the original three-hour version was far more interesting than the eventual release (Imamura 2004: 152).
2. The titles of the novel and the film are distinguished by the use of Chinese characters and katakana for denoting the word *kanzō* (liver), respectively.
3. Suitably published shortly after the abolishing of the Civil Censorship Detachment (CCD) in November 1949, *Dr. Liver* includes depictions of enemy attacks and critical

remarks that would certainly have been erased only months earlier on the basis of avoiding resentment toward the Allied occupation.
4. Ango, much like his older colleagues Sōseki Natsume, Ōgai Mori, or Kafū Nagai, is commonly known by his *nom de plume* rather than surname; his given name was Heigo.
5. These include *I Won't Give Up, Not Before Winning* (*Makeraremasen katsumadewa*, 1958, Shirō Toyoda), *Under the Cherry Blossoms* (*Sakura no mori no mankai no shita*, 1975, Masahiro Shinoda), and *Nonconsecutive Cases of Murder* (*Furenzoku satsujin jiken*, 1977, Chūsei Sone). In addition, *Tenmei Tarō* (1951, Tadao Ikeda) was based on a radio drama to which Ango contributed an episode. Subsequent adaptations include *The Idiot* (*Hakuchi*, 1999, Makoto Tezuka), *One Woman and the War* (*Senso to hitori no onna*, 2013, Jun'ichi Inoue), and an anime series *Un-Go* (2011, Seiji Mizushima).
6. According to film credits, *Dr. Akagi* has also drawn from two other texts by Ango, *Discourse on Decadence* and *Drifting Clouds, Flowing Water*. While the character of Sonoko clearly originates in the latter, the influence of the former can at best be detected in terms of its general tone.
7. The doctor's given name Fuū (literally, wind and rain) is an allusion to Kenji Miyazawa's (1896–1933) universally known poem "Ame ni mo makezu" (Be not defeated by the rain), which is mentioned on several occasions in relation to how the doctor perceives his own profession.
8. Subsequently, an older Emoto has been cast in similar roles such as in Kaneto Shindō's final feature *Ichimai no hagaki/A Postcard* (2011), where he is the father who hangs himself after both his sons are killed in combat.
9 David Desser has pointed out a stronger thread of such issues, an "anxiety of influence [with] Oedipal overtones" at the very core of Imamura's filmmaking, which from the very beginning has sought to reject his initial training at Shōchiku. In the director's words: "I wouldn't just say I wasn't influenced by [Yasujirō] Ozu. I would say I didn't want to be influenced by him" (Desser 1988: 44).
10. The trilogy includes *The Most Terrible Time in My Life* (*Waga jinsei saiaku no toki*, 1994), *Stairway to the Distant Past* (*Harukana jidai no kaidan o*, 1995) and *The Trap* (*Wana*, 1996).
11. Unit 731 has been captured on the screen in several horror films that include *Men behind the Sun* (*Hei taiyang* 731, 1988, Tun Fei Mou) and *Philosophy of a Knife* (2008, Andrey Iskanov).
12. For more on Imamura's relationship with Kawashima, see Imamura 1997: 133–44.
13. The same words are used for the title of Imamura's book-length tribute to Kawashima, *Sayonara dake ga jinsei da: Eiga kantoku Kawashima Yūzō no shōgai* (Life Is But Farewell: The Life of Film Director Yūzō Kawashima), 1969.
14. Although action was moved from Izu Peninsula to the Inland Sea, apparently to make the ending possible, Imamura admits that the mushroom cloud of Hiroshima would not have been visible from as far as Okayama prefecture (Kakii and Imamura 1998: 96).

Works Cited

Bock, Audie (1997). "Shohei Imamura: No Confucianist." In *Shohei Imamura*, ed. James Quandt, 149–53. Toronto: Toronto International Film Festival Group.

Desser, David (1988). *Eros plus Massacre: An Introduction to the Japanese New Wave Cinema*. Bloomington: Indiana University Press.

Dr. Akagi [*Kanzō sensei*]. Dir. Shohei Imamura. Japan: Imamura Purodakushon/Tōei/ Tōhoku Shinsha/Kadokawa Shoten, 1998.

Imamura, Shohei (1997). "The Sun Legend of a Country Boy." In *Shohei Imamura*, ed. James Quandt, 133–44. Toronto: Toronto International Film Festival Group.

Imamura, Shohei (2004). *Eiga wa kyōki no tabi de aru: Watashi no rirekisho* [Cinema Is a Journey of Madness: My Résumé]. Tokyo: Nihon Keizai Shinbunsha.

Kakii, Michihiro, and Shohei Imamura. (1998). "Imamura Shōhei kantoku intabyū: Yakusha o oikonde ikeba, karera wa chan to ugoku to iu koto ni ki ga tsukimashita" [Interview with director Shōhei Imamura: I realized that when driven into a corner, the actors will start to move properly]. *Kinema Junpō* 1269 (2083), November: 95–97.

Kanazawa, Makoto, and Emoto Akira (1998). "Emoto Akira intabyū: 'Nande mo iwanai' Imamura enshutsu ga hijō ni omoku kanjirareta" [Interview with Akira Emoto: I felt very impressed by Imamura's "say nothing" direction]. *Kinema Junpō* 1269 (2083), November: 98–99.

Katori, Shunsuke (2004). *Ningen dokyumento: Imamura Shōhei densetsu* [Record of a Human: The Legend of Shōhei Imamura]. Tokyo: Kawade Shobō Shinsha.

Murakawa, Hide (1998). "'Jūkigeki' ni kuwaerareta tōmei de chōmei na bigaku" [The Transparent and Crystalline Aesthetics of "Serious Comedy"]. *Kinema Junpō* 1269 (2083), November: 100–101.

Muramatsu, Tomoshi (2003). *Imahei hankachō: Imamura Shōhei to wa nanimono* [Imahei's Criminal Record: Who Is Shōhei Imamura]. Nihon Hōsō Shuppan Kyōkai.

Nakata, Toichi, and Shohei Imamura (1997). "Shohei Imamura Interview." In *Shohei Imamura*, ed. James Quandt, 107–24. Toronto: Toronto International Film Festival Group.

Quandt, James (1997). "Pigs, Pimps and Pornographers: A Brief Introduction to the Films of Shohei Imamura." In *Shohei Imamura*, ed. James Quandt, 1–5. Toronto: Toronto International Film Festival Group.

Richie, Donald (1997). "Notes for a Study on Shohei Imamura." In *Shohei Imamura*, ed. James Quandt, 7–43. Toronto: Toronto International Film Festival Group.

Sakaguchi, Ango (1986). "Discourse on Decadence." Trans. Seiji M. Lippit. *Review of Japanese Culture and Society* 1, no. 1: 1–5.

Sakaguchi, Ango (1990). "Kanzō sensei" [Dr. Liver]. In *Sakaguchi Ango zenshū*, vol. 7, 320–61. Tokyo: Chikuma Shobō.

Sato, Tadao (1982). *Currents in Japanese Cinema*. Trans. Gregory Barrett. Tokyo: Kodansha.

Chapter 13

Time Out of Joint: Shohei Imamura and the Search for an "Other" Japan

Bill Mihalopoulos

In memory of Peter Williams (1953–2015)

From the release of *Kami gami no fukaki yokubo/The Profound Desires of the Gods* (1968) until his return to feature filmmaking with *Fukushu suru wa ware ni ari/ Vengeance Is Mine* (1979), Shohei Imamura spent nine years primarily making documentaries. During this period, he made three documentaries for Tokyo Channel 12 that are the focus of this essay: *Mikikanhei o otte: Marei-hen/In Search of the Unreturned Soldiers in Malaysia* (1971); *Mikikanhei o otte: Tai-hen/ In Search of the Unreturned Soldiers in Thailand* (1971); and *Muhōmatsu kokyō ni kaeru/Outlaw Matsu Returns* (1973). The documentaries were made at a great personal financial sacrifice for the Imamura household; all were bankrolled by his wife's production company that created artwork for animation films (Nakata 1999: 120).

All three documentaries were made for a Japanese audience and were framed by the politics of *Beheiren*—the Citizens' League for Peace in Vietnam (*Betonamu Ni Heiwa O! Shimin Rengo*). The broad historical context that provided the framework for the documentaries was: (1) Japanese involvement in the Vietnam War; and (2) concern by Japanese citizens that cooperation with American Cold War conflicts in Asia provided the foundation for Japan's postwar affluence. From February 1965, when Lyndon Johnson approved of Operation Rolling Thunder, the US military was dependent on the unrestricted use of its 148 bases across the Japanese archipelago for their sustained bombing campaign against North Vietnam. Moreover, most of the 400,000 tons of monthly supplies needed to sustain the US military presence in Vietnam passed through the US bases stationed at Yokosuka, Sasebo, and Naha (Havens 1987: 85–87).

Many Japanese citizens saw their government's cooperation in allowing Japan to be used as a base for US war-making in Vietnam as unlawful and a violation of Japanese sovereignty. US bombing raids originating in Japan were a prohibited contravention of Japan's 1947 postwar constitution, which renounced

Japan's right to use force in settling international disputes (Article 9) on the premise that demilitarization was essential for the rehabilitation and reentry of Japan as a peaceful member of the community of nations (de Bary, Gluck, and Tiedemann 2005: 1029–36). Moreover, Articles IV and VI of the 1960 Treaty of Cooperation and Security between the United States and Japan explicitly stated that the Japanese government had to be consulted before US troops based in Japan were to be sent into combat.

Antiwar movements such as *Beheiren* led by the writer Makoto Oda and philosopher-historian Shunsuke Tsurumi did not buy into the fiction peddled by Prime Minister Eisaku Satō that US troops received their combat orders once they were outside Japanese territory (Havens 1987: 12–13). Instead, student and citizen antiwar groups saw the collaboration of the Japanese government elite with US war objectives in Vietnam as a violation of popular sovereign will. From mid-1967 to 1970, 18.7 million Japanese took to the streets to demonstrate their disapproval (Havens 1987: 133). The demonstrations acted as a tribunal of public opinion, the streets becoming the theater for the mass denunciation of the ruling elite, with an attempt by citizens to reinstate democratic rule over a government that saw itself above the will of the people (Havens 1987; Marotti 2009).

Fiscally, however, the Vietnam War was a boon for the Japanese economy. Japanese manufacturers supplied the everyday commodity goods demanded by the enlisted men of the Allied forces and the necessary equipment and materials for the US war effort against enemies of South Vietnam. It was estimated that one billion American dollars per year entered the Japanese economy because of the Vietnam War from 1966 to 1971. Moreover, between 1965 to 1968 Japanese exports to Southeast Asia increased 18 percent annually. By 1970, Japan had surpassed the United States as the leading trading power in Southeast Asia (Halliday & McCormack 1973: 54–56). Prominent *Beheiren* activists produced a series of exposés uncovering a list of "Hyena Corporations" feeding off American military involvement in Vietnam with fixed plans to heavily invest in South Vietnam's postwar economy. The most prominent names of corporate Japan made up the list: Mitsui Bussan, Mitsubishi Shōji, Marubeni, Toyota, and Sony, to name a few (Avenell 2010: 143–44). To the antiwar activists, the support and indirect participation of the Japanese government in the Vietnam War and the rise to prominence of Japanese companies in Southeast Asia felt uncannily familiar. They took the Japanese businessmen who started to appear in the cities of Southeast Asia in the 1960s as representing the shock troops of Japan's new imperialism (Kaji 1973; Shimizu 1973; Imamura 2001: 236). The Imperial Army may no longer be marching through Asia, but it seemed that the actions of corporate Japan in the region were driven by the same will to dominate that drove Japanese imperial ambitions in the first half of the twentieth century.

Beheiren activists drew attention to the fact that Japanese rapid economic growth and the Vietnam War were inseparable. Makoto Oda and Yoshiyuki Tsurumi in particular claimed that under the Japan-US Security treaty, Japan was a client state of the United States. They pointed to the fact that the supply of special procurements for the Vietnam War by corporate Japan was a permanent and institutionalized feature of the Japanese economy and made possible the prosperity and material comforts enjoyed by most Japanese (Avenell 2010: 143). *Beheiren* spokespeople urged Japanese citizens to critically address the fact that Japan was once again perpetrating aggression against an Asian nation—this time by logistically supporting the US military in Vietnam.

In Search of the Unreturned Soldiers in Malaysia, *In Search of the Unreturned Soldiers in Thailand*, and *Outlaw Matsu Returns* are framed by the politics of the *Beheiren* movement in three distinct ways. First, the narrative of the documentaries subscribes to an anti-state agenda. The documentaries adhere to the idea that the workings of power are secret and hidden, concealed by the scenery of public appearances, and that the state and agents of political power are to be treated critically and with caution.

Second, each of the three documentaries interrogates how Japan's contemporary relations with its Asian neighbors were malformed by the unfinished history of the Pacific War: a war that is not a problem of yesterday but of today.[1] In the documentaries, Imamura investigates how the specter of the war lies heavy on the present, not only for the Japanese people, but also for the peoples who inhabited the regions occupied by Japan that became the bloody battlefields of the Pacific War.

Third, following the cues of *Beheiren* activists, Imamura incorporated a victim-aggressor dynamic in his documentaries based on the critique that for Japan to find peace with its Asian neighbors, individual Japanese needed to resist the state locked into supporting the US war in Southeast Asia; otherwise they would remain victims of the state while simultaneously the victimizers of fellow Asians (Avenell 2010: 106–47). In his documentaries, Imamura attempts to locate the origin of this victim-aggressor dynamic in the actualization of belief; the emotional investment and leaps of faith that infused and affirmed the lived present with possibility and an agenda of action. Belief for Imamura was bound up with choices in a mode of existence, and a notion of self that could not be understood in isolation from its social and relational contexts. Politics and culture were inseparable. In the unreturned soldiers Imamura sought to find an untapped embodied experience of the Pacific War, a knowledge and memory that moved beyond the retelling of events. The documentaries begin with a simple supposition that challenges the dominant place-bound formation of Japanese identity, which chains culture, community, and ethnicity to the delimited territory of the Japanese state. Namely, why did soldiers who sacrificed all for the emperor choose to remain in Southeast Asia rather than return to Japan? In his search to find what motivated unreturned soldiers to turn their back on Japan, Imamura hoped to unearth the beliefs that gave meaning and direction to their lives, and in the process have his audience actively relive an unalloyed experience of the Pacific War in order to understand the real-life uncertainties confronting Japan in the present (Imamura 2001: 234–38).

Imamura and Documentary Style in Fiction Film

Japanese studios of the 1950s and 1960s organized film production around the motto "quickly, cheaply, and lucratively" (Tachibana 1988: 1–2). As a result, directors had little say in the films the studios would allocate them, which were a mixture of genre fare and star vehicles. The director's main role was to maintain production schedules, manage costs under budget, and to make popular films for a general audience. This was especially true for Nikkatsu film studios, which Imamura joined in 1954. Nikkatsu production was tailored around its stars, not its directors, and was renowned in the sixties for releasing low budget double features every week (Schilling 2007).

The film studios gave directors little artistic choice in genre. Imamura chafed at the narrative structures imposed by Nikkatsu and the demands to work on vehicles for studio stars. He thought the emphasis on stories built around the expectation of resolution and closure produced a heavily clichéd, stagnant cinema that bored rather than captivated. From early on his career, Imamura was keenly aware that the power of cinema lay in making the visual images on the flat screen more tangible, real, and believable via its composition, acting, set, sound, and lighting (Imamura 2004: 60). Inspired by the work and theories of avant-garde documentary filmmakers Toshio Matsumoto (Raine 2012; Matsumoto 2012) and Susumu Hani (Mellen 1975: 179–97), Imamura embraced documentary film methods to give his work a sense of "reality." Imamura quickly broke from the dictates of Nikkatsu studio production. He insisted on shooting the majority of *Nianchan/My Second Brother* (1959), his fourth feature film for Nikkatsu, outside the confines of the film studio. This saw Imamura and his production crew experimenting with the latest technological advances in audio recording and film cameras to shoot outdoors on location. Imamura's production crew proved highly innovative. *Nippon konchuki/The Insect Woman* (1963) was the first Japanese feature film to be entirely produced on location since the advent of the talkies (Imamura 2004: 40; Satō 1997: 70–73). Imamura departed fully from studio practice and chose not to record the sound track of *The Insect Woman* on Nikkatsu's soundstages. Instead, he had the actors fitted with wireless microphones and synchronized sound recording with filming (Imamura 2004: 118; Satō 1997: 74).

Imamura also broke studio procedure with his preference to work with non-professional actors rather than studio stars. He valued the "raw" performances of untrained novices as a way of shredding the artifice of the actor. He valued the unconscious and accidental elements that penetrated the performance of untrained actors because it enabled subjective representations that exceed expectation to be captured by the camera (Imamura 2004: 100).

Imamura's experimental and documentary style fiction filmmaking was ill suited to the high-volume, low-budget production regime of Nikkatsu studios, however. He always insisted on conducting intensive, time-consuming background research. Imamura placed great value in understanding the time, place, cultural context, and beliefs (point of view). He saw background research as providing the raw material from which to build the narrative arc and character developments that would give a film its singularity and keep the audience engaged (Sato 2012: 3). Moreover, he preferred to work by rehearsing each scene extensively, and would use substantial amount of film by shooting multiple takes for one scene. This way of shooting went against the frugality demanded by the studio, where production costs were calculated to be about one-third of all film-related expenses. Imamura soon became renowned within the upper echelons of Nikkatsu for not working to budget. In fact, as punishment for willfully exceeding production costs for his 1961 feature *Buta to gunkan/Pigs and Battleships*, the studio forbade Imamura from directing another feature film for two years.[2]

Imamura's move from fiction films to documentaries is well documented (Mes and Sharp 2005: 28–30). No longer willing to work within the regimented production values of Nikkatsu studios, he set up his own production company in 1965. Being a producer found Imamura becoming entangled in the everyday administrative side of film production. He learned that overseeing production and budget added another layer of complexity in his relationship with crew and actors. Imamura discovered that balancing the needs of each actor and crew with his overall vision for a project undermined his ability to work with them as collaborators (Imamura 2001: 235–36).

The pivotal moment in Imamura's career arguably was the financially disastrous *Kamigami no fukaki yokubo/Profound Desires of the Gods* (1968). Production difficulties and the film's poor box office return encouraged Imamura to turn his back on mainstream cinema and commercial distribution companies. Shot on location in Okinawa, consistent bad weather delayed production. The eighteen-month protracted shooting schedule gave rise to frustration and conflict among Imamura and his cast and crew. While waiting for the weather to clear, Imamura was happy to immerse himself in the beliefs of the local Okinawan culture. The actors, however, reportedly had little interest in using the delay in production to explore and experience the culture and values of local inhabitants in order to give authenticity to their performance. This indifference immensely frustrated Imamura, who wanted his actors to go beyond affectation and surface expression and seek the subconscious, unseen forces that motivate action.[3] Imamura put down the actors' indifference as a product of their vocation. The primary concern of an actor was their screen presence. Success lay in pleasing an audience and not on any criteria of authenticity. As a result, Imamura felt they were nihilistically fixated on the surface expressions of their performance and the superficiality of their public persona with little interest in the world "as it was" (Imamura 2001: 236).

Imamura's interest in local customs and beliefs was motivated by the desire to engage with the actuality of belief which infused and affirmed the lived present with possibility and an agenda of action. For Imamura, the leaps of faith that individuals took in the game of life revealed the essential relations at work even though they were not found in the world of anterior facts. He expanded on this topic in a conversation with Audie Bock. Imamura noted that to understand the whole of contemporary Japanese life, one needed to notice the rooftop shrines or household altars (*kamidana*) dedicated to the local tutelary deities that sat atop all the high-rise buildings of large Japanese conglomerates and the smaller factories that pock the landscape of urban Japan. For Imamura, these "little shrines" embodied the belief that pervade "the Japanese consciousness under the veneer of business suits and advanced technology." Custom, practice, and faith self-assured the mighty Japanese conglomerates and imbued them with the conviction to invest resources and manpower in business ventures (Bock 1978: 287).

Embittered by the commercial failure of *Profound Desires of the Gods* and his experience with actors during shooting on location in Okinawa, Imamura retreated to documentary filmmaking and his aesthetic quest to capture on camera the connectedness between the inner mental state of the protagonist and the world they inhabited—that is, a cinema that would dissolve the binary between objective and subjective truth, between fact and fiction.

In Search of the Unreturned Soldiers

The two companion-piece documentaries *In Search of the Unreturned Soldiers* typify Imamura's new direction. Imamura frames the lived experience of the unreturned soldiers as a counterpoint to postwar Japanese narratives of stability and economic development that effectively tied Japan's prosperity to the United States' global strategic policy of containing communism via military involvement in East and Southeast Asia. This included, among other things, trade arrangements enabling Japanese firms to export manufactured commodities and industrial resources to a less economically developed Southeast Asia, while US military forces selectively bombed them.

With *In Search of the Unreturned Soldiers*, Imamura attempts to locate the possibility of an alternative Japan that does not play handmaiden to the United States and does not seek to dominate the rest of Asia economically. The consciousness of the marginalized unreturned soldiers was appropriated and utilized to produce a critique of the moral and cultural trajectory of postwar Japan. The unreturned soldiers embodied a disjunction of time and history; the difference of today with respect to yesterday in terms of the transformations in Japanese character and sociability. For Imamura, the lived history of the unreturned soldiers held the possibility of a recoverable "reality" with the potential to offer the values and template for a Japan that could live together with other Asian countries without being the cause of war or economic and political friction.

Despite the passing of twenty-five years, the unreturned soldiers continued to live out the Pacific War. In the documentaries, Imamura takes the embodied experience of the former soldiers to reveal a world of multiple pasts and a present where time has literally come off its hinges. The content of soldiers' lives was a fork in time that diverged from the experience of a postwar Japan, crystallized around dominant public narratives stressing economic growth, consumerism, and postwar prosperity while eschewing any responsibility for the Pacific War and the bloody civil conflicts and wars of independence that erupted across Asia in the wake of Japanese defeat. In the contemporary national narratives of postwar Japan, Japanese public memory was selective. The dominant narratives of the Pacific War crystallized around suffering and victimhood: the trauma of American fire-bombing Japan's major cities, the nuclear holocausts of Hiroshima and Nagasaki, the shock of surrender, and the struggle to find food and rudimentary consumer goods in the wake of defeat. In contrast, in the lived experience of the unreturned soldiers the Pacific War never ended. Their direct experience fighting as Japanese Imperial soldiers in Southeast Asia was the moorings that gave meaning and purpose to the lives they led in Malaysia and Thailand, away from their homeland and ethnic community.

Imamura brilliantly presents to the audience the disjunctive nonsynchronic present by unchaining and separating the visual from the audial. The dissonance between sight and sound make visible the gap in time between the lived present of the unreturned soldiers where the Pacific War never ended and a postwar generation of Japanese who have little to no memory of Japanese aggression in Southeast Asia. By cutting the direct association between image and language,

Imamura challenged the audience to go beyond the clichéd stories of the atomic bomb and Japanese victimization, occupation, recovery, economic growth, and stability, and to engage directly with the unresolved and still unfolding consequences of Japanese actions and choices in the Pacific War.

In Search of the Unreturned Soldiers in Malaysia focuses on Imamura's search to find Japanese soldiers who chose to remain in Southeast Asia after Japan's surrender. The narrative and dramatic arc of the documentary is organized around the following question: Why would a soldier of the Japanese Imperial Army choose not to return to his homeland after Japan's formal surrender in September 1945? Imamura's search for such an individual unfolds via the use of interviews and carefully choreographed visuals. *In Search of the Unreturned Soldiers in Malaysia* is both a riveting exposé that unearths the silenced and overlooked events of the Pacific War and a powerful reflection-cum-investigation into the inconstancy embedded in the history, memory, and lived experience of the Pacific War.

The documentary exhumes a series of discomforting facts about the war for its intended Japanese audience. In his investigations, Imamura uncovers that some of the fiercest resistance to the Japanese invasion in February 1942 was by the 1,500 communist political prisoners, released by the British authorities in the final days before the fall of Singapore, who fought the invading Japanese army to the last man. This is a jarring revelation if juxtaposed with the facts presented in standard textbooks that write that General Arthur Percival, the British commander in Singapore, arranged for the surrender of 100,000 Commonwealth troops, or the factual digression found in the footnotes of accounts covering the fall of Singapore that chronicle the commander of the Australian forces, Lieutenant General Henry Bennet, escaping under cover of darkness while instructing the 15,000 men under his command to remain at their post.

Imamura's odyssey also revealed that for many Japanese soldiers stationed in Singapore and Malaysia, the war did not end in with the official surrender of Japanese forces to Lord Mountbatten, the Supreme Allied Commander of the Southeast Asian Command, on September 12, 1945, in Singapore. Kenichi Sasaki, whom Imamura found working as a travel guide, did not put down his weapon with Japan's surrender. Instead he fled deep into the mountains of Malaysia's interior with 300 other Japanese soldiers and kept fighting. They aligned themselves with Japan's former enemy—the communist-led Malayan People's Anti-Japanese Army, which had transformed itself into the Malayan National Liberation Army—in armed resistance against British colonial control.[4] However, after three and a half years of fighting, Sasaki came to realize that the Malayan National Liberation Army cause did not benefit Japan, and he ceased being a guerrilla fighter. Other Japanese soldiers chose to remain, however. Sasaki literally bristled at the thought that many in Japan regarded him an army deserter (*dassōhei*) who chose to remain in Southeast Asia rather than return home and face punishment. The Japanese government classified the many unreturned soldiers that Sasaki represented as traitors who put down their weapons and absconded in the final stages of the war, denying them military pensions and humiliating their families in the process. In response, Sasaki squarely faces the camera and with a steely glare fervidly pronounces that he was first and foremost a patriot; all his actions were motivated by his love and willingness to risk all for his country.

The documentary also captures the consternation of the local Japanese population who felt that, by asking Singaporeans about their experience during Japan's military occupation, Imamura and his film crew were raising the war dead. While long-term Japanese residents wanted to lay their collaboration with the Japanese military to rest, the lived memory of the systematic liquidation of predominantly Chinese men between the ages of eighteen and fifty by the Japanese *kempeitai* (military security force) continued to disturb the present.[5] The memory of the massacre haunted every nook and cranny of the city. In front of one of the main spots where the killing occurred, Mr. Won, Imamura's Chinese informant and guide, recalls to the camera in inarticulate, broken Japanese the horror of seeing the beheaded bodies of family, friends, and acquaintances littering the squares, beaches, and main thoroughfares of Singapore. For a Japanese audience in the 1970s, this would be a shocking revelation as the details of such events were erased from the Japanese collective memory of the Pacific War.

Imamura's odyssey ends with the discovery of Akeem, a former Japanese soldier wholly integrated into a close-knit Muslim community. Akeem provided Imamura with the voice he has been searching for to critique the "false progress" and "empty democracy" of postwar Japan (Imamura 2004: 158–59). Facing the camera, Akeem says that he feels pity for the "disadvantaged people" of Japan who work long, hard hours for shallow economic success. The Japanese had indeed developed economically faster than the "materially poor Malays" not because they were superior, but because they lacked any moral bearings. Economic success came easily to the Japanese because Japanese society was organized around satisfying base desires void of any higher calling or sense of "virtue or justice." For Akeem, it was the ignoble values of greed and instant gratification that underpinned the Japanese economic miracle.

Imamura, however, found Akeem's ire unsatisfactory. It did not account for the passions and forces that brought Akeem to the Malaysian peninsula to kill others. For Imamura, Akeem's adopted faith lacked "conviction" (Imamura 2001: 236). The trauma of the war and Japanese surrender left Akeem without

Figure 13.1 Akeem (left), a former Japanese soldier who converted to Islam and lives in a close-knit Muslim community in Malaysia. (Photo courtesy of Icarus Films.)

belief and isolated. He was without identity and community. He was literally saved by the local Muslim community, which took him in and treated him as one of their own. In return, Akeem uninstalled one system of prescriptions in the name of the Divine merely to install another. His need for certitude drove him to replace the glory and divine quality of the Japanese Emperor/Living Sun God with another set of religious convictions. However, the quality and force of his belief remained unchanged. The name of the Divine may have changed, but his want and need for an ordained natural order, a language of illumination and righteousness, and access to a wrath for any worldly deviation that strayed from the Divine plan remained the same.

Imamura continued his quest to find out what drove ordinary Japanese to war and how the unreturned soldiers coped with the trauma and memory of their actions in the companion documentary *In Search of the Unreturned Soldiers in Thailand*. The documentary was constructed around a meandering conversation, sustained by a healthy intake of alcohol, between three unreturned soldiers of differing background and temperament. Despite lacking any narrative arc, the documentary is a fascinating study on how morality has its own psychological faculty that outstrips rational thought.

Each of the three men found themselves fighting in Southeast Asia as a direct result of the prevalent "race war" discourse that played a significant role in informing and shaping Japanese imperialism, namely the political historicism of Japanese pan-Asianism, which stressed the 300 years of injustice the Europeans had inflicted on the peoples of Asia, and lionized the Japanese presence in China and the Pacific as the means for righting these long-inflicted wrongs (Hotta 2007; Saaler and Szpilman 2001). The rhetoric of Japanese Pan-Asianism found its crescendo on August 1, 1940, when Foreign Minister Yōsuke Matsuoka announced the Japanese government's policy to build a "Greater East Asia Co-Prosperity Sphere" (*Dai TōaKyōeiken*) that would liberate the "Asiatic" people from the colonial yoke of "White" domination (Dower 1986: 203–90). The term "Greater East Asia" implied that in addition to Japan, Manchukuo, and China, regional "co-prosperity" would include Southeast Asia. Clad in the language of "liberation," the new policy to expand the boundaries of Japan's empire beyond East Asia was an attempt by the Japanese leaders to seize the opportunity offered to them after France and the Netherlands fell to Nazi Germany in late spring 1940, thus forfeiting their colonies in Southeast Asia. Japan subsequently advanced into French Indochina in June 1940. When diplomacy proved futile in lifting economic sanctions imposed by the United States and British colonies and domains in the Pacific, Japan attacked Pearl Harbor on December 7, 1941. At the same time the Japanese invaded the Malaysia peninsular. Many Japanese were convinced their actions were freeing fellow Asians from European domination.

At its most potent, *In Search of the Unreturned Soldiers in Thailand* traces how the Pacific War was still being lived out by the three unreturned soldiers. In the documentary Namio Nakayama, a wealthy doctor, refuses to talk about the war or criticize the Emperor/Living Sun God.[6] Yet the trauma of the war was inscribed directly upon his body. Tattooed on his back were a series of Buddhist-related blessings and protective spells.

Matsukichi Fujita, a small land-holding peasant farmer near the Thai-Burma border, remained wholly invested in his identity as an Imperial liberation fighter. With joyful abandon, Fujita retells bloated stories of atrocities he carried out in the name of the emperor, the kill-or-be-killed theater of war still giving his life meaning and dignity thirty years after it ended. In contrast, Ginzaburō Toshida served the local poor as a lay doctor, his profoundly personal way of making amends for the violence Japan inflicted upon the region. Only Toshida speaks about the Pacific War as an exercise in futility and a waste of human life, while simultaneously condemning the Japanese emperor and his military cronies for demanding blind compulsion and obligation to a cause he did not and could not believe in.

Figure 13.2 The "wild boy" from Nagasaki, Fujita Matsukichi. (Photo courtesy of Icarus Films.)

Imamura never hints to the audience which account of the Pacific War he favors. Each man stands steadfast by his subjective version of reality and the truth about the war. Yet they do share a commonality. Each refuses to assume any burden of responsibility for his actions during the war. Toshida blames his involvement on a war-mongering emperor; Fujita excuses all his actions by saying he was a loyal soldier simply following orders; Nakayama deflects any accountability by enigmatically remaining silent.

The documentary ends with an unresolved question: How did a reckless youth from Nagasaki, a poor farmer from Ibaraki,[7] and a tinsmith from Osaka become the agents of brutal atrocities? The viewer is challenged to take up the vexing question: What are the Japanese youths who do not have direct experience of the war becoming? The final shot reveals a plane window framing a panorama of the Japanese landscape through cloudy skies. The voiceover factually states: "The sky over Japan is cloudy."

Outlaw Matsu Returns

The emperor-loving "wild boy" Matsukichi Fujita's return to Japan thirty years after the war is the focus of *Outlaw Matsu Returns*. The documentary conceptually and aesthetically differs subtly from the *In Search of the Unreturned Soldiers* series. Conceptually, Imamura frames Fujita as a metonym for "the discarded" (*kimin*): Japanese people who gave valuable service to the state only to be discarded by the government in the processes of "reforming" and "rationalizing" postwar Japan.[8] Fujita stands in for the sacrifice extracted from the rural poor as objects of state manipulation. Postwar Japan is conceptualized as a political power obsessed with economic progress that favors the interests of the political and commercial elite at the expense of the true interests of the ordinary individual such as Fujita. The narrative and characterological emphasis of the documentary falls heavily on the tragedy of Fujita caught in circumstances beyond his control or understanding. Aesthetically, the documentary reverts to the practices of *Ningen johatsu/A Man Vanishes* (1967). While employing many of the "fly on the wall" techniques associated with *cinéma vérité* to deliver a sense of authenticity, *Outlaw Matsu Returns* is anything but neutral. Imamura stages footage and shamelessly manipulates Fujita, manufacturing conflicts with his brother and attempts at a clumsy, cringe-worthy romantic subplot by introducing Fujita's youthful crush to heighten the dramatic arc of the documentary. In many ways, *Outlaw Matsu Returns* is the harbinger of Reality TV programming, which blends the aspiration to document events occurring before the camera as they happen with the tendency to imagine

Figure 13.3 Thirty years since he was dispatched abroad as an Imperial Japanese solider, "Outlaw Matsu" returns to Japan.
(Photo courtesy of Icarus Films).

reality because of the necessity of a coherent narrative structure to produce effects such as suspense and drama for the viewing audience.

Outlaw Matsu Returns is organized around two narrative strands. One strand is the domestic drama between Fujita and his brother Fujio on his return to his native home. Through a juxtaposition of the psychological makeup of Fujita and his brother, Imamura aims to convey the whole experience of Japan's postwar transformation into an economic power. On the one hand, Fujita embodies the Japan of yesteryear: honest, fiercely loyal, and driven by a strong sense of obligation and duty to family. His grief at the cemetery for his parents and brother's family who died in the nuclear holocaust unleashed on Nagasaki is sincere. His concern for his younger sister Fujiko, divorced from an abusive husband and neglected by Fujio, is heartfelt. Fujio, on the other hand, represents the changes in personality and sociability of the Japanese during the two decades of postwar recovery and economic growth. He embodies the impersonal historical forces that give shape to Japan's economic miracle—a love of money, the language of self-promotion, and the transformative power of an economy that robs things of their innate value and distinction by making everything interchangeable with money. The documentary strongly links Fujio's love of money with his decision to abandon his younger sister to destitution, and his "conspiracy" with Fujita's childhood friend to have Fujita pronounced dead so that he did not have to share his parents' inheritance.

The other narrative strand of the documentary is Fujita's growing awareness that he no longer has a place in the land of his birth despite his fierce loyalty to the emperor and willingness to die for his country.[9] He literally does not exist. His country has proclaimed him dead, a victim of the Pacific War, his uncultured Japanese and outdated notions of loyalty and obligation treated with contempt. His visit to Yasukuni Shrine, one of the iconic symbols of Japanese nationalism built in 1869 to commemorate all who died in the service of the emperor, leaves him underwhelmed. He has no investment in the nationalist trappings and imperial myths associated with the shrine. They are the symbols of an aristocratic and military elite. The imperial narratives proclaiming the glory of Japan are not meant for, nor do they include, a simple "wild boy" from Nagasaki. The only time Fujita feels at home in Japan is when he meets his superior officer. Their friendship is one forged by the heat of battle and, for a moment, as he hears his officer's voice again over the phone, time forks and Fujita's fanatical loyalty to the emperor returns to take over the workings of his body, the passion ripping a pledge from his lips to "join the Third Operation again to once more kill the British and Chinese."

The climax of the documentary is Fujita taking a guided tour of the imperial palace with Imamura and his film crew. The imposing size surprises Fujita, as does the guide's revelation of the expense to build and maintain the imperial palace. The camera captures the feelings of betrayal that erupt from Fujita. How could the emperor live in such opulence when loyal subjects such as he lived in poverty abroad? Infuriated and confused, Fujita wildly speculates that the emperor started the Pacific War for money, too. The realization that he has been used and abandoned by the emperor, sacrificed for the sake of vulgar material accumulation, cuts Fujita to the bone, leaving him staring dazed into the camera. Fujita's nationalist fervor can no longer hide from him that his personal sacrifices in the name of the emperor have no home in postwar Japan. He is an example of "the discarded"—Japanese who loyally served the emperor and Japanese state only to have both turn their backs on them in their time of need—*par excellence*.

Imamura's History Lesson

At the heart of Imamura's three documentaries for Tokyo Channel 12 is a curiosity about the changing nature of the present in its own right. The documentaries expose the history of postwar Japan by juxtaposing what the Japanese are ceasing to be with what they are becoming via an exploration into the "reality" of the Pacific War and the subjective self that finds itself enmeshed in the questions of identity and history. Imamura's analysis begins with the "what is" and proceeds to deduce the conditions out of which the real developed.

At the heart of Imamura's quest is a deep-seated skepticism for any politics of transcendence. The promise of universal peace under the providence of the emperor encapsulated in the wartime slogan *hakkō-ichiu* (eight corners of the world under one roof) led the Japanese people to sacrifice their present, only to be repaid by the Imperial Japanese state in the currency of war, death, and destruction. Imamura also sees the postwar calls for the Japanese to surrender themselves to the higher values of free market democracy as fatally compromised. In the process he gives a diagnosis of the "economic animal" the Japanese have become by tracing how individual and communal relations were transformed, from associations founded on emotional attachments and reciprocal obligation to social relations based on calculations and tradeoffs with exclusive reference to the means/ends of making money.

The power of the three documentaries lies in the way they disorient the contemporary audience by telling a history of the present that is not narrated from the fixed viewpoint of the Japanese state. They confront the audience not with one single history but with many, each with its own duration, speed, evolution, and "truth." Imamura uses the power of cinema to render visible the way the human body of the unreturned soldier, via the associations it made with its environment and other bodies, was a site of multiple temporalities incompatible with chronological time/history organized around a series of linear events that solidify the Japanese nation-state. Imamura entrusts the visual medium of cinema to capture the authentic "moment" of postwar Japan, bringing the audience into contact with a whole new unconscious optics that would reveal the true situation of the present and, in the process, lead the audience away from their zone of passive entertainment to a space of critical enjoyment.

Notes

1. The Japanese entered what later became the Second World War in 1937 with hostilities against the Republic of China. Some Japanese historians date Japanese involvement in the Second World War even earlier, with Japan's invasion of Manchuria in September 1931.
2. Imamura fared better than the producer who was sacked.
3. Imamura has articulated this point further: "In my work . . . I want to enter a character's heart. I want to capture the smallest action, the finest nuance, the most intimate psychological expression because filmmakers must concern themselves with much more than facades" (Imamura 1999: 126).
4. These events are remembered as the Malayan Emergency (1948–1960). The conflict was between predominantly Malayan Chinese communist guerrillas and British Commonwealth forces. The term "Emergency" describes the events from the British colonial government's perspective. British authorities declared a State of Emergency in the newly created Federation of Malaya on June 18, 1948, after guerrillas assassinated three European plantation managers in the northern state of Perak.
5. The Japanese are estimated to have killed between 6,000 and 40,000 Chinese civilians in the Sook Ching Massacre carried out in the first month of the occupation.
6. The Japanese emperor is believed to be the direct descendent of the celestial sun goddess Amaterasu-ōmikami (Great Divinity Illuminating Heaven).
7. Ibaraki prefecture is located to the northeast of Tokyo along the Pacific coast. Once farm land, many of the major cities of Ibaraki prefecture are now part of the Greater Tokyo Area.
8. In contemporary academic circles, the term *kimin* is usually associated with Japanese immigrants who were mostly neglected by the Japanese government and left to fend for themselves. Here Imamura seems to have appropriated this term as it was used to represent people callously discarded once they no longer had a role to play in the Japanese state's ambition to turn the nation into a leading power in Asia and the Western Pacific. Imamura's other documentary dealing with *kimin* is *Karayuki-san, The Making of a Prostitute* (1975), where he discovers that Kikuyo Zendō, a former *karayuki-san*, chose not to return to Japan because of the prejudice she faced coming from a discriminated community (*tokushu burakumin*).
9. Fujita's experience may well have inspired the ending of *Zegen* (1987), where the patriotic Iheij Muraoka has set up his own Japanese colony in Malaysia by surrounding himself with a throng of submissive offspring, only to be brushed aside in his efforts to greet the invading Japanese troops as another "simple native."

Works Cited

Avenell, Simon (2010). *Minding Japanese Citizens: Civil Society and the Mythology of the Shimin in Postwar Japan*. Berkeley: University of California Press.

Bock, Audie (1978). *Japanese Film Directors*. New York: Kodansha International.

de Bary, Wm. Theodore, Carol Gluck, and Arthur L. Tiedemann, eds. (2005). *Sources of Japanese Tradition, Volume 2*, 2nd ed. New York: Columbia University Press, 1029–36.

Dower, John (1986). *War without Mercy: Race and Power in the Pacific War*. New York: Pantheon Books.

Halliday, Jon, and Gavan McCormack (1973). *Japanese Imperialism Today: Co-prosperity in Greater East Asia*. New York: Monthly Review Press.

Havens, Thomas R.H. (1987). *Fire across the Sea: The Vietnam War and Japan, 1965–1975*. Princeton, NJ: Princeton University Press.

Hotta, Eri (2007). *Pan-Asianism and Japan's War, 1931–1945*. New York: Palgrave Macmillan.

Igarashi, Yoshikuni (1998). "The Bomb, Hirohito, and History: The Foundational Narrative of United States-Japan Postwar Relations." *Positions* 6, no. 2: 261–302.

Imamura, Shohei (1999). "My Approach to Filmmaking." Trans. S. Erviel and M. Cousins. In *Shohei Imamura*, ed. James Quandt. Toronto: Toronto International Film Festival Group, 125–28.

Imamura, Shōhei (2001). *Kannu kara Yamiichi e, Toru* [*Take: From Cannes to the Black Market*]. Tokyo: Kōsakusha.

Imamura, Shōhei (2004). *Eigawa Kyōki no Tabi de aru: Watakushi no Rirekisho* [*Film Is a Crazy Journey: My Personal History*]. Tokyo: Nihon Keizai Shinbunsha.

Kaji, Etsuko (1973). "The Aftermath: Japan in Southeast Asia." *AMPO: Japan-Asia Quarterly Review* 16: 11–18.

Marotti, William (2009). "Japan 1968: The Performance of Violence and the Theater of Protest." *American Historical Review* 114, no. 1: 97–135.

Matsumoto Toshio (2012). "A Theory of Avant-Garde Documentary." Trans. Michael Raine. *Cinema Journal* 5, no. 4: 148–54.

Mellen, Joan (1975). *Voices from the Japanese Cinema*. New York: Liveright.

Mes, Tom, and Jasper Sharp (2005). *The Midnight Eye Guide to New Japanese Film*. Berkeley: Stone Bridge Press.

Nakata, Toichi (1999). "Shohei Imamura Interview." In *Shohei Imamura*, ed. James Quandt, 107–24. Toronto: Toronto International Film Festival Group.

Raine, Michael (2012). "Introduction to Matsumoto Toshio: A Theory of Avant-Garde Documentary." *Cinema Journal* 5, no. 4: 144–47.

Saaler, Sven, and Christopher W.A. Szpilman, eds. (2011). *Pan-Asianism: A Documentary History, Volumes 1–2*. Lanham, MD: Rowman & Littlefield.

Sato, Tadao (1997). *Imamura Shōhei no Sekai* [*The World of Imamura Shōhei*]. Tokyo: Gakuyō Shobō.

Sato, Tadao (2012). "The Documentaries of Shohei Imamura." Trans. J. Winters Carpenter. *Icarus Films*, 1–4. http://icarusfilms.com/other/filmmaker/ima.html. Accessed September 9, 2017.

Schilling, Mark (2007). *No Borders, No Limits: Nikkatsu Action Cinema.* Godalming: FAB Press.

Shimizu, Tomohisa (1973). "Nippon Koei: Engineering Colonialism from Korea to Vietnam." *AMPO: Japan-Asia Quarterly Review* 19, pp. 35–38.

Tachibana, Takeshi (1988). "Imamura Shōhei to Watanabe Kunio." In *Kōza Nihon Eiga 8: Nihon Eiga no Tenbō [Lectures on Japanese Cinema 8: Perspectives on Japanese Cinema],*" ed. Shohei Imamura et al., 1–2. Tokyo: Iwanami Shoten.

Chapter 14

Promotional Discourses and the Meanings of *The Ballad of Narayama*

Rayna Denison

After *Narayama Bushikō/The Ballad of Narayama* received the Palme d'Or at the Cannes Film Festival in 1983, *Cahiers du Cinéma* critic Charles Tesson declared, "*The Ballad of Narayama* places us in the presence of a *physical* Imamura, a filmmaker characterised by consumption, by excess. Excess of project, excess of filming, excess of construction" (1983: 159, emphasis in original). Part of a comparison between the "cerebral" Nagisa Oshima and the more "physical" Shohei Imamura, Tesson's account of Imamura situates the director as an early example of extreme filmmaking from Japan. This tactic, which equates Imamura's excesses as a filmmaker with his aesthetic and thematic concerns, shows how tightly defined and understood Imamura's authorship became as he entered the global stage in the 1980s. Imamura himself played a significant role in this process, famously self-identifying his cinema as "messy" (Quandt 1997: 3) and claiming to "force a union between questions of the lower half of the body and the daily culture of Japan's lower class" (Standish 2011, citing Matsushita 1964: 7). These proclamations, and others like them, have shaped much of the discussion about Imamura and his cinema.

The latter quotation, for example, is provided on the inside cover of James Quandt's (1997) edited collection on Imamura, and it also acts as an epigraph to the fourth chapter in Isolde Standish's more recent book on Japan's avant-garde cinema. I argue that this immediate and insistent relay between the director and his critics means that many of the debates that could have been had in relation to Imamura's filmmaking practices and processes are underexplored and worthy of revisiting.

In the broadest terms, Standish argues that we "should not ignore the socio-political and economic conditions that at times impact on practice" in filmmaking (2011: 128). Standish's work is perhaps the most critical reappraisal of Imamura's relationship to the critical community, and, through her analysis, she questions his proclamations about the links between class, gender, and ethnographic filmmaking methods. Standish's attention to the contextual details of production enable her to challenge the existing impression of *The Ballad of Narayama* as straightforwardly exemplary cinema. Instead, she argues that the film "feeds into conservative discourses on *nihonjinron* (discussion of Japanese identity) which became increasingly popular in the 1970s and 1980s. This would in part explain the exotic appeal of *The Ballad of Narayama* to the audience at Cannes in 1983" (2011: loc. 2244). Following Standish's example, in this chapter, I revisit the construction of Imamura's authorship by taking an alternative look at his working practices. Through an examination of the promotional discourses around *The Ballad of Narayama*, I inquire into how the contemporary promotional media in Japan worked to exaggerate, qualify, and even challenge our existing understandings of Imamura's major themes and concerns.

The Ballad of Narayama is used here because of the way it has come to act as a shorthand for Imamura's directorial acumen. Standish's contention is all the more remarkable because elsewhere, as in Dave Kehr's (1983) and Allan Casebier's (1983) contemporary assessments of Imamura's authorial presence, *The Ballad of Narayama*'s success on the international film festival scene was previously used to assert his significance as a director in more general terms. By contrast, *The Ballad of Narayama* is useful here because it sits *awkwardly* within discourses about Imamura's authorship, most obviously because it was an adaptation that had been filmed once before. Shichirō Fukazawa's 1956 novella, about a remote village where poverty has become so extreme that the elderly are abandoned on the top of a nearby mountain to help everyone avoid starvation, was immediately recognized artistically on its release (Hung 2003), and was first adapted into film by Keisuke Kinoshita in 1958. Lee Wood Hung (2003) has produced a detailed analysis of Imamura's version of *The Ballad of Narayama* in which he focuses on Imamura's originality as an adapter. Hung notes that Imamura amalgamated two Fukazawa stories within his film version of *The Ballad of Narayama*, and that it was Imamura's addition of other new materials that helped to exaggerate his own concerns about class, women's place in Japanese society, and nature-informed allegories within his adaptation.

By comparison, this chapter is more concerned with how Imamura's adaptation process was discussed at the time of its release and how those discussions might confirm or challenge the perceptions of *The Ballad of Narayama* and Imamura that developed after the fact. I focus on how these discussions can help to clarify both Imamura's primary roles as a filmmaker and his approach to his thematic concerns. I argue that promotional discourse, particularly behind-the-scenes coverage, has the potential to reveal a more nuanced account of Imamura-as-filmmaker.

Analyzing the processes and products of filmmaking in this instance requires a methodology that compares the production and promotional discourses with textual analysis of the finished film. Furthermore, reconsidering Imamura's process requires a reflexive stance toward discourse analysis and especially toward the often optimistic accounts of filmmaking seen in promotional material. To this end, I adopt a reception studies method, viewing the release of *The Ballad of Narayama* as an event, rather than as a text, and considering how the promotional materials reveal the construction of Imamura as auteur director, including those aspects of production that are disguised or elided (Klinger 1997; Staiger 2000).

Discussing the usefulness of promotional discourse to a project like this one, Barbara Klinger has argued:

> Films circulate as products, not in a semantic vacuum, but in a mass cultural environment teeming with related commercial significations. Epiphenomena constitute this adjacent territory, creating not only a commercial life-support system for a film, but also a socially meaningful network of relations that enter into the arena of reception around it. Promotion thus represents a sphere of intertextual discourse that helps explain the complex relation between commodity discourses and reception. (1989: 5)

The extensive coverage of *The Ballad of Narayama* in *Kinema Junpo*, Japan's foremost film magazine, will be used to establish part of the "sphere of intertextual discourse" that positioned Imamura's film for the Japanese marketplace. I use this source both because of the wide range of coverage it devoted to *The Ballad of Narayama*, but also because I am interested in how Imamura was regarded within his own industry and *Kinema Junpo* tends to act as an analytical trade-oriented publication for the Japanese film industry. In May 1983, Imamura appeared on the cover of *Kinema Junpo*, and the issue provided audiences with a copy of Imamura's screenplay for *The Ballad of Narayama*, along with his synopsis of the production (Imamura 1983). Additionally, they produced a roundtable "symposium" discussion by the film's stars and a production diary, as well as more generalized reporting (Anon 1983a; 1983b). This extensive coverage of the film, alongside the trailers used to promote its release, form the basis of the interrogation of Imamura's creative methods in this chapter. These commodity discourses enable a comparative analysis with the finished text, revealing the myths built up around *The Ballad of Narayama*, but also showing how carefully constructed the image of Imamura's cinema had become by the 1980s.

Understanding Imamura: *The Ballad of Narayama* and Academic Discourse

Although the win for *The Ballad of Narayama* at Cannes provided Imamura with a cache of international success, bolstering his reputation within critical circles, surprisingly little academic attention has been paid to this seemingly pivotal film in his career. Indeed, the auteur approach to Imamura has been so dominant that relatively few of his films have received detailed analysis, certainly when compared to the numbers of scholarly texts detailing Imamura's themes and providing commentaries on his body of work (for examples, see Desser 1988; Richie 2005; Standish 2005). In this section I analyze the wider scholarship on Imamura in order to identify clusters of academic scholarship around his filmmaking practices. These key concepts are then used to form the starting points for the sections that follow.

Perhaps the most influential of these has been David Desser's structuralist analysis. In one significant summary, Desser extends Allan Casebier's earlier assessment of Imamura's themes:

> Casebier has isolated a series of oppositions which characterize Imamura's work: irrational vs. rational; primitive vs. civilized; spontaneous vs. conventional; the lower classes vs. the upper classes; authentic vs. contrived. To these we might add documentary vs. fiction. (1988: 82)

Casebier and Desser's interpretations of Imamura's themes sit neatly alongside the director's own declarations about his desire to reveal the "real" Japan (Nakata 1997), rather than the "traditional" view of Japanese culture usually depicted in Japanese cinema. They also align with Imamura's proclamations about the messiness of his cinema and his desire to reveal the untainted sensuality of Japan's lower classes.

Desser's work thereby feeds into discussions of Imamura's representation of "naturalism." The concept of "natural culturalism" is also the focus of Hung's analysis of *The Ballad of Narayama*, one of the few academic studies of the film to date. Hung defines natural culturalism as "the natural characteristics of the Japanese culture, as portrayed by Imamura" (2003: 147), arguing that Imamura's most significant adaptive additions to *The Ballad of Narayama* are those he made in order to "paint his vision of Japanese culture, using points of symbolic detail to clearly demonstrate structural features of Japanese culture" (2003: 160).

Naturalism is thereby read through Imamura's representations of people and Japanese culture in relation to the natural world. Similarly, Standish argues that "Imamura's approach is underscored by a 'naturalist' viewpoint derived from the study of the natural sciences and ethnography" (2011: 176). However, Hung's assessment complicates the idea of Imamura-as-ethnographer by asserting that Imamura makes symbolic uses of the natural world. Through these means, Hung suggests that Imamura's filmmaking practice contrives connections between the natural and the cultural.

Hung's concept of "natural culturalism" is reflected elsewhere in the critical reception of Imamura's filmmaking. In relation to other films, most particularly *Kamigami no Fukaki Yokubō/Profound Desire of the Gods* (1968), critics have argued that Imamura's representations of animals parallel the behavior and plights of his human characters. For example, Antoine de Baecque argues that the animals "replay the fable of humans" ([1990] 1997: 155). Scott Nygren goes so far as to claim that "Imamura's animals, from pig to insect to carp, work to deterritorialize nationalist narratives of history founded on primitive origins and generate counter-histories of [modern Japan] next to official versions" (2007: 185). Like Standish, then, Nygren sees artificiality in Imamura's use of the natural world, or at very least the incursion of culture into Imamura's well-documented ethnographic sensibilities (Standish 2011). These observations suggest a useful set of debates that will be evaluated further in relation to *The Ballad of Narayama*: from the ways natural imagery, location shooting, and documentary aesthetics are deployed, to the ways those images and techniques relate to Imamura's deeper thematic concerns about how to reveal hidden aspects of Japanese society.

In this respect, Desser's observations about documentary stylistics within Imamura's filmmaking sit in useful contradistinction to the director's allegorical uses of animals and location spaces. Documentary and ethnography within Imamura's cinema have been highlighted repeatedly as an ongoing challenge for those attempting to unpack Imamura's meanings. Alastair Phillips (2007: 232), for example, argues that Imamura's cinema blurs the lines between documentary and fiction techniques, something to which Isolde Standish also attests. She argues that Imamura's "documentary-styled films represent an alternative and an altogether more effective challenge to mainstream history by narrating a view of the past from the memories of female characters on the margins of society" (2011: loc. 2248). In this analysis, Standish unites the debates around Imamura's fluctuating use of documentary aesthetics (noting the blurred line between documentary and fiction) with another important theme, his perceived feminist stance.

Several other scholars have investigated Imamura as a champion of Japanese women, even citing Imamura as a *feminisuto* (feminist) director (Desser 1988: 122; Richie 1997: 11; Standish 2011). However, none of the previous studies have investigated how Imamura's actresses talked about working with him. In this chapter, therefore, I analyze the discussion of Imamura by the stars of *The Ballad of Narayama* in order to reevaluate these claims in relation to off- as well as onscreen treatment of women. These concepts—naturalism in production, feminism, and Imamura's uses of documentary aesthetics—are used hereafter as the investigative starting points for my analysis of the promotional discourses circulating around *The Ballad of Narayama* and the ways they can be arraigned to make sense of the finished film. I argue that these commodity discourses can challenge our perception of Imamura's major themes, and that a closer examination of his working practices as depicted in these various materials has the potential to reveal a more complex, and more contradictory, filmmaker.

From Up on the Mountain: Discourses of Extremity and the Production of Realism

> The director himself is writing the screenplay and his stated aspiration is to "not tell a simple story of illusion, but to have complete realism, and to freely depict severe physical labour and sex." (Anon 1983a: 12)

Imamura's declaration about his search for "complete realism" was enthusiastically seized upon within the promotional coverage of *The Ballad of Narayama*. Different to the idea of "naturalism" highlighted by scholars, which refers to the depictions of the natural world, here Imamura foregrounds the aesthetics of "realism," in this context invoking his desire to capture action of all kinds using an unfettered documentary aesthetic. Informing that discourse on realism, however, is another about extremity that returns us to the opening quotation from Tesson. Consequently, within the commodity discourse around *The Ballad of Narayama*, Imamura's authorship became closely conjoined to discussions of his working practices in relation to both realism and the lengths Imamura was willing to go to achieve it. For *The Ballad of Narayama*, Imamura's insistence upon location shooting in a mountainous portion of the Tohoku region of Japan became the nexus point for debates about his extreme search for realism versus his heroic authorship—directing *The Ballad of Narayama* in the face of unseasonable weather and local resistance. In this section, therefore, I focus on the film's theatrical and television trailers, and *Kinema Junpo*'s production diary for *The Ballad of Narayama*.

Within this commercial intertext, the admixture of commercial and avant-garde aspects of the filmmaking became the core of the promotional campaign for *The Ballad of Narayama*. An explanatory trailer details how filmmaking was undertaken: "On a closed set in an abandoned village at 1000m, amidst both the warmth and hardship of nature," and it later lingers on a freeze-frame of the village taken from a helicopter as the credits appear onscreen.[1] Similarly, earlier

Figure 14.1 Location shooting.

"Explanatory Notices" for *The Ballad of Narayama* emphasize Imamura's behind-the-scenes presence by including shots of him directing actors. In addition, they include information about its three-year filming duration as evidence for the film's quality. One of these "Explanatory Notices" goes as far as to cite Imamura as a "genius" (*tensai*) director, using him as a legitimating presence for this new adaptation of *The Ballad of Narayama*. The direct promotion of the film thereby selectively promotes Imamura as an authorial presence whose use of location shooting is part of a discourse of "genius." Moreover, by emphasizing the duration and hardships, the trailers collapse the discourses from the production into the text itself to heighten Imamura's proclamations of "complete realism."

For example, within the production diary in *Kinema Junpo*, journalist Yasuo Yamamoto relates his visit to the location shoot near Minami Kotani in 1982, emphasizing hardship:[2]

> When we alighted in an unthinkable mass at the small station, sunset was drawing near on December 3rd. In our party were lots of people who looked like the stars I see a lot on television, but no-one thought it possible that Ken Ogata and Tonpei Hidari would travel with us . . . But, before long those people started climbing the mountain just like ordinary people, in the midst of a blizzard of snow. (1983: 52)

Thrown together, the journalist journeyed up the mountain accompanied by the film's male stars, Ogata and Hidari, with the worsening weather conditions playing up the seemingly fantastic elements of his production story. Yamamoto's

Promotional Discourses 253

commentary thereby plays up Imamura's reputation for immersive and extreme filmmaking, indicating that even the stars had to walk up the mountain with everyone else. Moreover, Yamamoto's presentation of the events also takes on a mythologizing tone as he describes the extremity and harshness of the working environment, with the blizzard conditions taking on contradictory notes of realism and fable.

Jirō Tomoda, the co-author of the production diary, recounts the trip's logistics in a similarly mythologizing fashion. In the introductory statement below, Tomoda's language suggests how the remote and previously abandoned location shoot served to mythologize *The Ballad of Narayama*'s production:

> Alight at Minami Kotani station, then go up a steep slope for one hour and forty minutes. In this place, there used to be about ten households, but the villagers left this place one after another because the location is so remote, and now the place has become a ghost town. Of course, you travel by road from the station for about four kilometres, but it's not a road as such, and cars can't reach the high ground. (1983: 52)

Tomoda's account of the remoteness of the main location is phrased in language that echoes Fukuzawa's short story, and character dialogue from the film, about traveling up the mountain on a road that is not really a road. Tomoda thereby links the original to the new adaptation through his own journey to the shooting location. Additionally, in Tomoda's account, the location's actual historical abandonment is used to create an impression of authenticity around the production, while also signaling Imamura's ability to overcome the hardships that had driven away the original community. The loss of the "real" village to history is also significant for the way it allows Imamura's version of *The Ballad of Narayama* to occupy a position outside of contemporary Japanese culture, becoming part of the location's "ghost town" environment. In these ways, both production diary accounts of the location for *The Ballad of Narayama* work to separate the film from normal Japanese filmmaking, mythologizing it and, with this mythologization, suggesting reasons why Imamura should be recognized as an auteur-style director.

This is a feature of Imamura's filmmaking that Yamamoto aligns with Imamura's ethnographic sensibilities. Yamamoto states:

> The director enjoys investigations by his nature. When he was moving house, he took the opportunity to talk with them about the reality of being a real estate agent. Helping with a friend's funeral, he did behind-the-scenes research at a funeral home ... This time, *The Ballad of Narayama* has this kind of tone. (1983: 51)

The use of "tone" is interesting in this account, implying that Imamura's ethnographic research complexly informs his approach to filmmaking. These production commentaries invoke the ethnographic work Imamura had been undertaking in the previous decade, which resulted in documentaries like *In Search of the Unreturned Solidiers in Malaysia* (*Mikikan-hei o otte: Marei-hen*, 1970) and his 1975 film *Karayuki-san: The Making of a Prostitute*. Additionally, the everyday ethnographer described as lurking within Imamura in this production account is used here to authenticate his authorial vision, and to explain his insistence upon a search for "complete realism."

However, the production diary also brings Imamura's filming problems to the fore. In doing so, Yamamoto and Tomoda demonstrate that *The Ballad of Narayama*'s production was not as "authentic" as Imamura had intended, nor was his search for "complete realism" without its drawbacks. Tomoda reveals that before the filming began tensions arose with the landowner for the location: "Right away, the landowner began discussions, really opposing them [the filmmakers], saying, 'In this village, we won't cooperate with a film about abandoning parents'" (1983: 52). However, Imamura is shown to have taken on a strong personal leadership role in response to this confrontation. Tomoda continues by saying that "the director strongly persevered, holding a town meeting, and was able to persuade them as a matter of course, just managing to get their consent" (1983: 52). Nevertheless, Imamura was forced to compromise, with the production being required to use far fewer of the original local buildings than he had hoped for, and instead having to construct an extra two buildings in which to film scenes. This incident suggests that Tesson's observations about Imamura's excessive production process has merit. However, this is not an uncontrolled version of extremity; rather, Imamura's desire for "complete realism" is here presented as the impetus behind his efforts to personally overcome obstacles to production. The director thereby becomes the star or hero of the production-process narrative.

Other difficulties faced by the production also work to nuance this presentation of Imamura as the hero behind the production of *The Ballad of Narayama*. One of the more significant difficulties the production faced were continual unexpected and extreme weather events. Weather was of paramount importance to the production, with Yamamoto relating, "Everything that appears in this film is real. The spring is spring, and they continued filming in the middle of the natural summer for summer" (1983: 51). This idea, that "everything that appears in this film is real," reinforces the discourse of "complete realism" begun by Imamura. But it is also framed as a problem throughout the production of *The Ballad of Narayama*, with inclement weather repeatedly affecting the production schedule. Most significantly, an initial lack of snow into the winter of 1982, followed by an unseasonably late and lingering snowfall, reached a staggering depth during the spring of 1983.

Yamamoto relates about the initial lack of snow:

> When films are made, they normally use fake man-made snow, but Imamura's insistence on realism would not accept that. Until the end, they were on alert until it snowed. However, ironically, there was an unusually warm winter in the Northern provinces. They normally had fine weather every day, when in an average year it would have snowed. (1983: 54)

This meant that Imamura had to continue filming long after he had intended, getting pick-up shots well into the time he had planned for editing. His response was extreme and included taking two bulldozers, in pieces, up to the mountain by helicopter and reassembling them so that they could move snow to and from the location sets. These accounts help to reinforce the impression of Imamura as both extreme and as the protagonist in a tale about overcoming adversity. Yamamoto and Tomoda's descriptions of such challenges are used to generate an image not of failure, but of determination and commitment to an authorial vision. Imamura is, in this account, a director whose search for realism cannot be forestalled even by natural disasters.

Viewed from one perspective, this kind of discourse suggests a filmmaker at the avant-garde end of the auteur spectrum, an artist whose obsessive desire for a particular aesthetic drives him to extreme working practices. Viewed from a more pragmatic perspective, however, Imamura's ability to overcome these obstacles is also suggestive of a filmmaker whose budget was large enough to extend to a lengthy production schedule with unexpected cost—the latter indicating an otherwise undiscussed commercial aspect to the production of *The Ballad of Narayama*. The production diary, consequently, begins to show how Imamura's authorship was understood at the time of *The Ballad of Narayama*'s release, as both an artistic endeavour and a commercial, highly mediated, and promoted one.

Imamura's authorial vision, and his search for realism, goes essentially unquestioned in *The Ballad of Narayama*'s commodity discourse. More importantly, much of the promotion supports and even exaggerates the image of Imamura as avant-garde filmmaker. This can be seen, for example, when Tomoda declares that *The Ballad of Narayama* is "a film that was made with sweat and tears and heart by a director who was in the midst of it with his staff and crew who banded together in a common cause and a common destiny, thoroughly breathing life into the strange sorrows and joys of people, desiring to sing a paean to life" (1983: 54). Once again, here, Imamura's presence is made *physical*, his body becoming the spark behind

Figure 14.2 Imamura as the exaggerated center of *The Ballad of Narayama* in teaser trailer, framed by cast and crew.

The Ballad of Narayama's soul, indeed becoming something he sings into life while trying to describe the essence of human existence.

This imagery, based as it is on the film's title, has the potential to disguise the industrial processes that were also involved in realizing Imamura's adaptation. For one thing, the discourse around the difficulties overcome by Imamura, which function as the presentation of Imamura as a heroic figure holding his production together, is something seen not just for avant-garde auteurs, but also for directors who work in more mainstream cinema (see, for example, Kapsis 1992). For another, Imamura's choice to film on location in a remote area was the cause of many of the problems the production would face, making him less a hero than the villain of the piece, though *Kinema Junpo*'s coverage does tend to celebrate his achievements, rather than dwelling on Imamura's risk-taking. In the end, by creating and then solving these problems, Imamura is discursively transformed into both the genius behind, and arch publicist for, his film.

The Performance of "Unconscious" Acting: Imamura's Feminism

If the discussions of Imamura's approach to location shooting helped to affirm his status as an avant-garde filmmaker, his treatment of actors was a more qualified success. Fujio Tokita (who plays Jinsaku) describes Imamura's approach to acting as unmannered and naturalistic, beginning a debate among the actors in *Kinema Junpo*'s symposium with the film's stars: "Tokita: As for Imamura, he really sees the difference between conscious and unconscious acting. We were aiming for unconscious performance" (Anon 1983b: 45). Unconscious acting is something that Tonpei Hidari (Risuke) defines by saying that when "acting, there are unconscious moments, and there is acting without calculation. Those would be good cases" (1983b: 46). Additionally, the actors all mentioned Imamura's tendency for multiple takes before letting them move on. In this sense, "unconscious acting" was something achieved through repetitive re-performances to engender naturalistic acting. These techniques were praised by the actors themselves for running contrary to their perceptions of more usual, mannered styles of acting.

Within these discussions of repetition and a search for a more naturalistic performance style, however, come revelations about Imamura's treatment of actors that run contrary to claims made about his feminist depictions of women onscreen. For example, the actresses involved in the symposium discuss the attempts at generating a naturalistic approach to sex scenes. Discussing her sex scene with protagonist Orin's (Sumiko Sakamoto) smelly and sexually frustrated son, Risuke, Kiyokawa states:

> When we did that [sex] scene a lot of mass media reporters seemed to show up. They came and tried to watch on the set because we said that only staff would be allowed for this scene. However, I declared that "I'm not going to cover up, because I'm going to be unashamed. I'm not pasting thin, undignified patches over my private parts." But, at the cut when people were staring at me *there*, it was intolerable and I shouted, "Stick the covers on me!" (46)

This frank discussion of the impact of outsiders on the filming process is interesting because it suggests the limits of Imamura's instance upon the free depiction of sex within *The Ballad of Narayama*, and the kinds of pragmatic decisions that layered artifice upon the naturalism of the acting style he sought. On one hand, this example provides evidence for the collaborative nature of filmmaking and for actors' agency within that process. On the other, it describes a situation in which a sex scene was used to draw journalists to the location shoot, thereby creating tensions between the commercial and artistic aims of the production. The exploitation of Kiyokawa, then, is at odds with the Imamura's feminist aesthetic onscreen, making it important to allow such alternative voices into the debates around Imamura's filmmaking.

Imamura's feminist legacy is also qualified by his treatment of the actresses playing Orin. While Sumiko Sakamoto, a singer turned actress, is given full credit for the role, she was not Imamura's first choice. The production diary reveals that "Sanae Futaba, playing Orin, collapsed [on set in the summer of 1982]. Afterwards, clearly it was hard for her to return to the location. They held a quick staff meeting and started to work through the selection of candidates for this important role" (Yamamoto 1983: 52). Viewed positively, this behind-the-scenes information illustrates further the collaborative approach to the production of *The Ballad of Narayama*, and a flexible approach to scheduling. Viewed negatively, this is the only time Futaba's name is mentioned, and her withdrawal from the production is discussed only inasmuch as it impacted on the overall filming schedule, rendering her almost invisible within the film's production history.

Further to this report, the production diary also relates another on-set collapse on September 6, 1982:

> Sumiko Sakamoto was brought down the mountain on a stretcher and was admitted at once to the hospital in Omachi. It was the second time an accident had been visited on Imamura's troupe. In the end, they weren't able to film in September, and the staff spent the time filming animals at the next location. (Yamamoto 1983: 53)

These on-set collapses add more weight to the discourse about the difficulties faced by Imamura within the production diary, but they also highlight the extreme working conditions and the varying levels of commitment from the central actresses. Interestingly, neither incident is mentioned in the cast symposium, with the attention focused instead on other extreme aspects of the filmmaking.

The most obvious example of "extreme" commitment to *The Ballad of Narayama* once more comes through narratives about Sakamoto's transformation for the role of Orin, especially her decision to have her four front teeth pulled. Tomoda writes that "because there weren't any people of the actual age of her predecessor . . . the 46-year-old Sakamoto Sumiko had to become a 70-year-old, and so she did dozens of make-up tests, and had four of her teeth pulled and, above all that, she started on a diet to lose 10 kilos" (1983: 52). Artifice once again creeps into the acting discourse here, with Sakamoto's age exaggerated by makeup, weight loss, and cosmetic dentistry in order for her to undertake the role. Sakamoto, in the actor symposium, comments:

> Because I'm a fool, when I was told they [my teeth] would be pulled out I forgot that people would be able to see that they had been pulled . . . All of my friends have said that only I would do something like this. But, myself, I think that I am not that extreme a woman. But I'm not someone who is filled with common sense. (1983b: 44)

Sakamoto frames her decision as an impulsive, but not extreme one in these comments. Thus, she resists the discourse of extremity around Imamura, while also suggesting her commitment to the role of Orin. If the illnesses on set suggest an approach to acting that punished his actors, Sakamoto's comments suggest that the actors were keen adherents to Imamura's strict regime of realism.

The presentation of *The Ballad of Narayama* through its promotional campaign also does little to draw attention to potential feminist aspects of Imamura's filmmaking process, despite academic claims that Imamura was one of the most feminist directors of the era (Desser 1988). Women's voices are heard less frequently than men's throughout the campaign, which is perhaps surprising given the centrality of Orin to the narrative. The first of the film's two trailers is perhaps the most explicit about the possibilities for feminist content in the film, with intertitles over the top of footage from the film explaining that Orin has decided to go up the mountain and is passing her last days with her family. The trailer then asks, "What does it mean to be a woman, still full of zest for life, living in strict accordance with their laws?" This sequence of titles plays out over the top of the murder of a whole family of villagers, and a woman's voice (Matsuyan, played by Junko Takada) is high in the sound mix. It ends on a shot of Orin and Tatsuhei in front of the tree Tatsuhei buried his father under, with the sound of wind blowing as the tree sways unnaturally (an effect produced by the use of a helicopter's downdraft). This is the most overt feminist question asked within the promotional discourse, and it remains unanswered by the trailer. In one respect,

Figure 14.3 Tatsuhei and Orin in helicopter downdraft.

this trailer simply draws attention to Orin's centrality to the narrative, but a more holistic reading would suggest that a generalized feminist discourse can be seen in the contemporary epiphenomena, a discourse that seems to have been embraced in later scholarship.

Sakamoto's presence is also important in the second of two trailers for the film, in which she is seen and heard singing one of the film's central ballads, and then narrating significant plot points, including Orin's desire to leave the village for the mountain in the winter. Sakamoto's performance fragments here work to generate the impression of naturalism sought by Imamura. However, from this point onward, the trailer's focus shifts to documentary imagery shot during the filming, including a shot of a helicopter flying up the mountain in the snow, and another of the main cast bundled up in snow gear getting on board the same helicopter. These final images of the trailer are especially interesting in the way they contradict the consistent messages in the production discourse about the cast and crew being required to walk up the mountain, even in blizzard conditions. It challenges the idea of a cast and crew living and working together within the remote location site and indicates that some of the details of the production (the less difficult and challenging) may have been omitted.

Nevertheless, the actors' comments about unconscious acting commingle with other aspects of production that work to exaggerate and enhance the perception of realism, even as they are constructed through artificial or extreme means. Hung notes that the characterizations are themselves non-naturalistic, with Orin becoming an extreme portrayal of the village's traditional culture and Tatsuhei becoming an exaggeration of the sentimentality and weakness of mankind (Hung 2003). The filmmaking process accords with, and qualifies, some of Hung's observations, showing how artifice crept into the production culture through the stars' performances.

Imamura's contradictory directorial persona comes through in the actors' symposium, which offers evidence of the way he both encouraged and pressured his actors during production, and it is perhaps in these instances that Imamura's extreme filmmaking is most obvious. However, it was an extremity that the stars claim to have been prepared for, despite the need for everything from explicit sex scenes to surgery. Nor was Imamura's extreme treatment limited to the actresses; Ken Ogata is reported to have suffered from frostbite while filming external scenes during the winter months on the location shoot (Yamamoto 1983). In these ways, the unconscious acting desired by Imamura was frequently enacted through the real-life suffering of his actors. While this pain is in evidence for both sexes, it is interesting to note that none of his actors discussed the importance of feminism to his filmmaking style, preferring instead to call attention to their suffering and commitment on the director's behalf.

Documentary, Realism, and the Use of Animals

The human actors were only part of the production story on *The Ballad of Narayama*, with animals playing important, often symbolic, roles. Hung relates that the scenes featuring animals were one of Imamura's main additions to his version of the story (2003), while Standish is clear that "the many scenes of animals mating and nature link the social world of the village and rules governing familial relations to primitive needs for survival" (2011: loc. 1729). By contrast, I argue, that Imamura's presentation of nature is in many respects the least natural aspect of his filmmaking style. It is in his need for symbolic images of nature that Imamura most blurs the line between documentary, realism, and artifice.

Even the briefest glance at the production of *The Ballad of Narayama* attests to Imamura's constructed depiction of animals. Two separate animal handling and training companies are cited in the end credits for the film: Ōtake Animation Productions and a more specific citation for crow handler and keeper, Tsuguo Kuroda. The involvement of these companies makes the construction of the film's animal images plain, not least the inclusion of the many crows that appear at the top of the mountain at the climax. The crows flutter and call in large numbers around the rocks surrounding Orin, suggesting that she will die and be devoured by nature. These unnaturally inserted animals take on the burden of visual metaphor and become symbolic of death's repercussions, extending Hung's observations about the use of exaggeration of character within Imamura's version of *The Ballad of Narayama*. However, the non-natural insertions of animals into the film are never mentioned in the promotional discourses, nor do they feature in the academic scholarship around *The Ballad of Narayama*. Therefore, they begin to create what Janet Staiger calls a "structuring absence" within the film's commercial discourses; a purposefully concealed aspect of production that is used to exaggerate the seeming naturalism and documentary aesthetics at its heart (2000: 163). Consequently, I would argue that the blurring of lines between documentary footage of animals and their aestheticization presents a challenge to Imamura's professed search for "complete realism."

In particular, there are obvious joins between documentary footage of birds of prey and sequences like the one in which an owl watches Orin and Tatsuhei leave for the mountain. This relatively long take, using racking focus to shoot from behind the owl's perch and over its shoulder, frames the departure of Orin and Tatsuhei. This indicates a complex staging of action that would have required pre-planning. The owl's presence had to be predicted, offering just one example of the symbolic and non-documentary use of animal imagery. The fact that neither the actors, production diary, nor Imamura's own comments within *Kinema Junpo* mention these sequences suggest that the audience is meant to assume that they were part of the documentary filming undertaken by the crew during delays and cast illnesses. In this way, the emphatic presence of animals contradicts their lack of discussion by *Kinema Junpo* and the cast and crew, generating an absence that appears all the more significant for being purposefully elided.

Further evidence for the symbolic and purposeful use of animals in *The Ballad of Narayama* can be found in Imamura's screenplay, which was very specific about the kinds of animal images he wanted. For example, near the start of the film, Imamura's screenplay describes the following images at the protagonist's home:

> Japanese rat snakes hibernate under the floor in a hole, two or three tangled together.
> A brown rat approaches, sniffing the smells. (Imamura 1983: 55)

The requirement for specific, rather than generic, animal imagery would have necessitated the inclusion of tamed, or at least purposefully positioned, animals during filming. It is this specificity in the face of the unpredictability of animals that lends greater weight to the idea that Imamura's animal imagery was as much staged as it was documentary-style footage. But within the promotion for the film, this is never made clear. In one of the few mentions of their animal co-stars, Sakamoto argues during the cast symposium that there is "no distinction drawn between human sexual activity and animal mating and birth . . . Fukazawa did seem to discuss this, but his was not a work which captures the divinity of humans and animals to the same extent" (1983b: 46). Her comments show the embedded and symbolic uses to which *The Ballad of Narayama* puts its animal stars, but remains silent on how these images were obtained.

Animals were also significant and symbolically used within the trailer campaign, which heavily features animal imagery, as when, in the second of the two trailers, the opening image of the green mountainside cuts to a shot of a hare running, only to be caught by a bird of prey. An intertitle proclaims moments later that the story takes place "amidst the warmth and hardship of nature," over the top of a long take of nesting house martins. Following the film's title, Tatsuhei is shown trying to convince his new wife to sleep with his brother, a conversation interrupted by an image of mating mantis and a subsequent shot of crabs at a riverside, both of which work to link the conversation to the natural order. This is immediately followed by shots of two birds of prey which act as a visual buffer between Tatsuhei pleading with his wife and Orin's appearance singing a ballad. As she sings, the film cuts to a sequence of shots—a snake giving birth, a tanuki at night, an owl in flight and a spider whose long legs are illuminated by seeming-moonlight—matched to invocations to the audience to recognize the fragility of mankind. In this trailer, then, the use of animal imagery is distinct and repurposed from its appearance within the film. Animals are used to punctuate, to provide intellectual gaps between disparate concepts dealt with by the film. At other times, their presence seems intended to augment a sense of revulsion, as when the mantis appear.

The final montage is perhaps the most closely aligned with the use of the imagery within *The Ballad of Narayama* itself, with these nocturnal images appearing in connection with the film's central thematic concerns. The insertion of animal images in the trailer, however, are typically jarring and do not always act in obviously symbolic ways. In this regard, the commodity discourse of the film suggests that *The Ballad of Narayama* may be most artificial when depicting its most "natural" animal stars.

Conclusion

Even the highly specific view of the production-side discourses attempted here shows how major themes like naturalism, documentary, and feminism can be reevaluated when analyzed through the documents that surround film production. Starting with three of the central themes that have been associated with Imamura's version of *The Ballad of Narayama*, I have explored how the presentation of the film to audiences in the 1980s worked to exaggerate his role as author but can add nuance to perceptions of his feminism and can even challenge thematic concerns like naturalism and documentary in his aesthetics. Using these sources, we can see how there tends to be resonance between academic accounts about Imamura, Imamura's own proclamations, and the commodity discourse that surrounds his films. Sometimes, however, there is more ambivalence in the presentation of the themes. Through the elements that are exaggerated by promotional discourses but, equally, by the discursive absences in promotion, the aspects of production hidden from view and from critical notice can be brought into focus.

Consequently, there is more to Imamura's cinema, and more to his version of *The Ballad of Narayama*, than has previously been acknowledged. He is shown in this instance to have been a contradictory filmmaker—kind but pressurising, consistent in vision but inconsistent in execution of filming, highly idealistic about complete realism but completely pragmatic when the weather and other challenges are presented. This is a version of Shohei Imamura that deserves far greater attention, and one whose significance to Japanese film culture can be heightened by the addition of further contextualizing analysis of his filmmaking process.

The Ballad of Narayama has provided a useful lens through which to begin to reexamine the debates around Imamura and his central thematic concerns. The promotional materials produced for the film's release usefully demonstrate that Imamura played an important role in setting the central terms of the debates that have subsequently positioned him within the history of Japanese filmmaking. However, this film's promotional discourse also reveals the tensions around those crucial terms—that in Imamura's documentary aesthetic there was necessary artifice; that his control over his productions was not absolute, but was generously supported by industry, that his treatment of women onscreen was almost completely separate from his treatment of actors during production. These adjustments to our understanding of Imamura are significant for the way they outline his negotiation of the complex industrial landscape of filmmaking in Japan in the 1980s. More contextualizing evidence might also reveal further tensions and qualifications of our understanding of Imamura as auteur. For example, the post-production recording of sound, the addition of musical score, the special effects sequences, and the art design for the film all deserve a closer look. In this way, *The Ballad of Narayama* is less an exception to Imamura's filmmaking than it is representative of his constant attempts to negotiate his status as an avant-garde figure within the Japanese film industry.

Notes

1. All the trailers analyzed herein are provided on the *Eureka! Masters of Cinema* DVD and Blu-ray release of *The Ballad of Narayama*.
2. This production diary was recently translated into English by Craig Keller for the *Eureka! Masters of Cinema* distribution label, but it seems that he is taking his translation from the French version published in *Positif*, which was apparently abridged, and the translation therefore does not contain some of the passages translated herein. All translations are the authors own, but my thanks to Sachiko Shikoda for her guidance and help.

Works Cited

Anon (1983a). "Narayama bushikō" [*The Ballad of Narayama*]. *Kinema Junpo* 5A: 859, March: 11–15.

Anon (1983b). "Narayama bushikō: kankyaku to kyouyū shitai wasure-enu omoide! Hidari Tonpei, Kiyokawa Nijiko, Tsuneda Fujio, Takejo Aki, Sakamoto Sumiko" [*The Ballad of Narayama*: Unforgettable Memories That You Want to Share with the Audience! Tonpei Hidari, Nijiko Kiyokawa, Fujio Tsuneda, Aki Takejo, and Sumiko Sakamoto]. *Kinema Junpo* 5A: 859, March: 44–50.

Casebier, Allan (1983). "Images of Irrationality in Modern Japan: The Films of Shohei Imamura." *Film Criticism* 8, no. 1 (Fall): 42–49.

De Baecque, Antoine (1997 [1990]). "The Profound Desire of the Gods: Murder of the Pink Pig." In *Shohei Imamura*, ed. James Quandt, 155–56. Toronto: Toronto International Film Festival Group.

Desser, David (1988). *Eros plus Massacre: An Introduction to the Japanese New Wave Cinema*. Bloomington: Indiana University Press.

Fukazawa, Shichiro (1964). *Narayama bushikō* [*The Ballad of Narayama*]. Tokyo: Shinchosha.

Hung, Lee Wood (2003). "Natural Culturalism in *The Ballad of Narayama*: A Study of Shohei Imamura's Thematic Concerns." *Asian Cinema* 14, no. 1 (Spring/Summer): 146–66.

Imamura, Shohei (1983). "Narayama bushikō: Kyakuhon" [*The Ballad of Narayama: Screenplay*]. Kinema Junpo 5A: 859, March: 55.

Kapsis, Robert E. (1992). *Hitchcock: The Making of a Reputation*. Chicago: University of Chicago Press.

Kehr, Dave (1997). "The Last Rising Sun." In *Shohei Imamura*, ed. James Quandt, 69–87. Toronto: Toronto International Film Festival Group.

Klinger, Barbara (1989). "Digressions at the Cinema: Reception and Mass Culture." *Cinema Journal* 28, no. 4 (Summer): 3–19.

Klinger, Barbara (1997). "Film History Terminable and Interminable: Recovering the Past in Reception Studies." *Screen* 38, no. 2: 107–28.

Matsushita, Keiichi (1964). "Nippon Konchūki to Nihon Seiki." *Eiga Geijutsu* 12, no. 2 (February).

Nakata, Toichi (1997). "Shohei Imamura Interview." In *Shohei Imamura*, ed. James Quandt, 107–24. Toronto: Toronto International Film Festival Group.

Nygren, Scott (2007). *Time Frames: Japanese Cinema and the Unfolding of History*. Minneapolis: University of Minnesota Press.

Phillips, Alastair (2007). "Unsettled Visions: Imamura Shōhei's *Vengeance Is Mine*." In *Japanese Cinema: Texts and Contexts*, ed. Alastair Phillips and Julian Stringer, 229–39. London: Routledge.

Quandt, James, ed. (1997). *Shohei Imamura*. Toronto: Toronto International Film Festival Group.

Richie, Donald (2005). *A Hundred Years of Japanese Cinema: A Concise History*. Rev. ed. Tokyo: Kodansha.

Richie, Donald (1997). "Notes for a Study on Shohei Imamura." In *Shohei Imamura*, ed. James Quandt, 7–44. Toronto: Toronto Film Festival Group, 1997.

Staiger, Janet (2000). *Perverse Spectators: The Practices of Film Reception.* New York: New York University Press.

Standish, Isolde (2005). *A New History of Japanese Cinema: A Century of Narrative Film.* New York: Continuum.

Standish, Isolde (2011). *Politics, Porn and Protest: Japanese Avant-Garde Cinema in the 1960s and 1970s.* London: Bloomsbury. Kindle

Tesson, Charles (1997). "Pigs and Gods." Trans. Claudine Quinn. In *Shohei Imamura*, ed. James Quandt, 159–63. Toronto: Toronto International Film Festival Group.

Yamamoto, Yasuo, and Jirō Tomoda (1983). *"Narayama bushikō: Oyama mairi ha karaugozansu"* [*The Ballad of Narayama*: Going to the Mountains, There Is Happiness]. *Kinema Junpo* 5A: 839, March: 51–54.

Chapter 15
Boundary Play: Truth, Fiction, and Performance in *A Man Vanishes*

Diane Wei Lewis

Shohei Imamura's documentary *Ningen jōhatsu/A Man Vanishes* (1967) follows thirty-two-year-old Yoshie Hayakawa (nicknamed "Nezumi," or mouse) on her quest to locate her missing fiancé, Tadashi Ōshima. The actor Shigeru Tsuyuguchi accompanies Yoshie and assists her with her interviews. Imamura's planning meetings with cast and crew are also incorporated into the film. Onethird of the way into *A Man Vanishes*, the filmmakers have tracked Ōshima to his last known position but are no closer to determining Ōshima's fate, nor the reasons for his disappearance. From this point on, the film focuses increasingly on Yoshie and her sister Sayo (whom the crew nicknamed "Usagi," or rabbit; Imamura 2004: 136) while Imamura begins to question the nature of the "reality" documented by the film.

A Man Vanishes generated public outrage on the eve of its release when it became known that Imamura used hidden cameras and sound recording equipment without the sisters' knowledge. Surreptitious recordings exposed the women's actual attitudes toward the investigation. In particular, Imamura went out of his way to show that Yoshie was putting on a "performance" for the cameras and fancied herself an "actress" in the film (Imamura 2004: 135–36). Yoshie was filmed confessing her love for Tsuyuguchi and throwing temper tantrums, while Tsuyuguchi is shown cozying up to Sayo in a bar. By the second half of *A Man Vanishes*, the search for Ōshima appears to be a pretense for exploring how the Hayakawa sisters react to being filmed. The longtime enmity between the sisters supersedes the hunt for Yoshie's missing fiancé. Imamura gives a performance of his own, deceiving the sisters in the name of "truth." His pronouncements in the film link the deliberately unflattering footage of the sisters to the central theme: What we think is reality is often actually fiction. However, many commentators argued that this critical project was not sufficient justification for including damaging depictions of the Hayakawas and

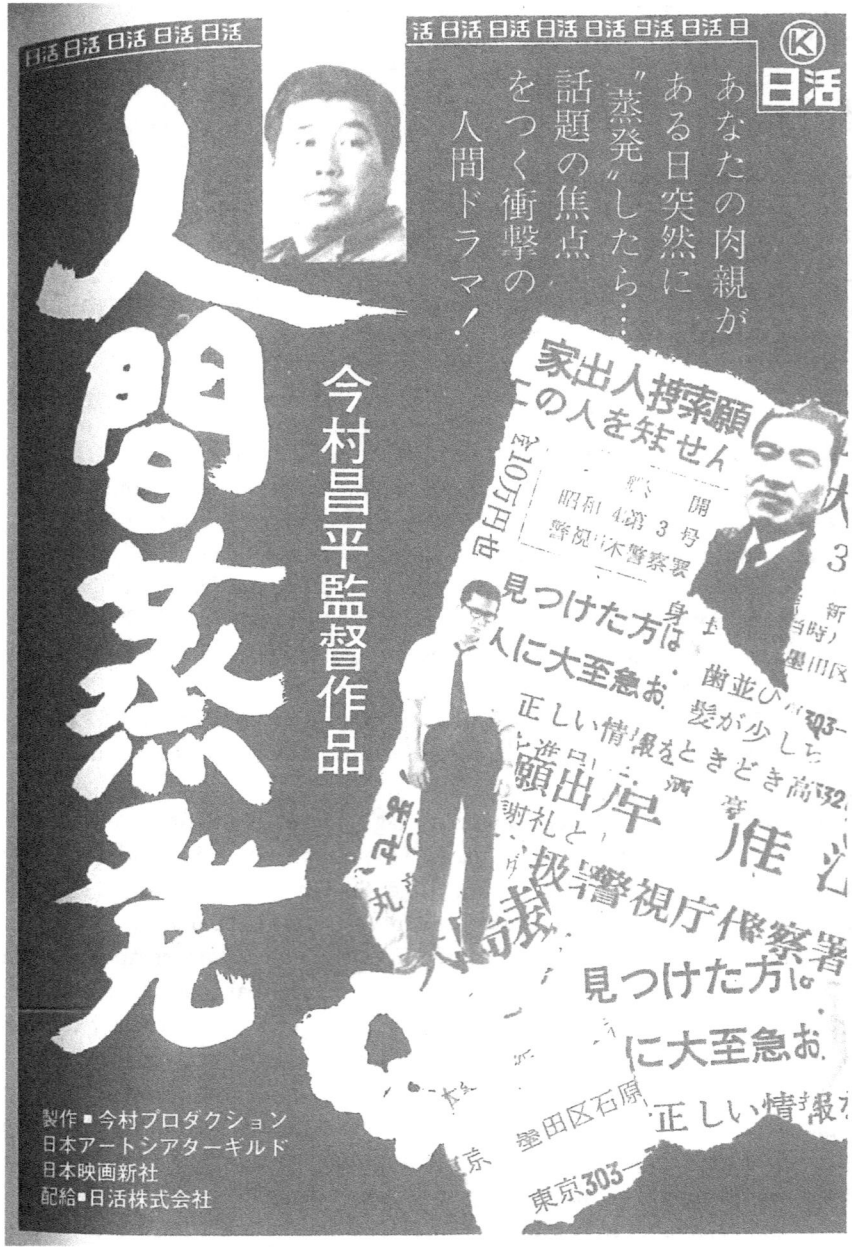

Figure 15.1 An ad for *A Man Vanishes* in the August 1967 issue of *Eiga hyōron*.

violating their privacy. Imamura's gambit fueled debates among Japanese critics about documentary filmmaking ethics. Many journalists argued that Imamura crossed the line in exploiting the women's excitement to be involved in a film. They asked whether Imamura hadn't tricked these "amateurs" with promises of stardom, exposing them to cruel scrutiny and ridicule that beloved celebrities are usually shielded from.

In the discussion that follows, I examine how *A Man Vanishes* takes Imamura's longstanding fascination with realism and human psychology to new extremes. In *A Man Vanishes*, Imamura tests his subjects, their assertions, and their motivations—and even reality itself—using interviews, mock situations, and covert observation. These experimental tactics showcase Imamura's interests in sociology and ethnology, which was sparked by his discovery of folklorist Kunio Yanagita (1875–1962) in the early 1960s (Imamura 2004: 105). The film also exemplifies the mixture of fiction and documentary found in much late-1960s and early-1970s Japanese independent filmmaking, which was strongly influenced by direct cinema, *cinéma vérité*, and, as Yuriko Furuhata has shown, postwar Japanese theoretical discourse on "actuality." This discourse was influenced by the rise of television and mass media journalism and defined above all by a critical engagement with reality. As Furuhata describes in *Cinema of Actuality*, medium-specific concepts of cinema came under scrutiny with the growing ubiquity of television, which became the primary site of moving-image actuality in the 1960s. Televised demonstrations against the ANPO treaty, militant student activism, and police standoffs and hostage crises strengthened television's associations with reportage, liveness, and contingency. Thus, Furuhata writes, "The proximity between cinema and journalism became a focal point of discussions precisely around the time when television began to threaten cinema with its strong appeal to actuality" (Furuhata 2013: 65). Responding to this crisis of the cinematic image, political filmmakers used methods borrowed from documentary, television, and investigative reporting, testing and contesting the mainstream news media's claims to actuality. Furuhata's analysis focuses on modernist filmmakers and the "mediatization of politics" (Furuhata 2013: 56), but it is fair to say that the critical debates and oppositional practices that she discusses were part of a more general trend in 1960s-1970s Japanese filmmaking and global cinema.

In addition to thinking about *A Man Vanishes* and experimental documentary form, this chapter also explores how the notion of the "auteur" shaped critical responses to Imamura's film. As early as the 1920s, discourse on film authorship in Japan was firmly centered on the film director as the driving creative force behind a film. As an auteur, Imamura (like any other prominent film director) was viewed as creating a persona through his films, which were not only marked by common stylistic features and common themes, but also seemed to be driven by a specific subjectivity—by the director and his orientation toward the world. Critics viewed Imamura's film style as an extension of his individualistic personality and uncompromising worldview. This emphasis on *kosei* or "individuality" in Imamura criticism is typical of how many new, young postwar directors were discussed by film journalists in the 1960s. This emphasis can in part be related to the postwar political-philosophical discourse on *shutaisei* (subjectivity) (Koschmann 1996; Standish 2011; Raine 2012a), which featured prominently in influential leftist film journals such as *Kiroku eiga* and *Eiga hihyō*.

Yet, just like the discourse on actuality, Japanese discourse on the auteur was also shaped by television and mass media. Some film critics—including renowned critic Akira Iwasaki—were circumspect about the emphasis being placed on *kosei*, *shutaisei*, and persona, which they viewed as a product of *masu komi* (mass communications) and mass media celebrity, and less a sign of political engagement. Michael Raine observes that even filmmaker and critic Toshio Matsumoto believed that "*shutaisei*, a term central to the debate on postwar subjectivity among occupation-era literary critics and echoed by later filmmakers such as Oshima Nagisa and Yoshida Kiju . . . had been reduced by repetition to a mere 'attitude'" (Raine 2012a: 147). This dilution of *shutaisei* was a problem for Matsumoto, who argued that "the task is to engage with the world as *taisho*, the active thing in the world . . . set in opposition to the subjective existence of the filmmaker" (Raine 2012a: 146). Similarly, director Nagisa Ōshima demanded that filmmakers engage directly with social reality and ask difficult questions about real conditions: "only the maintenance of a state of tension with reality and the discovery of a new method of perpetual active involvement will enable [the filmmaker] to make works that are a true expression of himself. Thus the filmmaker must always seek a new tension with reality and constantly negate himself in order to continue to create a new artistic involvement" (Ōshima [1960] 1993: 48). However, as Raine points out, Ōshima maintained his cultural relevance long after his emergence as one of the leading directors of the New Wave by becoming "a public intellectual, writing a column for the prestigious *Asahi* newspaper and appearing regularly on television in the 1980s and 1990s" (Raine 2012b: 147). Raine argues that this public visibility and collaborations with other celebrities are what made Ōshima successful as a "cultural provocateur" (Raine 2012b: 148). Similarly, my chapter on *A Man Vanishes* will examine Imamura's public persona and analyze the conflation of Imamura's critical project with his bad boy celebrity in the reception of the film.

In Search of the New: Mixing Documentary and Fiction

In a two-part article "Documentary and Fiction" published in 1967, Jun Watanabe noted a remarkable rise in the use of reportage and documentary strategies in film, television, and literature. Commenting on the popularity of the Italian "cruel film" (*zankokumono*) or mondo film, the "documentary dramas" of playwrights Heinar Kipphardt and Jean Vilar, and the rise of *cinéma vérité*, Watanabe suggested that documentary works had become a major current in contemporary culture. For Watanabe, this trend appeared to signify a crisis in art, as art usually derives its power from fiction, and the new documentary works were not simply concerned with "fact" or "truth" but attempted to ground fiction in documentary and create new, hybrid forms of fiction. His essay suggested that a moribund Japanese cinema endangered by the rise of television would be enlivened by new genres that combined fiction and documentary (Watanabe 1967a; 1967b).

"Documentary and Fiction" was published in the mainstream, mass-circulated film magazine *Kinema junpō*, which remains a popular venue for film criticism for a general audience today. In the 1960s and 1970s, new experiments with documentary realism were widespread and not limited to oppositional and avant-garde cinema, but also found in Japanese box office smashes such as *Mondo Cane* (Paolo Cavara, Franco Prosperi, and Gualtiero Jacopetti, 1962) and, later, *jitsuroku* (true record) yakuza films such as *Battles without Honor or Humanity* (Kinji Fukasaku, 1973). Although *A Man Vanishes* is often treated as a very experimental documentary, it reflects broad trends in 1960s Japanese cinema—in particular, the search for alternative models of film production, distribution, and narration in the era of television, which led to declining theater attendance and drastic cutbacks in mainstream commercial studio production.

Co-produced by Imamura Productions and the Art Theatre Guild (ATG), *A Man Vanishes* was among the first films to be co-financed by ATG, which was established as a theater chain and foreign film distributor in 1962. ATG played a major role in the exploration of new modes of film production, distribution, and exhibition in the 1960s (Domenig 2004, 2012; Furuhata 2013; Hirasawa 2012; Yomota 2003; Zahlten 2017). In the first years of its existence, ATG distributed such major European and Soviet art films as *Umberto D* (Vittorio de Sica, 1952), *Wild Strawberries* (Ingmar Bergman, 1957), *Cleo from 5 to 7* (Agnes Varda, 1962), *Shoot the Piano Player* (François Truffaut, 1960), *Andrei Rublev* (Andrei Tarkovsky, 1966), *The Seventh Seal* (Bergman, 1957), *Last Year at*

Marienbad (Alain Resnais, 1961), *8 ½* (Federico Fellini, 1965) and *Pierrot le fou* (Jean-Luc Godard, 1965). However, in 1964, when as part of trade liberalization, the ceiling on profits made from foreign films was lifted, driving up the bidding on non-Japanese films, ATG determined it would be cheaper to go into domestic production than to distribute foreign films (Domenig 2012: n.p.).

Go Hirasawa has suggested that *A Man Vanishes* is "difficult to classify as an ATG production as it was planned completely by the director and then shown at Nikkatsu-run theaters after only a short run at ATG" (Hirasawa 2012: n.p.). *Death by Hanging* (Nagisa Ōshima, 1968), made the following year, is usually treated as the first ATG production, since it was the first film made as part of an ATG initiative to co-produce Japanese independent films on a meager ten-million-yen budget (approximately 28,000 USD at that time). ATG put up half the funds for the "ten-million-yen films," and each production received a guaranteed four-week run in ATG theaters (Ogawa 2015: 306). Since it has not been grouped with these productions, *A Man Vanishes* has perhaps not received the attention it deserves, despite being an important forerunner of many independent productions, including later ATG films, that to varying degrees mix fiction with real-life events and utilize a documentary film style. For instance, like *A Man Vanishes*, films such as *Three Resurrected Drunkards* (Ōshima, 1968), *Funeral Parade of Roses* (Matsumoto, 1969), *Diary of a Shinjuku Thief* (Ōshima, 1969), and *Throw Out Your Books and Go into the Streets* (Shūji Terayama, 1971) include interview segments that were common in *cinéma vérité* and seen increasingly on Japanese television programs, such as in the award-winning TBS documentary program *Anata wa . . .*

In planning *A Man Vanishes*, Imamura searched through a list of 80,000 missing persons and found himself drawn to case of missing person Tadashi Ōshima, who struck Imamura as an utterly unremarkable person. It was the era of high economic growth, and young people like Ōshima flocked to metropolitan areas from their rural farming village hometowns, hoping to find happiness while contributing to Japan's economic miracle. Many of these youths later mysteriously disappeared. Imamura wondered, where had they disappeared to and how did this impact the rural communities where they were from (Imamura 2004: 134)? Filming *A Man Vanishes* took the form of an open-ended investigation that deliberately eschewed the conventions of the fictional narrative film. Director and screenwriter Kirio Urayama, one of Imamura's collaborators on *A Man Vanishes*, notes that few of the production's crew had experience working on fiction films. Cinematographer Kenji Ishiguro was a still photographer who specialized in depictions of youth. He was assisted by Masaki Mizuno, a young Nichiei technician with a background in documentary film. Sound recorder Kunio Takeshige was self-taught, and his three assistants were Waseda

University students. The filmmaking was a collaborative process that evolved daily with the crew's ongoing research and new developments, giving rise to an ever-changing understanding of the film's subject matter. Nightly planning meetings in the one-room office of Imamura Productions went on until consensus was reached among all staff and crew, including the most junior members, typically at around 2:00 am (Urayama 1967: n.p.).

Despite being Imamura's first full-fledged documentary, *A Man Vanishes* is not unlike earlier Imamura films such as *The Insect Woman* and *The Pornographers*, which bring fictional drama into close proximity with unstaged reality. In these earlier films, Imamura delights in transgressing the boundary between fiction and reality. For instance, street scenes in *The Insect Woman* are shot with hidden cameras, and unsuspecting bystanders react to the staged drama without realizing that the strange interactions they are witnessing are not real. We delight in their candid shocked expressions, which are not unlike the credulous reactions of unwitting victims on hidden camera shows. In this sense, *The Insect Woman* creates what we might call "performance situations" using one of the definitions of performance proposed by Richard Schechner, who suggests that what we understand as performance involves reality in the subjunctive and may also involve bringing together or overlaying "different orders of experience" (Schechner 1985: 97). Imamura excels in creating performance situations. He uses diverse cinematic strategies (freeze frames, voiceover, news footage, intertextual citations and more) to demarcate different registers of reality in his films.

In essays on *A Man Vanishes* in *Kinema junpō* and *Eiga hyōron*, critic and novelist Hideo Osabe postulated that Imamura's dialectical explorations of the tensions between the urban and the rural, the modern and the premodern, and fact and fiction were influenced by the *minzokugaku* (folklore studies) of Kunio Yanagita, the philosophy of Kiyoteru Hanada, and the plays of Pirandello. Osabe argued that beginning with *The Insect Woman*, Imamura put into practice Hanada's method of "sur-documentarism": "Using the conventional documentary as a negating medium, Imamura attempts to surpass modern drama (fiction); using fiction as a negating medium, Imamura attempts to surpass documentary" (Osabe 1967: 58). Osabe observed that in *A Man Vanishes*, as the extent of Imamura's intervention in the reality before the camera becomes increasingly unclear and the film becomes increasingly focused on Yoshie Hayakawa's posturing, "the lie (*uso*) appears to be truth (*honto rashiku*) and the truth (*honto*) appears to be a lie (*uso rashiku*)" (Osabe and Satō 1967: 20).

Indeed, the reality represented in *A Man Vanishes* is incredibly layered and unstable. Midway through *A Man Vanishes*, Yoshie confesses her feelings for

Shigeru Tsuyuguchi, feelings that weaken her resolve to find her fiancé while perversely strengthening her commitment to the film. Later, during a heated confrontation between Yoshie and Sayo, whom Yoshie suspects of having had an affair with Ōshima, Imamura breaks down the set to reveal that the argument is not taking place in a private room (as it seemed) but on a soundstage in a Nikkatsu studio. By the end of the film, Yoshie is convinced that her sister is hiding something from her and may have been involved in Ōshima's disappearance. A scattering of mysterious, foreboding scenes suggests the irrational, supernatural power of Yoshie's suspicions. For instance, the crew visits a spiritual medium who channels Ōshima's spirit and asserts that he is three months dead but refuses to answer any other questions. Yoshie describes a dream in which she chased two cats, slashing them with a knife, capturing them in a crate, nailing it shut, and piercing their eyes. In the second half of the film, Imamura inserts several dramatic shots of the medium dancing with fans in front of an altar in a pitch-black space. Strong overhead lighting creates deep, crawling shadows over the medium's white robes and around her feet. The film becomes increasingly surreal. Yoshie begins to investigate Sayo, taking the filmmakers to neighborhood businesses that Sayo frequented around the time of Ōshima's disappearance. While Yoshie questions a stylist at the Asakusabashi Pearl Beauty Salon, one of Imamura's cameramen literally pushes his way into the shop, squeezing through the doorway between Yoshie and Tsuyuguchi, and pushing them out of the frame. In a subsequent shot, three crewmembers, including a soundman wearing headphones, are seen crammed into the doorway behind Yoshie and Tsuyuguchi. The cinematic interrogation of reality and Yoshie's emotions now take precedence over Ōshima as the subject of the film.

Toward the end of *A Man Vanishes*, several locals report seeing Ōshima with Sayo at the apartment where the sisters used to live. A fishmonger claims that he saw them walking together. In the last scene, Imamura shoots their old neighborhood as Yoshie and eyewitnesses attempt to reconstruct the hotly disputed incident in which Sayo and Ōshima were allegedly spotted together. Imamura, Tsuyuguchi, and a battery of camera operators and sound technicians mill about the scene, collecting film footage and sound, while Yoshie supervises a reenactment of the disputed incident. Throughout *A Man Vanishes*, Imamura and Tsuyuguchi have continually debated who is in command of the production: Is it the filmmakers or their subject? In this scene, Yoshie literally becomes a metteur-en-scène who tries to produce meaning by overseeing the reenactment of the alleged tryst. However, competing with Yoshie's efforts to assert authority over the proceedings, nearly every shot in this sequence reveals the haphazard recording activities of camera operators, sound technicians, and assistants, with Imamura looking on. Crew can be seen gathering coverage from all distances and angles. They stand at street level, on rooftops, and on objects in between. The audio track includes the audible whirr of filming cameras and the repeated sound of clapboards clacking. The multiplicity of viewpoints conveyed in this scene is not limited to those of the feuding participants in the reenactment; with the use of editing and disjunctive sound, Imamura also makes us conscious of the production and post-production manipulation of the film's "reality." This is a clearly a synthetic reality, made up of multiple visual and aural points of view, with a sound track that contains both sync and wild sound, recorded on location as well as after the fact. As a result of these techniques, our understanding of who is directing (who is in control), what is under investigation, and which layer of "truth" is primary becomes hopelessly confused. The proliferation of frames within frames within this scene underscores a multiplicity of competing viewpoints, which remain unresolved even as the film draws to a close.

This is not the first Imamura film to use such reflexive framing. In *The Insect Woman*, in addition to using documentary film tactics such as on-location sound recording, handheld cameras, hidden cameras, high-power telephoto lenses, and wireless microphones, Imamura uses frames within frames, or aperture framing, in order to create competing areas of interest and strong visual contrasts. Aperture framing refers to the use of architecture, interposing objects or other elements to literally frame actors in the image (Bordwell 2005: 104–5). In *The Insect Woman* this technique is used frequently, though not exclusively, in rural scenes. Windows and doorways that open onto bright sunlit spaces only increase the sense of darkness and enclosure in rustic interiors. Used repetitively and conspicuously, aperture framing is self-reflexive: it makes us aware of the camera and the composition of the image, thus drawing our attention to both the literal and rhetorical framing of the material.

In *The Pornographers*, Imamura's first independent film production, aperture framing underlines the theme of voyeurism, which is narrativized through the main character Ogawa's business of making and distributing stag films, as well as his furtive sexual interest in his live-in lover's daughter. Within this narrative, aperture framing makes the film viewer conscious of their own as well as the characters' desire to see into other worlds. Frames within frames also suggest how characters are hemmed in by their situations and must operate within a restricted set of social relations. For instance, when Ogawa visits an office building to peddle pornography to male managerial workers, Imamura films the scene from the roof of a nearby building through a telephoto lens. Two distinct spaces within the company are visible through the windows: a well-appointed sitting room in which Ogawa passes around his wares and an adjacent office in which rows of female clerical workers are absorbed in their work. Here, aperture framing provides a commentary on the (not entirely successful) containment of sexuality in the modern workplace and its redirection toward consumption during the period of high economic growth.

Imamura's use of aperture framing contributes to the creation of performance situations. In his films, noticeably strong compositional elements serve to remind us that these are fictional cinematic worlds, worlds that have been posited by the filmmaker. Using reflexive framing, Imamura self-consciously shows reality in the subjunctive. Even when Imamura films in a documentary style that is characterized by the use of "all-location" shooting, hidden cameras, and amateur actors, the strong formal qualities of Imamura's *mise-en-scène* remind us that these images are *representations* of reality and not simply an objective recording of the world. *A Man Vanishes* continues Imamura's exploration of frames within frames, going even further than *The Insect Woman* and *The Pornographers* in its use of framing as a reflection on the activity of filmmaking. For in *A Man Vanishes*, Imamura films his own crew filming and has filmmaking increasingly become the subject of the film itself.

This use of reflexive framing and blending of fiction and nonfiction could be compared to classic documentaries that impose "an acting frame around a nonacting circumstance," such as Edward Curtis's *In the Land of the Head Hunters* (1914) and Robert Flaherty's *Nanook of the North* (1922). These films "combine people sometimes going about their ordinary tasks, sometimes restoring behaviors of a recent past, and sometimes acting for pay in fictive situations in an 'on-location' set wearing costumes and saying lines written for the occasion" (Schechner 1985: 97). However, *A Man Vanishes* deliberately foregrounds the use of staging, fictionalization, and other forms of intervention. Imamura's film is self-conscious and self-reflexive in a way that Curtis's and Flaherty's films are not. For instance, at the outset of the last scene, Imamura describes *A Man Vanishes* as a "dramatic film" (*geki eiga*) and a work of "fiction" (*fikushon*). His assertions draw our attention to the problem of reenactment in documentary films. As Bill Nichols points out, reenactments are often used as an "attempt to resurrect people and lives no longer available to the camera" (Nichols 2008: 74). Reenactment "complicates the literal, linear, and binary logic . . . that sets out to determine what really happened" (Nichols 2008: 78). In order for a reenactment to be legible as such, the viewer must understand that the reenactment is not identical with the original, irretrievable event, and as a result, the reenacted event introduces a fantasmatic element that an initial representation of the same event lacks. Put simply, history does not repeat itself, except in mediated transformations such as memory, representation, reenactment, fantasy—categories that coil around each other in complex patterns. (Nichols 2008: 73)

Rather than simply reconstructing what really happened, reenactments foreground desire, imagination, and loss.

The culmination of *A Man Vanishes* in an inconclusive reenactment is crucial. In its critical examination of "actuality," *A Man Vanishes* combines elements of documentary and fiction, and although it is not an expressly political film, it uses many of the techniques found in films examined by Furuhata in *Cinema of Actuality*. It foregrounds form and the medium, using artifice to break the viewer's absorption and encourage active spectatorship. Of the various kinds of reenactment that Nichols identifies, the type most applicable here is "Brechtian Distanciation," which "greatly increases the separation of the reenactment from the specific historical moment that it reenacts, giving greater likelihood that the fantasmatic effect will come into play" (Nichols 2008: 85). Imamura asks us to examine seemingly self-apparent, obvious truths, including the realism of the cinematic image, playing with the boundary between event and representation. As Osabe wrote, Imamura is an artist much like Pirandello whose work is situated in the space between truth and fiction (Osabe and Satō 1967: 21).

Though Imamura does not think of his work as overtly political (Imamura 2004: 105), Stephen Heath's analysis of Nagisa Ōshima's films could also apply to *A Man Vanishes*:

The *intensity* of Oshima's work lies in a "going beyond" of content that constantly breaks available articulations of "form" and "content" and poses the film in the hollow of those breaks ... Split *in* the narrativisation, the films are thus out of true with—out of "the truth" of—any single address: the subject divided in complexes of representation and their contradictory relations. (Heath 1976: 109)

However, whereas Ōshima uses modernist strategies that trouble realist representation and foreground form in order to critique state ideology and examine the legacy of Japanese imperialism, Imamura uses similar techniques to get at the dark unknowability of human desire. (In Ōshima's films, sexuality and desire tend to be the vehicle rather than the object of analysis.)

Examining the film's themes and documentary methods, contemporary critics readily situated *A Man Vanishes* in relation to Imamura's oeuvre as well as global trends in modernism, documentary, and documentary-influenced filmmaking. However, they asked, was Imamura's artistic ambition just cause for deceiving the Hayakawa sisters?

The Ethics of *A Man Vanishes*: Critics Respond

A Man Vanishes can be related to postwar Japanese auteur discourse on two levels. First and most obviously, critics understood the film within an auteurist framework: they related *A Man Vanishes* to previous Imamura films and emphasized the appearance of typical Imamura themes and methods, even when examining the ethics of the film. This auteurist understanding of Imamura's oeuvre became the basis for interpreting his use of documentary technique and self-reflexive cinematic form to analyze human behavior. However, there is another, more crucial sense in which the film can be tied to debates on the film director as a creative intelligence and public figure. *A Man Vanishes* does not simply confirm and reinforce Imamura's public image as a maverick director with specific preoccupations; *A Man Vanishes* also explores the creation of media personalities. The film was widely discussed as a self-reflexive examination of how the mass media creates personas, blurring the boundaries between public and private and confusing what is authentic with what is a performance. This aspect of the film is most obvious in the Hayakawa sisters' transformation in front of the camera and their participation in reenacting and sometimes even faking events for the film. In addition, Imamura's ability to engage the sisters in this way, to deceive them and even be celebrated for it, reflected Imamura's own celebrity. In many ways, *A Man Vanishes* and its reception allow us to explore the thorny connections between auteurship, self-presentation, and the mass media.

The auteurist understanding of Imamura's oeuvre is well established by the time of *The Insect Woman*. Imamura was known for firmly grounding his characters within richly described physical and social environments. Films such as *Stolen Desire* (1958), *Endless Desire* (1958), and *Pigs and Battleships* seemed to regard their characters' wild urges and foibles with a dry and analytical yet humorous perspective. Michizō Toida's 1963 analysis, published in *Kinema junpō* in anticipation of *The Insect Woman*, is typical in its description of Imamura's methods, tone, and themes. Toida writes that Imamura affirms desire and celebrates the primitive robustness of human beings who openly express their needs. His films imply that "there exist things of such impenetrable darkness that they cannot be logically explained, which are rooted in depths that cannot be illuminated by the light of human reason" (Toida 1963: 68). Imamura fixes his gaze on the dark underbelly of humanity and history. His characters are essentially irrational but also powerfully shaped by social and historical circumstances. Despite Imamura's preoccupation with dark instincts and desires, however, Toida also understood Imamura's films as characteristically "postwar," because they were "light and dry" and characterized by a distanced, analytical perspective. This contrasted with the "damp," wallowing, emotional introspection of prewar films and literature (Toida 1963: 67).

When it came to *A Man Vanishes*, critics were both fascinated and disturbed by Imamura's treatment of the Hayakawa sisters, whom they perceived as typical Imamura heroines. *A Man Vanishes* seemed to revel in a very troubling relationship between the filmmaker and his cast. In his memoir, Imamura reveals that he never got along with Yoshie, whom he found "egotistical and self-centered." She infuriated Imamura by impeaching him with shrill accusations, questioning his real motivations for looking for her fiancé. Imamura insists that he always intended to find Ōshima. However, "While having these conversations with Nezumi [Yoshie], I thought that if for some reason I couldn't hunt down Ōshima, I'd make a film investigating this woman's interiority, and without giving her any warning, I'd begin by insinuating myself into her day-to-day life, in order to rip off Nezumi's mask" (Imamura 2004: 135). When Yoshie quit her job at a Tokyo hospital before filming started, Imamura sent one cameraman to the farewell party and put one camera on the roof of a nearby building with a telephoto lens. Without warning Yoshie, Imamura had Tsuyuguchi enter the party unannounced. His entrance created a huge disturbance among Yoshie's flabbergasted coworkers, who had no idea she would be shooting a movie with a famous actor and director. Imamura kept the cameras rolling as Yoshie burst into tears, enraged, waiting for Yoshie to betray her true self (Imamura 2004: 135). To Imamura's dismay, as filming continued, the presence of the cameras seemed to transform Yoshie into an actress rather than destroy her façade. Imamura became "hellbent on baring Yoshie, the human being" (Imamura 2004: 136). This motivated him to "take the film to another level, an emotional level." If Yoshie intended to become an actress, there were strategies—hidden cameras and hidden microphones—for dealing with that (Imamura 2004: 136).

Controversy over Imamura's methods first erupted after a test screening in which the Hayakawa sisters viewed the complete film for the first time. Yoshie was shocked to learn that her private meetings with Tsuyuguchi had been secretly recorded (Satō 1980: 110). The Hayakawas' complaint was reported to newspapers, which then widely publicized the sisters' objections to the film, leading to calls to ban the movie. Nikkatsu's publicity department fanned the controversy, hoping the furor would make the film an even greater sensation (Satō 1980: 108–9). It was even reported that Yoshie destroyed the film by setting it on fire, while critics debated whether this was a PR stunt (Osabe and Satō 1967: 27–28).

The debates over *A Man Vanishes* took up legal and ethical questions about art, privacy, journalism, and "the people's right to know" (Okamoto 1967: 33). The film magazines *Kinema junpō* (August 1, 1967), *Eiga hyōron* (September 1967), and *Eiga geijutsu* (September 1967) all ran special sections on *A Man Vanishes*, but the *Kinema junpō* articles paid especially close attention to the relationship between *A Man Vanishes* and its contemporary media context. In this issue, Yoshio Shirai wrote that the film seemed aimed at "the destruction of the privacy of a certain kind of petit bourgeois" and described *A Man Vanishes* as "a film that experiments on live human subjects." He wrote, "After the film is over, one is left with an awful, hollow aftertaste. One senses that what the film captures, the treacherousness of the characteristic Japanese environment (*Nihon-teki na fūdo no inshitsusa*), is a trait of the film itself" (Shirai 1967: 35). Media critic and philosopher Sadayoshi Fukuda was both fascinated by how the relationship between Imamura and Yoshie was portrayed as well as deeply critical of the film, which he found "unethical." He believed that while Imamura's tactics were indefensible, the film opened up a necessary debate on the ethics of filmmaking. For Fukuda, the problem at the center of *A Man Vanishes* was essentially a question of the relationship between Imamura as a film professional and Yoshie as an amateur participant (Fukuda 1967: 31–32). In his article, Akira Iwasaki regretted that the Hayakawa sisters did not pursue a lawsuit, which he believed would have set an important precedent for how civil rights issues are handled in film. Nonetheless, he was fascinated by Imamura's extremism. His palms broke out in a sweat during the riveting confrontation between Yoshie and Sayo that was later revealed to have been staged in a Nikkatsu studio. He was shocked when the studio lights went up, revealing the space to be an illusion. He suggested that Imamura's pronouncements that what appears to be reality is actually fiction were an "extremely ingenious alibi" that surely helped protect Imamura against legal action (Iwasaki 1967: 37). Shirai suggested something similar when he referred to Imamura's philosophical musings as the "director's excuse" (Shirai 1967: 35). In this climactic moment, as the set is being struck, Imamura gives this speech:

> When you think you're telling the truth, everything looks real to you . . . For instance, this is a set. No ceiling, no roof. But we've been talking as if in a real room. You probably felt like it was a real room . . . Looks can be deceiving. This is fiction. This drama developed because Oshima went missing. It didn't occur spontaneously. It evolved as we planned . . . The camera is trying to film you, and you know it. Tomorrow, another fabricated film drama will play out here. But it's not necessarily that fiction is false, and non-fiction is true. This is fiction, too. (Imamura [1967] 2012)

Although this speech initially gave Iwasaki the shocking impression that the film was not in fact a documentary but that the Hayakawa sisters were "starring" in a "fiction" by Imamura and playing along with his games, the sisters' accusations gave him pause: "In the words of Hayakawa [Yoshie], this is a 'human guinea pig' problem. The question is whether this guinea pig gave consent, of her own will, within limits that she herself set" (Iwasaki 1967: 37).

Finally, for Sadayoshi Fukuda, *A Man Vanishes* showed how filming transforms the reality in front of the camera. However, his problem with the film was that only the "amateurs," or the ordinary people who are in front of the camera, seem to change. The "professionals," the specialists who work in front of and behind the cameras, emerge from the film unscathed. For Fukuda, this discrepancy reflected the unbalanced relationship between the mass media and the average individual. The presence of Imamura's camera prompted performances from ordinary people who were highly conscious of being filmed, making legible a quotidian kind of artificial self-presentation that often goes unnoticed in everyday life. At the same time, once raised to the status of public figures, these amateurs became subject to the derision of film viewers who could no longer imagine the film's participants as part of their ordinary world. Wasn't this an ethical problem? he asked. The real importance of *A Man Vanishes*, Fukuda argued, was its potential to make spectators think about their relationship to media. Accordingly, he wrote, "We can re-specify that the central problem of the film is not simply 'What is film?' but 'What is film for us?'" (Fukuda 1967: 32).

Several essays on *A Man Vanishes* in *Kinema junpō* focused on the practice of journalism and the power of weekly magazines. The following month, in the August 15 issue, journalist Hiroshi Okamoto described how his sense of professional duty was the only thing that kept him from leaving a screening of *A Man Vanishes* in disgust. His obligation as a reporter overrode his shame at being party to the treatment of the interview subjects. As the screening continued, he grew increasingly angry that viewers around him, whom he assumed were free of his professional obligations, were somehow able to sit silently and tolerate its injustices. At the same time, Okamoto felt exposed, for what he saw in the film was not so different from what he and other newspaper reporter friends did on the job. Okamoto thought the film was phenomenal in the way it held up the darkest, most loathsome aspects of the media to public scrutiny (Okamoto 1967: 32).

Similar concerns were raised in other publications. In *Eiga geijutsu* (November 1967), Nagisa Ōshima issued a warning to Japanese film directors and film critics in the article "Those Who Only Discourse on Method Are Corrupt." Although not directly addressed to Imamura or *A Man Vanishes*, Ōshima harshly criticized the normalization of brutality on television and the complicity of television directors who, simply documenting without questioning developing events, act as accomplices. He criticized attitudes such as "while we're filming something will happen" and "while we're investigating something will come up" as "anti-subjectivity, anti-critical, and an affirmation of the status quo" (Ōshima 1967: 24). According to Ōshima, this trend was most evident in the work of mediocre television directors who got their ideas from newspapers and weekly magazines. They passively filmed, feeling self-satisfied and revolutionary, indulging the notion they had pioneered "a televisual manifestation of the happening." Ōshima sneered, "The documentary weeps, the happening weeps—there is nothing revolutionary here at all" (Ōshima 1967: 24).[1] Whether or not Ōshima was covertly criticizing *A Man Vanishes*, he added his voice to the growing uproar against documentary filmmakers drawing from mass media and using mass media as a platform, acting irresponsibly toward their subject matter as well as the public.

In *Kinema junpō*, despite general condemnation of Imamura's ethics, the criticism of *A Man Vanishes* was ultimately tempered by the contributors' interest in situating *A Man Vanishes* within Imamura's oeuvre. After all, Imamura had already achieved acclaim for the very qualities that made *A Man Vanishes* problematic: he was famous for his unique perception of reality, his quasi-ethnographic or sociological perspective, and his wry view of the instinctual drives, which were vividly embodied by lusty, uninhibited protagonists. His films were already associated with a documentary sensibility that contributed to the investigative quality of his films. These characterizations are made so emphatically, repeatedly and early on in Imamura's career, that it is difficult not to view *A Man Vanishes* as deliberately playing upon Imamura's established public persona. As early as 1962, one even finds discussion of Imamura's work in terms of "truth" and "actuality." Heiichi Sugiyama observed that Imamura's films reveal the unintentional comedy of the darkest, most terrifying aspects of humanity with humor that borders on the macabre. He noted that Imamura's "natural, somewhat strong sense of humor derives from a new, exceptional sense for reality (*genjitsu kankaku*) . . . From this sense for reality, he arrives at a truth (*shinjitsu*) that goes beyond 'actuality' (*jijitsu*)" (Sugiyama 1962: 44). Similarly, essays on Imamura in *Kinema junpō*'s 1963 "New Director Studies" series underscored the strong anthropological flavor of his work and its role in producing the probing, investigative quality of his films. Michizō Toida used terms such as *Nihon fūdo* and *Nihon fūzoku*—"Japanese climate" and "Japanese customs"—to characterize Imamura's rough, folksy, and matter-of-fact realism (Toida 1963: 69). For Toida, what distinguished Imamura from other filmmakers was his dedication to analyzing human desire in relation to historically and geographically situated forms of social organization. Toida argued that

Imamura's films were also rooted in the director's own subjectivity and his relationship to contemporary Japan.

> Customs are the appearance of the age, but they are not the age. A description of customs is surely not sufficient if we want to grasp the age. The age is deeply rooted in the existence of the creator himself, in this case the existence of director Shōhei Imamura himself, and it is through the process of grasping the creator himself, and in the process of how we describe him, that the age is revealed. Scenes that reveal his personality, where his personality is active, are scenes where the age is active and is revealed. (Toida 1963: 69)

In this type of criticism, Imamura's persona and his cinematic style were inextricable.

The powerful influence of the media on Imamura's work and his reception—in particular, the media's role in shaping Imamura's image as an auteur who reveals his worldview through a critical engagement with reality, as mediated by the camera—has not been given enough attention. This form of celebrity was examined critically in *Kinema junpō* long before *A Man Vanishes* was made. In 1962, *Kinema junpō* ran a special collection of articles on Nagisa Ōshima, Susumu Hani, and Shohei Imamura as three new directors who promised to overturn the old conventions of Japanese filmmaking. Contributor Iwasaki Akira offered a sober assessment of their fame, suggesting that their ability to remain in the spotlight would depend heavily on the whims of the market. He noted that *masu komi* (mass communications) had made Ōshima, Hani, and Imamura stars, and it was possible that the rollercoaster of fame would cast them down into obscurity as fast as it had lifted them up. Iwasaki suggested their success could be attributed to the public's thirst for novelty as much as anything else. One thing these directors all had in common, he wrote, was a natural ability to strike well-timed dramatic poses for the news cameras. He warned that if they didn't move fast enough, they would be mugging in the dark (Iwasaki 1962).

Iwasaki's essay anticipates the media frenzy surrounding *A Man Vanishes*. The film itself is a study of the rollercoaster of fame and the impact of the mass media on self-presentation. Iwasaki may have been mistaken to suggest that Ōshima, Hani, and Imamura were just a passing fad, but he was correct in identifying a special relationship between new Japanese filmmakers who operated outside the Japanese studio system and postwar *masu komi*. The *A Man Vanishes* controversy illuminates the connection between New Wave–era iconoclasts and the news media. In the film and subsequent controversy, Imamura plays the role of sociological filmmaker and gadfly to the hilt, actively courting public controversy, reinforcing his auteurist image by taking his public persona to ridiculous, even ethically questionable, extremes. The film and the controversy are revealing for what they suggest about the seductive power of celebrity, for the famous filmmaker iconoclast as well as for the unsuspecting amateur.

The early critical reception of Imamura's films—in particular, the terms in which his authorship was defined in the 1960s—allowed critics to emphasize continuities between his fiction productions and his first documentary feature film, sometimes at the cost of fully exploring the ethical and legal questions at the heart of *A Man Vanishes*. The director's interrogation of Yoshie's persona only confirmed his artistic reputation and shielded him from the repercussions of making an unethical film. As Iwasaki Akira suggests, Imamura was protected by the alibi of an auteurist *modus operandi*. *A Man Vanishes* shows how the interaction between New Wave directors and the mass media contributed to new ideas of authorship—and exonerated new directorial extremes.

Note

1. My thanks to Roland Domenig for pointing me to Ōshima's article in *Eiga geijutsu* and suggesting the connection between Ōshima's criticism and the controversy surrounding *A Man Vanishes*.

Works Cited

Bordwell, David (2005). *Figures Traced in Light: On Cinematic Staging*. Berkeley: University of California Press.

Domenig, Roland (2004). "The Anticipation of Freedom: Art Theatre Guild and Japanese Independent Cinema." *Midnight Eye*, June 28, www.midnighteye.com/features/the-anticipation-of-freedom-art-theatre-guild-and-japanese-independent-cinema/. Accessed September 1, 2018.

Domenig, Roland (2012). "The Art Theatre Shinjuku Bunka and the *Bunka* of Shinjuku." In *Place and Space in Japanese Cinema: From Inside to Outside the Frame*, ed. M. Downing Roberts. UTCP Booklet 23: 57–69.

Fukuda Sadayoshi (1967). "Tsūyoku o hakaishita furinsei: *Ningen jōhatsu* no eigateki miryoku" [An Immorality That Destroyed the Banal: The Cinematic Allure of *A Man Vanishes*]. *Kinema junpō*, August 1: 31–33.

Furuhata, Yuriko (2013). *Cinema of Actuality: Japanese Avant-Garde Filmmaking in the Season of Image Politics*. Durham, NC: Duke University Press.

Heath, Stephen (1976). "Narrative Space." *Screen* 17, no. 3: 68–112.

Hirasawa, Go (2012). "Underground Japanese Cinema and the Art Theatre Guild." *desistfilm*, October 9, www.desistfilm.com/atg/. Accessed May 27, 2016.

Imamura Shōhei (2004). *Imamura Shōhei: Eiga wa kyōki no tabi de aru* [*Shōhei Imamura: Film Is a Wild Ride*]. Tokyo: Nihon Keizai Shinbunsha.

Imamura, Shōhei [1967] (2012). *A Man Vanishes*. DVD. New York: Icarus Films.
Iwasaki Akira (1962). "1960 nendai shinjin no sakka konjō" [The Personality of 1960s Newcomer Auteurs]. *Kinema junpō*, March 1, pp. 38–41.
Iwasaki Akira (1967). "Zannen datta soshō torisage: Geijutsu to puraibashii" [Too Bad They Dropped the Suit: Art and Privacy]. *Kinema junpō*, August 1, pp. 36–37.
Koschmann, J. Victor (1996). *Revolution and Subjectivity in Postwar Japan*. Chicago: University of Chicago Press.
Nichols, Bill (2008). "Documentary Reenactment and the Fantasmatic Subject." *Critical Inquiry* 1, no. 35: 72–89.
Ogawa, Shota T. (2015). "Reinhabiting the Mock-Up Gallows: The Place of Koreans in Oshima Nagisa's Films in the 1960s." *Screen* 56, no. 3: 303–18.
Okamoto Hiroshi (1967). "*Ningen jōhatsu* no gimon o kenshōsuru: Imamura Shōhei e no kōkaijō" [Examining Doubts about *A Man Vanishes*: An Open Letter to Shōhei Imamura]. *Kinema junpō*, August 15: 32–35.
Osabe Hideo (1967). "Ōshima Nagisa, Imamura Shōhei." *Kinema junpō*, September 1: 56–58.
Osabe Hideo and Shigechika Satō (1967). "Imamura Shōhei no genwakujutsu" [Shōhei Imamura's Art of Enchantment]. *Eiga hyōron*, September: 19–35.
Ōshima Nagisa (1967). "Hōhō dake o ronzuru mono wa taihaisuru" [Those Who Only Discourse on Method Are Corrupt]. *Eiga geijutsu*, November: 23–25.
Raine, Michael (2012a). "Introduction to Matsumoto Toshio: A Theory of Avant-Garde Documentary." *Cinema Journal* 51, no. 4: 144–47.
Raine, Michael (2012b). "Nagisa Oshima: Paradox and Perversion in the 1960s Avant-Garde." In *Directory of World Cinema: Japan 3*, ed. John Berra, 146–49. Bristol: Intellect.
Satō Tadao (1980). *Imamura Shōhei no sekai* [*The World of Shōhei Imamura*]. Tokyo: Gakuyō Shobō.
Schechner, Richard (1985). *Between Theater and Anthropology*. Philadelphia: University of Pennsylvania Press.
Shirai Yoshio (1967). "'Nihon' tankyū no seitai jikken: *Ningen jōhatsu* to Imamura sakuhin no kaku" [Experimenting on Live Subjects in Search of "Japan": *A Man Vanishes* and the Crux of Imamura's Films]. *Kinema junpō*, August 1: 34–35.
Standish, Isolde (2011). *Politics, Porn and Protest: Japanese Avant-Garde Cinema in the 1960s and 1970s*. New York: Continuum.
Sugiyama, Heiichi (1962). "Dokusō o mamoritoosu michi" [The Way to Keep Protecting Creativity]. *Kinema junpō*, March 1: 41–44.
Toida Michizō (1963). "Imamura Shōhei ron: Rekishi no naibu no kurayami o saguru" [Theory of Shōhei Imamura: Fumbling through the Darkness of History]. *Kinema junpō*, October 1: 67–69.
Urayama Kirio (1967). "*Ningen jōhatsu* (kadai) taidōki" [Record of Traveling with *A Man Vanishes* (Tentative Title)]. *Eiga hyōron*, June, n.p.
Watanabe Jun (1967a). "Kiroku to kyokō (jō)" [Documentary and Fiction (Part I)]. *Kinema junpō*, March 1: 36–39.

Watanabe Jun (1967b). "Kiroku to kyokō (ge)" [Documentary and Fiction (Part II)]. *Kinema junpō*, March 15: 106–9.

Yomota, Inuhiko (2003). "Deux ou trois chose que je sais d'ATG." Trans. M. Raine. In *Art Theatre Guild: Unabhängiges Japanisches Kino 1962–1984*, ed. R. Domenig and A. Ungerböck, 30–35. Vienna: Vienna International Film Festival.

Zahlten, Alexander (2017). *The End of Japanese Cinema: Industrial Genres, National Times, and Media Ecologies*. Durham, NC: Duke University Press.

Chapter 16

Why Not? Imamura, Nietzsche, and the Untimely

David Deamer

I show true things using fictional techniques but maintaining truthfulness . . . I'd like to destroy this premise that cinema is fiction. (Imamura 1997b: 130)

Insofar as it stands in the service of life, history stands in the service of an unhistorical power. (Nietzsche 2006: 67)

A Cinematic Encounter with the Untimely

They come, dancing, singing: women and men of East Ryogoku. Hundreds upon hundreds of people, in crazy costume and outlandish makeup: filthy beggars careering, lustful demons carousing, men dressed as clowns and as women, women dressed as men or bare-breasted. From all corners of the entertainment district of Edo: show-folk, thieves, pimps, whores, laborers, vagabonds. They chant the refrain *"ee ja nai ka"* ("Why not?" or "We don't care!" or even "What the hell!"). This exhortation comes in response to sung calls: "What if we take our clothes off?" / "What if we are all fools?" / "What if we were to die?" The crowd confronts the newly established Japanese infantry, who—upon command—shoulder their rifles. The people fall silent, become still. A few of the showgirls push their way to the front. They form a line, turn their backs upon the riflemen, hike up their kimonos, bare their asses, and piss hot piss on to the ground. Laughter from the crowd, the dance begins again, the singing again commences, and the carnival surges forward. The soldiers retreat . . .

Such is the image of anarchy at the climax of Shohei Imamura's cinematic period epic *Eijanaika/Why Not?* (1981). Set over the summer and autumn of 1866 and the winter and spring of 1867, the film explores an escalating crisis within Japanese society, a fundamental ungrounding of a highly stratified culture. This crisis comes in the wake of the opening of Japan in 1853: an event that led to the end of *sakoku* (the country's centuries-old isolationist policy) and the collapse of a way of life that had endured for over 250 years. This is the milieu of *Why Not?*—the situation that Imamura will explore through the events of the film and its characters. Yet Imamura would appear less concerned with a descriptive historiography of this moment from Japan's past than attempting to seize the sensations of the rupture: capturing and expressing the effects of anarchy. To do so, Imamura employs a disruptive cinematic praxis at every level of the film: image, narration, and narrative. Imamura creates discordant images, composes a disjunctive narration, and produces a dissonant narrative.

Imamura will create discordant images: wide shots as long takes or sequences that encompass the crowd as a cacophonous multitude, with action dispersed across each of the planes that take us from mid-ground to background. The *mise-en-scène* will be obscured by obstructing structures; interiors will remain unlit and in darkness concealing characters, their faces, and actions. Imamura will fashion shots that trouble recognition. Such images compose a cinematic collage. The film is replete with spontaneous events. Sometimes it is as if Imamura allows the narration to meander, to wander and lose itself. Or disparate instants along a staccato trajectory succeed one another helter-skelter. Elisions efface days, weeks, or perhaps months; stymying any conclusion to a series of images; jumping the tracks and orientating us in a new direction. Such a disjunctive narration produces a dissonant narrative—an ambiguous, equivocal, and oblique story world necessitating active interpretation. Imamura gives us a dizzying array of characters, encompassing all strata of society captured through and capturing up multiple perspectives: the stories of farmers, fishermen, samurai, gangsters, whores, show-folk, merchants, politicians, military, and domain lords. These characters inhabit and traverse a series of diverse locations: vibrant Edo (the capital, seat of the government or *bakufu*, controlled by the Tokugawa Shogunate); demure Kyoto (where the spiritual figurehead of the emperor and resurgent court reside); cosmopolitan Yokohama (the seaport opened to the Americans and international trade); and the ramshackle villages of the countryside in between (where the peasantry eke out their meagre existence). *Why Not?* is alive with multiplicity, riven with ellipses and opacities; the film is allusive, elusive, and illusive.

And it is the *eijanaika* procession that is the consummation of such disruptive cinematics. Wide shots capture the swarming mass crossing the river over Ryogoku Bridge and in dozens of small boats; pushing onward across the marketplace, structures collapsing in their advance. Among the people, a mobile camera weaves between bodies, body upon body, bodies dancing, in movement, overwhelming the frame. Frontal reverse tracking shots of the carnivalesque insurgency are given from multiple disparate perspectives. Imamura positions these anarchic images of the Japanese crisis as the concluding salvo of the narration; joyous rebellion ascends to become the dominant narrative theme. Order, however, will return. The troops fire into the air, over the heads of the people. And the *eijanaika* event is over. The procession begins to disperse, to fall back, and return to the East Ryogoku enclave. Even so, the Tokugawa officials command the infantry to shoot into the retreating crowd. People begin to fall. Blood soaks the earth. This is the devastating finale to the *eijanaika* uprising of *Why Not?* Yet this event never happened.

Accordingly, the *eijanaika* procession is the disruptive event par excellence of *Why Not?* Imamura fundamentally ungrounds the historiography of the film, undermines the historical veracity of the movie, weakening the link of image, narration, and narrative with the Japanese past: the end of *sakoku* and the consequent and escalating conflict between Shogunate *bakufu* and the emperor's court. Thus the purpose of this chapter: to interrogate Imamura's cinematic exploitation of the past in the context of his disruptive filmic praxis. To do so, I employ Friedrich Nietzsche's philosophy of history.

Turning to the philosophical thought of Nietzsche in a consideration of the cinematic art of Imamura may seem immediately problematic, and for any number of reasons. Imamura is a postwar twentieth-century Japanese filmmaker, Nietzsche a late nineteenth-century German philosopher. In the first instance, we encounter the problem of deploying cinema as exemplar, the film becoming a passive event for the mere illustration of a philosophical system or concept. More troubling still, there are the differences that times, spaces, and subjectivities throw up: committing the crime and conjuring the specter of a Eurocentrism, using a European philosophy to explore an Asian cinema, a reification of sociopolitical power and domination. However, neither of these problems are conclusive, in theory. Lúcia Nagib responds to the latter in "Towards a Positive Definition of World Cinema" (2006). The cinema of the world must be considered as having no center. Cinema is an acentered multiplicity that will cohere as an assemblage according to the approach of any theoretical perspective that resists othering and affirms collaboration (Nagib 2006: 35). Furthermore, with Nietzsche the problem may not be as acute as it first appears, for the philosopher has long been known to the Japanese. The first essay on Nietzsche was published as early as 1898 and translations of his books soon followed, beginning with the first of five versions of

Thus Spoke Zarathustra (1883–1891) in 1911 (Parkes 2008: xxxiii). A little later, the novelist Natsume declared the text—complicating matters still further—to be fundamentally un-European; and in 1913 the philosopher Watsuji Tetsurō published a seminal study of Nietzsche that remained influential with Japanese philosophers, including the prominent Kyoto School, for many years (Parkes 2008: xxxiii). We do not know if Imamura read Nietzsche. However, we do know the director studied Western history at Waseda University and was fascinated by existentialism—a philosophy that took inspirations from and would be unthinkable without Nietzsche (Kim 2003). No doubt, the complexities of cultural power relations can never and should never be shrugged off; but neither should transcultural collaboration and affirmation be silenced. Indeed, the very problematic nature of such encounters can be productive: would not such an approach appear fitting when exploring discord, disjunction, and dissonance?

Yet, in truth, we discover many resonances, correspondences, and correlations between Imamura's filmic praxis and Nietzsche's philosophy, and perhaps nowhere more so than in the question of the capturing and release of the past through history. In an early foundational essay entitled "On the Uses and Abuses of History for Life" (1874)—the second of his four *Untimely Meditations* (1873–76)—Nietzsche analyzes, as the title suggests, the purpose of history, its benefits and ills for the individual and society, and how such ills can be ameliorated and benefits accentuated. Historical research and historiographic knowledge are essential for producing an image, narration, and narrative of the past, present, and future as a continuum, delimiting and demarcating a geographical space, and determining cohesive subjectivities (the emotions, acts, and thoughts of people and peoples). Yet—according to Nietzsche's analysis—such a capture concomitantly fossilizes the past, preserves but does not engender, inspires repetitions of the same, encourages seductive nationalisms and fanaticisms, cements and exceptionalizes values, culture, and society, fosters and provokes ressentiment and revenge. And this is Nietzsche's still-controversial conclusion: the past must necessarily be transformed, shaped, and exploited. Accordingly, the historian must embrace transformation, shaping, and exploitation and become an artist. For the fundamental purpose of art is not to represent (re-present) but to create. Art creates and in so doing problematizes: the most beautiful and eternal of artworks complicates, challenges, confronts—these disruptive processes engendering thought. And this was Nietzsche's wider project: to unground philosophy through art. Nietzsche's philosophy and philosophical method *in toto* is itself problematizing. Nietzsche's writing is elliptical and opaque. Nietzsche's philosophy affirms discord, disjunction, and dissonance pre-echoing Imamura's disruptive cinematic praxis; and Nietzsche's philosophy of history—so I claim—will thus allow an interrogation of the *eijanaika* event in *Why Not?* While cinema needs not philosophy, and philosophy needs not cinema, when allowed to resonate these two disciplines can collaborate to produce, together, an adventure in thought. And such an adventure occurs between Nietzsche and Imamura through the ungrounding of history—the untimely.

Imamura and Disruptive Cinematics

With *Why Not?* and Imamura (as with all filmmakers and films), the encounter begins with cinematic technique: with the form and function of images and their coalescence as narration—framing, the shot, montage, color, and sound. For the narrative (the story and story world) is emergent. Screen images are sensed by bodies and thought through minds. To explore and reflect upon cinematic technique (the creation and coalescence of images) is thus to theorize in the wake of an empirical encounter. Yet the director immediately challenges us: "the techniques which I use cannot be theorised" (Imamura 1997a: 125). Why this disavowal? Disingenuously, Imamura explains "my films are messy" (Imamura 1997b: 131). The context of such a statement is essential to understanding Imamura's cinematic approach.

Imamura will tell of the time he was apprenticed as assistant director under Yasujiro Ozu. Ozu began as a filmmaker during the 1920s and became famous for creating cinematic masterpieces from the banalities of everyday Japanese family life. Working at first in the black and white silent cinema, Ozu developed a unique visual method that he consolidated and refined even as he resisted, adapted to, and then adopted (later than most directors) sound and color. Ozu's most celebrated images concern the suspension of movement, action, and human presence and have been named variously by Paul Schrader as "cases of stasis," Donald Richie as "still lifes," and Noël Burch as "pillow shots" (see Deamer 2018: 261–63). These images can be seen as having two essential coordinates. In the first place, a sequence will be bookended with a number of emptied-spaces such as landscapes, townscapes, street scenes, or interiors; in the second place, there will be a singularity within this sequence, a moment focusing upon an object or event, a vase, a clock, rain on a roof, falling blossoms, a table set for a meal. These two asynchronous processes, one centrifugal, the other centripetal, act at the level of narration. A succession of images is separated into a delimited sequence that coheres around and is overwhelmed by an amorphous affect, and these sequences form a series that structure the film. In other words, emptied spaces and singularities are disruptive images—but in tandem are productive of a flow, a continuum. "My early, shocking discovery when I worked with Ozu," writes Imamura, "was that a director could give disparate scenes continuity" (Imamura 1997a: 127). This composition of narration is but the most palpable of Ozu's processes. The director would reset the camera for each individual shot, even for the simplest of procedures such as a back and forth between two people in conversation; there was no reliance upon the repetition of framing. Or, the camera would be positioned low, seizing the characters and the world in a perception that does not cohere to naturalized human vision. Bodies would be captured in frontality with characters looking into the camera—troubling the fourth wall. Eyeline matches would not match, dissimilar objects graphic match. There was the use of 360 degrees, cinematic space consequently difficult to trace. And dialogue could be of imprecise topics, full of repetitions and silences. Famous examples of Ozu's disjunctive continuum include the opening shots of *Floating Weeds/Ukikusa* (1959) with the lighthouse in the background and the bottle in the foreground, the two shapes of the structure and object different but echoing one another. Or the false continuity in *Early Summer/Bakushû* (1951), when the woman leaves the main room of a restaurant and there is a cut to a corridor where she then appears, which we soon realize to be in another space and time entirely.

Ozu's disjunctive continuum is very different from the organic laws established through classical cinematic continuity. In the latter, the spectator is captured in the flow of images, in the flow of movement. Chronological time across comprehensive spaces constitute coherent subjectivities: spatiotemporal and sensorimotor continuity. And it is from this narration that the spectator encounters a rational and logical narrative as story world and plot. As Brian Henderson summarizes: classical cinematic techniques create images and compose narration "in order to reconstitute" the narrative "in highly organized, synthetic emotional and intellectual patterns" (Henderson 2004: 58). Against this conception of the cinema of recognition Henderson identifies another procedure: collage. "Collage does not do this"; rather, "it collects or sticks its fragments together in a way that does not entirely overcome their fragmentation" (Henderson 2004: 58). Chronological time is disturbed to problematize individual and collective memories and histories; comprehensive space is displaced to unground and question the links between bodies, and between bodies and the world; coherent subjectivities are challenged and identities contested. This is the shock Imamura encountered in the cinema of Ozu.

Yet at the same moment, Imamura will critique Ozu's method. Ozu's films explore but do not sustain discordance, disjunction, and dissonance. Ozu's techniques—the sequence-shots (with their emptied-spaces and singularities), the resonating of forms, the aberrations of perception, and so on—are "well conceived and beautifully detailed" (Imamura 1997a: 126). Ozu employs a disruptive cinematic praxis to establish a sublime mastery, presenting the glorious triumph of cosmos over chaos, permanence over crisis, order over anarchy. Despite exploring the fragmentation of the family, a husband and wife, society, the everyday is transcended—everything is as it is and as it ever was and will be. A "cinematic nirvana" in Imamura's words: Ozu "wanted to make film more aesthetic," the director continues, whereas "I want to make it more real" (Imamura 1997b: 130). Accordingly, Imamura does not follow Ozu, nor even accentuate his teacher's method. We could say, after Henderson, Ozu's collage tends toward mosaic, while Imamura's collage tends toward abstract expressionism. Imamura reverses the procedure: order is always under attack from anarchy. Imamura fragments the image, explodes the narration, and disperses the narrative. This is what Imamura means when he says his films are messy: "When I look at life through my viewfinder, I choose long shot when I want long shot, and close-up when I want close-up"; "I freely observe human beings" (Imamura 1997a: 125–26). This is what Imamura means when he says his cinematic techniques cannot be theorized: the rejection of a preestablished and *a priori* procedure for creating an image, composing the narration and producing the narrative. Imamura's techniques resist codification. Of course, that is not to say the director has no theoretical paradigm. Imamura's films are a cinema of disruptive forces: image, narration, and narrative are an assemblage of spontaneous, diverse, and anarchic drives.

Disruptive cinematics ungrounds the frame, the shot, montage, and even sound and color; and in *Why Not?* Imamura employs such disruption from the very beginning of the film. For instance, the opening sequence begins with a series of images capturing the bawdy wonders of a carnival before venturing out into the dangerous and tumultuous streets of East Ryogoku to then capture a bizarre event on the vast bridge that spans the river separating the show district from downtown Edo. This sequence is thus divided into three differential passages: the first a staccato serialism in static framing; the second a snaking long take with a mobile camera; the third a succession of shots along a linear trajectory.

The first passage of the film sees Imamura frame a series of tableaux vivant: a wrestling match, a snake eater, a long-necked woman, an eye-popping man, and a fire-eater. We pass from tent to tent, from scene to scene, each moment an event in itself. An old man in a *mawashi* (loincloth) and a heavy bare-breasted woman wrestle while a demon dances around them and a hawker cajoles the drunken audience. Imamura shoots the spectacle with a static camera from a high angle, the people filling the frame and surrounding a rough *dohyō* (circle for sumo matches) marked in the dirt. There is erratic movement everywhere: the wrestlers moving clockwise, the demon counterclockwise, the hawker confronting the spectators, these people (some sitting, some standing) a mass of disparate bodies. There is a cacophony of sound— the grunting of wrestlers, the laughing of the demon, the shouting of the showman, and the jeering of the crowd. Imamura throws us into this scene with a brutal cut from a sustained moment of pre-filmic silence on a blackened screen. And before we can even begin to take in this tableau, Imamura cuts from the colorful exterior to a dark enclosed interior, as a woman in front of a black curtain slashes the head from a snake, then sucks upon its decapitated form while drinking down its blood. Then on to a woman who is plucking the strings of a biwa; as we watch, her neck extends, and Imamura zooms his camera in upon her head as it shoots upward, out of and away from her body. Then a man holds his breath, his face goes red, and his eyes pop out of his face on long stalks. Then a woman takes a swig of some flammable liquid and breathes fire toward the camera. This series of five static staccato images are immediately and deliberately disorientating.

The second passage—very different from the first—is once again disorientating, but in its own way. Imamura begins in the street: the camera from on high frames a crowded thoroughfare in intense summer daylight, tumble-down wooden buildings tower in upon one another, and the scene is overwhelmed by people moving in every direction and swarming every space. Action occurs on every plane through an active depth of field. Eventually, Imamura will pan the camera. What appears as an unmotivated movement will, however, reveal itself to be a loose framing of a man as he pushes through the people and interacts with various hawkers. Suddenly there is a commotion, a chase through the street. Imamura leaves the man behind to follow the action—the camera now tracking laterally along a side street. A beggar is being pressganged into the Shogunate's army, beaten, slapped, and strangled into acquiescence. Then a group of gangsters moves across this scene, and Imamura tracks the camera back as they talk about having purchased a young woman for their brothel. A pickpocket is pursued through their little coterie, interrupting the conversation, before a throng of onlookers follows in their wake. Imamura pans and tracks the camera this way and that, eventually following in the direction of and overtaking this mass movement, tilting to frame Ryogoku Bridge in portrait framed between the sides of two buildings. Something is happening over there . . .

Once again—as in the first passage—Imamura has created discordant images, this time through the long take, a moving camera, depth of field and an overloaded *mise-en-scène*. The third and final passage of this opening sequence is of more traditional composition—a succession of interrelated shots focused upon a unitary center; nonetheless, Imamura will discover ways to unground the image. For at the center is an animal, a camel, a beast never before seen in Japan and thus the cause of some commotion. As the camel is led from Ryogoku Bridge into the show district by its Arab handlers, Imamura uses a succession of shots with a fixed camera, each panning from right to left to keep the animal in the center of the frame. However, these shots come from deep within the crowd, and the center becomes obscured and lost in the sea of bodies that surround it. This third passage concludes the opening sequence of *Why Not?* and while this sequence serves as an establishing shot (just as in classical cinema or Ozu's emptied spaces), it functions not to orient the viewer but to disorient. And while Ozu would compose the image as a suspension of movement, action, and human presence, Imamura foregrounds and overwhelms the screen with such forces of life.

Disruptive cinematics ungrounds the frame, the shot, montage, sound, and color. Not the representation of spatiotemporal order nor bringing a sublime order to chaos; but presenting anarchy—the assemblage of spontaneous, diverse, and fragmented images. Imamura's films are concerned with fundamental forces, drives, desires—all-pervading and immanent—that lie beneath and engender, that are corralled and dominated to create the seemingly serene surface of Japanese behavior, values, culture, and society. "The omnipresent and general principles of life," as Charles Tesson sees it, embodied through the "swarm of characters" where the "forces come from below (from the lower classes and from the genitals)" (Tesson 1997: 160). And, as Gilles Laprévotte, after Tesson, echoes, "From the people but also from the body, from sex" (Laprévotte 1997: 102). Perhaps Imamura puts it best of all: natural, animal drives. "Animals and humans are similar in the sense that they are born, they excrete, reproduce and die" (Imamura in Laprévotte 1997: 101). "Nevertheless," Imamura continues, "I ask myself what differentiates humans from other animals" (Laprévotte 1997: 101). The director has studied—he tells filmmaker Nakata Toichi—sociology and social anthropology, "which took me a lot further in my understanding of human beings" (Toichi 1997: 116). However, "all scientific approaches" for Imamura "have their limits" (Toichi 1997: 116). "What is a human being?" asks the director, and he responds, "I don't think I have found the answer . . . I look for the answer by continuing to make films" (Laprévotte 1996: 101).

Imamura emerged as director at the beginning of the symbiosis of mainstream and avant-garde cinema during the 1960s known as the Japanese *nūberu bāgu* (New Wave), and his films must be seen in the context of the heady postwar radical, progressive, anarchistic, and revolutionary political scene. Such diverse political coordinates inspired activists, artists, and the young alike. This was a time of riots and confrontations with the state. David Desser writes that "*open* rebellion was a blow against the façade of peacefulness, against the picture of placidity and homogeneity the Japanese like to project" (Desser 1988: 77; emphasis in the original). Exploring humans and the human world through the forces, drives, and desires of bodies becomes—for Imamura—not simply a way of disrupting the coordinates of traditional cinematic practices, but expressing the irrational forces that motivate life. Imamura's irrational—according to Allan Casebier—should not be understood in the negative, as a "pejorative" term, but in a "positive way," as "intuition, instinct, emotional response, where life itself . . . is ultimately mysterious and incapable of explanation by any mode of rational activity" (Casebier 1997: 90). "You may think all that is real," Imamura says to Audie Bock, surveying a Japanese cityscape, "but to me it's all illusion"; rather, "the reality is . . . the irrationality that pervade[s] the Japanese consciousness under the veneer" of the permanence of order and cosmos (Kim 2003). Imamura's disruptive cinematics discovers vital, anarchic forces. And in *Why Not?* Imamura will bring his disruptive cinematics to historiography: to the image, narration, and narrative of history.

The past is composed of an infinity of heterogeneous forces that are made to cohere as history, as homogenous anthropocentric space-time. "Historical knowledge streams in unceasingly from inexhaustible wells, the strange and incoherent forces its way forward" writes Nietzsche; and such forces "are in conflict with one another and it seems necessary to constrain and control them if one is not oneself to perish in their conflict" (Nietzsche 2006: 78). Nietzsche's analysis of history—writes Gilles Deleuze in *The Movement-Image* (1983)—"seems to us still valid today and applies in particular to a whole category of historical films" (Deleuze 2002: 237n10). Classical historiography—just like classical cinematic continuity—attempts to render the image, narration, and narrative of the past in the present and for the future as a continuum, cohering geographical space, and capturing up unified and unifying subjectivities. Imamura responds to such an idea of history with *Why Not?*

In the Wake of the Black Ships

Black ships on the horizon, framed between sea and sky. Masts with sails lashed down, at anchor upon the calm dawn waters. A longboat ploughs its way toward the shoreline, straining at the oars half a dozen or so American sailors. Waiting on the beach there is a contingent of Japanese officials, dressed in the robes of the Tokugawa elite. Before the boat hits land, one of the passengers leaps into the surf. This Japanese man, wearing a similar uniform to the American sailors, splashes clumsily through the shallow waters and throws himself to the ground. He crawls and rolls in the sand as if overwhelmed by an instinctual need to bury himself in the earth of the land that has long been lost to him. The captain of the American ship steps with poise from the now beached longboat and approaches the officials—who are doing their best to ignore the antics of their countryman. Greetings are exchanged, a polite address to the Japanese officials who bow in response. The captain explains: this man is Genji, a Japanese sailor lost at sea some five years previous, rescued by the Americans, taken to the USA in their homeward-bound vessel, and who signed on as crew in order to make the journey home. After the Americans leave, Genji is immediately arrested and thrown into jail. So begins *Why Not?*

This opening scene refers to the crisis of the *kurofune*, the beginning of the end of feudal Japan. As Marius B. Jansen puts it in his rightly renowned *The Making of Modern Japan* (2000): "It was the crisis of the foreign presence that provided the explosives for the bakufu's demise" (Jansen 2002: 332). On July 2, 1853, four black ships—the *kurofune*—appeared in Japan over the horizon, anchoring in Edo Bay. The American ships were under the command of Commodore Matthew Perry, and were so named by the Japanese in part due to previous encounters with Western vessels. In 1543 the Portuguese had arrived in carracks with hulls painted black with pitch, a first contact that led to the extension of European and Asian trade routes. The term *kurofune* thus came to refer to all European vessels, a reference reinforced by the later coal-fired steam engines from which black smoke billowed.

The arrival of the American ships under the command of Perry at the capital was immediately seen as it was meant: as provocation and threat. In the seventeenth century the Tokugawa Shogunate had implemented *sakoku*—the locked state, a policy of isolationism. When the Portuguese first began to trade with the Japanese, Catholic missionaries had tagged along for the ride, and within a few decades Christianity began to take root in the southern islands and lands. However, a local rebellion in 1637–1638 near Nagasaki, during the early days of the Tokugawa Shogunate, was blamed on the spread of Christianity that had first been ruled against in 1587 (Jansen 2002: 75–77). Such rulings eventually fed into the five principle decrees that underpinned *sakoku* (1633–1639). Jansen summarizes: "The first . . . forbade the sending of Japanese ships overseas . . . decreed death for Japanese who, having been overseas, returned . . . ordered the reporting, and offered rewards for identification of *kirishitan*" (Jansen 2002: 78). The subsequent decrees only strengthened such measures and led to the violent expulsion of proselytizing Catholic European nations and ambivalence toward the more ambivalent Protestant European countries. Within a short time, only a small outpost belonging to the Dutch remained (more from habit than profit), restricted to Dejima Island at Nagasaki. Fast-forward 200 years: the Americans arrive with four vessels filled with a thousand men and mounted with over sixty cannons. Perry sends a message to Edo outlining America's demands (at this point simply the right to use Japan for safe harbor and the replenishment of ships, although during negotiations trade will enter the dialogue). The letter is accompanied with a clutch of white flags. Refusal "would bring upon a war that Japan would most assuredly lose, and in that case the white flags of surrender would be useful" (in Jansen 2002: 277). A treaty was—eventually—signed (the following year). It was this event of the *kurofune* that brought to an end to *sakoku*. However, two centuries of isolation meant that the *sakoku* feeling continued to permeate society long after official decrees were superseded by events.

In *Why Not?* accordingly, when Genji returns to Japan after his sojourn with the Americans he is treated with suspicion and jailed. This sequence subtly captures the spatiotemporal and sensorimotor coordinates of the period which the film will explore. At the surface of the actual image: the *mise-en-scène* of the Japanese seascape, shoreline, and ocean with the American ships and longboat, the ceremonial dress worn by the various characters, the tone of the dialogue between the captain and the officials. Yet the image is also an allusive rendering of the past as history: the black ship on the horizon, the meeting of the Americans and the Japanese, the imprisoned sailor. In the dark, uterine cell in which he finds himself, Genji tells a fellow prisoner that the bureaucrats suppose he is now a Christian. Imamura's actual images at the beginning of the film thus beautifully capture and express this moment of the Japanese crisis: the portent of the black ships, the opening of Japan, the deep retention of the *sakoku* feeling. The heart of this problem concerned the treaty that had been negotiated with the Americans. Acquiescence was seen as inevitable, a pragmatic reaction by the Shogunate *bakufu* at Edo. The secluded and idealistic emperor's court at Kyoto, however, saw the signing of the treaty as the ultimate betrayal of Japan. Over the next fifteen years the peaceful state imploded and entered into an ongoing and escalating crisis.

It is into this crisis that Imamura throws Genji in *Why Not?* Escaping from his Yokohama prison, the returnee sets out for Kawanishi Village in Joshu. It is revealed, in this way, that Genji has returned to Japan to find Ine, his wife. Upon reaching home, however, he discovers she was long ago sold into prostitution by her family to the gang boss of East Ryogoku. So Genji travels to Edo. Ine, meanwhile, has worked out her contract and is enjoying her life in the big city, now famous among the show-folk of the enclave as having found a niche with a ribald spectacle named "tickling the goddess." The wife is as pleased to see her long-lost and presumed-dead husband as he is her; and they share stories—over sake and sex—with Genji telling of the United States, where farmers can make a good living without feudal domination, and where the country has now freed the slaves. Asking his wife to go to America with him and awaiting her decision, Genji is left to explore Edo, now riven by the conflict between *bakufu* and court—the creation of the Shogunate army with infantry and rifles replacing samurai and swords; the machinations of Chōshū and Satsuma agents in a not-so-secret alliance with the emperor at Kyoto. It is in this way that Imamura captures and releases the Japanese past through the images, narration, and narrative of *Why Not?* The film appears grounded upon the dual center and founding duel between court and *bakufu* as historiography.

History is a capturing of the past, of what has passed. In this way, the past when captured will always be released as history. The essential question is thus never "What is history?"—the answer to which is simple. Rather, it is a question of praxis. Or such is Nietzsche's contention in "On the Uses and Abuses of History for Life." Nietzsche isolates what he sees as three modes of such praxis: antiquarian history, monumental history, and critical history. Antiquarian history sustains cultural traditions; monumental history explicates great events; and critical history appraises past values. These three types of history interweave, cohere time, space, and humanity to allow an image of the past in the present for future; of territories, states, and cultural values; of the affects, acts, and thoughts of the people and their figureheads. This is universal history: chronological time across comprehensive space for coherent subjectivities.

In the first place, universal history concerns temporality: the antiquarian, the monumental, and the critical are three ways of capturing the past in the present for the future; and each approach is marked by the ascendancy of what we might name pastness, presentness, or futureness. Antiquarian history foregrounds pastness. The present is the present due to the saturation of past traditions, behaviors, landscapes, architecture, cuisine, drink, dress, customs—specific species of archival affects. The past is in the blood, of the body, felt in every breath, in the air that is breathed. Nietzsche writes "by tending with care to that which has existed from of old," the antiquarian "wants to preserve for those who shall come into existence after him the conditions under which he himself came into existence" (2006: 72–73).

Monumental history foregrounds presentness. It empowers the human to escape the mundane, trivial, habitual reality of the present in the present. The deeds of the great of the past are exemplars. The reward is a place in the future pantheon of heroes, a place where the act in the present can one day inspire others who come after. This is history as struggle. Struggle against, as Nietzsche puts it, the "apathetic," the world resistant to change where "everything else that lives cries No" (2006: 68). Again and again, glorious bodies will arise and triumph, or die trying. Critical history foregrounds futureness. It sanctions the past in the present for the future. The past—every past, immediate or remote—is brutal, horrific, barbaric. Nietzsche writes that critical history has the aim and purpose of bringing the past "before a tribunal, scrupulously examining it and finally condemning it" (2006: 76). Critical history is an analytic; it performs an autopsy on the corpse of the past. The traditions and actions of the past are accentuated, brought into relief, highlighted, and used to attack a culture, its values and behaviors, its beliefs. The present is thus the stage upon which critical reflection takes place and where the conditions are created for a more vital future.

In the second place, universal history concerns spatiality: antiquarian, monumental, and critical history are three ways of capturing space—"This is a universal law: a living thing can be healthy, strong and fruitful only when bounded by a horizon" (2006: 63). This horizon has three features: a space becomes geography (lands of the tribe, the nation, the people); a space coheres upon a center (the state, the capital, the figurehead); a space refines its spirit (the essence of the tribe, the nation, the people embodied in an earthly center that is a representation of an ideal). It is only through the coherence of these three aspects of space that history does not disperse. The territory expands over distance; the center gives the territory depth; and the spirit binds territory and center through intensity. Antiquarian history captures the territory through race and its artifacts. Monumental history sustains the center through a continual renewal. Critical history coheres the actual territory and its center with respect to the always pure (and thus always unobtainable, but always utopian) idea.

In the third place, universal history concerns humanity, people, consciousness organized through the sensorimotor trajectory: affect → action → thought. Antiquarian history captures up the affects of the past; it is a feeling, a belonging, a homeliness. Monumental history inspires actions that renew the nation. Critical history reflects upon the affects and actions of the past. "Only through the power of employing the past for the purposes of life and of again introducing into history that which has been done and gone," writes

Nietzsche, "did man become man" (2006: 64). History creates and sustains the coherent subject.

The crucial point is this: the past is composed of diverse heterogeneous forces that cohere in history as homogenous anthropocentric space-time. The name of universal history names the taming of the raging past. And the more the past rages, the more necessary the need for it to be tamed. Our recounting of the Japanese past as a conflict between Shogunate and court can thus be seen as just such a marshaling of antiquarian, monumental, and critical functions composing universal history. We have had the constitution of a chronological timeline (albeit with—nondisruptive—flashbacks and flash-forwards) emerging from prehistory to the modern period. Antiquarian history privileges traditions and is enshrined in *sakoku*, while monumental history divides into the ongoing duel between court and *bakufu*, emperor and shogun; and each in turn will employ a critical history upon the other to foreground their own ideas on the future of Japan. This history similarly describes the coalescence of the space of Japan, the lands becoming organized and the control of a center at Edo, with the court in Kyoto as spiritual ideal, while the affects of the Japanese past sustain the present, the actions of great figureheads and reflections upon the political forces that determine the very nature of the Japanese project for the future.

Yet in *Why Not?* Imamura immediately problematizes such historiographic praxis. While the confrontation between the Shogunate *bakufu* and the Chōshū and Satsuma rebellion permeates the atmosphere of the film, inspiring the *mise-en-scène* through which the characters move, Imamura is not concerned with a cinematic description of the past in order to resolve the crisis. Genji—awaiting Ine's decision—becomes acquainted with the East Ryogoku gang boss, Kinzo. Seen as being useful due to his knowledge of the Americans and his ability to speak English, the returnee is put on Kinzo's payroll. Kinzo is being handsomely paid and promised a great future for ongoing political interventions. On the one hand, the gang members have been ordered by representatives of the Shogunate to quell unrest on the streets; on the other hand, agents from Chōshū and Satsuma want the gangs to foment dissent amongst the peasants. Kinzo takes money from both sides: "Who cares!" He orders his crew to agitate and ferment uprisings but at the same time keep the rioters from doing any real damage. Kinzo's gangsters are confused: "But that's the opposite!" Kinzo is nonchalant: "So what?" *So what?—Who cares!* Such would appear to be Imamura's response to the given coordinates that inspire a universal history of Japan. *Why Not?* refuses to foreground the functions of antiquarian, monumental, and critical historiography to explicate the crisis in order to describe its resolution. There is little nostalgia for the past, there are no heroes to save the nation, and the people do not even need saving. The historicist dimensions of the film rather seem to be the ground for an ungrounding. In this way Imamura will explode the narration: through Genji and Ine we encounter not only Kinzo, but Itoman and Furukawa: the former a fisherman from the southern islands bent upon revenge against the Chōshū and Satsuma armies that have ravaged his homeland and killed his family, the latter a now masterless and disgraced samurai become ronin. We encounter the madam and aging prostitute Oko, and Omatsu, a young woman sold into prostitution (continually) by her peasant family. Imamura takes these characters—and many others—and disperses them across Japan: to Kyoto, to Yokahama, to Joshu. *Why Not?* is composed of forking pathways; it is a maze, a carnival funhouse of distorted mirrors, a labyrinth.

Such an ungrounding—for Nietzsche—is necessary to avoid the harms of universal history, one harm corresponding to each of the functions. The harm of antiquarian history: the encircling of the past is restrictive, it will sustain but a mere portion of the past, and does so with only retroactive understanding. It will also overvalue one set of artifacts at the expense of others. In this way "the historical sense no longer conserves life but mummifies it . . . Man is encased in the stench of must and mould . . . it knows only how to *preserve* life, not how to engender it . . . it always undervalues that which is becoming" (2006: 74, 75; emphasis in the original). The harm of monumental history: the patterns of the past have all differences annulled and are seen as dialectical repetitions of the same. "How much of the past would have to be overlooked," comments Nietzsche, "how violently what is individual in it would have to be forced into a universal mould and all its sharp corners and hard outlines broken up in the interest of conformity!" (2006: 69). Monumental history is deceptive; it requires analogies and can have horrific outcomes: "With seductive similarities it inspires the courageous to foolhardiness and the inspired to fanaticism" (2006: 71). The harms of critical history: we—from our lofty standpoint in the present—see the whole of the past as horror. Every past, writes Nietzsche, "is worthy to be condemned,—for that is the nature of human things: human violence and weakness have always played a mighty role in them. It is not justice which here sits in judgement . . . it is life alone, that dark, driving power" (2006: 76). Ressentiment, revenge, the belief that we are somehow more moral, more refined, more worthy of life—in the now.

Accordingly, the use of universal history reveals the abuse of antiquarian, monumental, and critical functions. Nietzsche's solution is the unhistorical. As Craig Lundy asks and responds, "How is one to escape the suffocating power and attraction of history and historical knowledge? Nietzsche offers two antidotes" (Lundy 2009: 192). These are the two moments of the unhistorical, the untimely. First, history emerges out of the night, out of the fog of our animality. Nietzsche asks us to consider the cattle in the field and how simple their lives appear to us, how we can become jealous of not having to drag the past after us like trailing distended, expelled, and rotten innards. The animal is the master of forgetting, and it is forgetting we need to master within ourselves. This is seen by Nietzsche "as being more vital and more fundamental, inasmuch as it constitutes the foundation upon which alone anything sound, healthy and great, anything truly human, can grow" (2006: 63). Forgetting (the ahistorical) must, however, be augmented by the suprahistorical (2006:65). Nietzsche writes: "We may use the word 'suprahistorical' because the viewer from this vantage point . . . would have recognized the essential condition of all happenings—this blindness and injustice in the soul of him who acts" (2006: 65). The past is all accident, contingency, serendipity, chance. Humans do not make history—history is what happens to humans. As John Gray writes of Nietzsche's position: "If you believe that humans are animals, there can be no such thing as the history of humanity"; accordingly, "Looking for meaning in history is like looking for patterns in clouds" (Gray 2003: 48). All historiography is founded upon the ahistorical (the animal)— the forgetting of aspects of the past. Universal history, however, effaces this forgetting in order to create chronological time across comprehensive space for coherent subjectivities. The suprahistorical—in distinction—actively uses and abuses history. It resists the linearity of chorological time, the creation of comprehensive space and the determinations of coherent subjectivities. The suprahistorical is disruptive of history.

Nietzsche's suprahistorical is an antidote to historiography, the historian as convalescent "cured for ever of taking history too seriously" (2006: 65). *Cured for ever of taking history too seriously*—surely here we discover as essential feature of Imamura's *Why Not?*—the endeavour being to create discordant images, compose a disjunctive narration, and produce a dissonant narrative. *Why Not?* does not aim to represent the past through history, but rather expresses an encounter with the problem of history, the discords, disjunctions, and dissonances that the praxis of universal history would tame and annul. Which returns us—finally—to the disruptive event of the *eijanaika* procession.

Eijanaika!

"No scene in Imamura's work," writes Nelson Kim, "better sums up his vision of the amoral, apolitical, anarchic life-force that pulses beneath the seeming stability of the social order" (Kim 2003). The moment of the *eijanaika* procession—for some writers—is thus both exemplary and a consummation of Imamura's cinematic oeuvre. "The explosion of *Eijanaika*," according to Dave Kehr, "is the culmination of 20 years' consideration of one idea" (Kehr 1997: 85). For Gilles Laprévotte, the concluding scenes of *Why Not?*—with the "crowd teeming with life and vital energy"—"could be a summary of Shohei Imamura's cinema" (Laprévotte 1997: 101). The showgirls dance in hybrid kimono/can-can costumes, singing: "Life is so uncertain these days / Will Tokugawa win? / Satsuma and Chōshū? / We can't tell / But who cares? / Both want to reform the world / Why not?" *Eijanaika*! Ine and Genji—showgirl and traveler—are captured up and subsumed in the carnivalesque procession that coalesces from the streets, brothels, markets, and entertainments of East Ryogoku. The people—the dispossessed, the enslaved, the poor, the uneducated—have arisen. Joyous and celebratory anarchy reigns. The conflict of court and *bakufu* no longer describes the situation. A spontaneous insurgency of the people ungrounds the coordinates of the state.

Eijanaika carnivals occurred in Japan during the year of 1867, arising all over the main island of the country. However, as Thomas Keirstead and Deidre Lynch attest, "The people danced, authorities by and large paid them no heed, things returned to normal" (Keirstead and Lynch 1995: 65–66). In his *Making of Modern Japan*, Jansen mentions the "*ee ja nai ka* movement" just once and only in passing (Jansen 2002: 302). However, this moment references a passing discussion on "'world renewal' (*yonaoshi*), vaguely millenarian, movements [that] swept major urban areas" during "the last few decades of Tokugawa rule" (Jansen 2002: 236). "On such occasions," continues Jansen, "rumours flew that divine signs had been seen to fall mysteriously [from the sky] . . . This would spark rejoicing, dancing, and celebration"; however, such amulets in reality came "from the homes of the wealthy . . . [who] found it prudent to share their goods, particularly drink, with the throng: the resultant enthusiasm could sweep an entire region" (Jansen 2002: 236). In *Why Not?* this idea of world renewal similarly arises when such amulets first appear. "What's wrong with scattering charms? Why not!" laughs one of Kinzo's gangsters: "some come from gods; some come from men." On a stage in a tent in East Ryogoku, Ine and her showgirls dance, more amulets fall, the carnivalesque procession begins. "One looks in vain for truly 'revolutionary' purpose" in such movements, comments Jansen; "their net total was as often ludicrous and carnival" (Jansen 2002: 236). Yet, despite this, the *eijanaika* movement reveals a whole hidden history of spontaneous protest (*ikki*). "A great deal of writing about Japan emphasizes a 'consensus' model that would lead one to anticipate a smoothly functioning social organism," comments Jansen, but "the facts do not bear this out" (Jansen 2002: 232). Drawing upon studies by Aoki Kōji and James White, Jansen briefly explores 7,331 "instances of social conflict and political protest" between 1590 and 1877 appearing through "waves of *ikki*" (Jansen 2002: 236). These waves of *ikki* are spontaneous uprisings by the people. Yet while Jansen mentions *ikki*, *yonaoshi*, and *eijanaika* events, he does so only in parentheses. For Imamura, if universal history effaces the people, his cinema and *Why Not?* must allow the people to arise. For Keirstead and Lynch, such a move accordingly "refuses history its accustomed role"; *Why Not?* is a "critique of the practice of history" (Keirstead and Lynch 1995: 66). "In *Eijanaika*," Imamura tells Donald Richie, "I was really making a 'documentary' period film. I am more like [a] historian (Imamura in Richie 2007: 41). And in an essay Imamura writes: "I have a preference for shooting true things" (Imamura 1997b: 131). Yet as Kehr observes, "Though *Eijanaika* is based on [a] historical incident, Imamura doesn't have much interest in historical detail . . . he even flaunts his indifference." The film is "full of unsettling anachronisms" (Kehr 2007: 82). Such paradoxes are a sign, for Casebier, of Imamura's "blurring of the distinction between fiction and reality" (Casebier 1997: 91). Imamura creates a suprahistorical cinema, the truth of cinematic art. Rather than the story of the Tokugawa Shogunate and the emperor's court, Imamura is after something else. "My greatest obsession was individual freedom—the condition that the state had denied us absolutely" (Nakata 1997: 111). Imamura allows the people to arise. In a restaurant across the river the Satsuma and Chōshū infiltrators become concerned by the *eijanaika* insurgency: "We are the ones to crush the Shogunate! Not commoners!" The Tokugawa Shogunate will—however—massacre the people. The coordinates of court and *bakufu* will reassert themselves.

Yet Imamura has one more ungrounding in *Why Not?*—there will be no explication of how the situation between Shogunate and emperor was resolved. *But who cares?* The final image of the film is of Ine; she has returned to the scene of the carnage that brought an end to the *eijanaika* procession and where Genji was shot and killed. Echoing the opening scene of *Why Not?*, Imamura has Ine throw herself to the ground. She crawls and rolls in the dirt overwhelmed by a need to commune with the earth and Genji's blood. *I won't stop*, she whispers into the wind, *I won't give up* . . .

Works Cited

Casebier, Allan (1997). "Images of Irrationality in Modern Japan: The Films of Shohei Imamura." In *Shohei Imamura*, ed. James Quandt, 89–100. Toronto: Toronto International Film Festival Group.

Deamer, David (2018). "Look? Optical / Sound Situations and Interpretation: Ozu—(Deleuze)—Kiarostami." In *Reorienting Ozu: A Master and His Influence*, ed. Jinhee Choi, 249–68. New York: Oxford University Press.

Deleuze, Gilles (2002). *Cinema I: The Movement-Image*. Trans. Hugh Tomlinson and Barbara Habberjam. London: The Athlone Press.

Desser, David (1988). *Eros plus Massacre: An Introduction to the Japanese New Wave Cinema*. Bloomington: Indiana University Press.

Henderson, Brian (2004). "Toward a Non-Bourgeois Camera Style." In *Film Theory and Criticism: Introductory Readings*, 6th ed., ed. Leo Braudy and Marshall Cohen, 54–64. New York: Oxford University Press.

Imamura, Shôhei (1997a). "My Approach to Filmmaking." Trans. S. Erviel and M. Cousins. In *Shohei Imamura*, ed. James Quandt, 125–27. Toronto: Toronto International Film Festival Group.

Imamura, Shôhei (1997b). "Traditions and Influences." Trans. S. Erviel and M. Cousins. In *Shohei Imamura*, ed. James Quandt, 129–31. Toronto: Toronto International Film Festival Group.

Gray, John (2003). *Straw Dogs: Thoughts on Humans and Other Animals*. London: Granta Books.

Jansen, Marius B. (2002). *The Making of Modern Japan*. Cambridge, MA: Belknap Press of Harvard University Press.

Kehr, Dave (1997). "The Last Rising Sun." In *Shohei Imamura*, ed. James Quandt, 69–88. Toronto: Toronto International Film Festival Group.

Keirstead, Thomas, and Deidre Lynch (1995). "*Eijanaika*: Japanese Modernization and the Carnival of Time." In *Revisioning History: Film and the Construction of a New Past*, ed. Robert A. Rosenstone, 64–76. Princeton, NJ: Princeton University Press.

Kim, Nelson (2003). "Shohei Imamura." *Senses of Cinema*, July 27, http://sensesofcinema.com/2003/great-directors/imamura/. Accessed August 12, 2018.

Laprévotte, Gilles (1997). "Shohei Imamura: Human, All Too Human." Trans. L. Fitzgerald. In *Shohei Imamura*, ed. James Quandt, 101–6. Toronto: Toronto International Film Festival Group.

Lundy, Craig (2009). "Deleuze's Untimely: Uses and Abuses in the Appropriation of Nietzsche." In *Deleuze and History*, ed. Jeffrey A. Bell and Claire Colebrook, 188–205. Edinburgh: Edinburgh University Press.

Nagib, Lucia (2006). "Towards a Positive Definition of Word Cinema." In *Remapping World Cinema: Identity Culture and Politics in Film*, ed. Stephanie Dennison and Song Hwee Lim, 30–37. London: Wallflower Press.

Nakata, Toichi (1997). "Shohei Imamura: Interviewed by Toichi Nakata." In *Shohei Imamura*, ed. James Quandt, 107–24. Toronto: Toronto International Film Festival Group.

Nietzsche, Friedrich (2006). "On the Uses and Disadvantages of History for Life." In *Untimely Meditations*, ed. D. Breazeale, trans. R. J. Hollingdale, 107–24. Cambridge: Cambridge University Press, 57–124.

Parkes, Graham (2008). "Introduction." In *Thus Spoke Zarathustra* by Friedrich Nietzsche, ix–xxxiv. Trans. Graham Parkes. New York: Oxford University Press.

Richie, Donald (1997). "Notes for a Study on Shohei Imamura." In *Shohei Imamura*, ed. James Quandt, 7–44. Toronto: Toronto International Film Festival Group.

Tesson, Charles (1997). "*The Ballad of Narayama*: Pigs and Gods." In *Shohei Imamura*, ed. James Quandt, 159–64. Toronto: Toronto International Film Festival Group.

Chapter 17

Kuroi Ame: An Anthropology of Suffering

Dolores P. Martinez

> Throughout his films—from the assassination in *Vengeance Is mine* to the atomic bomb in *Black Rain*—a predator is at the heart of the story and nothing ever saves its victims. The weak die, beautiful under the camera's unfeeling gaze. (de Baeque 1997: 156)

Shohei Imamura as an Anthropologist

In an interview with Toichi Nakata, Shohei Imamura described his study of anthropology, an inquiry he pursued from the age of thirty through library research:

> I first tried to gain a sociological perspective and set out to analyse "reality" through social structures. It didn't take me long to realize that this was very limiting and so I turned my attention to social anthropology, which took me a lot further in my understanding of human beings. (1997: 115)

Social anthropologists tend to look down on library study, preferring fieldwork as the marker of good ethnography, and Imamura had that as well. Working in the postwar black market, Imamura had come to know the sort of people about whom he was most passionately interested in making films (1997: 111); thus he had a body of good empirical data to draw on when writing and directing. By anthropological standards, he had been through the fieldwork experience, or the important initiation period, necessary to earn the title of anthropologist. Interestingly, it is his "documentary" filming style that has brought his anthropological interest to the attention of critics, and this is the method that comes to the fore in *Kuroi Ame* (*Black Rain*), his film about the aftermath of the atomic bomb dropped on Hiroshima, which can be read as documenting how postwar Japanese communities treated the *hibakusha* (atomic bomb survivors).

Kuroi Ame is also considered an outlier film in Imamura's career. The reasons are various: in the late 1980s he could only recreate the scenes of chaos from August 6, 1945;[1] the screenplay he co-wrote with Toshirō Ishidō was based on the much-loved and lauded novel *Kuroi Ame* (1966) by Masuji Ibuse; and rather than being about the Japanese underclasses that Imamura found so compelling, it is the story of a rather elite household (the Shizuma) that is trying to find a husband for their niece Yasuko, a young woman who has been exposed to the black rain that fell in the aftermath of the bomb's explosion. Audie Bock sums up the general view of this film, whose heroine differs from the women that generally populated Imamura's work, as "a glaring exception to the ribald rule of Imamura's chaotic style . . . Uncharacteristically, this is a story in which tears may flow" (1997: 153).

In depicting the family's struggles with radiation sickness five years after the end of the Second World War, Imamura has also been critiqued for making a film in which the main characters are portrayed not as survivors but as victims (see for example Cavanaugh 2001; Todeschini 1996). Implicitly the criticism is that Imamura was being a historical revisionist for portraying atomic bomb survivors as victims.[2] The portrayal of Japanese postwar suffering, then, is seen to cast the US as the villain, when the dominant historical assessment is that the Allies were fighting a just war. The colonial excesses of the Japanese, the Rape of Nanking, the chemical experiments, the forced use of women as sex workers for the Japanese troops, and the abuse of prisoners of war (Japan had not signed on to the Geneva Convention) cannot be denied; nor are the Japanese Right's attempts to soften or rewrite that history acceptable.[3] Yet I disagree with the view that Imamura is trying to depict the Japanese as victims of the Allies in *Kuroi Ame*, nor do I wholly agree with Robert Feleppa (2004) that this film is a humanist effort, attempting to remind us all what it would mean to become a victim of war and atomic weaponry.[4]

In this chapter I argue three things. First, while Imamura's films often celebrated earthy, ribald Japaneseness, we also need to remember that much of his work features Japanese women as heroic in the harsh conditions of a postwar Japan in which the US presence is often subtly critiqued. Donald Richie notes that Imamura wanted to avoid stories about the suffering and pathos usually found in women's films (1997: 14) and preferred to portray women as wily manipulators and survivors. Second, it is important to keep in mind that "Imamura's world . . . is characterized by power, and by economic, political, and sexual difference" (Desser 1988: 123). If Imamura had a position on World War

II, it seems to be that all abuses of power are wrong (see Dorsey and Matsuoka 1996: 219).

Third, while it may seem odd that he made a film in which the heroine seems to share few qualities with the women of his earlier films, I will argue that *Kuroi Ame* is subversive in its portrayal of Yasuko and her fate. Imamura is not trying to make her an A-bomb survivor whom we must pity, but rather to depict, without too much sentimentality, the travails of a woman who is nothing like his preferred healthy, robust, and sexually active heroines. That she is a *hibakusha* is almost inconsequential, although, true to Imamura's anthropological bent, the depiction of her illness is fairly realistic. To make these points, it is necessary first to discuss what an anthropology of suffering is.

> After the nuclear event of Hiroshima and Nagasaki, the *hibakusha* who survived experienced something beyond comprehension... No one understood, at first, what the symptoms were symptoms of. (Deamer 2014: 136–37)

> [An] anthropology that is concerned with breakdown and repair. (Davis 1992: 149)

The anthropology of suffering is not an anthropology concerned just with the culturally different ways in which people suffer—although this is how the concept came to be taken up in the sub-discipline of medical anthropology. As John Davis outlined in the article that set the parameters for the topic, it is research into how people deal with the trauma of lived experience, or what Davis terms "the normality of pain" (1992: 150) as well as with cases of exceptional catastrophe. The fact that pain or trauma is a part of human existence challenges a "comfortable sort of anthropology" (1992: 150), which has tended to ignore both how cataclysmic events can become recurrent conditions (drought, famine, migration) and how the breakdown of normal social experience that takes place during war becomes embedded in social memory for generations afterward. Both types of suffering are "continuous with ordinary social experience; people place it in social memory and incorporate it with their accumulated culture" (1992: 152). David Deamer also follows this line, albeit through the work of Gilles Deleuze, in his overview of postwar Japanese cinema:

> Traces of the atom bomb imagery appear in Japanese film as symptoms and figures. These could be said to be cinematic symptoms: films which, while not depicting the *pika* or the *hibakusha*, appear permeated with the nuclear legacy... It is if the nuclear event is haunting Japanese screen-images and the cinematic horizons of Japanese history. (2014: 121)

Whilst sharing Davis's idea that catastrophic events become embedded in a society's subconsciousness, Deamer acknowledges the fact that having been defeated in the war, the Japanese memory and representation of the atomic bomb has had to kowtow "to political suppression and mass psychological repression" (2014: 1). Using Gilles Deleuze to discuss the historicity of film in general and thus seeing all Japanese films of the second half of the twentieth century as postwar, Deamer is less interested in the trauma and suffering of the immediate postwar era than he is in the atomic event itself.

For Imamura, contrastingly, it was the occupation years (1945–1952) that fascinated him. He lived through that era as a young man and, as already mentioned, it was a time when he threw off his upper-class background to make a living in the black market, mixing with Japan's underworld of gangsters, pimps, sex workers, and bar hostesses. It was during this time that Imamura met people whom he believed embody the real Japan: working-class characters he admired because, as Richie argues, they remained "untouched by the rationalizations, hypocrisy and face-saving which so characterize(d) their betters . . . It [was] the determination, the will, and the honesty" that he appreciated (Richie 1997: 18).

Briefly put, it was an era that could be seen as one of breakdown and repair for the Japanese, a time of trauma and suffering, but for those reasons it was a particularly vibrant period as well. As a sort of documenting anthropologist, Imamura saw the response to those circumstances as particularly Japanese. The upper classes dealt with it through various rationalizations and accommodations, the lower classes by fighting and scheming their way to a more secure footing in life. Specifically, as Richie noted, it is Imamura's working-class women who often win the "game" of life although it is dominated by men; they not only often fight to achieve their own goals, but often they survive and prosper (1997: 15). Thus, in his pre-*Kuroi Ame* postwar films—*Buta to Gunkan* (*Pigs and Battleships*, 1961), *Nippon konchūki* (*The Insect Woman*, 1963), as well as the documentaries *Nippon Sengoshi: Madamu Onboro no Seikatsu* (*The History of Postwar Japan as Told by a Bar Hostess*, 1970) and *Karayuki-san* (*The Making of a Prostitute*, 1975)—the female protagonists may not always engage our sympathies, but they are vital and able to adapt to all vicissitudes of life, including the general corruption wrought by modern capitalism and the presence of the US military (see Tessier 1997).

Imamura's work speaks to how suffering is managed, contained, overcome, and even embodied in postwar Japan. The latter point is crucial to remember because much of this trauma had to be repressed. What does this mean? I am not positing that the Japanese be seen as the injured party because they were bombed and had lost the war. The trauma of World War II for the Japanese is much more complex and can be objectively understood as being constituted of various parts: it grew out of the war effort itself that took the lives of many and led to harsh living conditions even for those who were not directly fighting. It was an experience that, as all war seems to do (see Shay 1995), returned a surviving population of battle-shocked and war-hardened men to a "normal" society that did not (nor could it) recognize the symptoms of post-traumatic stress disorder (PTSD); and it involved the formulation of new types of knowledge in which all the narratives of the Japanese Empire were overturned. The Japanese were no longer heroes fighting a just war; they were the villains, the losers, and everything they had believed in was overturned by the presence of the occupying forces who brought "true" democracy and new forms of education with them (see Igarashi 2000; Bourdaghs 2005; Frühstück 2007; Seaton 2007; Galan 2008).

A major trauma for postwar Japan, then, was the shock of an apparent rupture with the past. Although Imamura always said that he saw persistent continuities with Japan's earthy premodern past throughout Japanese society, this more recent fissure had to be very carefully represented on screen because, from 1945 to 1952, the occupying forces censored movies and then the studios themselves enacted a sort of censorship based on political correctness throughout the 1950s. In principle, by the 1980s such restrictions were no longer in place, but in practice the example of *Kuroi Ame*'s critical reception, as well as that of Kurosawa's *Yume* (*Dreams*, 1990) and *Hachi-gatsu no Kyōshikyoku* (*Rhapsody in August*, 1991), illustrates how the wider world (or the US) is always quick to pass judgment on any representation that seemed to glorify Japan's imperial past or that demonstrated pity for its postwar citizens. To even appear to argue, as some Japanese revisionist historians do, that the war was the fault of the elites and that ordinary Japanese were just dupes is to be an apologist for the war; while an objective understanding of how dominant ideologies work within *any* nation-state seems impossible when it comes to Japan. Currently, many Japanese of the war era hold to the view that they were misled, and most young Japanese are not entirely sure what the war was about; this situation contrasts with the German case, where guilt has been actively embraced. The Allies' decision to punish only a few obvious war criminals, in contrast to the more active investigations and trials in Germany, paradoxically supports a view that not all Japanese were to blame (see Buruma 1994). Yet to portray *hibakusha* as suffering is to walk a fine line: one in which weapons of mass destruction are bad, but only if used by the "wrong" people. Under such circumstances, the vanquished nation must suppress any of its agony.

However, the repressed, as Robin Wood (2003) put it—following Freud, of course—always returns. While this statement is often understood in terms of individual suffering, Wood's discussion of the return of the repressed in relation to the horror film raises the issue to that of the larger group: the nation. How to represent that which may not only be unrepresentable (because it is embodied, buried within the mind, too horrific to recall) but which also *cannot* be represented (because it is unacceptable to show any fellow feeling toward the sufferers)? This is the problem in Japan's case. It is doubly an issue because as Ann Kaplan and Ban Wang argue, while "trauma consists in the unmaking of the world, the prohibition against representation blocks the way to the re-making of the world" (2008: 310). Deamer sees the Japanese mass media as struggling to overcome this obstruction to the repairing of the social (to use Davis's term) through decades of movies that grapple with the subject matter of the atom bomb, albeit symbolically.

Kuroi Ame is one of the films that Deamer sees as valiantly trying to overcome this obstacle even if somewhat indirectly: "It is a film that decentres the atomic attack both temporally and spatially; allows it to inhabit memories and bodies; allows it to be forgotten and repressed; disperses its meaning back into the Pacific War and forward into the Korean War" (2014: 257). The historian Yoshikuni Igarashi has a term, borrowed from the anthropologist Homi Bhabha, for this process: "re-membering." As he argues:

> The healthy body of the nation was dismembered as imperial Japan experienced a radical transformation, and these dismembered bodily images were assembled again in the postwar period in order to articulate the new statehood. Body parts were metaphorically sutured together to regain the nation's organic unity and to overcome its trauma; yet the suture left on the discursive body's surface served as a constant reminder of the trauma. (Igarashi 2000: 14)

Davis's discussion of the anthropology of suffering posits this as the norm for any (and thus every) postwar state; however, Japan cannot mention/represent the war unless it is to apologize and make reparations.[5] Thus Igarashi sees the Japanese mass media as the locus for indirect expressions of the nation's struggle to externalize this suffering in order, as Kaplan and Wang explain, to "create a less traumatic, less painful environment" constructing the "social imaginary" (2008: 320) that is necessary for a society's renewal and change. Kaplan and Wang differ from Davis by arguing that the devastation being dealt with through these representations is the very shock of modernity; for them "the catastrophic event" is a "symptom of [the] deep-lying contradictions of modernity, and the experience of modernity" is that of "living with shocks and suffering" (2008: 395).

From this perspective, *Kuroi Ame* can be read *not* as an attempt, in 1989, to depict the Japanese as victims, but as a film that endeavours to represent what it means to live through the predicaments of modernity. That there exist particular historical circumstances that we would describe as Japanese (the war, the bomb) obscures an important point about the suffering that trauma brings: at an individual level, as Freud found, much of the experience of trauma depends on the individual's previous suffering at the hands of society's structures of violence. In this case, these structures are not only those of the state—with its monopoly on legitimate force (the police, the judiciary) that is used over, and through (the military), its subjects—but also are the deeper, core or infra-, structures such as patriarchy that underpin modernity's culture. These are the social formations over which Imamura's women so often triumph; and they are the norms by which Yasuko, the heroine in *Kuroi Ame*, seems to be destroyed. To understand this, we need to turn to the film.

> The crucial question . . . is whether a culture is able to understand trauma as an episode in a longer chain of the structural mutations in modern systems that have accumulated a record of violence, suffering, and misery. (Kaplan and Wang 2008: 310)

> The main concern of the family now . . . is marriage. (Treat 1995: 286)

In his discussion of the novel *Black Rain,* John Treat points out that it begins almost as would a book by Jane Austen—the key concern of Shigematsu Shizuma, the family patriarch, is to see his niece Yasuko get married (1995: 286). There are differences between the Japanese novel and an Austen narrative, however. In contrast to the latter's heroines who are often too poor, socially inferior, less than "pretty," and frequently too intelligent to find a rich husband, Yasuko seems to come from a well-off family, she is pretty, and no mention is made of her intelligence or lack of it. She is neither an Austen heroine nor even a Tanizaki one—she is not like the younger Makioka sisters, who are either too refined or too wild to settle down and marry. In fact, as Reiko Tachibana (1998) notes in an insightful article on the film, the novel itself almost immediately leaves behind the problem of Yasuko's marriage to focus on her own, her uncle's, her aunt's, and a doctor's diaries describing the atomic bomb attack on Hiroshima and its aftermath. Tachibana calculates that the novel devotes about 70 percent of its narrative to the diaries and, increasingly, Yasuko fades from the story. She is almost engaged, she is rejected by her suitor's family, she becomes ill and is taken to the hospital—that is all noted. In contrast, Tachibana argues, the film restores the narrative to Yasuko, making her the central character. Or to develop

Treat's line on the novel, it continues in the vein in which it had begun: centering on the problem of arranging a marriage in postwar Japan.

Historically, we know, many a marriage was not made in the postwar era, as it seemed that women outnumbered men, and some were even marrying foreign men instead of Japanese, but more interesting is the era in which the film was made. Much has been made of 1989 as the peak of Japan's economic miracle, the epoch of "a Japan that can say no" (Ishihara 1992), and readings of *Kuroi Ame* that see the film through the lens of a more nationalist 1980s Japan often miss that this was also the period that saw the beginnings of the fall in marriages and births in Japan. Foreign researchers picked this problem up in the 1990s, but as early as 1984 I attended a feminist conference outside of Tokyo in which sociologists were already raising concerns about this trend. Japanese women were marrying later or not at all, and, if they married, they were having fewer than two children on average. *Kekkon kyohi shōkōgun* (marriage refusal syndrome) was already seen as a social issue in Japan—and Imamura, the anthropologist filmmaker, would have been aware of the newspaper articles on the topic at the very least.

The question then is this: If Imamura decided to rewrite large portions of the novel when making his film—adding a grandmother; Yasuko's father and mother (who died giving birth to her); a stepmother; half-siblings; a romance with a war-traumatized soldier, Yuichi; having a meeting between Yasuko and her would-be fiancé, Aono; and two entirely new women: Fumiko's mother, the town floozy, and her illegitimate daughter Fumiko, a nightclub singer—where has his documentary impulse gone? Why fictionalize a novel that was purportedly a realist account of the experiences and lives of *hibakusha*?

In an assessment of the plagiarism controversy that has plagued Ibuse's novel—did he just lift passages straight out of his informants' diaries?—Lin (2011) hints at a possible reason for Imamura's filling out of the narrative: there were copyright issues he did not want to wade into. There is also another possibility to explore, and that is the fact that while this film appears to be, as mentioned above, an outlier movie in Imamura's career, it is perhaps less so than normally imagined. We might see it as Imamura's anti-Ozu film. Imamura famously told Audie Bock about his first film mentor: "I wouldn't just say I wasn't influenced by Ozu... I would say that I didn't want to be influenced by Ozu!" (1990: 289). *Kuroi Ame* appears to be his final word on Ozu.

As if to make the point of how near and yet how far the film is from Ozu's own work, Imamura sets up certain shots in *Kuroi Ame* as Ozu would have done—filming within traditional houses, holding a certain stillness within scenes, and his outdoor countryside scenes are often bathed in sunlight—while also undermining any Ozu reference. Imamura's camera looks down or across to his kneeling actors in interiors; the peaceful countryside is contrasted with the horror and chaos of Hiroshima on August 6 or is interrupted by malicious gossiping women; his editing is more in line with Kurosawa's (whom Imamura admired), so the action in his scenes have a beginning, middle, and end, and so on. *Kuroi Ame* could be an Ozu narrative, he seems to be saying, but it is definitely not.

So if the film is neither a family drama in the style of Ozu's famous postwar films despite a superficial narrative resemblance, nor a documentary about the atomic bomb, what is it about? One answer to this question lies in the fact that Imamura's film confronts issues that Ozu left implicit in his great "Noriko Trilogy": the end of the war and Japan's occupation by the Allies. These are absent presences both in Ozu's trilogy and in *Kuroi Ame*, but the latter film does not need to refer to the war or the occupation in great detail; its very subject matter makes clear that this is the historical background against which the story unfolds. Ozu's indirect hints at the war (why is Noriko a widow in *Tokyo Story*?) seem unimportant compared to his delicate delineation of Japanese refined traditions and continuities. Imamura is also interested, as he himself says, in Japanese continuities, but not in the refined culture of the upper classes. The real Japan, for him, would be found in the characterizations of Fumiko's mother, her daughter, and their lovers. Yet these women seem marginal to his narrative. Or are they?

Let us return to the details that Imamura added to Yasuko's story. The film opens not with her uncle and his concerns about finding Yasuko a husband as in the novel, but with Yasuko herself narrating a section from her diary. On the day the bomb exploded, she was taking various "important" (*daiji-na koto*, subtitled "precious") items to the house in the country. These items include her uncle's good suit, her grandmother's wedding kimono, and more. In short, part of the list sounds like the contents of a wedding trousseau. Moreover, she is taking them to their house in the country—establishing the fact that this is a well-to-do family. Clearly, aged twenty, Yasuko is already being prepared to be married. She is living with her aunt and uncle, it is explained at a later point, to save her from having to work in a munitions factory, implying that she is too well bred for such hard labor. Yet, as Tachibana (1998) notes, and as would be obvious to any Japan expert, there is the issue of the continuity of the family at stake here: her uncle and her aunt Shigeko have no children of their own. In the 1940s, to take a niece into a childless household would be a familiar strategy to any well-off Japanese family—adopt her, find her a good husband, and adopt him as a *yoshi*, a son-in-law who will take on the family name, and together they will inherit the household and family property and be responsible for caring for the family ancestors.

Kuroi Ame: An Anthropology of Suffering 317

Figure 17.1 Yasuko with her aunt and uncle, making their way through Hiroshima.

Yasuko was not in Hiroshima on the day the bomb exploded but was caught in the black rain that was triggered afterward. She then made her away across the city to find her relatives, only to be dragged back across Hiroshima by her uncle to safety. In a nutshell, if the black rain was not radioactive enough to make her ill, two trips across the city alive with radioactivity should have caused enough harm. Clearly her uncle Shigematsu feels guilty about this and spends the movie working hard to keep not just himself and his wife healthy, but also trying to prove that Yasuko is free from radiation sickness. He feels it his duty to find her a husband and there is no discussion that the man need to become a *yoshi*; it is enough that Yasuko marry well. Shigematsu's efforts are constantly being undermined; first the certificate of good health for Yasuko backfires, making the prospective groom's family suspicious; then the rumors spread by their neighbors that Yasuko was in Hiroshima as the bomb came down seem to scupper a possible marriage with Mr. Aono.

The journey across Hiroshima to safety appears in a few key scenes. These are not just germane to the fact that Yasuko might become ill, but also significant as a psychological framework for Yasuko herself: she sees (along with the audience and her aunt and uncle) dreadful things throughout this trip. The scenes are graphic, sometimes Daliesque in their composition, but always grotesque and true to the horrors described in Hiroshima survivors' diaries. Yet no one asks if this has affected Yasuko in any way at all. It is only through the addition of the war traumatised Yuichi,[6] with whom Yasuko "feels comfortable talking about

Figure 17.2 Yasuko and her uncle Shigematsu see the king carp.

the war," do we get a sense that this lovely and placid young woman is traumatized. That there might be a different Yasuko, one more full of life, is hinted at near the film's end when she sees a king carp leap up out of the pond and cheers in a most unlady-like manner.[7] This is a woman with some joie de vivre in her, a different Yasuko from the woman who stiffly pulls away as if miserable at the intimacy when her suitor, Aono, kisses her passionately. This is a Yasuko with the gumption to first declare that she doesn't want to marry and then to accept a proposal from the socially inferior Yuichi. In the first case, Yasuko—like an Ozu heroine—declares that she won't marry so she can care for her aunt, uncle, and grandmother; in the second she seems resigned to marriage, but on her own terms. However, we learn later, she accepts the proposal after she has begun to suspect that she has already become ill from radiation sickness. Does she know she will not live to marry?

This is where I think that Imamura subversively allows Yasuko the sort of autonomy he so admires in his peasant and working-class women: her docility is not merely about refinement but also about trauma. She has been quiet because she is in psychological pain and if being healthy does not reflect her suffering, then she will become ill. In short: Yasuko does not want to marry. Whether it is because what she saw at Hiroshima filled her with despair about the future of humankind; or because her grandmother adds to her reluctance by telling her that if she marries she will die in childbirth as did her mother; or because she finds men uninteresting—she only seems to react to Aono when he trips and falls on a step, otherwise she seems rather distant with him—and frightening (she is certainly scared of Fumiko's gangster friend who mistakenly kisses her); or because she really just wants to stay home and take care of her relatives: whatever the reasons, Yasuko does not want to marry. Saying yes to Yuichi's proposal seems to be a concession to everyone else's obsession with finding her a husband. Perhaps she thinks he will be a good, brotherly companion. Perhaps she knows she will never see her wedding day, but Yasuko does not want to get married.

Why should Imamura be interested in this story, then? Given the rest of his work and its focus on the "real" Japan of vibrant, coarse, working-class heroes and heroines, this film might be a reflection on the end of an era. The countryside elite (who lost much land in the US-forced land reforms, shown in the film) had all but disappeared by 1989. The existence of the new middle class continued to depend on appropriate marriages and childbearing (or the social reproduction of class), and Japan's young women seemed to be rebelling against this in the 1980s; the situation is seen to have become still worse in the twenty-first century.

Seen from this perspective, *Kuroi Ame* seems to be less about the trauma of the Second World War and more about the ordeal of being modern. The war and the bomb are just symptoms of the evils of Japanese modernity, in which love is not seen as necessary for marriage and everyone declares themselves "middle class." Women are not full agents in postwar Japan, while the ideology of "good wives and wise mothers" still dominates the society despite the 1947 constitution's granting of equal rights to women.[8] Since the Meiji Restoration of 1868, a woman's "job" has been to produce more Japanese to serve the body politic, whether it be in its prewar colonialism, the war's military service, or in aiding the Japanese postwar recovery. Not only must she produce babies, but she needs to make sure that they become proper middle-class Japanese (see Hendry 1989)—the Foucauldian concept of biopower is clearly articulated in the Japanese case.

We see hints of this attitude throughout the film. That Yasuko might ever live an independent life is deemed impossible just fifteen minutes into the story. Her uncle tells her that she has been offered a job (note that the offer was made to him); then, without letting her get a word in edgewise, Shigematsu decides that she doesn't need it and that he will turn it down for her. Later we learn that she was taken in by her relatives in order to keep her from working in munitions (unlike more "common" girls is implicit). Finally, when Yasuko's father—who lives in a modern house, with a very modern-looking second wife—asks to have her move back home, it is again her uncle who speaks first, cutting off what her initial reaction might be. Reminded of the fact that she, her aunt, and her uncle are all "bound by the bomb," Yasuko then speaks only to confirm what her uncle says. She wants to stay with them in the village and to care for them—marriage doesn't really matter to her.

It is only with Yuichi, the film's extremely and visibly traumatized character, that Yasuko discusses what it was like walking through Hiroshima and what it means in terms of radiation exposure. This becomes the moment for Yuichi to act out his traumatic work experience,[9] an enactment that had its parallel in the opening scene that Yasuko narrated. Later, when Yasuko finally speaks fully and for herself—urging her uncle to accept Yuichi's marriage proposal made by his widowed mother to her uncle—she speaks of her respect for him, but also of how she can "talk about the bomb and everything with him."[10] By this point in the film, the audience knows that Yasuko is already ill with radiation sickness and has been, at the least, since returning from visiting her father in the city. From this point in the story it seems that Yasuko's fate is sealed—like her aunt, who suddenly became sick after the last marriage proposal was withdrawn, she becomes mortally ill. The question is: has Yasuko let herself become ill?

> Suffering may be a sign of truth ... At least it is self-evident; you cannot argue with it. (Lambek 2003: 50)

The full effects of the atomic bomb were not known until long after the explosions. We now know that radiation in large quantities sooner or later causes cancers and kills. Moreover, the original Yasuko, on whose diaries the novel was based, did marry, have children, and then died from radiation poisoning (Lin 2011). That Yasuko in the film is doomed adds to the sense that she is not a typical Imamura heroine: whatever the postwar era brought to them, his women often did not merely survive but triumph. In contrast, *Kuroi Ame* appears to be Imamura's version of a Greek tragedy, a story in which the audience knows full well the dramatic irony of the characters' hope of escaping their fates. By 1989 much more was known about the dangers of radiation sickness and the fates of *hibakusha*; moreover, the popular novel ends, as does the film, with Yasuko ill in hospital.

So why suggest that Yasuko has made herself ill? There are various changes to the novel that would appear to support this: Yasuko's aunt Shigeko does not die in the novel; nor does she consult a medium in the hopes of understanding why they cannot successfully arrange a marriage for her niece as she does in the film. Her husband, Shigematsu, is sure that she has become ill because she has allowed herself to be psychologically influenced by the medium's version of events: it is Shigeko's fault for not praying for her dead sister-in-law that has cursed the family. Thus, rather than the "rationality" of science—the doctor who keeps repeating that surviving after the bomb is all a matter of will power—she succumbs to age-old superstition in which ancestors can harm their descendants if not properly worshipped.

Why this addition to the story? I think it is a reminder of all the ways in which a supposedly modern Japan remains in the grip of older beliefs about family, ancestors, and post-1868 ideals relating to marriage among the new middle class.[11] Shigeko dies apologizing for not providing the household with an heir, and if they cannot find a husband for Yasuko, they will never have an heir—a point that is obvious to viewers who understand patterns of Japanese household inheritance. The continuity of the patriarchal household is everything, and this continues to be an issue in twenty-first century Japan as the nation's birth rate continuously declines. In 1989, however, Imamura's Japan was less concerned about birth rate than about the young women who were rejecting "traditional" marriage patterns. In many ways, Imamura's earlier heroines represent a prewar Japan in which working-class, peasant, and other women had much more choice in marriage, divorce, and how they lived their lives. These women were often less circumscribed by modern middle-class ideologies about womanhood; Fumiko and her mother are in the film to remind us that such women exist.

Yasuko, in contrast, resembles an Ozu heroine: kind, polite, keen to do her duty, and selfless in her choices. Or is she? We seem to have two Yasukos: the one described above, and another who bravely makes her way from the harbor to her uncle's house in Hiroshima in the aftermath of the bombing; a young woman who is not afraid to be kind to lower-class "crazy" Yuichi; the Yasuko who cheers vulgarly at the sight of the king carp, rejoicing at its "vitality" (*genki*, which is not translated in the subtitles). The irony is that at the film's end her uncle stands by the same pond and prays for a rainbow: if one appears, he knows Yasuko will survive; yet earlier, when Yasuko saw the carp—and a Japanese koi is often variegated—he literally dragged her home, away from her symbol of hope. In short, Shigeko's death, her loss of the will to live, prefigures Yasuko's. Both have been destroyed not just by the atomic bomb, but also by their (perceived) failure to live up to Shigematsu's (and Japan's) patriarchal norms. They, and all the film's characters, are victims of the structures of violence that make up any modern society: sexism toward women; the brutality of military training; and the unthinking acceptance of nationalist policies.

Kaplan and Wang (2008) argue that social trauma occurs not just as a result of a single catastrophe, but is symptomatic of the sufferings wrought by modernity, and which add to the pain that is a normal part of living in modernity. Contemporary warfare does not end the structures of violence endured by women and the underclass in any society—it just increases their suffering.

Moreover, in the case of World War II and the Japanese, one of the ways in which the nation "sutured" up its wounds postwar was to declare the continued subjugation of women a continuity with its past. Stoic Japanese women, feminine and supportive of patriarchy, dressed demurely in kimono or modern dress, were glorified as part of the modern nation's mythology: they were/are its good wives and wise mothers. Imamura has long rejected this view of Japanese women, seeing them as agents constantly working to survive their limiting circumstances. In adapting Ibuse's *Kuroi Ame*, he made additions that clearly demonstrate how the women who try to live up to social ideals suffer and how, ultimately, they are destroyed by the very men who profess that they will love and protect them.

Notes

1. In an interview with Hubert Niogret (2002:77), Imamura discussed his original plan to use documentary footage from the era but ultimately found it impossible to do.
2. In the postwar era, Western historians have battled over the decision by the US to drop two atomic bombs: was it necessary? Was Japan about to surrender anyway? If it wasn't necessary, was dropping the bombs, at best, a warning to the USSR about entering the Pacific conflict; or, at worst, was it just a cruel experiment in seeing how the bombs would work? Ide (2014) summarizes all three positions in this debate at http://www.hamptoninstitution.org/hiroshima-historiography.html#.VsHZGeYy6Uk.
3. See for example Jeans (2005), Bukh (2007), and Nozaki (2008).
4. Kurosawa's *Yume* (*Dreams*, 1990) and *Hachi-gatsu no kyôshikyoku* (*Rhapsody in August*, 1991) have also been critiqued for their portrayal of the Japanese as victimized.
5. The issue of apologizing for the war is another subject that is contentious in the Japanese case. No matter how many times any government in power (or even the emperor) has expressed collective guilt over Japan's colonial and war-era aggressions, it is never seen as heartfelt enough. Dujarric (2013) discusses this at http://thediplomat.com/2013/11/why-are-japans-apologies-forgotten/.
6. This character, as others have noted, is an addition brought in from another Ibuse (1971) short story. His PTSD in the story is the result of a rather silly argument with an officer, which ends with him falling off the back of a transport lorry. Imamura rewrites this backstory but still seems to put blame on Yuichi's commanding officer.
7. Imamura describes her as "exploding" (*explose*) in this scene (Niogret 2002: 79).
8. As well as the constitution, 1986 saw the implementation of the Equal Employment Opportunity Law in Japan, in an attempt to allow women to pursue full careers in the work place (about 51 percent of Japanese women worked only part-time and with no benefits), although the pressure on women to quit when marrying or having their first child meant that the law was virtually meaningless. Workplaces still do not provide enough nurseries, even though maternity leave laws were revised in 2010 to allow a woman up to a year's leave. However, taking leave and having a family always

puts a dent in promotion chances; in international Japanese companies, it becomes an excuse not to transfer a woman abroad. Such transfers are often necessary for climbing the company ladder.

9. I do not discuss this scene here, except to note that Yuichi's trauma, like that of many a PTSD soldier, is rooted in having to follow orders that put their lives in danger (see Shay 1994) in the most frightening of situations. In short, less than a plea for Yuichi to be seen as a heroic sufferer at the hands of the US, he is portrayed as the victim of the Japanese officer who kept telling him (and others) to advance against the oncoming US tanks.
10. This is glossed over in the subtitles as "frank and honest." In fact, the bomb, *pika*, comes up numerous times in this discussion of marriage with Yuichi, but this also is not translated.
11. Hendry (1981) well describes how different and varied marriage patterns were up until the 1970s in the Japanese countryside, where, until the 1960s, the majority of the Japanese had lived.

Works Cited

Bock, Audie (1990). *Japanese Film Directors*. New York: Kodansha International, Ltd.

Bock, Audie (1997). "Shohei Imamura: No Confucianist." In *Shohei Imamura*, ed. James Quandt, 149–54. Toronto: Toronto International Film Festival Group.

Bourdaghs, Michael (2005). "What It Sounds Like to Lose an Empire: Happy End and the Kinks." In *Perspectives on Social Memory in Japan*, ed. Yun Hui Tsu, Jan van Bremen, and Eyal Ben-Ari, 115–33. Folkestone: Global Oriental.

Bukh, Alexander (2007.) "Japan's History Textbooks Debate: National Identity in Narratives of Victimhood and Victimization." *Asian Survey* 47, no. 5: 683–704.

Buruma, Ian (1994). *The Wages of Guilt; Memories of War in Germany and Japan*. New York: New York Review of Books.

Cavanaugh, Carole (2001). "A Working Ideology for Hiroshima: Imamura Shōhei's *Black Rain*." In *Word and Image in Japanese Cinema*, ed. Dennis Washburn and Carole Cavanuagh, 250–71. Cambridge: Cambridge University Press.

de Beacque, Antoine (1997). "*The Profound Desire of the Gods*: Murder of the Pink Pig." In *Shohei Imamura*, ed. James Quandt, 155–56. Toronto: Toronto International Film Festival Group.

Davis, J. (1992). "The Anthropology of Suffering." *Journal of Refugee Studies* 5, no. 2: 149–61.

Deamer, David (2014). *Deleuze, Japanese Cinema, and the Atom Bomb: The Spectre of Impossibility*. New York: Bloomsbury.

Desser, David (1988). *Eros plus Massacre: An Introduction to the Japanese New Wave Cinema*. Bloomington: Indiana University Press.

Dorsey, John T., and Naomi Matsuoka (1996). "Narrative Strategies of Understatement in *Black Rain* as a Novel and a Film." In *Hibakusha Cinema: Hiroshima, Nagasaki and the Nuclear Image in Japanese Film*, ed. Mick Broderick, 201–21. London: Kegan Paul International.

Dujarric, Robert (2013). "Why Are Japan's Apologies Forgotten?" *The Diplomat*. http://thediplomat.com/2013/11/why-are-japans-apologies-forgotten/. Accessed September 19, 2018.

Feleppa, Robert (2004). "*Black Rain*: Reflections on Hiroshima and Nuclear War in Japanese Film." *Cross Currents* 54, no. 1: 106–19.

Frühstück, Sabine (2007). *Uneasy Warriors: Gender, Memory and Popular Culture in the Japanese Army*. Berkeley: University of California Press.

Galan, Christian (2008). "The New Image of Childhood in Japan during the Years 1945–59 and the Construction of a Japanese Collective Memory." In *The Power of Memory in Modern Japan*, ed. Sven Saaler and Wolfgang Schwentker, 189–203. Leiden: Brill/Global Oriental.

Hendry, Joy (1981). *Marriage in Changing Japan: Community and Society*. London: Routledge.

Hendry, Joy (1989). *Becoming Japanese: The World of the Japanese Pre-School Child*. Honolulu: University of Hawai'i Press.

Ibuse, Masuji (1971). "Lieutenant Lookeast." *Lieutenant Lookeast and Other Stories*. Trans. John Bester. London: Secker & Warburg.

Ibuse, Masuji (1966). *Black Rain*. Trans. John Bester. New York: Kodansha USA, Inc.

Ide, Derek (2014). "Dropping the Bomb: A Historiographical Review of the Most Destructive Decision in Human History." New York: The Hampton Institute. http://www.hamptoninstitution.org/hiroshima-historiography.html#.VsiI-7uYy6Ul. Accessed September 9, 2018.

Igarashi, Yoshikuni (2000). *Bodies of Memory: Narratives of War in Postwar Japanese Culture, 1945–1970*. Princeton, NJ: Princeton University Press.

Ishihara, Shintarō (1992). *The Japan That Can Say No: Why Japan Will Be First among Equals*. Trans. Frank Baldwin. New York: Touchstone Books.

Jeans, Roger B. (2005). "Victims or Victimizers? Museums, Textbooks and the War Debate in Contemporary Japan." *Journal of Military History* 69, no. 1: 149–95.

Kaplan, E. Ann, and Ban Wang (2008). *Trauma and Cinema: Cross-Cultural Explorations*. Hong Kong: Hong Kong University Press.

Lambek, Michael (2003). "Rheumatic Irony: Questions of Agency and Self-deception as Refracted through the Art of Living with Spirits." In *Illness and Irony: On the Ambiguity of Suffering in Culture*, ed. Michael Lambek and Paul Antze, 40–59. New York: Berghahn Books.

Lin, Yi-Ling (2011). "Plagiarism, Hiroshima, and Intertextuality: Ibuse Masuji's *Black Rain* Reconsidered." *Reitaku: Journal of Interdisciplinary Studies* 19, no. 2: 23–55.

Nakata, Toichi (1997). "Shohei Imamura Interview." In *Shohei Imamura*, ed. James Quandt, 107–24. Toronto: Toronto International Film Festival Group.

Niogret, Hubert (2002). *Shohei Imamura, Entretiens et Témoignages*. Paris: Dreamland éditeur.

Nozaki, Yoshiko (2008). *War Memory, Nationalism and Education in Postwar Japan: The Japanese History Textbook Controversy and Ienaga Saburo's Court Challenges*. Abingdon: Routledge.

Richie, Donald (1997). "Notes for a Study on Shohei Imamura." In *Shohei Imamura*, ed. James Quandt, 7–44. Toronto: Toronto International Film Festival Group.

Seaton, Philip A. (2007). *Japan's Contested War Memories: The "Memory Rifts" in Historical Consciousness of World War II*. Abingdon: Routledge.

Shay, Jonathan (1995). *Achilles in Vietnam: Combat Trauma and the Undoing of Character*. New York: Scribner.

Tachibana, Reiko (1998). "Seeing between the Lines: Imamura Shōhei's *Kuroi Ame* (Black Rain)." *Literature/Film Quarterly* 26, no. 4: 304–12.

Tessier, Max (1997). "Unagi: of Eels and Men." In *Shohei Imamura*, ed. James Quandt, 179–80. Toronto: Toronto International Film Festival Group.

Todeschini, Maya Morioka (1996). "'Death and the Maiden': Female *Hibakusha* as Cultural Heroines and the Politics of A-bomb Memory." In *Hibakusha Cinema: Hiroshima, Nagasaki and the Nuclear Image in Japanese Film*, ed. Mick Broderick, 222–52. London: Kegan Paul International.

Treat, John Whittier (1995). *Writing Ground Zero: Japanese Literature and the Atomic Bomb*. Chicago: University of Chicago Press.

Wood, Robin (2003). "The American Nightmare: Horror in the 70s." In *Hollywood: From Vietnam to Reagan . . . and Beyond*, 63–84. New York: Columbia University Press.

Chapter 18

The Symbolic Function of Water

Timothy Iles

René Wellek and Austin Warren, in their seminal *Theory of Literature* (1942), ask and proceed to answer a question central to considerations of Imamura's work, taken as a whole:

> Is there any important sense in which "symbol" differs from "image" and "metaphor"? Primarily, we think, in the recurrence and persistence of the "symbol." An "image" may be invoked once as a metaphor, but if it persistently recurs, both as a presentation and representation, it becomes a symbol, may even become part of a symbolic (or mythic) system. (Wellek and Warren 1942: 189)

It is this quality of the systematic recurrence of water in Imamura's films that elevates the image to symbolic status, and permits me to consider his films, taken as a whole, as constituting a mythic system in which themes and social critique remain consistent. From his earliest films such as *Buta to gunkan* (*Pigs and Battleships*, 1961) or *Erogotoshi-tachi yori: Jinruigaku nyûmon* (*The Pornographers*, 1966) to his final complete feature, *Akai hashi no shita no nurui mizu* (*Warm Water under a Red Bridge*, 2001), water recurs at key moments in the narratives to highlight particular emotional, fatalistic, or inevitable conditions. In this chapter, I analyze this use of water in several of Imamura's films, to create an interpretive context in which I situate *Warm Water under a Red Bridge* (hereafter *Warm Water*), to demonstrate the consistent though evolving function of water as a force for change in the lives of Imamura's characters, a force they neither can nor should resist. Water becomes an indicator of destiny, of time, of change, or the irrefutability of nature as a mechanism within the lives of the characters upon which Imamura focuses his formidable, sympathetic attention. In *Warm Water*, the symbolic value of water evolves to represent an equally powerful force, against which the protagonist neither can nor should struggle—the force of love, of redemption. I can certainly agree with Roland Barthes when he writes that "while I don't know whether . . . 'things which are repeated are pleasing,' my belief is that they are significant" (Barthes 1972: 12). Water imagery repeats and recurs so consistently at key moments throughout Imamura's films that it does, indeed, significantly facilitate the creation of a system, one I can characterize as mythic, and one we can analyze both in and of itself, and as a contributor to other recurring themes and motifs in Imamura's work.

I am concerned here fundamentally with the significance of water throughout Imamura's work, and so I may summarize my analytical method as primarily semiotic, in that "to postulate a significance is to have recourse to semiology" (Barthes 1972: 111). My own approach focuses on formalism, taking hints on the function of any given unit of narration from Barthes—and this, despite Barthes's embarrassing, profound inability to understand cinema.[1] Nothing in narrative (understanding film as narrative text) is accidental, although not everything has the same functional weight. As Barthes writes, "A function only has meaning insofar as it occupies a place in the general action of an actant, and this action in turn receives its final meaning from the fact that it is narrated, entrusted to a discourse which possesses its own code" (Barthes 1977: 87). When we encounter images that recur, across decades of artistic production, and in similar narrative situations, we have a tremendous starting point for the evaluation of text. This is what we find in Imamura's cumulative work—we may bring these films together, to a certain extent, as a single "text" that makes use of a specific image in a particular, symbolic fashion. Water is such an image. Further, as Carroll argues,

> the functional account regards film form as generative. Film form is that which is designed to bring about the point or the purposes of the film. This account uses the notion of a function to explain why the individual film is the way it is. It enables us to say why the film has the shape and structure it has. The form serves a function. It is designed to serve a film's purpose (or purposes), a means to securing its point or points. It is that which makes manifest the point or purpose of the film. The functionalist account explains why the film is the way it appears by showing that a formal element has been selected because that element realises the film's point and that the choice occurs in the work in order to realise its point. (Carroll 1998: 399)

This approach accepts intentionality in both narrative and the agents responsible for the creation of that narrative, as "narrator" and as "author," but it does so deliberately—and, here, effectively, given that my purpose is an interpretive analysis of water imagery throughout Imamura's films, focusing most extensively on *Warm Water*. Despite the theoretical insistence that these "agent[s] cannot be identified with the writer, painter, or filmmaker . . . [who withdraw and call] upon a fictitious spokesman, an agent technically known as the narrator" (Bal 1997: 8), we cannot look at Imamura's work without seeing a consistency—of interest, of subject matter, of presentation, and, indeed, of formal elements. While textual analysis focuses by necessity and rightly on texts themselves and the internal relations between the elements that constitute them, the functional analysis of Imamura's films—of any narrative—

> is dynamic in that it ties form to the motive force—the points and purposes—that explain a film's constellations of choices . . . Admittedly, the functional account is teleological. But it is not strange to treat objects of human design teleologically. We assemble such objects in order to fulfill certain purposes. In film analysis, the functional approach is sensitive to this feature; it assumes from the outset that films are the way they are as the result of human design. (Carroll 1998: 401)

Thus, methodologically, understanding the purposeful inclusion of specific, recurring functional features at related points across a set of narratives helps point us toward the meaning not only of those features but of the narratives themselves of which they are integral parts.

This chapter argues, therefore, that the deliberate presence of water imagery in Imamura's films serves as a concrete manifestation of the various forces his characters encounter. Water-as-force and force-as-water recur and point to the potential for transformation of the characters through immersion in a substance both greater than they are and yet less precise; eternal yet never static; sustaining yet never sedate. Water-as-force and force-as-water serve as barometers of a morality that, for its naturalness, remains amoral, transcending the limitations of the characters upon whom Imamura focuses his attention, while permitting them a chance for redemption, inclusion, happiness, and, indeed, even love. Against a backdrop of despair and dissolution, Imamura creates a world in which both wonder and hope are possible. The fundamental humanism of Imamura's work sustains a community in which communication, redemption, and forgiveness merge with the absurd, the perverse, and the fantastic, to demonstrate the dignity and value of each individual. The struggles of society's lowest strata provide the foundation for a reconceptualization of the contours of the human community, in which realization of aspirations becomes the shared project of all. My close textual analysis of *Warm Water*, situating it in a context of Imamura's earlier films, argues that through the imagery and symbolism of water, the film proposes an inclusive, sustaining circulatory system of love, capable of transforming individuals' lives and transporting them from despair to stability. Allegorically, the film also proposes the necessity of shared, communal experience to create a stable economic environment of development and prosperity. As such, the film presents a compendium of the features that make up Imamura's mythic system, dealing as it does with the issues that have run, as a stream, through his works.

Wellek and Warren suggest that images/symbols an author repeats with sufficient frequency may join with or constitute a system or a myth; how do we understand such a term within the context of a contemporary filmmaker whose mode, while flirting with the supernatural, is primarily realist? "Myth" does not imply something unrealistic, nor even impossible or unbelievable—and one point we must mention is that, despite the fantastical, even absurd, elements that repeatedly come into Imamura's films, his work is most decidedly not unrealistic. As Allan Hazlett and Christy Mag Uidhir argue, "Unrealistic fictions are a species of inconsistent fictions" (Hazlett and Uidhir 2011: 33) wherein the inconsistency may still serve a positive aesthetic function. The texts in question here, especially *Warm Water*, utilize fantastical elements quite consistently, even systematically, to overdetermine a particular structural feature and highlight its central, interpretive importance.

We may contextualize water as symbolic even beyond Imamura's work—or, more precisely, we can understand Imamura as borrowing quite deliberately the powerful imagery of water from canonical Japanese texts. One of the first sources of water imagery is in fact one of Japan's first sources of its sense of self and cultural identity: the *Kojiki*, the eighth-century compendium of creation myths that, among other political purposes, establishes and codifies a set of social hierarchies. The very opening passages of the *Kojiki* present the Earth as "young and like unto floating oil, drift[ing] about medusa-like" (Chamberlain 1919: "The Beginning of Heaven and Earth"), to which descend the gods Izanami and Izanagi, who

> standing upon the Floating Bridge of Heaven pushed down the jeweled spear and stirred with it, whereupon, when they had stirred the brine till it went curdle-curdle, and drew the spear up, the brine that dripped down from the end of the spear was piled up and became an island. (Chamberlain 1919: "The Island of Onogoro")

The islands of Japan, "Onogoro" here, are born of the water that the deities churn, concretizing the importance of water to an island land. Further, as a monsoon country, and one agriculturally dependent on wet-rice cultivation, water and its cycles help determine the wealth and viability of communities. So important is rice that, as Hasumi Yasushi argues, "we may say that the significance of the expression, *Mizuho no kuni,* 'Japan, the land of abundant rice' . . . is something which has transcended mere rhetoric to develop in the hearts of the people throughout the more than two-thousand-year history of our land" (Hasumi 1962: 13). Water is that which makes rice cultivation possible; water, as rainfall, is that which heralds the arrival of the planting and growing season. More: water has long served as a metaphor for the transience and changeability of human life, as Kamo no Chōmei so aptly notes in his *Hōjōki* (*Record of the Ten-Foot Hut,* 1212): "The flow of the running river is ceaseless, yet it is never the same water. The bubbles floating in the pools disappear or merge, but none last for long. The people of the world and their dwellings too are like this."[2] Water is time, is life, is change and inevitable transformation; against water, formless but tangible, and its flow, ever-present though never constant, nothing can stand. Water is emotion, too—sleeves ambiguously wet with tears or dew form one of the most common metaphors for sorrow in the *Kokinshū*, the tenth-century anthology that helped establish the *tanka* as the quintessential poetic form in both pre- and modern Japan. So affecting is the imagery of water that even in as dry a film as *Suna no onna* (*Woman in the Dunes,* 1964), Teshigahara Hiroshi creates powerful parallels between water and flowing sand, utilizing the resulting tension to highlight the stagnation of the village community as it resists the inevitability of change—the village community balanced between an ominous ocean on the one hand and engulfing dunes on the other. Here, too, water stands as a symbol for liberation and change, as the protagonist, the Man (Eiji Okada), whom the villagers have trapped at the bottom of the sand pit, discovers a mechanism through which he can access a ready source of fresh water, a mechanism that he refers to as his hope.

We find a correlation between this awareness of water-as-fate in *The Pornographers*, which also provides us with numerous instances of water-as-force. Interestingly, the presentation of water here is consistent despite the rapid and significant improvements in the Japanese economy and in access to financial stability for increasing numbers of Japanese that characterize the mid-1960s. Despite the tangible improvements in daily life that mark the moment of the film's historical context, Imamura retains his focus on the people who live at the margins of Japan's stabilizing situation. Of the improving Japanese economy in the period of *The Pornographers*, Shigeru Otsubo has written:

> The Japanese economy eventually entered an economic growth process with positively reinforcing feedback: demand expansion—production expansion—increases in income—consumption expansion—further income expansion—increases in savings—investment growth and an expansion of production capacity. The rapid growth period from the late 1950s to1960s was thus created. From 1955 to 1972, the Japanese real GDP grew by an annual average rate of 9.3%. (Otsubo 2007: 13)

Even though only specific industries received direct government attention during (at least) the initial period of Japan's economic recovery, for the most part

> this strategy was generally accepted by most Japanese as a "trickle-down approach" to raise incomes and living standards in Japan. In forming this consensus, [the] government's medium-term economic plans, particularly the National Income Doubling Plan of 1960, contributed significantly. (Otsubo 2007: 13)

So effective was the strategy of rebuilding the Japanese economy that urban populations also increased dramatically—economic development "increased [the] workforce of 15–24 years of age in Tokyo by 1 million during 1955–1965" (Otsubo 2007: 9). Even in this era of increasing prosperity, however, Imamura maintains his focus on the margins of Japanese society, looking here at characters whose line of work, while also developing rapidly, remains illegal and potentially immoral.

The character relations in *The Pornographers* are relatively straightforward, despite their emotional intricacy: Ogata (Shōichi Ozawa) makes and distributes pornographic films. He lives with Haru (Sumiko Sakamoto) and her son Kōichi (Masaomi Kondō) but desires her daughter, Keiko (Keiko Sagawa). Haru is a widow; she believes the spirit of her dead husband has reincarnated into a large carp she keeps in an aquarium in her home. Before he died, her husband had made her promise not to remarry. Haru believes the carp is keeping a watchful eye over her—to the extent that she has an abortion when she becomes pregnant with Ogata's child, because "the carp jumped." Ogata is skeptical, but Haru insists, explaining, "It's true! Whenever something bad happens, the carp jumps!"

What is most interesting throughout the film, however, and in this key scene in which Haru tells Ogata about having aborted his child, is the camera work that "submerges" both the viewer and Haru beneath the water of the aquarium, and the dominating figure of the carp, blocking our clear view of Ogata and Haru as they affirm their devotion to each other. Joan Mellen makes much of this carp, describing it as Imamura's method of "satirising the entire notion of ancestor worship, as well as the unnecessary waste and pain resulting from the injunction that widows not remarry" (Mellen 1976: 371). Semiotically, this scene places Haru into an impossible realm in which she cannot survive; it is a clever foreshadowing of her death and apparent reincarnation as a carp, rejoining her late husband, and an equally clever foreshadowing of Ogata's final drifting off on the waves, as his houseboat slips its moorings and transports him, unaware and alone with the project that obsesses him—the creation of a life-like, female sex doll—onto the wide-open ocean at the film's close.

Water thus dominates this sequence, with its themes of repressed though finally realized desire, and the possibility of new life springing from the union of these two people irresistibly drawn to each other. The function of water is similar to, though clearer than, its subtle use in the scene between Kinta and Haruko in *Buta to gunkan*, in which Haruko reveals her pregnancy to the protagonist. Water imagery dominates the scenes around Haru's insanity and death, as well, with Ogata attending a Shinto exorcism to purge the spirit of the carp whom Haru believes is haunting her. During the ceremony, Ogata sees a woman, her long hair streaming with rain water, who reminds him of his mother. A flashback shows a very young Ogata and his mother in a traditional bath together, the child struggling while the mother clutches him in the splashing water, a lascivious expression dancing on her face as she kisses the child. A quick cut gives us Haru's hospital death bed—however, we see this bed, Haru lying calmly, her black hair spread out on her pillow, as if we are floating directly above her. Between our view and Haru, a carp leisurely swims. We are thus floating, ourselves, above Haru, recalling the earlier scene in which Haru appeared submerged in the water of the aquarium. Ogata implores her not to die, not to "follow that carp." As Ogata asks Haru for title deeds and her seal, to take control of her finances, the carp flashes its tail, stirring the water through which we are looking and distorting the scene. A cut brings us parallel to Ogata and Haru, as Ogata exclaims, "*Itoshii na . . . itoshii na . . . ,*" "I love you, I love," his voice breaking with emotion. In the next scene, Haru has died. A quick cut brings us to her funeral, mourners in black along the right side of the scene, but the carp in its aquarium neatly divides the screen in the middle—it occupies nearly the entire left foreground. As the funeral continues, Ogata plucks the carp from its tank, carries it outside to the canal beside the house, and reviles it for haunting Haru until she followed it into death—and for making him impotent again. He flings the carp into the water. Immediately as he does so, his associate leans out of an upper window to tell him that their partner has run off, stealing the equipment with which they had made the pornographic films that constituted their livelihood.

The extreme emotionality of the scenes in this sequence, from Haru's deathbed to Ogata's confession of sincere and profound love for her, the funeral, and the loss of Ogata's means of production (in two senses!), occurs within a frame of water. This is literally true for the reading of Haru's will—we hear in voiceover Haru reciting the terms of her will, while the camera shows us two carp nestling side by side under water. Water once again functions as a complex multivalent symbol, one which we can associate with inevitability, fate, and even profound love.

The film's closing, too, makes powerful use of water and the protagonist's proximity to the ocean. Following Haru's death, Ogata devotes an increasing amount of energy and time to perfecting the mechanical, female doll with which he will replace real women. He has named this doll "Haru," and he talks openly and affectionately with it. Living in a small house boat floating where he had tossed the carp back into the canal, he has become withdrawn from the world around him, and even hostile to the people nearby. "All [Ogata] can do, having experienced Haru's death, is try, through his own efforts, to bring her back to life," writes Shimizu Masashi (2001: 427). When Haru's son, now employed by a manufacturing firm, brings an investor to purchase Ogata's doll, Ogata refuses even to consider selling his invention; he pushes the boat away from the bank, dumping the investor in the water. Later, the boat slips its moorings and drifts out to sea, "bearing [Ogata] and his ersatz Venus towards a receding horizon of oceanic ecstasy" (Young 1968: 648). Whether ecstasy awaits Ogata, or simply death, remains ambiguous; his meeting with his fate will take place on the water, that force against which he is powerless to struggle—literally so, for his houseboat has neither engine nor rudder. Water bears him to where it will; water symbolizes that which carries human beings toward their fate. As Mellen puts it,

> Ogata has gone the way of us all, from Oedipal childhood through insatiable middle years to the bewilderment of old age. His rudderless houseboat reflects the unguided, directionless course we all pursue through the channels of sexuality. In Imamura's depiction, it is a vital, frightening, and very funny voyage. (Mellen 1976: 375)

But this description focuses too exclusively on the issue—granted, a central one—of sexuality in the film. The final shots of Ogata's houseboat adrift give us more than a metaphor for the individual's relationship to the sexual world. The ships which the houseboat passes are part of the working world of contemporary Japan, part of the international commerce that sustains its economy, an economy that oppresses the characters in the film, but also provides them with their goals, their ambitions, and their struggles. Here, water symbolizes these aspects of their lives, as well. Water is that stratum of Imamura's mythos, the system of meanings he creates in his films, which represents the inevitable set of forces that antagonize, energize, sustain, and ultimately propel his characters. This stratum remains constant even in times of increasing economic prosperity, and we should note the repeated and explicit attentions that Imamura includes to highlight the improving wealth of Japan and segments of Japanese society throughout the film—Haru's beauty parlor does a steady and good trade, and

Ogata's business, too, depends on a specific access to disposable income among the more "legitimate" members of Japan's growing middle class. Nonetheless, both these characters are dependent on this middle class, peripheral to it and at the mercy of economic forces that carry them forward in their lives. Water here overlaps with the rising tide of "the macroeconomic development process of the postwar Japanese economy (the so-called 'Miracle Recovery')" (Otsubo 2007: 1), which can either permit or destroy Ogata's own prosperity.

While *The Pornographers* gives us the memory of an encounter between a mother and her son, a memory which the son's point of view endows with a potentially frightening sexual connotation, *Fuskushu suru wa ware ni ari* (*Vengeance Is Mine,* 1979) gives us a parallel scene between the father (Rentarō Mikuni) of the protagonist (Ken Ogata) and his daughter-in-law (Mitsuko Baishō). Both take place in the context of bathing—one, in the family bath, the other, in an *onsen*.

Taking these two scenes together allows us to point out a set of key features, the most obvious of which is the water in which the characters stand, sit, or recline. The first scene establishes a direct proportion between the characters' desire and the degree to which they submerge themselves in the water of the *onsen*. As their desire increases, so too does the extent to which water dominates their surroundings—Imamura goes so far as to flood the scene with water, in the form of the rain that falls with increasing vigor as the passion of the two characters increases. As Shizuo pulls away, however, breaking the moment and sending Kazuko inside because of "the cold," the rain suddenly stops. In the later scene, even though Kazuko's attention and vows to care for Shizuo in his old age have clearly moved him, Shizuo does his best to maintain his composure. Here, too, water stands in relation to the desire the characters have for each other, and stands, also, as a symbol of the power of that desire—but interestingly, by this point in the film, Shizuo has grown more in control of himself (even as Kazuko has grown more sure of the love she feels for him), and the level of the water here is much lower than in the earlier scene.

Water is therefore symbolic of powerful emotion in this film, as it functions in other Imamura works. The emotions it signifies are not always positive. As Phillips points out, it can operate also as an indicator of forces both negative and neutral, as well:

> In the telling scene between Enokizu and Haru's mother set in a forlorn eel hatchery just after the couple have visited a lower-class urban race gathering, the watery landscape becomes a metaphor both for the unstable elements in their personal relationship (she fears he intends to kill her) and for the shifting currents of the social world that surrounds them. After gazing at a single eel trapped against a twig, Haru's mother comments,

"the outside world has changed," followed by Enokizu's remark that "it sure has. It gets worse every day." The shot of teeming constrained eels in a subsequent image suggests the same kind of unnatural entrapment hinted at by their unsettling conversation. (Phillips 2007: 234)

The premonition of murder is, of course, accurate, for Enokizu does indeed murder both Haru (Ogawa Mayumi) and her mother (Kiyokawa Nijiko). In the context of the narrative, their deaths are inevitable; the premonition, and its close association with water, necessitates them. Water as force, but also water as emotion, and water as love—these aspects remain constant for Imamura, as does his attention to the marginal members of Japan's now-strong economy. Iwao slips easily into new identities, each more apparently prosperous and securely *middle class* than the previous, even while his own crimes remove him more fully from that stratum of society whose guises he assumes.

Ever consistent, Imamura in *Kanzō sensei* (*Dr. Akagi*; 1998) again creates scenes involving powerful emotion and declarations of love, and locates these in or on the ocean. The film gives us the story of Dr. Akagi (Akira Emoto), a physician obsessed with hepatitis—he sees it everywhere, in almost everyone he meets, and declares it to be the defining disease in Japan at the end of the Pacific war. But Dr. Akagi is also a dedicated, compassionate, and gifted physician who devotes his energy sincerely and totally to caring for his patients. So profound is his dedication that he wins the affection—equally profound and sincere—of a reformed prostitute, Sonoko (Kumiko Asō), who has come to work for and live with him. Sonoko has tried to give up prostitution, but times are tough, money is scarce, and her younger siblings beg her, in a letter she reads while sitting on the docks beside her small fishing boat, to return to her former employment. As a favor to the mother of a young man about to go off to war but who is still a virgin, Sonoko takes him under her wing, so to speak—later in the evening, as she swims exhaustedly in the ocean, his mother thanks her. The characters are silhouettes against the light of dusk on the limitless blue water, as Sonoko refreshes and revitalizes herself in the calm waves. This sequence overlaps a mother's love and worry for her son's physical safety, with her concerns—as a woman—for her son's becoming "a man." It also overlaps Sonoko's promise to herself to give up prostitution, with the responsibility she feels for both her siblings, and for the son of her friend, the woman who comes to ask of her this great favor. Inevitability also functions in this sequence—the son's necessity of going to war, the mother's fears of the certainty of his death ("they say virgins attract bullets!"), and the inevitability—from giving in to necessity—of Sonoko returning to her former work. In the system of Imamura's films, these events must happen near or in or on water, for water is the symbol, the substance, that propels characters forward in their lives. So, too, Sonoko's declaration of love for Dr. Akagi at the film's close must take place in her fishing boat on the ocean, after she has pulled herself from the water (having lost her clothing diving in to harpoon a whale). But the ending is tragic—this declaration of love comes on the morning of August 6, 1945, at 7:00 AM. From the fishing boat bobbing on the peaceful, green ocean, dripping wet in each other's arms, awash in the emotion that overpowers them, the two witness the atomic bombing of Hiroshima.

The consistent presence of water in Imamura's films and its function as a symbol for force, fate, and powerful emotion reaches its apotheosis in *Warm Water*. With this film, Imamura not only consolidates and affirms the value of water in the mythic system he creates in his work, but moves bodily into the realm of mythology itself. His characters here, while maintaining Imamura's interest in the lower half of Japanese society—the marginal, the working poor, the homeless—also cross the boundary marking this world from the other world, the world of legend, of myth, of spirits and *kami*. With *Warm Water,* Imamura transports us into the world of the *otogi-banashi*, the fairy tale, made real. Water serves as a constant presence in the film, and functions in many of the ways it has throughout Imamura's opus: as a force of destiny, of change and time and fate, but also here as a source of redemption, solidarity, community, and love.

Imamura released *Warm Water* in 2001, when Japan was immersed in recession and economic dismay. As Overholt writes of the situation facing Japan at the time,

> A major historical era is ending in Japan. Institutions that created the country's economic miracle a generation ago have now brought Japan to the verge of an economic debacle. And the changes needed to resolve that crisis will broadly affect the nation's economy, finances, politics, foreign policy, and family life. (Overholt 2002: 134)

Once again, Imamura focuses on characters at the edges of Japanese society, but now he seems to point out that anyone can end up at those edges. The film follows Sasano Yosuke (Kōji Yakusho), a former well-to-do, white-collar salaryman who has recently become unemployed, living alone in Tokyo, as he embarks on a journey at the behest of a now-dead homeless man, Tarō (Kazuo Kitamura). Tarō had been known as the "Blue Tent Philosopher" among the other elderly homeless camping along the banks of an unidentified river in Tokyo, because of his education and the high quality of the books he had read. He had often told Yosuke of a treasure he had left behind in a small town on the Noto peninsula, in a house beside a red bridge. After Tarō's death at the very beginning of the film,

Yosuke decides to accept his request that he go to claim the treasure in his place. Making his way to the village, he finds the house, and follows the woman, Saeko (Misa Shimizu), living in it. Within minutes of their meeting, the two begin a relationship, as Saeko implores Yosuke to help her release the water that builds up (*agattekuru*) inside her, which she can only release (as anything from a trickle to a high-pressure torrent) through doing something "wicked"—although shoplifting and making love are the only examples of this "wickedness" the film gives us. Yosuke stays on in the town, taking a job on a fishing trawler, and deepening his relationship with Saeko. Yosuke's wife, Tomoko (Toshie Negishi), having had to return to her family home away from Tokyo as a result of Yosuke's financial problems, asks for a divorce in her frustration at Yosuke's inability to find sufficiently remunerative employment, leaving Yosuke free to stay with Saeko in enduring, though dripping, happiness.

While other Imamura films have flirted with fantasy and the unreal, *Warm Water* whole-heartedly embraces them. This is most apparent in the character of Saeko, and her unearthly ability to gather into and release from her the water that wells up, apparently on its own, as she goes about her daily life. We also have here, however, instances of coincidence and confused identity that create an atmosphere of other-worldliness. Scenes of boundaries and border crossings abound, as do persistent reminders of Shinto and the world of *kami*. Yosuke's dream sequence soon after meeting Saeko, too, brings us into a realm that combines imagery of the cosmos and the womb, connoting both travel to a distant world, and rebirth—both of which Yosuke experiences. We have, also, a tremendous vitality and force of life running through the film, as well as a profound, animistic connection between the human and the nonhuman world—which we see when the water that has gushed out from Saeko runs its way to the river beside her house. Myriads of fish come to consume the water—Saeko describes the red bridge as the meeting point between the river and the sea, and therefore a favorite spot for numerous types of fish—but she seems oblivious to the attractive power that the water from her body has for them.

This is not the only one of Imamura's films to contain a strongly animistic component. In writing about the scenes of animal/natural sexual activity in *Narayama bushikō* (*The Ballad of Narayama*, 1983), Satō Tadao suggests that sexual activity "becomes the most fundamental image which equates to the animism repeatedly appearing in Imamura's works, affirming and confirming the power of life at the simplest dimension" (Satō 1997: 214). Also writing about *Narayama bushikō*, Hung argues that "behind all the explicit visual natural images lies Imamura's implicit assertion that in Japanese traditional farming life, the interrelation among the individuals, the *ie*, and the *mura*, is constructed in the image of nature" (Hung 2003, 154). While *Narayama* is the most "natural" or "animistic" of Imamura's films, the underlying argument is definitely true, highlighting one of the key features of Imamura's work as a whole—its affirmation of life. Further, David Desser connects the function of sexuality in Imamura's films with a drive for liberation, both personal but also gendered: "Imamura's women do indeed achieve a kind of transcendence, but it comes not through self-sacrifice, but through coming to terms with themselves as sexual beings ... and it is achieved in the here-and-now" (Desser 1988: 123). We find such a life force in Orin, the matriarch of *Narayama bushikō*, about to turn seventy but ashamed of her persistent vitality, as she apologizes to her new daughter-in-law for being so healthy and still having her teeth, as strong as rocks, as Tatsuhei says of them. The film concerns itself with time and the processes of transition it entails. The narrative highlights the cyclicality of the seasons, beginning and ending with aerial shots of the mountains in which nestle the villagers' homes, held in the grip of snow and winter. Throughout, as both Satō and Hung point out, are scenes of sexuality, both human and animal, but also scenes of change from winter to spring, summer to autumn and winter again. And, as ever, we find water. The camera focuses on a cinematic cliché, water as it trickles from the melting snows as spring arrives, but it also focuses on water as it trickles in an increasingly strong rivulet away from the Amaya home—the family whom the villagers catch and punish for stealing food. The flow of water and the snake leaving their hut signal the fate about to befall them—the force of retribution, of their "fatal" destiny, for their socially destructive actions.

Water and sexuality, as symbols of life, power, and irresistible force, also operate throughout *Warm Water*. Saeko's sexuality is insistent, absorbing, ever-present, and something from which Yosuke has no intention of fleeing. The water which their lovemaking releases streams into the river beside the house; the fish who come to revel in the water serve as targets for the elderly men who try to hook them; and the elderly men compose the community in the small village where Yosuke is able to find redemption with Saeko. It is the water that flows from Saeko which establishes and motivates this series of connections and interdependencies; as such, this water takes on a symbolic function new to Imamura's work—that of the sustaining, circulating, all-encompassing force of affection, of warmth, of love.

The sequence from the film's opening to Yosuke's and Saeko's first meeting, in typical Imamura fashion, is semiotically very rich, with repeated emphasis on water, the inevitable flow of life from one stage to the next, the irresistible influence of economic forces on the lives of individuals, powerless against them, and transitions or passages from one plane or sphere to another. A telephoto shot gives us an elevated roadway paralleling a broad, urban river. Traffic runs along the road; along the far bank of the river, a row of blue tents—the far too-common dwellings of the homeless in contemporary Japan. A cut shows us, from still across the river, two police officers descending a flight of steps toward the tents. We cut to a row of books on a shelf, with titles by or about Somerset Maugham, Pascal, the Mafia, Robespierre; another cut shows us an elderly man lying in shabby clothes, dead, his reading glasses still on his face. The camera shifts to show us a police officer leaning into the blue hut, while another elderly man explains that the locals had called the dead man Tarō, the "Philosopher of the Blue Tents." Yosuke arrives; he and two other homeless reminisce about Taro, and drink a cup of saké in his honor. A cut brings us to a very brief, and obviously futile, job interview for Yosuke; walking back along the river to the blue tent community, he has a telephone call from his wife, asking him for money; he slips back into memories of talking with Tarō. Deciding to take up Tarō's suggestion that he travel to seek out the treasure he had left behind, Yosuke travels by train to the Noto peninsula. He asks for directions from an elderly woman (Baishō Mitsuko), who, he later learns, lives with Saeko in the very house he seeks; the *mise-en-scène* places both of them directly beneath a Shinto *torii* as she points out to him where to go. He finds the red bridge, and the house on its far side. Following Saeko, he discovers her peculiarity. In returning an earring she had dropped, he begins his relationship with her.

Water is ever-present throughout this sequence. The image of the homeless in their temporary, though surprisingly durable, blue tents beside the river powerfully recalls Kamo no Chōmei's *Hōjōki*, with its analogy between human life and the bubbles that form and bust on the waters of rivers. The river, with its broad, incessant flow, forms the background for Yosuke's conversation with his disappointed and distant wife, and the train that takes Yosuke to the small town runs parallel to a vibrant and active sea. The house that he seeks stands immediately beside the river which brings the fish to enjoy Saeko's water, and the name of the business which Saeko and the elderly woman occasionally operate is *Suisen manjū*—"Daffodil Sweets," but the Chinese characters are quite interesting. The combination is *sui* and *sen*, designates "water" and "hermit" or "wizard." A *sen* is a person who lives deep in the mountains, and who has obtained knowledge of how to live on forever, without aging, and so the name of the shop conjures up an image of a "water wizard." Together with the other symbols and instances of fantasy, this word here helps bring us into the mythic realm. Saeko speaks eloquently about the different types of sweets she has made in the shop, but she emphasizes to Yosuke that it is the water which is of extreme importance in differentiating the varieties of manjū—water, she says, gives each one its particular flavor.

A further feature of the opening sequences also helps propel us into the realm of fantasy and mythology: this is the repeated crossing of boundaries or barriers between various characters. The very opening shot of the river with its blue tents establishes a boundary, for the camera stands on one side of the river, peering across to the other. The opening with its focus on the dead Blue Tent Philosopher also focuses on the boundaries between life and death, between the mundane and the ethereal, the intellectual; between affluence and poverty, and the short step which separates the two. When Yosuke receives the telephone call from his wife, the camera shows her speaking to him from her distant home—but a glass window stands between her and us. The train journey takes Yosuke from contemporary, urban Japan, to a small fishing village, definitely not urban and, visually, no longer contemporary: Yosuke has crossed a boundary in time. Asking for directions from Mitsu, Saeko's grandmother, the camera frames the two beneath the *torii* of a Shinto shrine—this is the boundary in Shinto belief between the mundane, human world, and the sacred world of *kami*. Yosuke walks directly through this *torii* on his way to find the red bridge, which he comes across immediately. As he walks halfway across the bridge, Saeko appears, walking from the house toward the side of the river on which Yosuke had stood. Saeko's red sweater matches the red of the bridge—these are the only two patches of color in this otherwise drab, primarily earth-toned scene of greys and browns. Mitsu, with whom Saeko lives, writes fortunes for the local *jinja,* the Shinto shrine near their home, and thus serves as an oracle, a proxy for the other world. The fortune she writes for Yosuke promises him that luck will come to him, which, of course, it does. Yosuke dreams of floating in a quantity of amniotic fluid as he drifts through deep space (before waking to discover that rain water is dripping onto him through a leaking roof). Later, we see Saeko's mother, a Shinto shaman, drown in the river that had brought industrial poisoning to the local village, and later still, we see Yosuke and Saeko explore a scientific complex for the investigation of neutrinos. The complex uses ultra-pure water to spy out these sub-atomic visitors from the cosmos.

These repeated boundaries and transports have water in common, and water, too, runs through the episodes which mark the increasingly strong, emotional relationship that binds Yosuke together with Saeko. Water is thus multiply symbolic throughout this film, and while its meaning is related to that which it has held throughout Imamura's earlier films, here the emphasis on water as an emotional force is far greater. Sign, symbol, myth, and, ultimately, part of the system that Imamura has created in his films—water functions as an indicator, an index of necessity, force, and emotion, operative in realist films but also in works of fantasy. The tremendous consistency of this symbol indicates its importance, and points, as well, to a meaning that emerges across Imamura's career. The force of life propels and compels us all; this force is irresistible, ever-present. For both high and low—the affluent, the poor, the homeless, the marginal, the mainstream—life and time flow on in ways unalterable, as the currents of the waters that run through the rivers of fate in ways against which we cannot struggle. Imamura's final vision of this irresistible force is of Yosuke and Saeko, clutching each other in the act of life, sheltering beside the immense ocean as sprays of water cascade around them, happy in each other's embrace and resigned, comfortably so, to the life that fate—water, current, the flow of time—has brought them. In this world, such happiness is possible, so long as one knows how to accept the inevitable, as one can accept the flow of the waters of life.

Notes

1. See, for example, "The Third Meaning," in *Image, Music, Text* for examples of Barthes's tortuous, hyperbolic attempts to understand "the filmic," attempts that amount to a failure to understand film as film, instead of a series of "stills" (Barthes 1977: 65).
2. *Yukukawa no nagare wa taezushite, shikamo moto no mizu ni arazu. Yodomi ni ukabu utakata wa, katsu kie katsu musubite, hisashiku todomaritaru tameshi nashi. Yo no naka ni aru hito to su to, mata kaku no gotoshi.*

Works Cited

Bal, Mieke (1997). *Narratology: Introduction to the Theory of Narrative.* 2nd ed. Toronto: University of Toronto Press.
Barthes, Roland (1972). *Mythologies.* Trans. Annette Lavers. New York: Hill and Wang.
Barthes, Roland (1977). *Image, Music, Text.* London: Fontana Press.
Carroll, Noel (1998). "Film Form: An Argument for a Functional Theory of Style in the Individual Film." *Style* 32, no. 3 (Fall): 385–401.
Chamberlain, Basil Hall, trans. (1919). *The Kojiki.* http://sacred-texts.com/shi/kj/index.htm.
Desser, David (1988). *Eros plus Massacre.* Bloomington: Indiana University Press.
Hasumi, Yasushi (1962). *Kome to jinsei* [Rice and Life]. Tokyo: Waseda shōbō.
Hazlett, Allan, and Uidhir Christy Mag (2011). "Unrealistic Fictions." *American Philosophical Quarterly* 48, no. 1 (January): 33–46.
Hung, Lee Wood (2003). "Natural Culturalism in *The Ballad of Narayama*: A Study of Shohei Imamura's Thematic Concerns." *Asian Cinema* 14, no. 1 (Spring/Summer): 146–66.
Imamura, Shōhei (2004). *Eiga wa kyōki no tabi de aru* [Film Is a Journey into Madness]. Tokyo: Nihon Keizai Shimbun Sha.
Kamo no Chōmei (1212). *Hōjōki.* http://www.aozora.gr.jp/cards/000196/files/975_15935.html.
Mellen, Joan (1976). *The Waves at Genji's Door: Japan through Its Cinema.* New York: Pantheon.
Otsubo, Shigeru (2007). "Post-war Development of the Japanese Economy—Development, Japanese/Asian Style." https://www.gsid.nagoya-u.ac.jp/sotsubo/Postwar_Development_of_the_Japanese%20Economy(Otsubo_NagoyaU).pdf. Accessed July 27, 2018.

Overholt, William H. (2002). "Japan's Economy, at War with Itself." *Foreign Affairs* 81, no. 1 (January-February): 134–47.

Phillips, Alastair (2007). "Unsettled Visions: Imamura Shohei's *Vengeance Is Mine* (1979)." In *Japanese Cinema: Texts and Contexts,* ed. Alastair Philips and Julian Stringer, 229–39. London: Routledge.

Satō, Tadao (1997). *Imamura Shōhei no sekai* [The World of Shohei Imamura]. Tokyo: Gakujo-shōbō.

Shimizu, Masashi (2001). *Imamura Shōhei o yomu: bosei to kaos no bigaku* [Engaging with Imamura *Shōhei: The Aesthetics of Motherhood and Chaos*]. Tokyo: Torikage-sha.

Wellek, René, and Warren, Austin (1942). *Theory of Literature*. New York: Harcourt, Brace, and World.

Young, Vernon (1967–68). "Poetry, Politics, and Pornography." *Hudson Review* 20, no. 4 (Winter): 643–49.

Index

8½ (1965), 272
10 Rillington Place (1971), 76
11'09"01/September 11 (2002), 1, 11

Abe, Shinzo, 182
Akai hashi no shita no nurui mizu see Warm Water Under a Red Bridge
Akai Satsui see Intentions of Murder
Akasen kichi see Red Light Base
Akaza, Etsuko, 180, 192–206
Akujo no kisetsu see Season of the Witch
American Beauty (1999), 154
Andrei Rublev (1966), 271
L'Année dernière à Marienbad see Last Year at Marinband
antiquarian history, 299–302
Aoyama, Shinji, 95, 96
Ashita (1995), 96
Audition (1999), 218
Austen, Jane, 314

Baisho, Mitsuko, 1, 6, 79, 102, 334, 339
Bakumatsu taiyōden (1957), 122
The Ballad of Narayama (1983), 6, 7, 17, 32, 68, 246–64
Ballad of Orin (1977), 7
Barthes, Roland, 22, 326, 327
Bazin, André, 93
Befu, Harumi 82
Bergman, Ingmar, 93, 122
  Wild Strawberries (Smultronstället 1957), 271
  The Seventh Seal (Det sjunde inseglet 1957), 271
Bhabha, Homi, 313

Black Rain (1989), 214, 308–16, 319, 320
Bock, Audie, 3, 5, 6, 59, 214, 233, 296, 309, 315
The Boston Strangler (1968), 76
Bounce Ko Gals (1997), 97
Brecht, Bertolt, 130–35
  The Good Person of Setzuan, 130
  Mother Courage, 130–32
  The Threepenny Opera, 130
Brooks, Richard, 76
Bungakukai, 214
Burai-ha (Decadent School), 214
Burakumin, 14, 180, 188, 190, 192, 196, 201, 205, 208
Burakumin League, 190
Burch, Noel, 291
Buta to gunkan see Pigs and Battleships

Les Cahiers du Cinéma, 23, 25, 246
Cardullo, Bert, 84
Carroll, Noel, 327
Casebier, Allan, 247, 249, 296, 305
Chahine, Youssef, 1
Chinpira (1966), 95
Cleo from 5 to 7 (1962), 271
critical history, 299–302

Darakuron see Discourse on Decadence
Davis, John, 310, 311, 313
Daydream (1964), 122
Dazai, Osamu, 214
De Baecque, Antoine, 308
De Sica, Vittorio, 271
Dejima Island, 298
Deleuze, Gilles, 296, 310, 311

Demme, Jonathan, 9, 10
Desser, David, 10, 12, 29, 73, 249, 250, 259, 296, 338
Dillard, Clayton, 81
Dines, Gail, 146, 150
Discourse on Decadence (1946), 214
Discover Japan, 129
Dr. Akagi (1998), 16, 213, 214, 217, 218, 220, 221, 223, 224, 335
Dreyfus Affair, 141, 142
Dyer, Richard, 22

Ebert, Roger, 10
Eiga Geijutsu, 23, 24, 25, 27, 33, 36, 280, 281
Eijanaika (1981), 287–89, 291, 296–99, 301–05
Emoto, Akira, 216, 217, 224, 335
Endless Desire (1958), 9, 21, 25, 26, 30–33, 35, 36, 45, 49, 224, 278
Eisenhower, Dwight, 41
Erogotoshi-tachi yori: Jinruigaku nyumon see *The Pornographers*
Eros and Civilization, 72
Expo 58, 127

Fassbinder, Rainer Werner, 71
Feleppa, Robert, 309
Fellini, Federico, 93
Flaherty, Robert, 276
Fleischer, Richard, 76
Forster, E. M., 15, 16
Foucault, Michel, 22, 208
Fujime, Yuki, 203
Fukazawa, Shichiro, 17, 247, 253, 262
Fukuda, Sadayoshi, 43, 280, 281
Fukushū Suru wa Ware ni Ari see *Vengeance Is Mine*

Gate of Flesh (1964), 152
Gatens, Moira, 203
Geneva Convention, 309
Gitai, Amos, 1
Godard, Jean-Luc, 133, 145
  Pierrot le fou (1965), 272
  Vivre sa vie (1962), 133

Gomel, Elana, 76
Gosho, Heinosuke, 2, 126

Hagerty Incident, 51
Hakujitsumu see *Daydream*
Hana-bi (1997), 97
Hanada, Kiyoteru, 116, 273
Hanare goze Orin see *Ballad of Orin*
Hani, Susumu, 127, 133, 231, 283
Harada, Masato, 97
Hasebe, Hideo, 49, 126, 131
Hashimoto, Mitsuru, 124
Hateshinaki yokubō see *Endless Desire*
Hayakawa sisters, 267, 278–81
Hayakawa, Yoshie, 17, 30, 267, 273
Heath, Stephen, 277
Helpless (1996), 96
Helter Skelter (1976), 76
Henderson, Brian, 292
Hibakusha, 18, 309, 310, 312, 315, 320
Hickey, Eric W., 82
Hidari, Sachiko, 31, 85, 116, 126, 127, 132
Hidari, Tonpei, 252, 257
Hijikata, Tatsumi, 126
Himeda, Ensaku, 31
Himeda, Shinsaku, 79, 128
Hiroshima, 15, 18, 188, 234, 309, 310, 314, 316, 317, 320, 321, 336
History of Postwar Japan as Told by a Bar Hostess (1970), 6, 11, 14, 15, 42, 180, 192, 311
Hitchcock, Alfred, 139, 140
Hōjōki (*Record of the Ten-Foot Hut*, 1212), 330
Hori Kyusaku, 44
Hsiao-hsien, Hou, 7, 93, 96
Hughes, Gordon, 82
The Human Condition (1959–1961), 181
Hung, Lee Wood, 247
Huston, John, 26

Ibuse, Masuji, 214, 224
Ichikawa, Kon, 2, 5, 126, 133
Igarashi, Yoshikuni, 313
In Cold Blood (1967), 76
In Search of the Unreturned Soldiers (1970–1973), 228, 230, 235

In the Land of the Head Hunters (1914), 276
incest
  The Insect Woman, 63, 124, 126
  The Pornographers, 13, 140, 157, 158
  The Profound Desires of the Gods, 14, 45, 161–64, 171, 174
Inárritu, Alejandro Goñzález, 1
The Insect Woman (1963), 5, 11, 14, 32, 45, 49, 51, 56, 61, 62, 68, 81, 85, 115–35, 218, 231, 273, 275, 276, 278, 311
Intentions of Murder (1964), 5, 31, 56, 81
Ishidō, Toshirō, 309
Ishiguro, Kenji, 272
Itami, Juzo, 69
Iwai, Shunji, 96
Iwasaki, Akira, 270, 280–84

Jacoby, Alexander, 8
Jansen, Marius B., 297, 298, 304, 305

Kamei, Fumio, 43
Kamigami no Fukaki Yokubō see *Profound Desires of the Gods*
Kamo no Chōmei, 330, 339
Kanesaka, Kenji, 118, 119, 130–32, 134, 135
Kanzō-sensei see *Dr. Akagi*
Kaplan, Ann, 207, 313, 321
Karayuki-san, The Making of a Prostitute (1975), 6, 15, 180, 192, 254, 311
Katō hayabusa sentōtai see *Kato's Falcon Fighters*
Kato's Falcon Fighters (1944), 222
Kawase, Naomi, 95, 97
Kawashima, Yuzo, 4, 27, 43, 122, 224
Kehr, Dave, 28, 247, 304, 305
Keirstead, Thomas, 304, 305
Kim, Nelson, 98
Kimura-Steven, Chigusa, 66
Kinema junpō, 213, 248, 251, 252, 256, 257, 262, 271, 273
Kinoshita, Keisuke, 2, 5, 6, 118, 247
Kipphardt, Heinar, 271
Kishi, Nobusuke, 41
Kitabayashi Tanie, 117, 125, 126

Kitagawa, Fuyuhiko, 26, 35
Kitamura, Kazuo, 84, 116, 126, 130, 165, 217, 336
Kitano, Takeshi, 95
Kiyokawa, Nijiko, 84, 257, 335
Klinger, Barbara, 120
Kobayashi, Masaki, 2, 152, 181
Kobayashi, Satoru, 152
Koji, Aoki, 305
Kokinshū, 330
Kokutai, 194, 195, 198, 201
Kozo Sawa, 66
Kracauer, Siegfried, 172, 173
Kuroi ame see *Black Rain*
Kuroi Ame, novel (1966), 18, 309, 315, 322
Kuroi yuki, 152; see also *Black Snow*
Kurosawa, Akira, 2, 4, 6, 7, 23, 25, 27, 50, 133, 223
  Akira Kurosawa's Dreams (Yume, 1990), 312
  Drunken Angel (Yoidore tenshi, 1948), 48, 49
  High and Low (Tengoku to jigoku, 1963), 115
  Madadayo (1993), 223
  Rhapsody in August (Hachi-gatsu no yōshikyoku 1991), 312
  Stray Dog (Nora inu, 1949), 49
  and Imamura 178, 316
Kyoto, 130, 288, 298–302

Lang, Fritz, 10, 18
Laprevotte, Gilles, 295, 304
Last Year at Marinband (1961), 272
Lelouch, Claude, 1
Lewis, Diane Wei, 17
Loach, Ken, 1
Love Letter (1995), 96
Lynch, Deidre, 304, 305

M (1931), 10
MacKinnon, Catharine, 146, 150
Makhmalbaf, Samira, 1
A Man Vanishes (1967), 17, 18, 30, 34, 36, 135, 217, 240, 267–84
Manhunter (1986), 9

Mann, Michael, 10
Marcuse, Herbert, 72
Maruyama, Masao, 123
Masumura, Yasuzo, 27, 122
Matsumoto, Toshio, 129–35
    Eizō no hakken (1963), 129
    Funeral Parade of Roses (Bara no Sōretsu, 1969), 272
    Ginrin (1955), 127
Matsushita, Keiichi, 120, 125
Mayuzumi, Toshiro, 130
Mellen, Joan, 3, 59, 60, 194, 197, 199, 331, 333
Mendes, Sam, 140, 154
Mifune, Toshiro, 23, 48, 49
Mihalopoulos, Bill, 17, 118, 124
Miike, Takashi, 6
Mikuni, Rentaro, 79, 162, 217, 334
Minamida, Yōko, 28, 30, 46
minzokugaku, 124, 273
Mishima, Masao, 47
Miyazawa, Kiichi, 94
Mizoguchi, Kenji, 2–4, 14, 23, 25, 63, 93, 118, 119, 203
Mizuno, Masaki, 272
Moe no suzaku/Suzaku, 95, 97
Molasky, Michael, 49
Mononoke hime/Princess Mononoke, 95
monumental history, 299–302
Murayama Tomiichi, 182
Murley, Jean, 75, 87
My Second Brother (1959), 9, 21, 24, 26, 34–36

Nagai, Frank, 31, 32, 35, 43
Nagai, Kafu, 224
Nagasaki, 7, 234, 239, 241, 297, 298, 310
Nagato, Hiroyuki, 27, 30, 46
Nair, Mira, 1
Nakata, Toichi, 77, 295, 308
Narayama bushikō see The Ballad of Narayama
Naruse, Mikio, 2, 14, 118, 119, 214
    Untamed Woman (Arakure, 1957), 122
    When a Woman Ascends the Stairs (Onna ga kaidan o agaru toki, 1960), 119

Nianchan see My Second Brother
Nichols, Bill, 206–08, 276, 277
Nietzsche, Frederich, 18, 289–91, 296, 299–303
    Thus Spoke Zarathustra (1883–1891), 290
Nihon no sugao, 128
Nikkatsu Corporation, 4, 5, 9, 21, 24, 28, 29, 31–36, 43–46, 70, 115, 117, 122, 127, 134, 164, 231, 232, 272, 274, 279, 280
Nikutai, 194, 195, 201, 203
Nikutai no mon see Gate of Flesh
Ningen Jōhatsu see A Man Vanishes (1967) 17, 18, 30, 34, 36, 135, 217, 240, 267–84
Ningen no Joken see The Human Condition
Nippon Konchūki see The Insect Woman
Nippon sengoshi: Madam Onboro no seikatsu see History of Postwar Japan as Told by a Bar Hostess (1970)
Nishi Ginza eki mae see Nishi Ginza Station
Nishi Ginza Station (1958), 21, 24, 25, 29, 30, 31–36, 43
Nishiguchi, Akira, 75, 77, 82
Nishimura, Ko, 29, 30, 187–90
Nobuaki, Takeda, 69
Non-fiction gekijō, 128
Noonan, Tom, 9, 10
Nusumareta yokujo see Stolen Desire
Nygren, Scott, 250

Obayashi, Nobuhiko, 96
Oda, Makoto, 229, 230
Oda, Sakunosuke, 214
Ogata, Ken, 6, 9, 10, 75, 83, 139, 260
Ogawa, Mami, 50
Ogawa, Mayumi, 335
Okaeri (1995), 96
Okamoto, Hiroshi, 281
Osabe, Hideo, 171, 171, 273, 277
Oshima, Nagisa, 2, 4, 5, 23, 27, 34, 132, 133, 246, 270, 277, 281–83
    Diary of a Shinjuku Thief (Shinjuku dorobo nikki, 1969), 272
    Forgotten Soldiers (Wasurerareta kōgun, 1963), 128

Index   347

In the Realm of the Senses (*Ai no korida*, 1976), 7
Three Resurrected Drunkards (*Kaette kita yoppari*, 1968), 272
Oshima, Tadashi, 267, 272, 274, 279
Otsubo, Shigeru, 330
Ouedraogo, Idrissa, 1
Ozawa, Shoichi, 30, 130, 331
Ozu, Yasujirō, 2–5, 7, 15, 23, 27, 31, 34, 43, 69, 71, 72, 101, 123, 178, 223, 291–95, 315–18, 321
  Early Summer (*Bakushu*, 1951), 292
  Floating Weeds (*Ukigusa*, 1959), 292
  Good Morning (*Ohayo*, 1959), 71, 72
  Late Spring (*Banshun*, 1949), 69
  Tokyo Story (*Tokyo monogatari*, 1953), 4, 178, 316

The People of Sunagawa (1955), 43
The People of Sunagawa: Wheat Will Never Fall (1955), 43
Perry, Matthew, 297, 298
Phillips, Alastair , 78, 250, 334
Pigs and Battleships (1961), 5, 11, 36, 41–53, 127, 232, 278, 311, 326
Pirandello, Luigi, 273, 277
La politique des auteurs, 23
The Pornographers (1966), 5, 13, 79, 81, 102, 140, 144, 145–48, 152, 157, 224, 273–76, 326, 331–34
Profound Desires of the Gods (1968), 2, 5, 14, 45, 68, 77, 161–64, 168–73, 217, 221, 224, 228, 233, 250
Proust, Marcel, 140–44
  The Guermantes Way, 142
Psycho (1960), 76

Quandt, James, 3, 35, 56, 59, 64, 65, 246

Raine, Michael, 14, 270
Rayns, Tony, 78, 81, 83, 87, 172
Record of Blood: Sunagawa (1956), 43
Red Light Base, 43
Renoir, Jean, 93
Resnais, Alain, 272

Richie, Donald, 59, 75, 148, 152, 178, 186, 216, 218, 291, 305, 309, 311
Ryūketsu no kiroku: Sunagawa see *Record of Blood: Sunagawa*

Sakaguchi, Ango, 48, 213, 214
Sakamoto, Sumiko, 257–62, 331
Saki Ryuzo, 14, 77
Sanae, Nakahara, 46
Sandakan No. 8 (1974), 186
Sato, Tadao, 14, 117, 118, 163, 222, 337
Schrader, Paul, 291
Season of the Witch (1958), 26
Shall We Dance? (1996), 95
Sharp, Jasper, 8, 19, 21, 95
She and He (1963), 127
Shibuya, Minoru, 26
Shimizu, Misa, 102, 337
Shimizu, Masashi, 124, 162–64, 333
Shimura, Takashi, 48
Shinada, Yukichi, 24–26, 30–32, 36, 161
Shinoda, Masahiro, 7
Shinozaki, Makoto, 96
Shochiku, 4, 5, 24, 27, 28, 34, 42, 43, 122, 178
Shomin, 14, 116, 133
Shoot the Piano Player (1960), 271
shutaisei, 161, 270
The Silence of the Lambs (1991), 9
Silverman, Kaja, 202
Sirk, Douglas, 71
Slaymaker, Douglas, 194, 195, 203
Standish, Isolde, 29, 192, 193, 201, 205, 246, 247, 249, 250, 261
Stolen Desire (1958), 2, 5, 9, 21, 24, 25, 27–29, 32–35, 43, 49, 278
Sugiyama, Heiichi, 25, 33, 36, 126, 182, 282
Suna no onna see *Woman in the Dunes*
Sunagawa no hitobito: kichi hantai tōsō no kiroku see *The People of Sunagawa* (1955)
Sunagawa no hitobito: mugi shinazu see *The People of Sunagawa: Wheat Will Never Fall*
Suo, Masayuki, 95

Suvari, Mena, 154
Suzuki, Seijun, 152

Takamine, Hideko, 119
Takechi, Tetsuji, 122
Takenaka, Naoto, 97
Takeshige, Kunio, 272
Tamotsu, Hirosue, 123
Tarkovsky, Andrei, 271
Tengan, Daisuke, 1, 218
Terayama, Shuji, 126
Teshigahara, Hiroshi, 14, 66, 169, 330
Tesson, Charles, 246, 251, 254, 295
Throw Out Your Books and Go into the Streets (1971), 272
Toida, Michizo, 282
Toko, Kon, 27
Tokugawa Shogunate, 67, 178, 179, 288, 297, 305
Tokyo, 28, 32, 33, 35, 42, 43, 45, 48, 82, 93, 94, 106, 108, 116, 126, 140, 166, 168, 218, 315, 331, 336, 337
Tokyo 1958, 127
Tokyo Biyori (1997), 97
Tomoda, Jiro, 253–58
Tomorowo, Taguchi, 1
Tono, Eijiro, 51
Tonoyama, Taiji, 46, 82
Treasure of the Sierra Madre (1948), 25
Treat, John, 314, 315
Truffaut, François, 271
Tsumura, Hideo, 122, 133
Tsurumi, Shunsuke, 229
Tsurumi, Yoshiyuki, 230
Turim, Maureen, 23
Two Punks see *Chinpira*

Uchida, Hyakken, 223
Ueno, Chizuko, 199–201
Ueno, Kōshi, 122
Ugetsu (1953), 103
Umberto D (1952), 271

Uraoka, Keiichi, 83
Urayama, Kirio, 47, 272
Ushikubo, Megumi, 94

Varda, Agnes, 271
Vengeance Is Mine (1979), 6, 9, 10, 11, 16, 68, 75–81, 86, 89, 139, 140, 145, 217, 228, 308, 334
Vilar, Jean, 271

Wang, Ban, 313
Warm Water under a Red Bridge (2001), 7, 63, 218, 326
Warren, Austin, 326, 329
Washburn, Dennis, 68, 80, 84, 87–89
The Waves at Genji's Door, 2
Wellek, René, 326, 329
White, James, 305
Wollen, Peter, 22
Woman in the Dunes (1964), 14, 66, 169, 170, 172, 330
Wood, Robin, 312
Why Not? see *Eijanaika*

Yakusho, Koji, 1, 98, 111
yakuza, 44, 46, 48, 49, 83
Yamada, Koichi, 147, 183
Yamamoto, Kajirō, 222
Yamamoto, Satsuo, 5
Yamamoto, Yasuo, 252–56
Yamanouchi, Hisashi, 43
Yamauchi, Akira, 46
Yanagisawa, Shinichi, 28–30
Yanagita, Kunio, 116, 122–24
Yamazaki, Tomoko, 186, 190
Yoshida, Kiju, 4, 7, 270
Yoshimoto, Mitsuhiro, 21, 22
Yoshimoto, Takaaki, 123
Yoshimura, Jitsuko, 44, 46, 116
Yoshimura, Akira, 98

Zendo, Kikuyo, 177, 180, 183, 184, 188

EU representative:
Easy Access System Europe
Mustamäe tee 50, 10621 Tallinn, Estonia
Gpsr.requests@easproject.com

www.ingramcontent.com/pod-product-compliance
Lightning Source LLC
Chambersburg PA
CBHW070010010526
44117CB00011B/1501